D1559524

Passage through Hell

Frontispiece. Robert Rauschenberg. *Canto III: The Vestibule of Hell, the Opportunists.* Illustration for Dante's *Inferno* (1959–60). Transfer drawing, torn and pasted paper, watercolor, pencil, and wash. 14⅜ × 11⅜″ (36.7 × 29.1 cm) (slightly irregular). The Museum of Modern Art, New York. Given anonymously. © 1996 Robert Rauschenberg/ Licensed by VAGA, New York, NY. Photograph © 1996 The Museum of Modern Art.

Passage through Hell

Modernist Descents, Medieval Underworlds

DAVID L. PIKE

Cornell University Press

Ithaca and London

Copyright © 1997 by Cornell University

All rights reserved. Except for brief quotations in a review, this book, or parts thereof, must not be reproduced in any form without permission in writing from the publisher. For information, address Cornell University Press, Sage House, 512 East State Street, Ithaca, New York 14850.

First published 1997 by Cornell University Press.

Library of Congress Cataloging-in-Publication Data

Pike, David L. (David Lawrence), b. 1963
        Passage through hell : modernist descents, medieval underworlds /
David L. Pike.
        p.   cm.
    A revision of the author's thesis.
    Includes bibliographical references and index.
    ISBN 0-8014-3163-8 (cloth : alk. paper)
        1. Hell in literature.   2. Literature—History and criticism.
I. Title.
PN56.H38P55 1996
809'.93382—dc20   96-18284

Printed in the United States of America

This book is printed on Lyons Falls Turin Book,
a paper that is totally chlorine-free and acid-free.

Cloth printing   10   9   8   7   6   5   4   3   2   1

Contents

Preface

HOW DO YOU illustrate Dante's *Commedia?* Robert Rauschenberg suggests a strategy of reflection: his silkscreen montage of canto 3 of *Inferno* includes the photograph of a skyscraper with the inscription from the Gate of Hell superimposed along with the word "WELCOME." Reflected through the transfer process of Rauschenberg's silkscreening, theological certainty is translated into the infernal irony of capitalist society. It is a no less ominous greeting than Dante's, for Rauschenberg's *Inferno* is populated by images clipped out of the the late fifties: Nixon, Kennedy, and Adlai Stevenson, soldiers in gas masks, Olympic wrestlers, astronauts, and televisions; the character of Dante is a man with a towel wrapped around his waist, Everyman measured up by a height scale in a series of advertisements for golf clubs. We can call this the beginning of postmodernism, pop culture taking over the classics, Dante for the video era; but Rauschenberg is an equally relevant starting point for positing a more complex, more contextualized appropriation of the weight of the past accumulated behind the façade of the Gate of Hell we see flattened onto a skyscraper.

By suggesting in the *Thirty-Four Drawings for Dante's "Inferno"* (1959–64) that illustration—an illustration moreover based solely on a montage of borrowed images periodically scribbled over as in a graphite rubbing—is as significant an art form as Dante's poetry, Rauschenberg did not simply support a pop art reductio ad absurdum of high culture. Rather, he implicitly claimed that such an apparently parasitic medium was able accurately to reflect the textual complexity of its model within the entirely alien context of America in the fifties. Just as Dante's terza rima introduced trinitarian structure into the very fabric of the poem, so Rauschenberg's transfer process—in which a collage of printed images is transferred (in reverse image) onto a flat surface—introduced structures of ideology into the visual texture of the illustration. Pop art prided itself on flattening all levels of art onto a single plane of aesthetic value; Rauschenberg flattened contemporary society into the system of Dante's hell as mirror images of itself. So, for example, the inscriptions on the Gate of Hell are reversed: reflection changes meaning without changing anything else.

Hell is the place of those who in life chose *not* to reflect (as Dante's Vergil puts it, those who have lost "the good of the intellect" [*Inf.* 3.18]). Rauschenberg's technique of illustration decodes the signs of hell, representing Dante's imagery by reflecting the raw material of contemporary society onto a silkscreen. The doctrines of the death of the artist (Rauschenberg strictly delimits his creative control over the work) and the illusory nature of truth (society is simply reflected) are already here, but allegorically, as products of their culture. Dante and his oeuvre are not the father to be killed in the art of the son but a site for reflection on the mediation between history and myth, a metaphorical structure within which to compile a critical inventory of contemporary culture. If meaning can be generated out of reflection on the material of present-day society, so can an authorial voice emerge by reflecting the disappearance of the artist within the work, and so an image of truth can emerge from the artistic reflection of its negation.

This is a key lesson of Dante's hell: critical reflection on the loss of hope engenders hope, immersion in images of falsehood reveals truth, descent leads to return. The distinction lies in Vergil's "ben de l'intelletto"— in the conversion undergone by the pilgrim. Conversion is the narrative structure of the mythic descent to the underworld, and Dante's *Inferno* has immeasurably conditioned its modern reception. Rauschenberg's drawings remind us of the historical complexity that the *Commedia*'s mediation interjects into any attempt to give a simple reading of this myth. When he reminds us of the obvious, "[Dante] was the hero *and* the author, the man who made the world he described," Rauschenberg stresses both the allure and the contradictions of the descent to the underworld.[1] On the one hand, by going into the past, the artist recreates whatever has gone before her. On the other hand, in order to validate the recreated history as myth, the artist must represent herself as divinely authorized. These are the stakes, I argue, that persist in determining the secular translation of divine authorization: the artist must either elevate the aesthetic sphere beyond the realm of artifact or remove the artifact beyond the aesthetic sphere.

As mere illustrations, however, Rauschenberg's drawings invert this structure: they remain faithful to the narrative and textuality of the *Inferno* while paradoxically rendering it nearly unrecognizably modern.

---

[1] Quoted in Calvin Tomkins, *Off the Wall: Robert Rauschenberg and the Art World of His Time* (New York, 1980), 160.

Rather than the myth of creation, Rauschenberg plays on its converse, the myth of reflection: the myth that his drawings affect neither the aesthetic nor the artifact, but that they precisely mirror Dante's poem in their content and precisely mirror society in their form (transferred images out of magazines and newpapers). They remain highly self-conscious of their mythmaking and remind us that Dante's text may be equally so; they stress the double meaning of *reflection,* asking that we reflect on the myth of unmediated reflection, the myth that translation, illustration, compilation, and allusion involve the unmediated transference of meaning.

What follows is a reevaluation of the *descensus ad inferos,* the descent to the underworld, in medieval and modern literature. Although structured around a repeated motif, it is not a motif study; even less would it claim to be a history of the genre of the *descensus.* Rather, it explores the means by which motifs are constantly revised and transformed, and influences constantly rewritten and configured, how history is made into myth and myth into history. Classical and medieval literature are interpreted through the lens of their construction in and by modernism, and modernism is viewed anew in light of a medieval model freed of that construction. The book follows a series of paths back and forth between modern and medieval in order to trace the reciprocal effects of each descent on its past and on its future. It maintains that Louis-Ferdinand Céline's reading of Dante revises our reception of the latter, and equally that Christine de Pizan's reading of Dante transforms our reception of Virginia Woolf. This is particularly the case with Dante, the book's center of gravity, the nadir of its descent, for he takes what had become the Christian structure of *descensus* and gives it the form in which it would be legible to the historical exigencies of modernism. He provides the vehicle whereby the world may be remade and described in the same moment of descent through the underworld: the autobiographical voice, the voice that can say simultaneously "this is what I see as history" and "this is what I am creating as myth."

Here is the transcendent narrative of the *descensus ad inferos;* Rauschenberg reminds us that at the same time, there is another, nonlinear, nonnarrative movement documented by the work of illustration, compilation, commentary, translation, allusion. In the drawing for *Inferno* 25, where the thieves, who in life stole the substance of others, are punished by having constantly to steal and then guard their own forms from others, he illustrates the transformations with a progression of images from left to right: a photo of a man, a technical drawing of a hermit crab, and a lizard. A space is created for the illustrator within the supposedly unmediated transference from text to image. The hermit crab has no shell of its own but makes its home in whatever abandoned shell it may find. Just so, the illustrator, along with fellow practitioners of marginal activities, moves into the abandoned shell of Dante, picks up the cast-off material of society like a beachcomber in order to adorn the newly discovered home. The thief's hellish punishment is recreated as the illustrator's artistic strategy. Needless to say, the illustration also points back to the presence of the same strategies in Dante's text; for does not the poet preface his virtuoso descriptions of transformation with a gesture toward the predecessors he will efface with his creation: "Be silent Lucan . . . be silent Ovid" (25.94–97)?

The figures of Dante and Vergil are present at the top of the drawing, encased in scuba diving gear out of a sporting goods advertisement. Like the hermit crab's shell, the suits give protection, in this case from the depths to which they have descended in the eighth circle. This is the suit of creative authority, for diving deeply into the creation of a master narrative; the illustrator, who merely moves along the shore, describes what is already at hand. Writers at work in marginal genres or with the motif in a partial manner—in this book we see the examples of Bernard Silvestris, Céline, Christine, and Woolf—appear to refuse or disallow the deep descent; like Rauschenberg, they prefer the myth of the shore dweller, the commentator, the one who reflects.

Whether it is the creation or the description of the narrative that is stressed, the same issues of myth and history, descent and return, rewriting as remaking are involved. The narrative does not explicitly change—it remains the myth of descent to the underworld. What does change is the history that determines what is to be retrieved by the descent. And there is a final element that is perhaps the most compelling: the undertow, the retrospective recreation of the purportedly eternal myth that occurs every time the historical object of descent changes. By telling us what it is looking for, the autobiographical voice simultaneously recreates its past as the place in which such a thing could have come into being.

In Chapter 1 I establish the necessary context for a reading of the descent to the underworld and the autobiographical voice as they are constructed between the poles of myth and history, past and present. The *Odyssey* and the *Aeneid* form the core of an introductory exposition of the descent in antiquity and in contemporary criticism; Augustine and Bernard rewrite that exposition within a Christian framework, revealing in each other the intertwining myths of divine authority and of simple reflection, each constituting itself as history by mythifying its predecessor as opposite. The subsequent example of Céline in Chapter 2 problematizes the ambiguous moral and political stance of the descent, arguing that its efficacy as a device for historicization is inseparable from its efficacy for mythification. Consequently, any reading of the allegory of conversion and descent to the underworld must account for both effects together. In Chapter 3 the pairing of Peter Weiss and Dante addresses the modernist construction of the descent from the vantage points of hindsight and foresight. The postwar writer Weiss outlines the contours of a modernist Dante by casting him as part of the same *entre-deux-guerres* past to which he must descend in order to rewrite a present that is no longer modernist. Once removed from a modernist context, Dante's negotiation of myth and history as a tension between poetry and Scripture becomes legible in a form unavailable to the polarizations of a stubbornly modernist critical reading. The pairing of Christine and Woolf in Chapter 4 suggests further possibilities of the *descensus ad inferos* as a site for critical reflection on the transmission of the past. Christine's creation of an authorial voice out of opposition to a monolithically constructed Dantean tradition of descent helps decipher Woolf's staging of her equivocal role within the traditionally received critical accounts of modernism. In Chapter 5 I propose Walter Benjamin's work on Paris, allegory, and contemporary literature as starting point for a reading of modernism able to account for the issues raised by the previous chapters. In the concluding chapter I address the implications of this reading for present-day literature and criticism, focusing on recent work by Seamus Heaney and Derek Walcott. The postwar mythicization of modernism as its past suggests that postmodernism is less a historical development of the last decades than the flip side of the modernist master narrative. Consequently, modernism must itself be reinterpreted in light of such a simultaneous, not sequential dialectic, and postwar literature must be accounted for as something other than simply postmodern.

In *Passage through Hell* I attempt to escape from the morass of competing claims to formalism on the one hand and historical relevance on the other. I argue that what we need now are strategies of reading that establish unforeseen connections and associations. Fundamentally a means for negotiating the antinomies of the past, the descent to the underworld suggests ways of incorporating insights of recent theory without dissolving the literary text altogether. This is the Vergilian image of "rousing the world below": furious at Aeneas's audacious descent to the underworld, successful return, and arrival at Latium, and seeing the Trojan leader now armed with everything necessary for the conquest of Italy and establishment of the Roman empire, the goddess Juno has lost the patience to go through proper diplomatic channels in order to petition Jove to change his plans. Instead, she exclaims, "If I can sway no heavenly hearts, I'll rouse the world below."[2] She summons the fury Allecto to wreak havoc all around. Following on the destined, eschatological march of history embodied in Aeneas and his descent to the underworld in book 6, Juno's fury presents a counterblast of protest that, if not able to change the end result, is instrumental in obstructing, and thus determining, the narrative leading to it. This is the story of the last six books of the *Aeneid*. It is no accident that Freud placed these verses as the epigraph to his epoch-making modernist text *The Interpretation of Dreams* (1900), suggesting the realm of the unconscious as a power to be reckoned with in the master narratives above. Here is the compelling double valence of the topos of the underworld: it encompasses within the inflections of its metaphorics both the master narratives and their countercurrents, both the will to transcendence and the movement toward entropy. The pages that follow plot this double movement at work within the antinomies of modernism and the Middle Ages and suggest the means for interpreting it.

TO THE DEGREE that this book can be said to remain my creation, it has received much of its present shape through the commentary of the many people who have been so kind as to reinvent it in one of its many forms. I want to start by thanking the members of the Medieval Guild of Columbia University, and Sarah Kelen in particular, for patiently following and directing the unfolding of the medieval material. I also want to thank the following friends, colleagues, and mentors for their comments and support: Teodolinda Barolini, Renate Blumenfeld-Kosinski, Susan Buck-Morss, Antoine Compagnon, David Damrosch, Priscilla Parkhurst Ferguson, Robert Hanning, María Rosa Menocal, Carol Jones Neuman, Claudia Ratazzi Papka, Sandra Prior, Michael Riffaterre, Robert Stein. I am especially grateful to Joan Ferrante for introducing me to and guiding me through the intricacies of medieval allegory. My thanks go to the Society of Fellows in the Humanities at Columbia University, in particular the director, Marsha Manns, and chairs, Elaine Sisman, Karl Kroeber, and Esther Pasztory, for granting me the time, space, funds, and atmosphere necessary to complete the transformation from early to final version. Bernhard Kendler and the readers and editors at Cornell University Press were instrumental in helping me find the form of that transformation. I am grateful to my editors Carol Betsch and Kim Vivier, and to the many other persons involved in the production of the book. A Mellon Research Award

---

[2] "Flectere si nequeo superos, Acheronta movebo." *Virgil*, trans. H. R. Fairclough, rev. ed., 2 vols. (Cambridge, Mass., 1978), 7.312; Virgil, *The Aeneid*, trans. Robert Fitzgerald (New York, 1990), 7.425–26.

from the College of Arts and Sciences of American University permitted the inclusion of illustrations.

My debt to Andreas Huyssen for his direction and encouragement at every stage of the project is immeasurable. Without his unwonted confidence, it would certainly never have come this far. The last words of these acknowledgments are reserved for Ana—to whom, as she well knows, the book is dedicated.

PORTIONS OF THE second chapter have been substantially revised from an earlier version published in *Lectura Dantis*. Excerpts from *Seeing Things* and *Station Island* by Seamus Heaney. Copyright © 1991 by Seamus Heaney. Reprinted by permission of Farrar, Straus & Giroux, Inc., and Faber and Faber Ltd. Excerpts from *Omeros* by Derek Walcott. Copyright © 1990 by Derek Walcott. Reprinted by permission of Farrar, Straus & Giroux, Inc., and Faber and Faber Ltd. The manuscript was completed too soon to make use of the forthcoming translation of the works of Walter Benjamin by Harvard University Press; the author and publisher gratefully acknowledge Suhrkamp Verlag and Harvard University Press for permission to use the author's own translations.

DAVID L. PIKE

Washington, D.C.

Abbreviations

Note on Texts and Translations

Primary and secondary sources are cited in translation, with words in brackets in the original language when necessary for my interpretation. Passages of poetry are printed in both languages. All translations are my own unless otherwise noted. My goal in translating has been to follow the syntax and meaning of the original as closely and literally as possible within a generously conceived notion of the bounds of acceptable English usage. When I have used existing translations, I have sometimes modified them according to the same guidelines. When page numbers are cited, the first reference is always to the passage in the original language edition cited, the second to the base text for translation (when one exists).

Passage through Hell

I

The Persistence of the Universal: Critical Descents into Antiquity

HERMES: . . . You're like the man in the street, Charon; there isn't even a trace of the poet about you. Now our noble Homer has made a "gateway to heaven" for us with just two verses—that's how easily he stacks mountains. I'm amazed that you consider these things so extraordinary. Certainly you know about Atlas—he's only one man and yet he holds up heaven with all of us on it. And you've probably heard how my brother Heracles once took over for that very Atlas and gave him a bit of a rest from drudgery by shouldering the load himself.

CHARON: I've heard these stories. But whether they're true or not—you and your poets would know about that.

HERMES: They're absolutely true, Charon. Why would wise and intelligent men tell lies? So let's pry up Ossa first, just the way the poem and our poet-architect tells us, and then

> pile upon Ossa
> Well-wooded Pelion.

See how easily just a bit of poetry did the trick?

— Lucian, *Charon*

At the entrance to science, as at the entrance to hell, the demand must be posted: *Qui si convien lasciare ogni sospetto; Ogni viltà convien che qui sia morta.* ["Here must all hesitation be left behind; here every cowardice must meet its death."]

— Karl Marx,
"Preface to *A Critique of Political Economy*"

THE ANCIENT MOTIF of descent to the underworld, while it has never
lost its defining role of exploring the passage between life and death, has
over the millennia gathered around itself an ever-increasing constellation
of meanings. Such an accumulation cannot, however, be described simply
in an archaeological manner, one layer at a time. An account of the descent to the underworld must keep sight of the guiding figurative structure: the topographical movement of descent and return within the motif
equally describes the accretion of meaning to it in history. This is what
makes the descent a fundamentally allegorical form: the core fact of death
is imbued with the hero's individual past, the past of his society, and the
past of the motif itself.

It is not a static process; rather, each descent rewrites and transforms
past images. The descent to the underworld functions simultaneously as a
repository for the past and as a crucible in which that repository is melted
down to be recast as something other than what it had been. The most
characteristic strategy of the descent is to stress its own complexity and
novelty in contrast with a simple and outmoded past, a past newly recon-
stituted as such by the new act of descent. In other words, the newest
elements in the constellation are legitimated, rendered as the dynamic
description of a historical present, when the previous constellation is represented as a single and static mythic past that is being surpassed.

The issues raised by the descent to the underworld as allegorical mode
are emblematic of metaliterary motifs in general and can lead to an account of literature and the criticism of it that would chart not only a
diachrony of movements and influences but a synchrony of the past newly
constituted by each moment out of a self-defined set of predecessors. Take,
for example, the vagaries of Walter Benjamin over the past half-century.
The celebrated verse "Tout pour moi devient allégorie" (Everything for
me becomes allegory) from Baudelaire's "Le Cygne" was taken over by
Benjamin to describe nineteenth-century allegory in his *Passagen-Werk*
(Arcades project). Since the 1970s, it has been joined with the now infa-
mous phrase from Benjamin's earlier study of baroque allegory, *Ursprung
des deutschen Trauerspiels* (1928; *Origin of German Tragic Drama*),
generally rendered in English as "Anything, anywhere, can mean anything else," to become the clarion call of the poststructural and postmodern definition of allegory as an antisymbolic play of language figuring
language.[1]

---

[1] Walter Benjamin, *Ursprung des deutschen Trauerspiel*, in *Gesammelte Schriften*,
ed. Rolf Tiedemann and Hermann Schweppenhäuser, 7 vols. (Frankfurt, 1991), 1:350;
trans. John Osborne, *The Origin of German Tragic Drama* (London, 1985), 175;

Mistranslation and decontextualization aside, why is it anything more than pedantry to complain about a strong misreading of the past? After all, that is the epitome of postmodern thought to begin with. The problem is essentially one of misrepresentation. The practice of strong misreading is synonymous with the strategy of the descent to the underworld and has nothing in particular to do with a postmodernism that would characterize itself as allegorical and the past millennia of literary practice as symbolic, mythic, or simply traditional. The particular period of the recent past at stake—in this case generally some version of romanticism or realism—is projected into the past as a hypostasized literary history overturned by the modernist (and especially postmodernist) project.

Modernism indeed constituted itself on some manner of surface repudiation of that recent past, but it did so by asserting its permanent modernity in opposition to a permanently outdated medievalism. The poetics whereby modernism refused the nineteenth century are appropriated from a medieval past it created as the negation of its own vision of the present. It will be impossible to contextualize modernism as something no longer present—that is, to determine its range of meanings in a postwar era that is no longer identical to it—until we can better grasp what it cast itself against and the means by which it constructed the medieval past as its negative. The most persuasive and enduring myth of modernism has been that it was always and continues to be *modern*.

Contemporary theory has rightly argued that in terms of artistic production a literary phenomenon known as modernism is no longer occurring. But the very desire to view literary history in terms of successive movements, each surpassing the other, is a specifically modernist phenomenon, by which I mean that it grows out of the artistic practices of a period broadly framed by the century between 1848 and 1945.[2] This is the legacy

---

hereafter cited as *TB* (following Benjamin's short title of *Trauerspielbuch*). The seminal postmodernist appropriation is Craig Owen, "The Allegorical Impulse: Toward a Theory of Post-Modernism," *October* 12 (Spring 1980): 67–86, and 13 (Summer 1980): 59–80; rpt. in *Art after Modernism*, ed. Brian Wallis (New York, 1984), 203–35. The central figures in the reception of Benjamin's allegory theory in poststructuralism are Paul De Man, *Blindness and Insight*, 2d rev. ed. (Minneapolis, 1983), esp. 173–74; Carol Jacobs, "Walter Benjamin's Image of Proust," *MLN* 86:6 (1971): 910–32; and J. Hillis Miller, "The Two Allegories," in *Allegory, Myth, and Symbol*, ed. Morton Bloomfield (Cambridge, Mass., 1981), 355–70.

[2] In terms of both aesthetics and politics, the year 1848, if too early a date for many scholars of British and American literature, remains the standard referent for Continental discourse on modernism and modernity. H. R. Jauss describes it as the "epochal transition" *(Epochenschwelle)* epitomized by Baudelaire's "aesthetic of mod-

of modernism, and the next theoretical move should be to question the extent to which such a succession can fully characterize the modernist period either, to question the degree to which it was a mythic account generated out of the self-representation of modernism, and to question the reasons behind such a self-representation.

These steps perhaps could be taken in the current critical climate. What is being realized much more slowly is that critical practice continues to labor under the myths of a modernism that, theoretically, it has pronounced as having been superseded by postmodernism. Witness the succession of theoretical schools, manifestoes and all, that has held forth, especially in the United States, since the late 1940s, mimicking a modernist practice at precisely the moment when modernism as a historical force was disappearing. It is to this belatedness of criticism, to an ongoing "modernism of reading," that this study is addressed. So, to return to the utility of recontextualizing Benjamin, it is with his appropriation as a *contemporary* that I take issue. Although criticism perhaps no longer considers itself quite so objective as it once may have done, it continues to represent itself in modernist terms and thus to view the practices of modernist cultural production unproblematically as its own.[3]

---

ernité—"politically . . . located on the horizon of the new experience of an industrial era in post-revolutionary society" and documented in Benjamin's *Passagen-Werk* ("The Literary Process of Modernism from Rousseau to Adorno," *Cultural Critique* 11 [Winter 1988–89]: 32–33). This should not belie the fact that this "almost canonized beginning of our modern age" (33) is far from fixed. That modernism and modernity did not spring fully formed out of the Second Empire is self-evident. As De Man has perceptively (if polemically) noted, "To write reflectively about modernity leads to problems that put the usefulness of the term into question, especially as it applies, or fails to apply, to literature" ("Literary History and Literary Modernism," in *Blindness and Insight*, 142). In other words, the definition of the term should be regarded as no more fixed than is any other aspect of modernist criticism.

[3] A striking example is to be found in the appropriation of Benjamin, Woolf, and Simone Weil as a "saintly trinity of self-defined outsiders" by the eminent Woolf scholar Jane Marcus. Reducing any difference between the three writers to the role of signifier of their respective "rational mysticisms," Marcus finds their relevance in our need, if we cannot emulate them, to strive to be their worthy successors: "Their studies of power and violence are invaluable to us; their ethical purity is unassailable. Their suicides—seemingly so socially determined as political acts—fill us with humility and rage. Did they mean to be scapegoats in self-slaughter or martyrs to the fear of fascism?" (" 'The Niece of a Nun': Virginia Woolf, Caroline Stephen, and the Cloistered Imagination," in Marcus, ed., *Virginia Woolf: A Feminist Slant* [Lincoln, 1983], 7–36; this quotation, 13). Marcus's martyrology, like those of early Christianity, negates any influence of ethnicity, class, or religious affiliation on its subjects and throws historical context to the wind in favor of a mythic hagiography. This is all well and good except when paired with the rhetoric of the committedly secular Marxist feminist scholar.

The act of appropriation certainly characterizes nearly every facet of modern capitalist society, and the field of criticism and theory is no exception: "Since the nineteenth century . . . excavation has served as a dominant metaphor for truth-seeking. . . . In this respect scientific inquiry retains an aura of the mythological, since the heroic quest for scientific truth has the pattern of a descent into the underworld."[4] We may either incorporate the myth at face value or seek to analyze its mechanism. Emblematic here is Freud's identification of the nineteenth-century excavation of Troy and invention of archaeology with the new science of psychoanalysis. Describing the successful conclusion of a patient's treatment, he writes: "Buried deep beneath all his fantasies, we found a scene from his primal period . . . in which all the remaining puzzles converge. . . . It is as if Schliemann had once more excavated Troy, which had hitherto been deemed a fable."[5] Freud's use of metaphors of antiquity to describe the mechanism of the unconscious—from Odysseus's summoning of dead souls to Juno's rousing the world below—displays the same complex awareness of the intertwined threads of individual memories, mythic pasts, and actual history apparent in his rereading of Sophocles' *Oedipus*.[6]

Such an "aura of the mythological," all too self-conscious in modernism and modernity, has lost its dialectical edge in a postwar climate content to appropriate the mythology of the modern without interrogating the dynamic function it first served. That dynamic function may not be so readily apparent in modernism, but it remains eminently observable in the generic descents of antiquity. Myth and history are the motor of the descent, but it is driven by the very nature of its narrative structure: to be found in the underworld, a person must be dead. Indeed, the vitality of each new descent depends on the mortification of its predecessors, that is

---

Marcus's ethical purity *is* unassailable, but, as always for the modernist critic, it is gained at the cost of the historical and cultural distance on which any affiliation of influence is necessarily predicated.

[4] Rosalind Williams, *Notes on the Underground: An Essay on Technology, Society, and the Imagination* (Cambridge, Mass., 1990), 49.

[5] *The Complete Letters of Sigmund Freud to Wilhelm Fliess, 1877–1904*, ed. and trans. Jeffrey Moussaieff Masson (Cambridge, 1985), 391–92 (12/21/1899). For the connection with archaeology, see Susan Cassirer Bernfeld, "Freud and Archaeology," *American Imago* 8 (1951): 107–28; and Donald Kuspit, "A Mighty Metaphor: The Analogy of Archaeology and Psychoanalysis," in *Sigmund Freud and Art: His Personal Collection of Antiquities*, ed. Lynn Gamwell and Richard Wells (New York, 1989), 133–51.

[6] For Odysseus, see *The Interpretation of Dreams*, vol. 5 of *The Standard Edition of the Complete Psychological Works of Sigmund Freud*, ed. and trans. James Strachey with Anna Freud, 24 vols. (London, 1953–74), 553; for Vergil, see 5:608.

to say, in the simple but absolute alteration caused by the transition from life to death. Life maintains a pretense of historical immediacy; death —and consequently the past invoked through it—can be known only mythically and indirectly, through interpretation. Beginning with the narrative dynamics, then, we can explore ways in the past in which the narrative logic of the descent to the underworld has been extended to an allegorical analysis of the generic structures of autobiography, commentary, translation, and criticism. Once viewed against such a background, the contours of a different modernism begin to emerge.

ANCIENT NARRATIVES of the descent to the underworld exhibit two tendencies, one mythical, the other historical.[7] The former, exemplified by the *nekuia* in *Odyssey* 11, involves a hero's rite of passage, a leave-taking from the past and orientation toward the future, and the prophetic voice related to it. Its origins are partly ritual, deriving from the shamanistic practice of *nekuomanteia*, the summoning of dead souls from the underworld.[8] This is the primary function of Odysseus's *nekuia:* to call the blind

---

[7] On the *katabasis* in ancient literature—pagan, Jewish, and Christian—see Ganschinietz, "Katabasis," *RE* 10:2359–2449; Pfister, "Unterwelt," in *Ausführliches Lexikon der Griechischen und Römischen Mythologie,* ed. W. H. Roscher (Leipzig, 1890–97), 6, 35–95; Albrecht Dieterich, *Nekyia: Beiträge zur Erklärung der neuentdeckten Petrusapokalypse,* 2d ed., annot. R. Wünsch (1893; Leipzig, 1913); Marcus Landau, *Hölle und Fegfeuer in Volksglaube, Dichtung und Kirchenlehre* (Heidelberg, 1909); Josef Kroll, *Beiträge zum Descensus ad Inferos* (Königsberg, 1922); Kroll, *Gott und Hölle: Der Mythos vom Descensuskampfe* (Leipzig, 1932); Mikhail Bakhtin, *Rabelais and His World,* trans. Helene Iswolsky (Bloomington, 1984), 368–436; Pierre Brunel, *L'Evocation des morts et la descente aux enfers* (Paris, 1974); Raymond J. Clark, *Catabasis: Vergil and the Wisdom Tradition* (Amsterdam, 1979); Martha Himmelfarb, *Tours of Hell: An Apocalyptic Form in Jewish and Christian Literature* (Philadelphia, 1983); Alison Morgan, *Dante and the Medieval Other World* (Cambridge, 1990); and I. P. Couliano, *Out of This World: Otherworldly Journeys from "Gilgamesh" to Albert Einstein* (Boston, 1991).

[8] Alfred Heubeck, *Books IX–XII,* vol. 2 of Heubeck and Arie Hoekstra, *A Commentary on Homer's "Odyssey"* (Oxford, 1989; hereafter cited as Heubeck), 71, 75–77, 84–85. On shamanistic roots, see Karl Meuli, *Gesammelte Schriften,* vol. 2 (Basel, 1975), 865–71; Agathe Thornton, *People and Themes in Homer's "Odyssey"* (London, 1970), 32 ff. On necromancy, see Reinhold Merkelbach, *Untersuchungen zur "Odyssee,"* vol. 2 (Munich, 1969), 185–91, 209–30; Geoffrey Stephen Kirk, *The Songs of Homer* (Cambridge, 1962), 236-40; Gerd Steiner, "Die Unterweltsbeschwörung des Odyssee im Lichte hethitischer Texte," *Ugarit-Forschungen* 3 (1971): 265–83; Karl Reinhardt, "Das Abenteuer des Odysseus," in *Von Werken und Formen* (Godesberg, 1948), 52–162 (this reference, 143); M. P. Nilsson, *Geschichte der griechischen Religion,* vol. 3, pt. 1 (Munich, 1967), 173–74. See Heubeck, 75–76, for further bibliography.

seer Tiresias to him so as to receive warnings and predictions about his future. The shamanistic myths may also be combined with the legendary material of a hero's descent, as in the case of Heracles. The other feature of the descent, the *katabasis,* or journey proper, is intertextual and frequently satirical, as for example in Aristophanes' *Frogs* and Lucian's *Voyage to the Underworld;* here, the underworld is a transparently social or political allegory of contemporary life on earth.

The categories are not mutually exclusive even in antiquity; we can read history into Homer and discover mythifying tendencies in the down-to-earth satire of Aristophanes or Lucian. The most influential rendering of them, *Aeneid* 6, brings these functions explicitly together as the thematic midpoint of the text. The epic hero Aeneas descends in order to receive his vocation and gain a prophetic vision of the future—his descendants and the city he is to found—from his father, Anchises; both vocation and vision are keyed to Vergil's own Augustan Rome. Descent as allegorical satire is translated into historical allegory: the relation of Aeneas's founding of Rome to the "peace of Augustus" is rendered typologically; that is, the former prefigures the latter in history, instead of merely commenting on it allegorically.[9] In a structural symmetry that has echoed to the present day, myth generates history, and history, myth.

It is not a question of once again reading *Aeneid* 6 as the point of origin of a particular structure of Western literature but rather to show how Aeneas's *katabasis* writes itself as that origin, while using its intertexts to provide a mythic foil, converging at the moment of Anchises' prophetic speech (6.724–885). It is a moment of dialectical tension, for the speech emerges simultaneously out of Vergil's historical situation as apologist and/or critic of Augustus *and* out of the narrative dynamics of the presentation by Aeneas's father of a dynastic heritage. Needless to say, the two are implicated one in the other: the heritage is a foundation myth of Vergil's own Rome, the historical intervention a mythification of the peace of Augustus.

The most visible form of this implication is found in the text's reception —here, the great divide of *Aeneid* criticism over the past one hundred fifty

---

[9] See the discussion below, pp. 22–24. The standard work on typology as a literary device remains Erich Auerbach, "Figura" (1944; rpt. in *Scenes from the Drama of European Literature,* trans. Ralph Manheim [New York, 1959], 11–76). In his resolution to distinguish Dante's *Commedia* from both theology and allegory, Auerbach significantly distorted his interpretation; this does not negate the seminal value of his research and insights, however. See David L. Pike, *"Facilis descensus Averno:* Allegory and the Autobiographical Voice, Medieval and Modern" (Ph.D. diss., Columbia University, 1993), 137–52.

years between those who read it as a dynastic epic concerned with the
means by which one founds an empire and masters one's self and those
who read it as a dark, paradoxical, and necessarily fragmentary meditation on the dissonance between the needs of the individual and those of
the state.[10] The dispute is symptomatic of an ambiguity at the heart of
Vergil's attempt to synthesize the two strands of the descent to the underworld; not coincidentally, it also mirrors both structurally and chronologi-
cally the broader conflicts of modernism discussed above.

This moment of ambiguity defines the mode of presentation I call the
autobiographical voice: it is autobiographical insofar as it appeals to a
diachronic moment in the writer's life; it remains a voice insofar as it
partakes of the narrative situation of the text. Moreover, it is allegorical,
for the Homeric *nekuia* and the tradition it represents are present in the
Aeneid as object of its satirical descent. Vergil makes his voice manifest in
large part through traces of his rereading and rewriting of Homer.[11] The
descent becomes emblematic of Vergil's endeavor as a whole, and the
literary dynamic a model of the rewriting of myth into history (Homer to
the *Aeneid*) and of history into myth (Roman history to the *Aeneid*). It
would be a mistake, however, to view *Odyssey* 11 as the mythic origin
of *Aeneid* 6; what I suggest is that it has been retrospectively cast as such
by Vergil's rewriting. The avowedly historical and contemporary thrust
of Aeneas's descent is achieved in large part through the redefinition of
that of Odysseus as timeless and ahistorical. Here, too, the effect is most
immediately legible in the reception. Robert Brooks, for instance, distinguishes between the "Odyssean adventure" on the one hand and the
"equivalent performance of the real death-journey" on the other (267).
This is the contrast constructed by Vergil's rewriting of the tradition of

---

[10] See W. R. Johnson's excellent summary in *Darkness Visible: A Study of Vergil's
"Aeneid"* (Berkeley, 1976; 1–16), which contrasts the optimistic Europeans such as
T. S. Eliot and Viktor Pöschl with the "pessimistic" Harvard school of Robert A.
Brooks, "*Discolor Aura*: Reflections on the Golden Bough," *American Journal of Phi-
lology* 54 (1953): 260–80; Adam Parry, "The Two Voices of Vergil's *Aeneid*," *Arion*
2:4 (Winter 1963): 66–80; and Wendell Clausen, "An Interpretation of the *Aeneid*,"
Harvard Studies in Classical Philology 68 (1964): 139–48.

[11] The critical literature on Vergil's relationship to Homer is extensive. For my
purposes, Eduard Norden's commentary remains the most thorough documentation of
the relationship, *Aeneid VI*, ed. and trans. (Leipzig, 1903). Ronald MacDonald takes
up the revision in book 6 in terms of attitudes toward narration and language in *The
Burial-Places of Memory: Epic Underworlds in Vergil, Dante, and Milton* (Amherst,
1987), intro. and chap. 1. Brooks discusses the descent in terms of religious verisimili-
tude. Johnson persuasively suggests adapting Auerbach's *Odyssey/Genesis* distinction
into one of Homer/Vergil.

the *katabasis* through Homer as the mythic origin of the prophetic history of Rome.

Consequently, though the *Aeneid* presents itself as the first text to have highlighted such an autobiographical voice, the appearance is due in large part to its having established a mode of comparative reading that tends to obscure traces of a similar dynamic in *Odyssey* 11. In fact, the Odyssean Hades already suggests what the *Aeneid* expresses more directly: that the descent to the underworld functions structurally both as the point of greatest deception, of greatest concentration of myth, and as the source of the greatest power over the audience, of the most control over the truth received, the history. It is noteworthy that the only time Odysseus breaks off the long first-person account of his wanderings that fills the two thousand-plus verses of books 9–12 is in the middle of the *nekuia* (11.328–84). The Phaiakian audience responds in this intermezzo by offering the storyteller gifts for his return home to Ithaca and requests that he continue by telling them about the other heroes of the Trojan War. The lore of the *nekuia* is presented as a repository of the past from which each poet draws whatever mythic or historical personages are required by each audience and context. In a broader sense, the descent to the underworld reveals itself as the site where the means and intentions of representation may be expressed and contextualized.

Aeneid 6 is not, then, as Brooks argued, the first descent to the underworld to revise through performance, and not "by adventure"; rather, the descent to the underworld produces the effect of performance by representing its predecessors as pure myth. In its turn, Odysseus's *nekuia* froze *its* predecessors into the past by mortifying them as souls in the underworld: the epic hero as defined by the figure of Achilles in the Iliadic tradition, and the *katabasis* tradition emblematized by Heracles. The account of Achilles' about-face on the subject of heroism ("I would rather follow the plow as thrall to another man . . . than be a king over all the perished dead" [11.489–91]) has often been remarked as central to the *Odyssey*'s redefinition of heroism from the Iliadic glorious death in battle to the safe return home.[12] When Achilles greets the storyteller, "Son of Laertes and seed of Zeus, resourceful Odysseus, / hard man, what made you think of this bigger endeavor, how could you / endure to come down here to Hades' place?" (11.473–76), we find an internal explanation for his retraction of Iliadic heroics: he grants Odysseus superiority by virtue of the latter's daring, the ability to rewrite the past, to descend to the underworld and return.

---

[12] Trans. Richard Lattimore (1965, 1967; New York, 1991). On Achilles, see in particular Gregory Nagy, *The Best of the Achaeans* (Baltimore, 1979), esp. 15–65.

The explanation holds true for the evocation of Heracles' *katabasis* in the concluding verses of the *nekuia* (601–26).[13] Odysseus recounts that Heracles recognized and addressed him: "Son of Laertes and seed of Zeus, resourceful Odysseus, / unhappy man, are you too leading some wretched destiny / such as I too pursued when I went still in the sunlight? / . . . One time / he sent me here to fetch the dog back, and thought there could be / no other labor to be devised more difficult than that" (617–24). Heracles has become the frozen symbol for all past *katabases:* he authorizes Odysseus, admitting him into the pantheon while equally demonstrating where he is outstripped by him; as in Achilles' speech, the Odyssean epithet *polumechanos* ("of many devices," "resourceful") sets the novel terms of the achievement.

If it is helpful to remind ourselves of the extent to which the Homeric *nekuia* gives evidence of the autobiographical voice the *Aeneid* sets itself up as inventing (and the extent to which it suggests that the earlier epics might, in an infinite regression, reveal similar surprises), it is equally important not to elide all generic distinctions between Homeric and Vergilian epic. One way of historicizing that distinction for current criticism is to compare the divide in Vergilian criticism with the "Homeric question" that was given its modern form by F. A. Wolf in the late eighteenth century.[14] Both disputes find fertile ground in the respective descents to the underworld. But if for Aeneid scholars the question has been one of a unified or fragmentary interpretation of an established text, for Homerists the problem has been the unity or fragmentation of the text itself. More specifically in terms of the *katabases,* if for Vergilians we must decide whether or not the prophecy presents itself as myth (ironically) or as history (imperialistically), for scholars of the *Odyssey* we must decide whether Odysseus is supposed actually to have descended into Hades in a physical *katabasis* or to have summoned the souls up from its outskirts in a *nekuomanteia.*[15]

---

[13] On the legend of Heracles' descent to Hades and the possibility of its existence in pre-Homeric epic form, see Ganschinietz, 2399–2400; Heubeck, 114; Peter von der Mühll, "Odyssee," in *RE,* Supplementband 7 (Stuttgart, 1893–), 696–768 (this reference, 727); Merkelbach, 190. See Hartmut Erbse, *Beiträge zum Verständnis der "Odyssee"* (Berlin, 1972), on the possibility of the episode as a self-conscious citation of the previous legend (31–33).

[14] See F. A. Wolf, *Prolegomena to Homer,* 1795; trans. and ed. Anthony Grafton, Glenn W. Most, James E. G. Zetzel (Princeton, 1985). For a summary of the issues and bibliography, see 5–35 and 250–52.

[15] Heubeck, 76; Victor Bérard, *Nausicaa et le retour d'Ulisse,* vol. 4 of *Les navigations d'Ulisse* (Paris, 1929), 346 ff.

A tentative distinction would be that where the *Aeneid* constructs its ambiguity on the level of theme, the *Odyssey*'s ambiguity is textually based: either we allow the seams of the oral traditions and various redactors to fragment it or we seek to draw significance out of the tensions any given redactor chose not to smooth over.[16] Whatever verdict each generation has reached on the question of orality versus literacy or of single versus multiple authorship, the symmetry of the disputes along fault lines of ambiguity suggests in both cases less a contradiction than the symptoms of reaction to either the historical or the mythic antinomy of an autobiographical voice.

Just as the poet of the *Odyssey* reified the Iliadic epic tradition into the shade of Achilles and the heroic *katabasis* tradition into the image of Heracles with an orally inflected voice, so Vergil uses Homer to personify the epic past he is redefining. The first gesture is a surface negation of any past at all, evident in the Homeric epic in the response Odysseus makes when first informed that he must make the descent: "Circe, who will be our guide on that journey? No one / has ever yet in a black ship gone all the way to Hades" (*Odyssey* 10.501–2). The gesture is then complicated through the language, diction, and incidental narrative of the descent itself. The surface conceit of any descent to the underworld is its novelty; the latent admission is its derivativeness. The result of the contradiction is to ground originality in the extent of the novelty of the revision. The *katabasis* is new because it surpasses whatever it represents its predecessor(s) as having done; its novelty is founded on the mythicization of the past as its antithesis.

The *Aeneid* plays in several ways on the *Odyssey*'s construction of this model. The first is to provide the guide that Odysseus did not receive from Circe. It seems now that Odysseus needed no guide partly because he did not really descend to the underworld. Indeed, the site of the *nekuomanteia* was reputed, especially following the appearance of the *Aeneid,* to have been not beyond the world-encircling Oceanus as recounted by Odysseus but at the same Lake Avernus through which Aeneas and the Sibyl descend.[17] The poem both denies and establishes Odysseus's priority at Aver-

---

[16] The latter approach was pioneered for Homeric studies by Nagy. A similar movement can be seen in the equally thorny and contested field of biblical scholarship, in particular of the Hebrew Bible. See in particular Robert Alter, *The Art of Biblical Narrative* (New York, 1981); and David Damrosch, *The Narrative Covenant: Transformations of Genre in the Growth of Biblical Literature* (Ithaca, 1987).

[17] See Strabo, writing at the turn of the millennium, "The people prior to my time were wont to make Avernus the setting of the fabulous story of the Homeric *nekuia;* and, what is more, writers tell us that there actually was an oracle of the dead here and

nus. When Aeneas makes his request for guidance to the Sibyl, he invokes
Orpheus, Pollux, Theseus, and Heracles—but not Odysseus, although he
has already been invoked as the arch-villain of the account of the sack of
Troy and has been present as overarching intertext from the shipwreck
of the wandering Aeneas at the start of book 1. The strongest token of
Vergil's subversion of the historical precedence of the Homeric model is
that he grants his hero no knowledge of the history of the Odyssean
journey. He effaces every trace of that journey by the very act of following
so closely in the footsteps of his predecessor.

When the Sibyl sets the terms of the descent—"facilis descensus Averno
. . . sed revocare gradum superasque evadere ad auras, hoc opus, hic labor
est" (Easy is the descent to Avernus . . . but to recall thy steps and pass
out to the upper air, this is the task, this the toil! [*Aen.* 6.126–29])—
she is rewriting the Odyssean version of difficult descent pronounced by
Odysseus's mother Anticleia (*Odyssey* 11.155–59), by Achilles (473–76),
and by Heracles (622–26). Vergil shifts the ground of the contradiction
from the level of fact (did he or didn't he) to that of narrative (was it easy
or difficult). "Facilis descensus Averno" encapsulates the shift in paradigm
of the critical dispute as well, apparently forcing a choice between two
interpretations. As Eduard Norden remarks, the phrase presents "a number of contradictions": the descent is easy only in the general (i.e., allegorical) sense of dying; but for someone still alive, it is actually quite difficult,
whence the elaborate preparation of sacrifices and the search for the
golden bough (159). Conversely, the return proves to be quite simple on
the literal level, even though its meaning may be recondite (ibid.). The
Odyssean intertext glosses the contradiction as a sign of a change in terms:
the heroism inheres no longer in the attempted visit (easy descent) but in
what is brought back out (hard return).

Aeneas's prophetic vision of the future Rome, the mythico-historical
teleology of the epic, is the novelty opposed by Vergil to the henceforth
aimless heroism of Odysseus. In other words, Aeneas needs guidance precisely because, unlike Odysseus, he is embarked on a learning process. Of
course, if we hold Vergil's Odysseus at bay and make a more objective
comparison, we can indeed recover a social meaning in Odysseus's desired

---

that Odysseus visited it" (*The Geography of Strabo,* trans. H. L. Jones, 8 vols. [Cam-
bridge, Mass., 1969], 5.4.5). Homer was absorbed into the Vergilian context, but as
pure myth. The earlier Lucretius, *On the Nature of the Universe,* 6.760–68, also links
the myths to the locale of Avernus so as even more strongly to deny them. See Bérard,
352–53; and Wendy Lesser, *The Life below Ground: A Study of the Subterranean in
Literature and History* (Boston, 1987), 34–41.

nostos ("struggling for his own life and the homecoming of his compan-
ions" [1.5]), but next to the imperial majesty of the *Aeneid*'s "So hard and
huge a task it was to found the Roman people" (1.33), any consideration
of Odysseus's power struggles on Ithaca must pale in comparison.

The *Aeneid* presents itself as a history-making enterprise, with the
Homeric poems constituting one element of that history. Take the first
encounter in the underworld, with the drowned and unburied helmsman
Palinurus (6.337–83). Vergil is working here with two givens: the Cape
of Palinurus on the coast of Sicily and Odysseus's encounter with the
unburied Elpenor in 11.51–83. Neither element is strictly necessary, but
the effect of Vergil's use of them is to make them appear to have been so.
The nomenclature of the cape provides Vergil with a ready-made topographical datum to legitimate etiologically the myth he is creating. By
grafting the retrospective myth onto a Homeric intertext, he glorifies the
historical, proto-Roman, and heroic Palinurus by contrast with a mythic
and pathetic Elpenor. The latter had fallen in a drunken stupor from
the roof of Circe's house to his death. The deflation of Elpenor's heroic
aspirations is completed by Odysseus's agreement to fix the rower's oar
on the burial mound (Heubeck, 82); Palinurus's status as sacrificial victim
to Neptune, as the one who will not come safely to Italy, and his subsequent immortalization as the eponymous cape are predicated on that deflation as a synecdoche of *Odyssey* versus *Aeneid*. The Homeric death is
base and meaningless, the burial promise a travesty of Greek heroism.
Palinurus, in contrast, suffers the hard fate of the Roman citizen, heart-
lessly sacrificed to the higher destiny of the foundation of the empire and
rewarded in kind by the immortal fame of that sacrifice. How we then
inflect the thematic ambiguity of the passage—whether as straightforward
mythmaking or as ironic criticism of the vagaries of empire—is a decision
made from within the now-established framework.

Also indicative of Vergil's textual strategy is the synthesis of Anchises
out of motifs from Odysseus's mother, Anticleia; the blind seer Tiresias;
and the king and general Agamemnon. The distinct roles of parent, seer,
and comrade-in-arms are conjoined into the proto-Roman pater familias.[18]
The reunion combines Odysseus's futile attempt to embrace his mother
with Agamemnon's tearful greeting of his former companion. In so doing,
it stresses the necessary inextricability of Aeneas's filial and civic duties. By
contrast, encountering his mother's shade was fundamentally incidental to

---

[18] Also striking is Vergil's construction of Dido's spurning of her faithless lover out
of the Homeric warrior's quarrel between Odysseus and Ajax and the final parting of
Hektor and Andromache (*Iliad* 6.495–96).

Odysseus; he had to deny himself the reunion until after he had heard out
Tiresias. Both Anticleia and Agamemnon gave Odysseus news and advice
about the situation on Ithaca; by combining such advice with the prophetic thrust of the Tiresian intertext, the reason for the Odyssean descent,
Vergil stresses that for Aeneas the personal news *is* the future of Rome;
his family *is* Rome-to-be.

At the same time, another part of the Tiresian intertext, along with
echoes of Circe's role in advising Odysseus, is shifted onto the Sibyl. In
particular, she takes over the mythic, shamanistic residue in the Vergilian
katabasis: she is the one possessed by the godhead, she demands the sacrifice, she negotiates with the creatures of the underworld. In a variation on
the strategy of mythifying Homer within the *Aeneid,* Vergil shifts away
from Anchises and Aeneas the archaic mythic elements he must retain in
order to represent a recognizably awesome descent to the underworld,
leaving father and son free to participate in what thereon is established
conversely as the historical substrate. Similarly, although Homeric intertexts predominate both quantitatively and thematically, Vergil derives
further material from the Orphic tradition (Norden, 270). Echoing Odysseus's narration of his own journey, Vergil has the Sibyl describe the
punishments of Tartarus. As if in homage to the invention of Odysseus's
travels, Vergil subtly distinguishes the most fantastic and most traditionally mythical part of the underworld—where the ancient figures are tor-
mented for their sins—from the (by opposition) credible regions actually
visited by Aeneas.

The following dialectic may thus be demonstrated in *Aeneid* 6. In order
to generate the mythico-religious authority necessary to legitimate Anchises' speech as prophecy, Vergil must retain and exploit the shamanistic
tradition of the *nekuomanteia.* Furthermore, to put that authority behind a
prophecy intended to rewrite the mythology of the origins and past of Rome
in a form that will carry weight as history, Vergil must invoke the poet's
authority as one able to generate truth out of language, meaning out of lies.
The archaic Homer is shifted onto the Sibylline narrative along with the religious and mythic material of the Orphic tradition. Simultaneously, Homer's
authority as a historical poet is shifted onto Aeneas, Anchises, and the encounters with souls in the underworld. As with the mythic material (for
example, the horrific description of the Sibyl's possession in lines 646–
55), the poetic authority is manifestly a negative contrast to the civilized
progress of the *Aeneid.* But the contrast not only aggrandizes Vergil's
poem by asserting its superiority while availing itself of the power of the
predecessors evoked; its definition of the tradition as mythic, archaic, and
false maintains the illusion of itself as historical, contemporary, and true
despite the mythic, archaic, and false means used to achieve that illusion.

I HAVE DWELLED at length on the Vergilian model because it set the framework for use of *katabasis,* allegory, and the autobiographical voice through to Dante's *Commedia;* and it is with reference to Dante that much of modernism and postwar readings of modernism derive their terms. A dialectical understanding of Vergil's rewriting of Homer makes far easier that of a tradition culminated (and thus defined) by Dante. Not surprisingly, a similarly informed understanding of Dante sets the stage for a corrective reading of both medieval and modernist literature. In particular, I am suggesting a certain medieval model of writing, the autobiographical allegory of conversion, as a source and intertext of modernism.[19]

This is not an unproblematic model—it is grounded in contradiction—but the questions raised by such contradiction and the ways in which it does or does not resolve them are precisely those that lie as unrecognized and unacknowledged antinomies within modern writing as well. Of modern critics, Benjamin has contributed the most toward such a model; his work is always involved in representing the antinomies it means to reveal in its object of study. The *Trauerspiel* book, for example, begins with just such a program: "It is characteristic of philosophical writing to take, with every turn [*Wendung*], a new stance before the question of representation" (*GS* 1:207; *TB* 27).

The particular "turn" with which this book is concerned entails leap-frogging back and forth over half a millennium. Such a step is partly polemical, intended to redress a relative neglect, while conversely not feeling so great a need to cover a field already well tilled.[20] It is also prompted

---

[19] Several writers have suggested comparative studies of the descent to the underworld: Carol Zaleski makes a connection with the contemporary mass-cultural phenomenon of near-death experience, *Otherworld Journeys: Accounts of Near-Death Experience in Medieval and Modern Times* (New York, 1987); Lesser discusses Vergil and Schliemann (poetry as archaeology and archaeology as poetry) and mythic vs. scientific descents in Vergil, Lucretius, and Jules Verne (50–76, 34–49). In *The Madwoman in the Attic: The Woman Writer and the Nineteenth-Century Literary Imagination* (New Haven, 1979), Sandra M. Gilbert and Susan Gubar propose the image of the cave as an ambivalent site of both patriarchal oppression and female power but then go on to split the ambivalence into opposed mythified images of either male journeys of initiation or female journeys into the "revitalizing darkness" (93–104). Beryl Schlossman uses *allegory of conversion* to refer in purely formalist terms to "the representation of an investment in style" (*The Orient of Style: Modernist Allegories of Conversion* [Durham, 1991], 4).

[20] In terms of medieval and modern allegory, several general studies of allegory include chapters on twentieth-century texts as supplements to medieval and Renaissance material, but from within a resolutely structural or linguistic paradigm. See Carolynn Van Dyke, *The Fiction of Truth: Structures of Meaning in Narrative and*

by the connection to a shift in predominance from a vertically to a horizontally constructed paradigm of the cosmos in Europe during the age of exploration, which appears to have shifted back again in the nineteenth century as exploration turned toward mining, underground construction, and other developments of industrialization (Williams, 8). A juxtaposition of the two periods in terms of their use of the descent to the underworld brings out a broader affinity between them.

This affinity is reflected on the literary battleground between allegory and symbol, which is laid out very differently in medieval and modern poetics than during the centuries in between, where traditionally there has been seen a progressive rejection of allegory in favor of symbol that culminated with the romantics. The extent and effects of that rejection are the matter of another book; what I maintain here is that the ascendancy of an allegorical mode from Baudelaire through the present is equaled in magnitude only by its medieval dominance.[21] This dominance is neither

---

Dramatic Allegory (Ithaca, 1985); and Maureen Quilligan, *The Language of Allegory: Defining the Genre* (1979; Ithaca, 1992). Jauss is the principal critic to have dealt at all comprehensively with medieval and with modern allegory and, to some degree, the relationship between the two. See especially *Alterität und Modernität der mittelalterlichen Literatur* (Munich, 1977) and *Studien zum Epochenwandel der ästhetischen Moderne* (Frankfurt, 1989). The strength of Jauss's studies—his emphasis on the reception and historical context of the texts examined—which brings out the affinity to begin with, is at the same time responsible for their drawback vis-à-vis the present book: there is little interest in a synchronic view to go with the documentation of reception.

[21] De Man's influential essay "The Rhetoric of Temporality" (1967; rpt. in *Blindness and Insight*) was instrumental in revising the evaluation of allegory but also maintained a periodization based in the romantic polarity. Other research has done much to complicate the modern critical reception of Renaissance, baroque, and early-nineteenth-century allegory as the negative pole of the privileged symbol while contextualizing an allegorical mode making sense of the decline of Christian paradigms of the Middle Ages and the resurgence of classical and, later, technological models of closure, resolution, and totality. Angus Fletcher, *Allegory: The Theory of a Symbolic Mode* (Ithaca, 1964), ranges widely and fruitfully over the entire terrain of Western allegory. The literature on Renaissance allegory, in particular the British and Italian epic, is especially rich; most useful in this context is Michael Murrin, *The Veil of Allegory* (Chicago, 1969) and *The Allegorical Epic* (Chicago, 1980). Antoine Compagnon, *La seconde main ou le travail de la citation* (Paris, 1979), treats the Renaissance in France. Benjamin's *Trauerspiel* book remains the standard study of baroque allegory. The frequent contradictions between theory and practice of allegory vs. symbol by Goethe, the British and the German romantics, and the American transcendentalists remain somewhat understudied, although the field has been expanding rapidly in recent years. See especially Benjamin's doctoral dissertation, *Der Begriff der Kunstkritik in der deutschen Romantik* (GS 1:7–122), and the collections *Formen und Funktionen der Allegorie*, ed. Walter Haug (Stuttgart, 1979), and *Allegory, Myth, and Symbol*, ed. Bloomfield.

identical in form nor without resemblance; rather, modernism took up issues that had lain comparatively dormant during the intervening centuries. Just as the current concerns are dialectically related to their earlier manifestations, so the autobiographical allegory of conversion, which is taken up again as a vehicle for expressing these concerns, remains dependent on its medieval predecessors.

In *Writing in Dante's Cult of Truth*, María Rosa Menocal suggests a related shift in critical strategy: "Where is the falsehood in the history that tells us that Borges as a young man learned about literature not from the Argentine short story writers who preceded him (that, perhaps, is a different story) but rather as he was riding back and forth on the trolleys of Buenos Aires, sitting next to Dante and his *Commedia?*" [22] Dante receives a new guide as Borges leads the poet in a trolley through the streets of Buenos Aires to work in the Municipal Library. The synchronic encounter between two authors in hell is inextricably linked to a diachronic mode that is defined not by the influence of Borges's predecessors ("literary history") but by the actual situation of reading.

The diachrony that brings together the material and the intellectual experience of literature is identical for our purposes to that defined above in the context of Vergil's *Aeneid:* the past is remade when reread and rewritten but also simply through the new context in which it is encountered. The predominance of such moments within the texts themselves documents the presence of the autobiographical voice, for they insist on a link to the diachrony of the voice of the writer while simultaneously insisting on textual autonomy from that diachrony.

The autobiographical voice is a particularly self-conscious variation on what Edward W. Said has defined more generally as the "worldliness" of a text:

> Even if we accept (as in the main I do) the arguments put forward by Hayden White—that there is no way to get past texts in order to apprehend "real" history directly—it is still possible to say that such a claim need not also eliminate interest in the events and circumstances entailed by and expressed in the texts themselves. Those events are textual too . . . and much that goes on in texts alludes to them, *affiliates* itself directly to them. . . . [T]exts are worldly, to some degree they are events, and, even when they appear to deny it, they are nevertheless a part of the social world, human life, and of course the historical moment in which they are located and interpreted. [23]

---

[22] *Writing in Dante's Cult of Truth: From Borges to Boccaccio* (Durham, 1991), 3.
[23] *The World, the Text, and the Critic* (Cambridge, Mass., 1983), 4.

The text's worldliness and what we could call its "wordliness," its identity as a linguistic creation, converge in the autobiographical voice. The author both signals the presence of the social world in the text and lays claim to control over it as language.

Now, if we may take it for granted these days that any text is worldly, it is something else entirely to demonstrate its active participation in that discourse of worldliness. The dominance of formalist accounts of allegory has led to an equivalent dominance of formalist accounts of modernism.[24] This has led, in turn, either to a vision of allegory as an ahistorical, formal phenomenon or to a severance of medieval from modern allegory on the grounds that the former was subservient to the religious world view of the time. To be sure, many valuable insights have emerged from such accounts, just as they have from more recent analyses of literature as one among many discourses—as purely political or social allegory, in other words. But what is needed now is a rereading of allegory as a mode of literature that foregrounds its participation in both accounts of allegorical discourse simultaneously, thus making it possible to discuss politics and aesthetics as distinct fields and as they converge within each text.[25]

This possibility cannot be realized solely through close attention to the present of the text, whether "present" be construed textually or historically. Words and concepts have complex histories; any contemporary appropriation of them invokes these histories by way of authorizing itself. In the fourteenth of his well-known theses "On the Concept of History," Benjamin raised this question with reference to the revival of Rome in the French Revolution: "Fashion has a flair for the topical, no matter where it stirs in the thickets of the long ago. It is the tiger's leap into the past, except that it takes place in an arena commanded by the ruling class. The same leap in the open air of history is the dialectical one, which is how

---

[24] I include in particular the sequence of theoretical schools from new criticism through structuralism down to deconstruction, as well as many varieties of postmodernism. Raymond Williams makes a similar argument in the posthumously published *Politics of Modernism: Against the New Conformists*, ed. Tony Pinkney (London, 1989), esp. 31–63.

[25] Andreas Huyssen raises the question of the dominance of formalist accounts of modernism in his essay "Paris/Childhood: The Fragmented Body in Rilke's *Notebooks of Malte Laurids Brigge*," in *Modernity and the Text*, ed. Huyssen and David Bathrick (New York, 1989), 113–16. According to Huyssen, the same problem arises in dealing with postmodern writers, where "neither the attacks nor the defenses of . . . the author and the person, ever r[i]se to the challenge of discussing politics and aesthetics both in their linkage *and* in their separation" ("After the Wall: The Failure of German Intellectuals," *NGC* 52 [Winter 1991]: 143).

Marx understood the revolution" (*GS* 1:701).[26] The two leaps—"the tiger's leap into the past" and "the same leap in the open air of history"—gloss the two returns at issue in the descent to the underworld and suggest a method for the analysis of both their medieval and their modern manifestations.

The first leap describes the descent into the past staged by the autobiographical voice as the rereading and rewriting of the tradition. It is synchronic; its signposts are Vergil, Augustine, and Dante; and it is governed by the whims of fashion and subject to ideological pressure in its very structure. It reconstitutes the present by means of a newly reinvented past, as we see in Marx's observation that his contemporaries idealize the most useful myths of their predecessors by projecting them backward as eternal forms. The recent past is appropriated for the present, "not as a historic result, but as history's point of departure . . . not arising historically, but posited by nature. This illusion has been characteristic of every new epoch to this day."[27] There are two ways of unmasking this mythic illusion of timelessness; both are characteristic of what Benjamin describes as the second leap.

The second descent into the past rereads the same text in order to "rouse the world below." Unlike the first, which is solely mythic, this descent corresponds to Marx's description of the dialectic, which "regards every historically developed form as being in a fluid state, in motion, and therefore grasps its transient aspect [*vergänglichen Seite*] as well."[28] Such a dialectical leap into the past is both self-conscious and critical, as we saw above in the case of Freud. It neither wishes away the power of myth nor attributes to it the illusion of history. It remains—and here it is indeed *modernist* in identity—acutely aware of the shaky ideological ground on which its claim to revolution rests as long as that claim continues to be constituted only through language.

Writing in the mid-nineteenth century, Marx had good reason still to be convinced of the possibility of an actual leap into the open air of history, of the necessity and the desirability of shaking off "the tradition of all the dead generations" that "weighs like a nightmare on the brain of the living."[29] Writing in the late 1930s, however, Benjamin retained pri-

---

[26] *Illuminations,* trans. Harry Zohn (New York, 1969), 261; hereafter cited as *I.*

[27] Karl Marx, *Grundrisse der Kritik der politischen Ökonomie (Rohentwurf), 1850–1858,* appendix to *Werke,* 41 vols. (Berlin, 1956–74), 5–6; trans. Martin Nicolaus, *Grundrisse: Introduction to the Critique of Political Economy* (New York, 1973), 83.

[28] *Werke* 23:28; *Capital,* vol. 1, trans. Ben Fowkes (New York, 1990), 103.

[29] *Werke* 8:115; *The Eighteenth Brumaire of Louis Bonaparte,* 1859, trans. Ben Fowkes, in *Surveys from Exile,* ed. David Fernbach (New York, 1974), 143–249; this citation, 146.

marily the heuristic force of the Marxian turn, taking "revolution" seriously in its linguistic sense, as a *turning back toward* what had already
happened but had not yet been comprehended. To restore history to that
first leap into myth required not just a return to the ghosts of the past but
a *new* turn to the more untimely and unlikely among them. Marx's claim
that the German economy could be best understood by studying England
is translated into Benjamin's characterization of French revolutionary history by way of the vagaries of fashion.

One way to uncover the mythic function of the descent to the underworld in modernism as well as to account for the mode in both its "transient nature" (diachrony) and its "momentary existence" (synchrony) is to
analyze it with reference to an epoch when its mechanism is far easier to
discern. For the mythically decisive return to "the open air" of Marxian
revolution is mirrored by the challenge presented to Aeneas by the Sibyl
when answering his request that she guide him through the underworld:
"Easy is the descent to Avernus . . . but to recall thy steps and pass out to
the upper air, this is the task, this the toil!" The descent into myth is
simple; some manner of return is the aim of all descents made through the
mode of the autobiographical voice. The ancient manifestation of Marx's
return to the upper air by the dialectical grasp of revolution is the creation
of a prophetic voice. Only by means of a critical reading of its modern
and medieval manifestations will we also be able to distinguish more
rigorously between them.

The roots of the medieval mode of descent are in Homer and Vergil,
but it takes recognizable form as divine inspiration in the autobiographical allegory of conversion developed by Augustine and Dante. The typology of Anchises' retrospective prophecy of the history of Rome opens up
the epic descent into historical allegory. The narrative line derived from
Homeric epic, which will take Aeneas through victory in the war against
Turnus's army, is outstripped by book 6's recitation of the legendary
genealogy of Rome. The same ground is covered as in books 7–12, as well
as the centuries between Aeneas's conquest and Vergil's composition of
the poem in 29–18 B.C.E. The autobiographical voice, and the historical
allegory projected by it, are manifest only in the latter narrative, although
it derives its mythic force from the epic concentration of the former.

In Christian rereadings and rewritings of the *Aeneid,* the narrative lines
are integrated within a single authorial voice as it speaks before and after
conversion. As John Freccero has put it: "The exegetical language seems
to structure experience, identifying it as part of the redemptive process,
while the irreducibly personal elements lend to the *exemplum* the force
of personal witness. Together, *exemplum* and experience, allegory and

biography, form a confession of faith for other men."[30] The moment of conversion calques the moment of Anchises' speech, rewriting the about-turn at the nadir of the descent as the temporal union of the two voices in the present of prophecy. Freccero's model of the allegory of conversion exemplifies the mechanism whereby Augustine and Dante establish the sense of presence that in a Christian model means being face to face with God; that is, with the revelation of truth. The discussion above of Vergil and Homer, however, makes clear that this moment, even if troped as prophecy, remains simply rewriting. The autobiographical voice intrudes at this moment as a means of heightening authority by creating the impression of historical, as opposed to purely mythic, presence.

The phenomenon of conversion itself represents a moment of convergence in which faith enters into and *turns* everyday life in a different direction. In fourfold allegorical interpretation, as we see below, conversion is the moral application of the Christ-event to the present-day. Cast into the dynamics of reading, conversion becomes the register of the text's ability to affect the reader and thus the token of its authority. Being linguistically based, it acts through the rhetorical means of persuasion, but the substance of its rhetoric is to persuade, and thus to prove by producing extratextual truth, that it is in fact more than mere persuasion. And it throws this mechanism of persuasion at the reader as a gauntlet, as an inevitable choice either to accept or to reject, but never to step outside, the theological reading.

This is how the ambiguity evident in the respectively textual and narrative disputes around the Homeric epics and Vergil's *Aeneid* manifests itself in a Christian context. It becomes an issue of theology versus art, of religious versus literary texts: either the *Confessions* is inspired Christian doctrine or it is the first work of literary autobiography; either Dante thought he was a divinely inspired prophet or he thought he was a poet imaginatively rendering an allegory. Now, this either/or choice is inherited to a large degree from modernist renderings of the past and obscures the fact that these allegories of conversion are constructed out of the force field created between the extremes of fiction and theology, between one leap and the other. This becomes clear with a closer look at the medieval construction of those two leaps as the tension between two modes of allegory.

PAUL AND VERGIL are the two great medieval authorities of the otherworld, the former for the vision alluded to in 2 Corinthians and the latter

[30] *Dante: The Poetics of Conversion* (Cambridge, 1986), 4. I am indebted to the insights of chaps. 1, 5, and 7.

for book 6 of the *Aeneid*. The figure of the Apostle emblematizes the
possibility of unmediated divine vision but also the prohibition of any
representation of it (2 Cor. 12:4). Vergil, in contrast, offers a poetic model
for depicting the afterlife and the historic truths that went with it, but a
model now damned because replete with pagan error. The ninth chapter
of Acts is paradigmatic of the relationship between the two exempla: the
conversion of Saul into Paul is followed directly by the conversion of one
"Aeneas" from a paralyzed pagan into a whole and sound Christian:
"And it came to pass, as Peter passed throughout all quarters, he came
down also to the saints which dwelt at Lydda. And there he found a
certain man named Aeneas, which had kept his bed eight years, and was
sick of the palsy. And Peter said unto him, Aeneas, Jesus Christ maketh
thee whole: arise, and make thy bed. And he arose immediately. And all
that dwelt at Lydda and Saron saw him, and turned [*conversi sunt*] to the
Lord" (Acts 9:32–35). The necessarily accidental nature of the conjuncture of the two converts is significant: *Aeneid* 6 makes its appearance with
regularity in medieval allegories of conversion, but always disclaimed as
pagan. Any identification with it must be read between the lines, as I
propose to do here with two examples of such accidental combinations:
the allegorical mode introduced by Augustine whereby Vergil and the
descent to the underworld were disseminated through the Christian Middle Ages, and the twelfth-century allegorical commentary on the *Aeneid*
wherein the Chartrian philosopher and poet Bernard Silvestris subtly exposed every inconsistency of the Augustinian model.[31]

    Through Aeneas and Paul we find the classical dialectic of myth and
history within the descent to the underworld recast in the Christian form
of the two allegories: *allegoria in verbis* and *allegoria in facto*. Their
precise meanings vary widely; I outline here the salient features that characterize the two allegories consistently as antinomial but inseparable
modes.[32] *Allegoria in facto*, or allegory in deeds, is a polysemous narrative
or event of which—and this is what distinguishes it from Vergil's use of
typology—not only the allegorical but also the literal level is taken to be
historically true. Traditionally, the only accepted author is God, and the

---

[31] For an extended exposition of the following material, see Pike, 25–118.

[32] For a brief introduction to the two allegories, see Jean Pépin, *Dante et la tradition
de l'allégorie* (Montreal, 1970) and *Mythe et allégorie: Les origines grecques et les
contestations judéo-chrétiennes*, 2d rev. ed. (Paris, 1976), 487–501. Particularly useful
out of an extensive secondary literature are Henri de Lubac, *Exégèse médiévale*, 4 vols.
(Paris, 1959–64); Beryl Smalley, *The Study of the Bible in the Middle Ages*, 2d ed.
(Oxford, 1952); Armand Strubel, "Allégorie *in verbis* et *in facto*," *Poétique* 23 (1975):
342–57; and Jon Whitman, *Allegory: Dynamics of an Ancient and Medieval Mode*
(Cambridge, 1988).

only "texts" are the events of world history and Scripture. In practice, *allegoria in facto* is an entirely interpretive mode that consists in giving symbolic meaning to actual events.

The levels of meaning are distinguished temporally, ranging from a basic division between past and present to what has become known as the fourfold method: one event is given allegorical meaning by a later one, which is thus said to have fulfilled it; together the two events constitute a single unit of meaning, the *figura*. These are generally called the literal and allegorical levels of meaning, although the three figurative levels are often also referred to collectively as allegorical. The subsequent levels are the moral or tropological—the application of the *figura* to the present-day life of the individual—and the anagogical—its application to the world to come. The paradigmatic form envisions world history as a narrative of the Christ-event: an Old Testament event, as for example the crossing of the Red Sea by Moses, is shown in retrospect to have prefigured Christ's salvation of his people by leading them out of damnation; the moral level would be the reader's conversion through faith in this message; the anagogical, Christ's leading his people into paradise after the Last Judgment. The *allegoria in facto* is thus a potent tool for the prophetic rewriting of history characteristic of the *descensus ad inferos;* the dilemma for the medieval writer is that divine authority is available only indirectly, by giving up poetic authority and becoming an exegete of God's creation.

The *allegoria in verbis*, or allegory of words, is the province of "poetic fictions," the narrative mode of personification that dominated medieval discourse. It dates back to Stoic readings of Homeric gods as abstract forces; as an interpretive practice I refer to it below as allegoresis. With the rise of Christianity, *allegoria in verbis* developed into a narrative genre, as in the *Psychomachia* of Augustine's contemporary Prudentius, where the phenomenon of conversion is externalized as an epic, Vergilian battle between assorted Vices and Virtues.[33] This is the narrative form through which the *Aeneid* was adapted as the autobiography of conversion; by the time of Fulgentius in the sixth century, the poem was being wholeheartedly Christianized, books 1–6 as the steps toward conversion, books 7–12 as the converted soul's battle against vice.[34] But if the conversion of Aeneas retained

---

[33] *Prudentius*, trans. H. J. Thomson, vol. 1 (Cambridge, Mass., 1969). On the subtlety and complexity of this much-maligned poem, see S. Georgia Nugent, *Allegory and Poetics: The Structure and Imagery of Prudentius' "Psychomachia"* (Frankfurt, 1985); see also Whitman, 83–91.

[34] Fabius Planciades Fulgentius, *De Continentia Vergiliana*, in *Opera*, ed. Rudolf Helm (Leipzig, 1898), 81–107; Fulgentius, *The Exposition of the Content of Vergil According to Moral Philosophy*, in *Medieval Literary Criticism*, ed. and trans. O. B. Hardison, Jr. (New York, 1974), 69–80.

the personal authority of the converted soul, it gave up the prophetic claim
to history of father Anchises' speech. Classical allegoresis could salvage
pagan texts as Christianized myth, and *allegoria in verbis* could give narrative temporality to individual experience and philosophical abstractions,
but they could not pretend even indirectly to extratextual authority.

As with myth and history in Homer and Vergil, however, the two
allegories appear not as independent and isolated modes but as inseparable antinomies. The extremes of Aeneas and Paul are played off each other
to negotiate a discursive space for creating divine authority through poetic
means. The pivotal moment of Augustine's *Confessions* conjoins the Vergilian journey and the Pauline act of reading. Pagan philosophy is troped
as bad epic; good epic is fitted out in doctrinal trappings:

> For it is one thing from the woody top of a mountain to see the land of
> peace, and not to come across the way thither; and in vain to travel
> through trackless ways [*per invia*], beset all around with these fugitives
> and deserters lying in ambush with their prince, who is both lion and
> serpent. It is another thing to keep on the way which leads thither,
> which is guarded by the care of the heavenly general, where there are
> none that deserted the heavenly army to exercise robberies, which they
> abhor as much as their very torment. These things did by wonderful
> means sink into my very bowels when I read that least of your Apostles,
> and had considered upon your works and had trembled.[35]

The new model derives its novelty from labeling the old model a perilous
myth; the Christian journey has authority, and that authority pits the way

---

[35] CCSL 27, 7.21.27. Hereafter cited by book, chapter, and paragraph number.
Trans. based on William Watts (1631; Cambridge, Mass., 1977) and R. S. Pine-Coffin
(New York, 1961). For general background on St. Augustine's relationship to pagan
literature, see Henri-Irène Marrou, *Saint Augustine et la fin de la culture antique*, 4th
ed. (Paris, 1958); Pierre Courcelle, *Les Lettres grecques en Occident de Macrobe à
Cassiodore* (Paris, 1948), 137–205; trans. Harry E. Wedeck, *Late Latin Writers and
Their Greek Sources* (Cambridge, Mass., 1969); and Courcelle, *"Les Confessions" de
Saint Augustin dans la tradition littéraire: Antécédents et posterité* (Paris, 1963), esp.
91–197. For the relationship with Vergil in particular, see Andrew Fichter, *Poets His-
torical: Dynastic Epic in the Renaissance* (New Haven, 1982); Harald Hagendahl,
Augustine and the Latin Classics (New York, 1967), 2:384–463; H. C. Coffin, "The
Influence of Vergil on St. Jerome and on St. Augustine," *Classical World* 17 (1923):
70–75; Domenico Bassi, "Sant' Agostino e Virgilio," *Annale dell'Istruzione Media* 6
(1930): 420–31; John O'Meara, "Augustine the Artist and the *Aeneid*," in *Mélanges
Mohrmann* (Utrecht, 1963), 252–61; Sarah Spence, *Rhetorics of Reason and Desire:
Virgil, Augustine, and the Troubadours* (Ithaca, 1988).

of Scripture against the *invia* of satanic fictions. But there remains as much of Vergil in one model as in the other; for, as we saw above, *Aeneid* 6 itself had already made a point of subordinating the "aimless" epic narrative of the *Odyssey* to its own prophetic reading of history.

Augustine employs a similar strategy in the *City of God* when he splits the *descensus* of *Aeneid* 6 into two versions, one acknowledged Vergilian, the other claimed as his own. Those things he cannot use, he explicitly rejects as Vergil's mythic model of return, proposing in its place a historical and true *imitatio Christi* that remains equally Vergilian, but this time only sotto voce. Augustine rewrites return to make it available only to a convert following in the footsteps of Christ, the only person ever to have descended and returned of his own volition and on his own authority. By combining imagery of the *descensus ad inferos* with figural vocabulary, Augustine makes hell the site of the earthly conversion of experience into exemplum, of history into *allegoria in facto*. Not only the Old Testament but the Jews themselves follow a figural pattern: "Otherwise, as long as Moses is read a veil is laid on their hearts; on the other hand, whenever anyone passes over from that people to Christ, the veil will be taken away. For we may be sure that the very aim of those who pass over is transformed from the old to the new, so that the aim of each is no longer the attainment of material, but of spiritual felicity."[36] As Old Testament is reinvented by New, so the converted Jews become living *figurae,* examples of how each life is a narrative authored by God, which become legible only when fulfilled by conversion.

Conversion occurs at the prophetic turning point in the pattern of Christ's life as a descent to the underworld and return to the heavens: "Thus he shall live and shall not see death; although he will first have died, but will have rescued his soul from the clutches of hell [*de manu inferni*], where he descended in order to undo the bonds of hell from some of the dead" (17.11; 740). The descent in order to harrow hell allows the Old Testament Jews to return to the heavens, revealing their deaths to have prefigured that very descent. Moreover, Augustine underscores the *imitatio Christi* as an autobiographical allegory of conversion: in order to ascend to God, we too must descend into hell and, following Christ, be converted, thereby rendering our past life as a legible narrative, a microcosmic parallel of the religio-historical scheme of world history of which the Christ-event is the crux.

This structure is the basic justification for the autobiography of the

---

[36] Cited by book and chapter number from *De Civitate Dei*, CCSL 47–48, 17.7; trans. Henry Bettenson, *The City of God* (New York, 1972), this quotation, 733.

Confessions: Augustine recounts his life as God's creation, in retrospect, from the point of view of one who, having been converted, sees clearly. He then uses the authority established from that conversion to authorize the interpretation of Genesis in the concluding books. The historical application in the *City of God* of the descent to hell as prerequisite to the ascent to the heavens is analogous to the use of the *descensus ad inferos* in the *Confessions* as a metaphorical foundation for the depths of the adolescent Augustine's wanderings and flounderings in the sea of iniquity exemplarized by his misuse of rhetoric. Indeed, he presents his state immediately preceding conversion as being asleep and dead: "Nor had I anything now to answer thee calling to me: Arise, thou that sleepest, and stand up from the dead and Christ shall give thee light [Eph. 5:14]" (8.5.12). For the central purpose of the Augustinian allegory of conversion, wherein the converted author leads the unconverted audience through the hell of paganism and sin by means of himself as allegorical everyman (specifically, as *imitatio Christi*), is to teach the correct means of reading, a dominant trope from the tears spilled over the *Aeneid* in book 1 to the child's whisper of "tolle lege" in book 8 to the concluding books of exegesis.

What Augustine's reformulation accomplished, beyond authorizing his own rewriting of the *descensus,* was permanently to slant readings of the *Aeneid* in favor of the first six books. The *Confessions* simply omits the narrative events from conversion until the present of composition as unessential. This short-circuiting of the narrative, which might have seemed peculiar to a pagan reader of the Aeneid, is easily accomplished by the introduction of the *imitatio Christi* into the narrative structure (and would remain a constant in medieval adaptations of the model).[37] For after his resurrection, Christ returned to heaven and fulfilled the meaning of history, just as the convert is now divinely inspired and beyond temptation. The epic narrative, the final six books of the *Aeneid,* persists, but only in

[37] The allure of truncation is evident: the sixth book had always exacted a disproportionately large amount of commentary, even in early non-Christian commentators such as Servius and Macrobius. The tendency to cut the *Aeneid* off at the sixth book remains significant within a Judaeo-Christian tradition of allegory and reading and, to the degree that one can generalize, primarily within a medieval and modern attitude to the dilemma. In the Renaissance, conversely, Maffeo Vegio added a thirteenth book (which was bound with copies of the *Aeneid* through to the eighteenth century), thus bringing true closure to the epic narrative thread and resolving the passion/duty conflict by depicting Aeneas's marriage to Lavinia and final ascent to the stars. See *Maphaeus Vegius and His Thirteenth Book of the "Aeneid": A Chapter on Vergil in the Renaissance,* ed. A. C. Brinton (Stanford, 1930); cf. Fichter, 44.

the form of the convert's lifetime battle against the vices of the world in expectation of the inevitable end.[38]

In Augustine's hands, the double structure creates a liminal space wherein the living writer has the rhetorical status of being already in heaven: he has followed Christ's life in history, his meaning as *figura* has been fulfilled, and his life is thus interpretable as an *allegoria in facto*. The narrative allegory of conversion leads us to this point; its role is to establish both the ability to read with it (by recapitulation of the steps it took) and the subsequent authority of its autobiographical voice to impose its own reading onto history or Scripture. In point of fact, Augustine's narrative works are self-fulfilling prophecies: Augustine needs God's authority to validate his rhetorical structure; he needs the rhetorical structure to assume God's authority. The autobiographical voice is the transformer, treating Scripture as myth when the narrative framework can pass as history (*Confessions* 1–9), and treating Scripture as history when the narrative framework is in danger of being revealed as mythic (*Confessions* 10–13). Augustine's success—the most absolute, if not the first or the most self-evident—set the terms under which the autobiographical allegory of conversion within a narrative of descent to the underworld was received. Whether the step to the open air, with all its contradictions and perils, is taken or whether it is invoked to be refused if not refuted, it is grounded in Augustine's myth of creation.

The paradox underlying Augustine's strategy became the central issue when Bernard Silvestris took up the Fulgentian tradition of allegorical commentary on the *Aeneid* and attempted, with philosophical as well as poetic rigor and consistency, to apply the conversion model of the stages of the life of man back onto the epic poem. Bernard was affiliated with the twelfth-century Neoplatonist School of Chartres; the commentary was developed as a tool for using the *Aeneid*'s narrative framework for teaching poetics, philosophy, and even physiology through the dynamics of allegoresis.[39] It consists of an influential methodological prologue, or *ac-*

---

[38] For the most influential allegorical reading of the last six books, see Fulgentius's allegoresis of the final six books as a psychomachia, the battle of the Christian converted in book 6 against the vices of temporal existence (103–7; 79–80).

[39] Neither Bernard's identity nor the attribution of the commentary is certain. For introductions to Bernard's oeuvre and to these issues, see Winthrop Wetherbee, *Platonism and Poetry in the Twelfth Century: The Literary Influence of the School of Chartres* (Princeton, 1972); Brian Stock, *Myth and Science in the Twelfth Century: A Study of Bernard Silvester* (Princeton, 1972); and Peter Dronke, *Fabula: Explorations into the Uses of Myth in Medieval Platonism* (Leiden, 1974).

cessus ad auctorem, and an allegoresis of each of the first six books of the *Aeneid,* including a narrative summary and a line-by-line exposition of that summary.[40] The first five books are dealt with concisely; the interpretation of the sixth book, conversely, occupies nearly three-fourths of the hundred or so pages of the printed version in what becomes very nearly a word-by-word gloss of Vergil's text.

The reading of what Bernard calls the *integumentum,* or "covering," of the *Aeneid* recounts the journey of the soul from its imprisonment in the body to its return to God; the *descensus* of book 6 marks the turn away from sin through the education of the mind.[41] The story of the *Aeneid* is rendered as a purely interior, psychological, and sometimes physical allegory. Bernard's reading is thematically coherent, if not literally faithful to Vergil's narrative. The storm of book 1 is rendered as an allegory of birth; books 2–4 as the sins of adolescence, from the affair with Dido to the fires of the "Babylonian" city Troy, to emblematic encounters with figures such as the Cyclops, who has only one eye because of excess consideration of temporal concerns at the expense of the spiritual; the funeral games of

[40] *Commentum quod dicitur Bernardi Silvestris super sex libros "Eneidos" Virgilii,* ed. Julian W. Jones and Elizabeth Frances Jones (Lincoln, 1977); hereafter cited by page and line number; trans. Earl G. Schreiber and Thomas E. Maresca, *Commentary on the First Six Books of the "Aeneid" by Bernardus Silvestris* (Lincoln, 1979); cited by page number with Vergil's words italicized. Dronke dates the commentary to 1125–30 in "Bernard Silvestre," *Enciclopedia Virgiliana* (Rome, 1984); Theodore Silverstein to ca. 1150 in his review of Jones and Jones's edition, *Speculum* 54:1 (1979): 157. A large percentage of critical study has been devoted to determining the validity of the attribution of the commentary to Bernard. The attribution is given in the single, late manuscript (Parisinus Latinus 16246, ca. 1480) used in Wilhelm Riedel's edition (Greifswald, 1924). Bernard Silvestris is also cited as author in a fifteenth-century library catalog. For a recent summary of the issue, see Julian W. Jones, "The So-Called Silvestris Commentary on the *Aeneid* and Two Other Interpretations," *Speculum* 64:4 (1989): 835–48.

[41] *Integumentum* is the Chartrian term for *allegoria in verbis,* in contradistinction to *allegoria,* which is reserved for *allegoria in facto. Integumentum* became current in the twelfth century as a description of allegorical practice based on Macrobius's definition of *narratio fabulosa,* combined with Augustine's and others' valorization of hidden truth in biblical enigmas. It ascribed a positive figurative sense to the term *involucrum,* which retained a more generic sense of myth in general. The two basic works on the topic are Edouard Jeauneau, "L'Usage de la notion d'*integumentum* à travers les gloses de Guillaume de Conches," *AHDLMA* 24 (1957): 35–100; and M. D. Chenu, "Involucrum: Le mythe selon les théologiens médiévaux," *AHDLMA* 22 (1956): 75–79. See also the later discussions in Wetherbee, 36–48 and passim; Stock, 31–62; and Dronke 1974, 23–28 and passim. There is general agreement on a translation as "myth" or "poetic myth."

book 5 for Anchises become the soul's remembrance of filial duty. Book 6, the soul's contemplation of past sins, reveals the commentary's commitment to the conversion narrative: only by recapitulating one's past errors as a narrative of descent is one able to convert and return to salvation. The commentary breaks off, apparently for no reason, at line 636 of book 6; that is, at the gates of the Elysian Fields, another significant accident to which we return below.

The crux of the commentary occurs at the beginning of the discussion of book 6, where Bernard starts equivocating between the descent as allegorization of the contemplation of earthly truths and the descent as an actual otherworld journey toward a meeting with God. Bernard consistently glosses Anchises as "dwelling in the skies" ("celsa inhabitans," 9.8–9). The gloss is faithful to the logic of the *Aeneid*, since the Elysian Fields are Vergil's paradise, blessed, although underground, with "greater air and light" ("largior . . . aether et lumine," 6.640), but it is fatal to the logic of Christian doctrine. Hence, glossing Aeneas's prayer to the Sibyl (6.108–9), Bernard outlines the descent to the underworld as an ascent toward the creator, the *integumentum* as an *allegoria*:

> *Ire:* We have taught before in the fifth book that the descent to the underworld must be made in order that Anchises (although he is elevated over all) may be seen, because knowledge of creatures leads to contemplation of the Creator. *Conspectum:* contemplation. *Ora:* presence, but first in this life one attains contemplation, and then in the other life one attains vision—that is, one sees face to face. *Doceas:* "teach"—this is indeed by understanding. *Iter:* the ascent through the knowledge of creatures . . . [the five steps, from inanimate things to the Creator, are listed]. . . . But, following the steps noted above, Aeneas cannot ascend without the Sibyl as guide. (51.26–52.19; 51–52)

Bernard presents a particularly succinct expression of the mechanism of the allegory of conversion with the words "Presence—but first in this life" ("presentiam. Sed prius in hace vita"). But does direct vision come at the moment of conversion or in the next life? We find Augustine's liminal space once again; for conversion conflates the two moments so that God himself is encountered at the nadir of the descent.

Bernard emphasizes the attempt to introduce divine vision into poetic fictions by the words "face to face," and not, that is, "through a glass darkly" (1 Cor. 13:12), alluding to Paul as the unmediated authority of *allegoria in facto*. That the sole appearance of Paul's name in the commentary comes in the gloss to "Facilis descensus Averno" begs the question

whether a pagan model can successfully represent the divine: "But although those who descend are infinite, nonetheless there are three kinds
who return: those whom Jupiter loves, those whom virtue raises up high,
and those who are demigods. It is said that he especially loves those
persons whom he has drawn unconquered [*invictos*] from temporal things,
such as Paul" (56.19–24; 56). The key word of the passage is *invictos*,
"unconquered," for it raises the specter of a direct journey to God, of the
figural events permissible only in the scriptural mode of *allegoria*.

   Refusing to discard completely the literal level of *Aeneid* 6, Bernard
preserves the option he has manifestly forbidden: that the *Aeneid* is an
allegoria in facto, Aeneas a figure for Bernard's own conversion, and the
descent of book 6 not just a salvaging project of pagan philosophy but the
"descent" of Bernard as poet and teacher into the hell of classical pagan
literature in search of divine truths. Consequently, the impending exposition of the meeting with Anchises in the Elysian Fields is established as the
moment Bernard, like Augustine before him, would assume divine authority for the *Aeneid*. Yet in the glosses of the gates of Vergil's paradise,
Bernard eschews the step into the open air, maintaining that this divine
figure would, like the others, also be a rhetorical "invention" (114.13–
155.5; 106–7).

   By bringing the commentary to a halt at the crux of his conversionary
reading of the *Aeneid*, Bernard has rewritten Augustine's myth of creation
to reveal why, logically speaking, it ought to have failed. The prophetic
authority necessary to transcend language, he argues, is available only
through a contradiction between nature and rhetoric; a philosophically
and poetically rigorous version may be portrayed only negatively, in a
figure such as the corrupt Salmoneus in Tartarus, founder of the renegade
city of Elis, damned by the attempt to emulate the Creator with faulty
materials and insufficient authority: "We read that Salmoneus reigned in
Elis and was so much Jove's rival that he made for himself his own world
having the four elements and lightning, thunder, and clouds. Here, he
signifies the tyrant and is so named Salmoneus, as if 'salmoneos,' that is,
the bringer of novelty. The tyrant brings novelty when he represents himself having divine power transcending the human" (109.8–110.2; 102).
These are the poles of meaning available to the *descensus ad inferos:* the
mythic version of the *Confessions* produces the inspired saint; Bernard
counters with the doomed tyrant, emulating the elements of God's creation with the human novelty of language.

   An awareness of the dialectic of myth and history in the medieval model
of descent demands not only an account of its residue in modernism but a
nuanced analysis of the tensions mustered by that residue. Modern writers

are appropriating a fundamentally religious model, and consequently we must take seriously the vocabulary and signifying structures of modernist literature, as for example Benjamin's "profane illumination" or the Joycean *epiphany*. Thus, Stephen Dedalus begins his descent into Nighttown by "flourishing his ashplant . . . shattering light over the world" with a gesture that invokes an *allegoria in facto* that is glossed in *verbis:* "Salvi facti sunt. . . . So that gesture, not music, not odours, would be a universal language, the gift of tongues rendering visible not the lay sense but the first entelechy, the structural rhythm."[42] Joyce's epiphany seeks to endow everyday experience with the authority of divine truth, just as Stephen's grandiloquently mythic walking stick would uncover "the structural rhythm of the world." The appearance of the two allegories at the entrance to Nighttown signals that the impending meeting between Stephen and Bloom will stage a modern version of the encounter between Aeneas and Paul, between the artist creating prophetic history out of profane language and the ad man's divine vision of the city of Dublin.

I suggest that we take these forms seriously not as religious per se but because the extratextual authority of mythified history manifested itself in medieval writing and was received in modernism through the Christian struggle between the two allegories. If we can observe that the sanctification of the successfully converted Augustine or Dante arises out of a side effect of the mechanism of descent and return, we can begin to understand how the hagiographical impulse in criticism of modernist writers—the unproblematic embrace of life and work into the present moment—arises from an analogous mechanism. Starting with texts where the full dialectical structure of the autobiographical allegory of conversion is more readily apparent, we can see the descent not only as a totalizing force of formal unity but as a staging ground for the dilemma posed by the twin desires of formal unity and historic truth.

The choice of modernist texts in this book is thus a second strategy for analyzing the mythic function of the descent to the underworld in modernism. The parameters of critical debate on the great novelistic monuments of the *entre-deux-guerres*—that is, what is generally called "high modernism"—did not arise fully formed out of postwar criticism; rather, they were set a priori from within the modernist oeuvres themselves. This phenomenon is visible in the powerful blend of classical mythology and Christian archetypes syncretically filtered through Dantesque medievalism which forms the thematic core of textual systems such as Joyce's recourse to Celtic myth and the classics, Eliot's Christianity and *Golden Bough,*

---

[42] James Joyce, *Ulysses* (1922; New York, 1961), 432.

and Pound's translations of Greeks and troubadours. Thomas Mann initiates the Joseph tetralogy with an extended prologue on the Bible and
mythology framed as a *descensus;* Proust's narrator begins his tale with
the descent into sleep: he makes his first effort at writing while following
a walk along the river Vivonne framed as a restaging of Dante's descent
into hell. The headiness of these modernist blends is demonstrated by their
success in determining the reception of their mythmaking as either a
world-dissolving aesthetics or an utterly failed effort at autonomy. We can
take *Finnegans Wake* as the limit case of this split: either choose to gloss
its difficult and alluring linguistic world or reject it as the height of her-
metic futility—it has successfully determined those antinomies.

Nevertheless, these same texts also offer the possibility of addressing
simultaneously the aesthetic world, the material means out of which that
world was created, and the relation between the two. One way to approach this possibility is to reexamine the Middle Ages appropriated by
these writers, but from outside their medievalist perspective; a second way
is to approach the canon of modernism obliquely, through the wrong
novels, through the theoretical and critical production of modernism, and
through its successors and precursors. The relation to classical literature
and to the Middle Ages is not simply one of myths and forms, and certainly not as those myths and forms have heretofore been received.[43] This
is the reason behind a similarly oblique approach to that other group of
modernists who took the Christian residue in the dialectic of myth and
history very seriously indeed in both their criticism and their fiction. I
mean, of course, C. S. Lewis, Charles Williams, J. R. R. Tolkien, and
Dorothy L. Sayers, although we could also mention the German critic
Theodor Haecker and writer Ernst Jünger, whom we encounter again in
the context of Benjamin.

In this case, the work of translation and criticism that was centered on
Dante and medieval epic was explicitly informed with the desire to redeem
society through the conservative Christian mythology of a romantic anti-
capitalism equally visible in the straightforwardly modern allegories of

---

[43] This is the strength of Theodore Ziolkowski's *Virgil and the Moderns* (Princeton,
1993), although it focuses exclusively on the direct transmission of Vergil to Modernism. First, Ziolkowski demonstrates an *entre-deux-guerres* reception of Vergil's writings
running the ideological gamut from Robert Brasillach's "proto-fascist" (38–48) to
Theodor Haecker's vision of Vergil as prototype of the pan-European that would later
influence Eliot and Broch (48–52). Second, Ziolkowski locates the height of Vergil's
influence between the wars (235–39) and attributes that influence to concerns at the
heart of modernism: "the descent to the underworld and the discovery of history"
(238).

their fiction. Consequently, the problem of reception is of a different sort. This criticism has been marginalized for not disguising its rewriting of the medieval past, and this fiction for the transparency of the desire to relate its aesthetic world to our own. If the high modernists have been overly successful in framing their reception within aesthetic questions, then the Christian polemicists brought questions of medievalism and religion far too successfully to the fore to be able to command any manner of extended aesthetic consideration.[44]

The choice of texts in the following pages, then, is motivated by the desire to raise the possibility of a different mode of reading both the modernist groups outlined above. It is a choice of oeuvres that approach the medieval obliquely and also pose unusual difficulties for standard postwar modernist criticism. We find motifs of the descent to the underworld in each case, and we find in each case that these motifs have set the parameters of critical debate on the relation between life and writings. The mechanism is synchronically related to the dialectics seen in Homer and Vergil, and Augustine and Bernard; but as we see in the following chapter on Céline, the modernist play of myth and history moves between the descent within the work and the descent that structures the methodology of that work. The autobiographical allegory of descent plots the tension between two literary as well as critical endeavors, and shows at work within the texts the issues that would become polarized in the later critical reception.

In Woolf's version of the same tension, writing meant being unable to descend as a woman into the language and parameters of a male tradition;

---

[44] See, however, Sebastian D. G. Knowles's reassessment of modernism, *A Purgatorial Flame: Seven British Writers in the Second World War* (Philadelphia, 1990). I find it not coincidental that Knowles's leading argument about periodization, "that Modernism did not expire in 1939, to return as Contemporary Literature in 1945" (jacket, front flap), takes the form of a study of Dantesque imagery in Woolf, Louis MacNeice, Eliot, Tolkien, Lewis, Williams, and Evelyn Waugh. Although Knowles sees in Dante mostly a primary source of a myth of purgatory, and views that myth as "chained to the force of history" (29), his book is instructive: not only does the investigation of otherworld imagery lead him to assert some manner of relation between myth and history in modernism beyond diametric opposition (25–35), but it results in a decidedly nontraditional canon and periodization of modernism itself. See also Norman Cantor, *Inventing the Middle Ages: The Lives, Works, and Ideas of the Great Medievalists of the Twentieth Century* (New York, 1991), esp. 205–44. Not surprisingly, Cantor's presentation of Lewis's and Tolkien's "transmut[ation] of their medieval learning into mythopoetic fictions" (208) is biographical and historical with little or no attention for the aesthetic.

for Benjamin, the critical descent into nineteenth-century Paris as the pre-history of modernity meant equally his own Marxian descent into the archives and economic facts of the time. For Céline, the means are the same, but the purpose is different: he did not strive to mediate the personal into the historical—to convert his readers into a revolutionary under-standing of their past and thereby of their present—but attempted to mediate the historical into the personal—to convert his readers into swal-lowing an expurgated version of his own past, the Céline myth, as history.

In return, Céline's manipulation of the ability to shift at ease between aesthetic and political discourses brings out the implications of Au-gustine's adaptation of *Aeneid* 6 to spiritual autobiography (*Confessions*) and to world history (*City of God*) and of Dante's to his *Commedia*. It ceases to be a question of believing or disbelieving Augustine or Dante, of being converted by them or not, but becomes a matter of grasping the mechanism whereby they simultaneously support a monolithic structure of Christian doctrine and establish a convincingly authentic and individual prophetic voice. Furthermore, once the mechanism is clear, we may ask ourselves conversely if they were not in fact also staging the essential impossibility of the same endeavor. This reading is implied already by Bernard Silvestris or Christine de Pizan, who rewrite their predecessors' success into inimitable monuments in order to excavate a different order of meaning out of their ruins.

Recontextualizing the dynamics of medieval literary strategies within the reception of modernists such as Céline, Woolf, and Benjamin can clarify the attitude of postwar writers such as Peter Weiss, Seamus Heaney, or Derek Walcott toward the peaks of modernism: not living in the past but journeying to it from a necessary distance; not emulating what now appear to be its unattainable glories but redefining them into a history that appropriately prefaces whatever is new about what they are doing. The modes of reading suggested by this model show how retrospec-tive readings reinvent the past. Once such strategic fault lines are recog-nized in medieval literature, in modernist literature, or between the two, the disenchanting insight can go in the direction either of praise or of blame, either toward mythifying history or toward innovations in using the mythifying power for a utopian objective. But such tendentiousness is more the reader's prerogative; for the most part, my aim is to clarify what lies behind the either/or of medieval and modern, of modernism and postmodernism, of allegory as history and allegory as myth.

2

"La Bataille du Styx": Céline's Allegory of Conversion

> Would not attributing *The Imitation of Christ* to Louis-Ferdinand Céline or James Joyce be a sufficient renovation of its tenuous spiritual counsels?
> —Borges, "Pierre Menard, Author of the *Quixote*"

IN MARCH 1945, Louis-Ferdinand Céline, his wife Lucette, and their cat Bébert arrived in Copenhagen after a journey as collaborationists across a war-torn Third Reich in the last throes of its defeat. In December of the same year, Robert Denoël, the publisher of Céline's novels and of the now dangerous anti-Semitic pamphlets, was shot down in the streets of Paris. Shortly thereafter, Céline himself was detained by the Danish authorities and incarcerated for the next fourteen months in either prison or hospital. He was released provisionally in June 1947 and in May of the following year settled with Lucette and Bébert in a primitive house near the sea at Körsor, where they remained for the next three years. At that time, thanks to his status as a wounded veteran of the First World War, he was pardoned for crimes in the Second imputed from the pamphlets, and allowed to return to Paris.[1] The central paradox of his life is that the only period

[1] Louis-Ferdinand Céline, *Romans I*, ed. Henri Godard (Paris, 1981), lv-lxxxix. For biographies of Céline, see François Gibault's exhaustive and hagiographical *Céline*, 3 vols. (Paris, 1977–85); Frédéric Vitoux's recent and comprehensive *Vie de Céline* (Paris, 1988), trans. Jesse Browner, *Life of Céline* (New York, 1992); and Patrick McCarthy's excellent critical biography *Céline* (New York, 1975). For materials relevant to Céline's involvement with the *collabos*, see *Céline et l'actualité, 1933–1961: Cahiers Céline 7*, ed. Jean-Pierre Dauphin and Pascal Fouché (Paris, 1986); hereafter cited as CC7.

of it in which Céline committed any truly damning acts also provided the autobiographical background for a trio of novels that in the late fifties effectively salvaged a career and a reputation severely damaged by that very past: *D'un château l'autre* (1957; *Castle to Castle*), *Nord* (1960; *North*), and *Rigodon* (posth. 1969; *Rigadoon* [a dance]).

Féerie pour une autre fois (1952; Faery for another time), written during his imprisonment and exile and the first of Céline's novels explicitly to address the Second World War, presents a rough draft for the reclamation project.

> I'm not after the guards or the prison walls! but the Classics, the thinkers before anything else! they've had it, magnificent and pus-breathing: Petrarch, Dantus, Homer, Prout Prout! End to end [*bout bout*]! iniquity through the ages! They just imagined Hell, we take you there! and with more than a few demons! hordes of them, mobs, countless! suckling on mouthfuls of sulfur! so the rats croak! . . . poor little beasts! . . . That's what goes on in the sewer . . . we are in the sewer, me Robignol and a thousand more, and a thousand others even more unfortunate, that no one talks about anymore, no one dares, who are croaking in the jails, who have paid in pain a thousand times over for all the crimes they didn't commit![2]

The narrator's voice identifies itself with the author's actual predicament as a prisoner and uses it to authorize his literary credentials for a descent into hell. On the one hand, he will surpass the "classics"—a canon defined from Homer through Dante to Prou[s]t—by virtue of the ability not just to represent hell but to journey down into it ("We take you there!"). The endeavor will succeed because of the current firsthand experience with hell, "the sewer" of the prison, and metaphorically that of his recent collaborationist past. At the same time, to shield himself from that past, he developed a postwar style based on the cheap thrills of modernity: the *descensus ad inferos* as cinematic rollercoaster. The postwar writings assert a rigorous separation between style and content; indeed, they assert a style that would bypass content to stimulate the nerves directly: "The reader of (. . .) one of my works in emotive style! (. . .) it seems to him (. . .) that someone is reading to him (. . .) right in the middle of his

---

[2] L.-F. Céline, *Féerie pour une autre fois* (1952), in *Romans IV*, ed. Henri Godard (Paris, 1993); this citation, 81; hereafter cited as *F1*. A note on citation in this chapter: the three periods (. . .) normally used to signal ellipses are an integral part of Céline's style. In quotations from Céline, any three periods marking my own ellipses are placed within parentheses; all others are Céline's.

nervous system! inside his own head!"[3] Pure sensation: Céline used the arsenal of high modernist poetics to reproduce the excitement and titillation of postwar popular culture.

Céline's oeuvre persuades the reader to choose between categories it has generated internally in order to evade the implication of their affiliation. In particular, Céline predetermines the categorization manifested later in the reception of his writings: there would be Céline the master of pure style, the technician of language whose life was unfortunately repellent; Céline the master of pure style who was not as bad as he looked; and Céline the master whose claims to pure style were irrevocably soiled by his politics.[4] Such polarized categorizations are endemic to modernism and continue to constitute what I have called the "modernism of reading" practiced by much of contemporary criticism. The example of Céline is both a salutary and a cautionary starting point for a rereading of modernism, for once we have recognized the dependence of such critical categorization on its construction within a writer's oeuvre, the next step must be to determine the means of, and motivation behind, that construction. Motifs of the descent to the underworld demarcate these artificial fault lines and help map the play of autobiography and fiction that delineates their contours. Now, the trajectory of Céline's career baldly displays the manipulative powers wielded by the conversionary structure of the *descensus ad inferos.* Unlike contemporaries such as Benjamin or Woolf, the only unified vision with which Céline sought to return from the world below was one that would protect his person and restore his reputation.

In terms of the descent to the underworld, Céline assumes alternately

---

[3] *Entretiens avec le professor Y* (1955), in *Romans IV*, 545; trans. Stanford Luce, *Conversations with Professor Y* (Hanover, N.H., 1986), 112–15; hereafter cited as *Y*.

[4] Céline as pure stylist is represented in contemporary form by Julia Kristeva's highly influential vision of the author as "an international writer, a prophet of apocalypse," the horror of the pamphlets subsumed within a mythic theory of the "abject," *Powers of Horror*, 1980, trans. Leon S. Roudiez (New York, 1982). See Alice Yeager Kaplan's groundbreaking study *Reproductions of Banality: Fascism, Literature, and French Intellectual Life* (Minneapolis, 1986) for a critique of Kristeva along these lines (35–46; quotation above, 120). The greater part of the criticism presents a version of the second Céline. As Philippe Muray self-consciously puts it, before proceeding to conform to the same pattern, "Following the chapters devoted to anti-Semitism, books on Céline ritually continue with observations about his writing style [*écriture*]" (*Céline* [Paris, 1981], 175). Those rejecting Céline are, needless to say, a minority of the specialists, if perhaps a majority of the nonspecialists. The extreme may be represented by H.-E. Kaminski, *Céline en chemise brune* (Paris, 1977). George Steiner was perhaps the first to suggest in a critically nuanced manner that the pamphlets irrevocably taint our reading of the novels ("Cry Havoc," 1971, rpt. in *Extraterritorial* [New York, 1976], 35–46).

the Dantean roles of guide and of pilgrim; he articulates their interrelation-
ship linguistically, through the use of a different sense of the French word
rame ("subway car" or "oar") to characterize each role. This is the hidden
dialectic that emerges in his postwar writings: as the pilgrim who would
be cleansed and reborn as the converted writer, Céline defined his soon-
to-be celebrated style as a "rame magique," a magic metro of streamlined
stylistic integrity, speeding unblemished through a sordid past; as permanent dweller of the underworld, amanuensis to the damned *collabos*, he
identified himself with Charon's *rame*, the oar with which the mythological ferryman beats souls that are tardy in mounting into his boat to be
taken across the Styx. Both words descend from the *ramus aureus* of
Vergil's *Aeneid;* together they constitute the golden bough that authorizes
Céline's descent. By tracing the two motifs as they come together through
the course of his oeuvre, I want to demonstrate that Céline actively places
himself within the tradition of the autobiographical allegory of descent
into the underworld, and that he compromises the so-called pure style
with the tainted truth of the other, historical time spent in hell.[5] Céline
manages to shift the historical weight of his guilt onto the fictional voice
of Charon and to settle the fictional weight of his revolutionary style onto
the autobiographical voice of himself as author.

The narrative self-presentation as author mirrors a growing convergence between autobiography and fiction that is thematized on a metafictional level. The three phases of Céline's career—from *Voyage au bout de
la nuit*, 1932 (*Journey to the End of the Night*); to the Nazi-era pamphlets
Bagatelles pour un massacre (1938), *L'Ecole des cadavres* (1938; The

---

[5] Such an itinerary is only a highly partial and selective one of a large and complex
oeuvre; nevertheless, the motifs to be traced here can serve equally as a means of
structuring such a reading so as still to maintain some measure of relevance to the body
of writing as a whole. Henri Godard, *Poétique de Céline* (Paris, 1985), is the best
general introduction, although Godard neglects to place his comprehensive and innovative analysis of Céline's language and style within the context of Céline's polemical
writings in particular and his role in history in general. McCarthy's remains the best
introduction in English. The critical literature is extensive: Nicholas Hewitt provides a
fairly up-to-date bibliography in *The Golden Age of Louis-Ferdinand Céline* (Leamington Spa, 1987); comprehensive ones are in Jean-Pierre Dauphin, *L.-F. Céline: Essai de
bibliographie des études en langue française consacrées á L.-F. Céline, I: 1914–1944*
(Paris, 1977); Dauphin and Pascal Fouché, *Bibliographie des écrits de L.-F. Céline*
(Paris, 1985); Charles Krance, "L.-F. Céline," in *The Twentieth Century, Part I*, vol. 6
of *A Critical Bibliography of French Literature*, ed. D. Alden and R. A. Brooks (Syracuse, 1980), 743–65; and Stanford Luce and William Buckley, *A Half-Century of
Céline: An Annotated Bibliography, 1932–1982* (New York, 1983).

school for corpses), and *Les Beaux draps* (1941; A fine mess), and novels *Mort à crédit,* (1936; *Death on the Installment Plan*) and *Guignol's band* (1944); to the postwar writings—can be defined in terms of the changing use of name for the first-person protagonist-narrators: from Bardamu in *Voyage,* to Ferdinand in the middle works, to a carefully prioritized postwar selection from among Céline (grandmother's name and his nom de plume), Destouches (his legal surname), Ferdinand, and Louis (his actual given name), depending on the interlocutor (Godard, 281–304).

With *Voyage,* Céline made his debut as a novelist pure and simple; Bardamu's adventures raised a critical storm from both left and right, for the ideology of the fiction was equally amenable or abhorrent to each camp.[6] Conversely, it is not coincidental that the first appearance of the name Céline within the diegesis of one of his texts occurs in the four-hundred-page pamphlet *Bagatelles:* the author's entry into his fictional topography is resolutely ideological in a way *Voyage* never was. This newly politicized voice remained nominally distinct from that of the novelist Ferdinand of *Mort* and *Guignol's band;* nevertheless, the direct intervention of the pamphlets gained authority from the voice of the author while the voice of the author took on added virulence from the convictions of the pamphleteer. And finally, after the writing had indeed landed the writer in prison, Destouches and Céline, Louis and Ferdinand were called into service as signs of the intricate interchange between life and fiction of the fifties and early sixties.

The vicissitudes of Céline's literary image and cultural reputation—from the nihilistic enfant terrible of the early years, to the apocalyptic jeremiads of the pamphleteer and wartime novelist, to the raconteur and stylist of the postwar novels *Féerie* and the trilogy—are framed within a metaphorics of the underground. I trace this movement through to the *rame magique* of Céline's style and the *rame* of Charon and *descensus ad inferos* of the postwar writings. Why does the word *rame* first appear only in *Guignol's band* and subsequently figure so prominently in the postwar writings? After all, Céline could simply have continued using the synonymous *métro* on the one hand and *aviron* on the other. Although he never explicitly related the *rames* to each other, it is difficult to suppose that such a meticulous stylist as Céline would have remained unaware of the homonymic and homophonic identity of two of the key motifs of his late fiction. I argue that the scene in *Guignol's band* establishes the motivation for the underlying postwar connection and confirms the presence in Cé-

[6] See André Derval, ed., *70 Critiques de "Voyage au bout de la nuit," 1932–35* (Paris, 1993).

line's oeuvre of an allegorical staging and subsequent apology and defense of the pamphlets. The one neither condemns nor justifies the other; rather, the stylistic brilliance of Céline's prose gains a large portion of its power from feeding off his autobiographical voice and, conversely, places that power in the service of exigencies of the author's historical predicament.

AN AETIOLOGY of the postwar *rames* begins with the image of the metro as it first appeared in *Voyage*. There is little resemblance here to the later *rame magique;* we find instead a site of filth and ordure to be avoided. The metro is further disparaged for its practicality, as the air-raid shelter to which Bardamu's lover Musyne wants to retreat: "She insisted on rushing somewhere deep underground and dragging me with her, into the Metro, the sewers, anywhere." [7] Bardamu, however, insists on keeping his distance from the antinomies of modern life. Much later, when he sets up a medical clinic in the petit-bourgeois Parisian suburb of "Rancy," the metro's combination of conformity and filth remains menacing: "Compressed like garbage into this tin box, they cross Rancy, stinking good and proper especially in the summer. Passing the fortifications, they threaten one another, they let out one last shout, and then are lost from view, the Metro swallows them up, limp suits, discouraged dresses, silk stockings, sour stomachs, dirty feet, dirty socks. Wear-ever collars as stiff as boundary posts, pending abortions, war heroes, all scramble down the coal-tar and carbolic-acid stairs into the black pit, holding their return ticket which all by itself costs as much as two breakfast rolls" (*V* 206; 239). As the air-raid shelter in the first quotation merged with the ancient mythology of the Parisian catacombs, so in this passage the archaic and the modern are combined in the threatening image of the metro. On the one hand, we find the organic images of ordure, of the metro as an enormous gullet, of the masses oozing *(dégoulinant)* down into darkness; but on the other, we find details of modern clothing and the final complaint about inflation.

The two other metro-related episodes in *Voyage*, both of which take place during Bardamu's earlier sojourn in New York City, lack the archaic, mythic lure of the abyss that would eventually draw Céline down into them back at home. The American images are travesties of the Parisian metro; purely modern in their negativity, they depict only the aspects of filth and danger. In midtown Manhattan, Bardamu attempts to follow in the tradition of Hugo's Jean Valjean by seeking refuge from the authorities in the sewers: "To the abyss! I say to myself" (*V* 168; 195). He enters

[7] *Voyage au bout de la nuit,* in *Romans I,* 69; trans. Ralph Manheim, *Journey to the End of the Night* (New York, 1983), 83; hereafter cited as *V.*

a hole, with stairs like the metro at home, but only to find a "fecal cavern," a public toilet. The promised abyss turns out to be just another place of filth that serves only to emphasize Bardamu's alienation: "To a foreigner the contrast was disconcerting. Such disorderly intimacy, such extraordinary intestinal familiarity, and up on the street such perfect constraint! I couldn't get over it" (V 169; 196). The other incident figures the metro in its menace but without the vaguest promise of a truth, not even the negativity of "the end of the night": "An Elevated Railway train [métro aérien] was passing. It bounded between two streets like an artillery shell, filled with trembling and hacked-up meat, and jolted from section to section of this lunatic city" (V 171; 198). In an unambivalent attack on the contemporary world, the vision of the metro as an exploding shell full of butchered meat proposes a metaphorical affiliation between urban modernity and the novel's earlier scenes of trench warfare.[8]

The metro participates in the central metaphorics of the novel both here and in the Rancy passage, where the descending mass of humanity is flowing "jusqu'au bout du noir," the nihilistic endpoint of Bardamu's journey "au bout de la nuit." If the archaic allure of Paris adds an ambiguity that would be exploited by the later novels, the underground in Voyage remains as irredeemable as the humanity surrounding Bardamu. This vertical division is equally at work on the metafictional level: in Voyage, the author does not yet show himself making the descent. To be sure, the narrator Bardamu is somewhat autobiographical, but explicitly he is not yet even partially identified with the author, and he is an observer, almost completely passive to the action around him. An unpleasant character, he remains clearly "other" from the masses, and his final vision of the end of the night consists of nothing more or less than his alienation.

Similarly, Céline's language and style have not yet themselves, so to speak, descended into the metro. In retrospect, Céline appears to have placed Voyage as the most recent in the category of "classics and thinkers," those who maintain a stylistic distance from their subject. As he put it after the war: "Petrarch, Dantus, Homer, Prout Prout! End to end [bout bout]. . . . They just imagined Hell, we take you there!" In these terms, Voyage continues to describe reality from an exterior vantage point. Beginning with Mort, Céline staked the claim he would later make for Féerie: pushing the stylistic and thematic elements of Voyage much further, he attempted to take his readers into hell, to express "le bout de la nuit" from within. The "end of the night" would now be rendered as the interior

[8] For the dependence of Céline's early work on the image of the Golden Age destroyed by the Great War, see Hewitt, esp. 3–14.

topography of the author Céline's mind, and hell as the exterior topography of the past life of Destouches.

We may trace this change in the transitional imagery of the metro that appears in the second of the three periods of Céline's oeuvre (including *Mort*, the pamphlets, and the two volumes of *Guignol's band*). The vertical movement refused in *Voyage* is now adopted by the scapegoating tactics of the pamphlets as well as by the thematics of the novels. In *Guignol's band*, we witness the symbolic birth of the postwar *style émotif* in the Underground under the sign of a murder; we see the historical context that would be excised from the later version to be found written into the *Entretiens*. *Guignol's band* bridges the two wars as well as the voices of Ferdinand and Céline: the narrative is based on a visit made by Céline to London between his discharge from the army and his journey to Africa, *Voyage* territory; the twenty-page prelude depicts a present-tense Céline recounting an ambulance drive to La Rochelle at the start of the Occupation and drops several allusions to the pamphlets before shifting to the past tense of the body of the London narrative.[9] Displaced from Montmartre to Soho, and from the present war to the previous, the novel lays bare the underground mechanics of the metaphorics employed so seamlessly by the unified front of the postwar writings.

The pressing historical concerns of the novel's prelude are translated into the thematics of a Ferdinand still working through his shell shock in Great Britain. Hence the allegorical initials of the title ("GB"); hence the stereotypically fat and greedy moneylender Titus Van Claben, the only major Jewish character in any of the novels, embodiment of Céline's paranoia about "the English judeocracy" (CC7 56).[10] Céline dramatizes the

---

[9] *Guignol's band I* (1944), in *Romans III*, ed. Henri Godard (Paris, 1988), 95–96; trans. Bernard Frechtman and Jack T. Nile, *Guignol's Band* (New York, 1969), 24; hereafter cited as *GB1*.

[10] Beyond scattered references in the pamphlets themselves (see esp. *Ecole des cadavres* [Paris, 1938], 283–89), the following answer to a survey by the anti-Semitic propagandist biweekly *La France enchaînée* (France in chains) gives a fair account of Céline's attitude toward England during the period of the composition of *Guignol's band:* "Thus will France be dismembered. We will draw first blood from the Germanic monster. We will play the 'banderillas.' Depending on the early results, *Judeo-Britain will either go or it won't.* (. . .) From *14 to 18*, England never stopped supplying Germany. *The war lasted four years solely on behalf and because of England,* this has been written a hundred times and never disproved. England is the only genuinely hereditary enemy of France. The English judeocracy already has at hand a compromise with Germany against us" ("Bagatelles for a Massacre: Céline's Opinion," *La France enchaînée* 26 [15–30 Apr. 1939], [1]; rpt. in CC7, 55–56; Céline's emphases).

polemic in a central scene of the novel. Ferdinand's friend Borokrom begins stuffing gold down the moneylender's throat; when they are unable to retrieve the pieces, he and Ferdinand smash in Van Claben's head. Anti-Semitic vitriol is carried over as a transparent metaphor into the fiction; like the pamphlets during the war years, the murder will haunt Céline for the rest of the first volume and throughout the second as well (*Guignol's band II*, 1944–47), before the body is finally heaved off a bridge into the Thames.[11] Fiction resolves politics: the body disposed of, Ferdinand crosses Tower Bridge into a safer quarter of London with his fifteen-year-old dancer companion, Virginia.

Criticism generally has it that a juncture has been passed: problematics crystallized in the First World War have been transcended and the way laid clear for the mature, stylistically innovative works following the next war.[12] And yet if ghosts of the thirties had already infiltrated the meta-phorics of a novel of the aftermath of World War I, how can the resolution of the narrative crisis be anything but wish fulfillment? A look at the second murder in *Guignol's band* shows that damnation and transcendence are not merely terms of Céline criticism but exist as counterparts of each other within the novel, just as *Guignol's band* mirrors the stylistics of the pamphlets.

The ending of *Guignol's band* may find Ferdinand dancing across Tower Bridge, but it remains predicated on the truly seminal scene of the novel, the descent into the underground. Once the delirious aftermath of the pamphlet-inspired murder of Van Claben has faded, Ferdinand encounters Mille-Pattes ("Centipede"), a dwarfish cripple whom he begins to suspect has betrayed his part in the murder. Mille-Pattes leads him into a tube station, and Ferdinand finds himself confronted with the very experience of modernity from which he had always kept his distance: "We're pushed into the elevator . . . smothered in the rush . . . suddenly I feel anxious! (. . .) Cooped up like that in this box! I'm palpitating! I'm palpitating! awfully crammed!" (*GB1* 254; 285). Céline stages a dually motivated apology of the pamphlets: Ferdinand's murderous attack might be fear of treachery, set off by the sight of Inspector Matthew across the tracks, but it may also be a sheerly physical attack of panic brought on by the press of people. Rationalizations for the pamphlets inflect the language

---

[11] First published posthumously in 1964 as *Le Pont de Londres: Guignol's band II*, rpt. in *Romans III;* this reference, 728–31; hereafter cited as *GB2*.

[12] Hewitt's is a recent version of this narrative: the important research and thesis on the meaning of the Golden Age in the early and middle works lead to a tone of successful exorcism in the analysis of *Guignol's band* (222–24).

and plot: that is, Céline was forced to descend into everyday facts by the worsening situation in France; he could keep quiet no longer; he lost his authorial distance. The pamphlets' descent into politics is mirrored by Ferdinand's descent into the London Underground. Whereas the nihilism of *Voyage* and *Mort* proposed no solutions and gave no hope of return, *Guignol's band* maintains that the open air of history is worth the pamphlets' descent into hell.

Ferdinand's murder of Mille-Pattes lays bare the quid pro quo of the recent past: escape from the depths came at the price of a corpse:

> So here we are waiting for the train . . . squeezed like that with all the people. I don't know why? . . . they're all stifling me! . . . I can't breathe anymore! . . . They're all there against me! I get myself free . . . Ah! I get free! . . . (. . .) They're waiting for the train [*la rame*] like us . . . We hear the train roaring . . . it's coming! . . . over there in the darkness . . . in the hole . . . to my right . . . Good! . . . Good! . . . Good! . . . the train's approaching. It's roaring fiercely, crashing and swelling up . . . "Brrrr Brrrroum! . . ." Good! Good! Good! . . . It's near . . . I'm looking at Matthew opposite . . . I feel the midget against me . . . he's got me by the arm . . . he doesn't want to lose me! . . . "BRRRR! . . ." the engine emerges and "Pfuuii! . . . PfUUii!" the whistle . . . Plouf! a kick in the ass and I send him flying! the midget! in the air! . . . The thunder lets loose, passes above! Whistle! Whistle! Whistle! . . . They're all yelling! all around! the whole station! . . . I pull clean back! I'm magnetized! That's the word! . . . positively! . . . I'm lifted up! . . . I'm light as a feather! I get going! . . . I'm snapped up by the exit! . . . the stairway! I'm sucked up! . . . I'm flying off! . . . It's instinct! flight! . . . (*GB1* 254–55; 286–87)

The delirium set off by the murder continues for quite a while along its vertical axis. No longer weighed down by worries, Ferdinand is transformed into a dancer, lighter than air; he practically floats up out of the tube station, his guilty secret concealed by the speeding train and the crowd.

Murder gives rise to dance; violence releases the brilliant emotion of Céline's style: this is the suppressed equation of the postwar division of the two *rames*. It is also the pattern of *Bagatelles*; indeed, the "coup de cul" with which Ferdinand sends the cripple flying is a precise translation into narrative of the central linguistic motif of the pamphlets. In *Bagatelles*, Céline develops obscene slang for sodomy (*enculer*) into a combinative prefix conforming all verbs to the economy of paranoiac delirium. Of the consequent neologisms, "enjuiver" (to enjew) is not surprisingly the most rampant and the most exemplary of Céline's meaning. To be sure, everything in Céline's world is susceptible of being turned into a verb, but in the era of the pamphlets the quid pro quo of *enculer* overwhelms the general process of linguistic creation.

Witness the opening salvo of *Bagatelles*, where Céline's category of Jew is already implicitly present in the first adjective, "refined" *(raffinés)*, and will further develop out of the tirade against the Academy:

A refined man, refined by right, by custom, officially, must out of habit at the least write like M. Gide, M. Vanderem, M. Benda, M. Duhamel, Mme Colette, Mme Valéry, the "French Theater" ... swoon over nuances ... Mallarmé, Bergson, Alain ... must anusify [*troufignoliser*] the adjectives ... goncourtify ... shit! bullshit [*enculagailler*] about flies' heads, obsess about Insignificance, write letters in fancy dress, puff himself up, beat his head like a nut about nothing ... (...) Me too, I could, I certainly could become a true stylist, an "appropriate" academician. It's a question of work, months of diligence ... perhaps years ... You can manage at anything ... As the Spanish proverb says: "A lot of vaseline, even more patience, Elephant sodomizes [*encugule*] ant." [13]

As in Céline's attitude to the murders in *Guignol's band,* the dialectic of aggressor and victim is highly unstable: in the first part of the passage, the "refined" writers are the ones who "enculagaillent" (Céline's neologistic variation on *pinailler,* "to talk in great detail about nothing"), just as later on France will be "enjewed"; in the second part, Céline, with his own literary pretensions (he would obsessively describe his work in all seriousness as an "effort of months or years," involving much "patience"), becomes himself the sodomizing "elephant." The assumed role of victim is never far from a self-presentation as aggressor: this is the pattern from *Mort* through the pamphlets to *Guignol's band.*[14]

Céline's literary ambitions are shown to motivate the anti-Semitic tirades of *Bagatelles.* Two of his ballets supposedly rejected by the 1937

[13] *Bagatelles pour un massacre* (Paris, 1937), 11; hereafter cited as *BM.* Needless to say, the anti-homosexual constellation goes hand-in-hand here with the imagery and ideology of anti-Semitism.

[14] The affinity, in fact, is historically supported by the reception of *Guignol's band* on its publication in 1944. Céline, who had been almost completely ignored by the press through most of 1943, was precipitously, and exclusively, reclaimed by the collaborationists in their reactions to his first novel in eight years (see the editors' discussion in *CC7,* 94–95).

World Exposition in Paris, Céline will have presented the polemic as a ruse of getting his creations into print, his rage a result of having been snubbed. The ballets are printed in full near the beginning of the pamphlet and contain sketches for the characters of Virginia the dancer and Van Claben (Bagaden here) in *Guignol's band*.[15] Moreover, near the conclusion of the pamphlet we discover the same soaring movement and the same dialectic of violence and release, descent and return, found in the London novel. Céline is reprising his ballet before a Russian Jew: "I surpass myself! . . . I am theater, orchestra, dancers! all of the ensembles at once . . . me all on my own! . . . I play the fool! . . . I skip about, I spring out of my chair! . . . I personify the entire 'Birth of a Fairy' . . . All the joy, the sadness, the melancholy . . . I am everywhere [*Je suis partout*]! . . . I imitate the violins . . . the orchestra . . . the seductive waves . . . (. . .) I advance quickly . . . develop . . . further entrances! . . . quadrilles! . . . I spring up again at the other end . . . bounce back . . . caper about! . . ." (*BM* 350). It is no accident that in the middle of the delirium Céline inserts an allusion to the Fascist journal *Je Suis Partout*, home of writers Lucien Rebatet and Robert Brasillach, which welcomed *Bagatelles* "with an enthusiasm knowing no reserve" (quoted in McCarthy, 135). But what Céline presented as inextricably linked would be in the reception quickly polarized between politics and aesthetics. When *Je Suis Partout* reprinted passages of *Bagatelles,* the editors excised the introductory narrative genesis of Céline's anti-Semitism and began with the battle cry that follows the text of the second ballet, "Now you're going to see some anti-Semitism!" (*BM* 41).[16] These allies did not welcome the ballets any more than Céline's publishers or his imagined Jewish producers did. Conversely, in a gesture indicative of the success of Céline's postwar strategy to separate the two aspects of his production, Gallimard fed a new public appetite for the writer by reprinting the three ballets on their own as *Ballets sans musique, sans personne, sans rien* (1959).

Once Céline had allowed himself to be drawn into the ordure of the metro, he also became open to the possibility of soaring to the skies, the vision of redemption; or, rather, once he wanted to soar, he needed first to go down. The descent of the pamphlets would make him a "political prophet" (*CC7* 85). Following a sixteen-month silence from the outbreak

---

[15] "La Naissance d'une fée: Ballet en plusieurs actes" (*BM* 17–26); "Voyou Paul. Brave Virginie: Ballet-Mime" (*BM* 30–40). The work also concludes with a ballet: "Van Bagaden: Grand Ballet-Mime et quelques paroles" (*BM* 375–79).

[16] Céline, "Morceaux choisis: *Bagatelles pour un massacre* (Le livre de la semaine)," *Je Suis Partout* (4 Mar. 1938): 8; see Kaplan's analysis, 126–27.

of war (although the previously banned *Bagatelles* and *Ecole* were on sale again as of late 1939), Céline's wartime production was fairly sustained: one article, twenty-six letters to editors, four responses to questionnaires, six interviews, one manifesto signature, and three prefaces (CC7 88). He made his debut with "Acte de foi" (Act of faith), in which, recounting the story of a girl who, impressed by the tale of Joseph, began dreaming of events the day after they had happened, he condemned all post-June 1940 articles as "the work of 'dreamers after the fact.' " [17] Judging from the disingenuous fuss he raised over the publication of the letter (CC7 218–21), Céline apparently wanted to isolate his from all others as the only authentically prophetic voice. Journalists are cowards (" 'Long live Pétain' shouted a hundred thousand times is not in practice worth a single little 'out with the Yids!' " [CC7 103]); he, in contrast, belongs to the true tradition of prophetic, pamphleteering loners ("A little bit of guts, in God's name! 'Guts after the fact' and less talk! . . . And I'll go find you Péguy and the Grand Méaulnes [sic] and the rest! . . ." [CC7 103]). Céline would bank his postwar maneuvering on the status he fabricated for himself during the war.

The postwar trilogy is less of a break than it may seem: Céline remained the prophet without fear in a world of cowards—but he had now made it a literary world. *Bagatelles* is framed with the pure beauty sought by Céline in the ballet; *Guignol's band* concludes with Céline strolling off into the London mist with his pure, beautiful Virginia; the wartime inferno depicted in the late novels is similarly bracketed by the novels' dedications: "For the animals, for the sick, for the imprisoned" *(F1);* "for the animals" *(Rigodon).*[18] The dominant persona of the late novels is a continuation of Ferdinand crossing Tower Bridge: the doctor Céline, always accompanied by Lili the dancer and Bébert the cat, always employing his métier no matter the circumstances, and always the suffering prisoner of *Féerie.*

The body of *Féerie* that the prison setting frames takes place in the spring of 1944, immediately following the real-life publication of *Guignol's band* by Denoël and immediately before Céline and his entourage fled for Denmark. It documents the end of his private life and the beginning of the necessity of taking political responsibility for the writings. The

---

[17] "Acte de foi de L.-F. Céline," *La Gerbe* 2: 32 (13 Feb. 1941), 1; rpt. in CC7, 102.

[18] *Rigodon* (1968), in *Romans II;* hereafter cited as *R.* The other two volumes of the trilogy have no dedications. The title *Rigodon* itself participates in this half of the polarity, nostalgically referring to a lively two-step dance, and its signature air of Provençal origin, popular during the seventeenth and eighteenth centuries.

same period saw Céline vacillating in taking the analogous step in his fiction. In September 1945 he was at work both rewriting the manuscript of *Guignol's band II* and starting a new project (*Féerie*). In March 1947, he declared *Guignol's band II* finished and put off the projected third part to dedicate himself to the new project. *Guignol's band* was a dead end, for the wartime writings had led to neither conversion nor transcendence. Both as a writer and as an actor in history, Céline had descended into hell and had not been able to find his way back out. Mentioning the *Féerie* project for the first time, he called it "a short memoir (. . .) The Battle of the Styx" (*Romans I*, lxxviii). In order to pull himself out of the hell of metro and pamphlets as his character Ferdinand had done in *Guignol's band*, Céline translated his descent into an autobiographical allegory aimed at converting those who accepted to read his books into accepting an authorized version of his innocence.

THE ROLE OF the *rame magique* in the new definition of Céline's style provides a context in which to view Charon's *rame:* in the narrative of the postwar novels it appears not as its opposite but as its dialectical counterpart. A closer look at the words themselves reveals the affiliation beneath the surface separation of Céline's postwar rhetoric. The original homographic and homonymic convergence of the two words in the French language, acknowledged by the Académie Française as of 1694, was coincidental.[19] The usage of *rame* to mean "oar" descends straightforwardly from the Latin *remus*, "oar," appearing in its present form in French by the end of the fourteenth century. It has spawned numerous figures of speech that appear in Céline's later novels as part of the celebrated metafictional asides: *être* or *tirer à la rame* (to work a lot, to be in a difficult situation); *ne pas en ficher, ne pas (en) foutre une rame* (to do nothing); *avoir la rame* (to be tired, to have no desire to work).[20] Guide and pilgrim are subterraneously related: the emblematic oar used to frame a *descensus ad inferos* conveys images of the process of composition and is thematically associated to the other *rame* ("subway train") with which Céline so closely identified his style; conversely, the metro car of the *style émotif* brings with it connotations of the physical act of writing, associated thematically with the framing *descensus* of Charon's oar.

The use of *rame* to describe the ensemble of a train, an engine with cars

---

[19] This analysis is based on material in the following dictionaries: *Trésor de la langue française*, the *Littré*, the *Grand Larousse*, and the *Robert*.

[20] For a list and discussion of such asides in Céline, see Godard, 305–40, "La présence du narrateur."

—and by extension a subway—first appears at the turn of the century, attributed to one of Céline's favorite writers, Henri Barbusse. It derives from the same source as the English *ream* (some five hundred sheets or twenty quires of new paper): the Arabic *rizmah,* through the Spanish *resma,* both also meaning *ream.* Here, too, we find motifs of Céline's autobiographical voice: "mettre un livre à la rame" means to sell by weight books that aren't moving quickly enough.[21] In a further resonance with the usage above, and probably by confusion between the two, the use of *rame* to describe a train derives from the sense of "ream" by way of its use to describe "a line of barges" (ca. 1855). Each usage thus comes to resonate with the other: the descent punctuated by the blows of Charon's *rame* with the process of composition, the metaphor of style with the mechanics of writing (Céline always emphasizes the physical act of putting pen on manuscript page) and the line of barges on the Seine within which Charon's *bateau-mouche, La Publique,* will appear in the prelude of *Château.*

The *rame magique* allows the writer unsullied access to his past; the *rame* of Charon contains its ordure and violence. Historically, in the hell of the novels of war, Céline will be the *rame*'s victim, threatened with Charon's oar crashing into his head if he delays entering the underworld. The metaphor is given further biographical weight through the increasingly frequent complaints about his head wound, the same relic of the First World War responsible for the 1951 pardon. On a metafictional level, the metaphor turns aggressive, repeating the dialectical flip-flop of *Bagatelles'* elephant and ant. As a learned allusion, a calque of Dante's Charon in *Inferno* 3.111 ("batte col remo qualunque s'adagia" [he beats with his oar anyone who delays]), it renews the insistently parodic pretensions to literary fame ("a place in the Académie!").[22]

Guignol's band presented the two roles implicated one in the other: the murders of Van Claben and Mille-Pattes allegorized the pamphleteer's descent into hell. That phantom remained stuck there, embodied in Charon and his *rame* as the ferryman of the underworld. And this is the role Céline assumed in the trilogy: he takes us across into the forbidden and clandestine world of the Third Reich and its *collabos.* As Muray has

[21] Céline's obsession with the monetary aspects of the writer's trade begins for our purposes with the rejected ballets in *Bagatelles* and reaches full bloom in *Entretiens,* which is predicated on the commercial and critical failure of the two *Féerie* novels.

[22] Muray notes the Dante allusion (212) and cites most of the relevant passages from the postwar books. His reading, however, moves in a different direction, toward apocalypse and toward Céline's language as the way to escape from it.

pointed out, the sound of Charon's oar ("et vlaouf! . . . vlaouf! . . .") on the heads of tardy shades punctuates Céline's writing from *Féerie* to *Rigodon* like the bombs continually falling around him (213–14), and, of course, like the "trois points" that punctuate the tracks of the metro, preventing it from derailing.

This is the analogy between the "métro-tout-nerfs-rails-magiques-à-travers-ses-trois-points" of *Entretiens* and the *ramus aureus*, the golden bough that guarantees Aeneas's protection from the oar of Charon as he descends into the underworld to receive the vocation of founding Rome, allowing Vergil retrospectively to rewrite the history of the peace of Augustus.[23] Here, the *rame magique* must protect Céline from himself, assert a distinction between victim and aggressor, innocence and guilt, and cleanse the writer's vehicle into an earth-shattering style that, like the author whose past it rewrites, has made its way through the war years without a trace of dirt.

We see this strategy at work in Céline's dialogic manifesto of his postwar stylistics, the *Entretiens avec le professeur Y*, where the liberating moment of truth in the London Underground reappeared transformed into an allegory of purely literary conversion. The first half of a two-pronged attack on the consciousness of his peers and public in response to the financial and critical failure of the two published volumes of *Féerie*, *Entretiens* stages an interview with a would-be novelist who is fishing for an introduction to Céline's publisher, Gallimard. Aesthetic points are made through comic exaggeration, mocking both author and supposed interviewer. The latter receives the brunt of the mockery, however, suffering an ever more Rabelaisian attack of incontinence as Céline's rhetoric takes off into his patented *délire* of style. We witness the *style émotif* in action through its physical effect on the professor.

As *Guignol's band* allegorized the pamphlets, here the characters personify Céline's style and model reader, respectively. This is his vision of the postwar style: the reader should be physically overwhelmed to the point that, unable to concentrate on the intricacies of the metaphor of the metro, by the end of the dialogue he is simply repeating the writer's dogma by rote. The express train of the *style émotif* renders ineffectual any lucid examination of its content: we descend into the station and are carried away without a stop and deposited at the other end—at the conclusion of the text, the narrator is walking home, planning to write his own inter-

---

[23] Although the current French translation for *ramus aureus* is *rameau d'or* (from the hypothetical popular Latin diminutive *ramellus*), the *rame* complex retains traces of *ramus* in the literary archaism *rame*, "tree branch" or "bough."

view, signed by himself and the professor. The reader gets a joyride but is refused any critical distance or input.

As the central paragraph of the manifesto shows, Céline's metro challenges the amusement park and the movies, an ultramodern, streamlined technological wonder:

> No "nonsense!" . . . I won't put up with your "nonsense" Colonel! . . . I'm giving you the truth, pure and simple . . . take advantage of what I'm telling you! . . . be forewarned: I'm leaving nothing to the movies! I've made off with all its effects! . . . all its fancy melodrama! . . . all its fake sensitivity! . . . all its effects! . . . decanted, refined, the whole bit! . . . right into the nervous system on my magic train [*rame magique*]! concentrated! . . . I stuff it all in! . . . my metro with "three dot ties" carries it all away! . . . my magic metro! . . . traitors, suspect beauties, foggy wharves, autos, puppies, brand-new buildings, romantic chalets, plagiarists, dissenters, everything! . . . (. . .) I've grabbed all the emotive stuff! . . . have I explained it, Colonel? . . . "Pigalle station to Issy" in the wink of an eye! . . . even the biggest sops feel moved! . . . (*Y* 543; 106–9)

Here are the basic components of the postwar *rame magique:* the metro is emotion, running beneath the surface of traditional literary language. Its rails are style, appearing straight but not so; that is, laboriously written so as to appear as if spoken language. The ties that hold down the tracks are the *trois points,* the three periods that propel Céline's prose from one phrase to the next with electrifying velocity.

The extended metaphor is carefully formulated and developed and grounded in the reality of Paris so far as to allow Céline to dissociate himself from it. The professor's first reaction to the paragraph above is utter panic. He mistakes the manifesto for reality and begins screaming that Céline is sabotaging the Metro. Hence, we are meant to respond to the fiction as if it were real in terms of the cinematic "suspension of disbelief," but not as if it were politically real. For the remainder of the book we find Céline pacifying the professor; just so the postwar novels oscillate between the provocation of presenting the (selectively blackened) reality of his guilt and reassurances that it is only literature, only meant to entertain, not to be taken seriously, that he is afraid he is boring us.

His account of the origin of the style plays along this axis. Céline models it on Pascal's famous conversion but sets it in the Pigalle Metro station, in the neighborhood in which he lived from 1929 until 1944, and where all the novels through *Guignol's band* were written. Bridge and

metro, the scenes of the two crimes in *Guignol's band,* are condensed into
a single authorizing image of tradition. In 1654, the horses of Pascal's
carriage went out of control on the Pont de Neuilly; two fell into the
Seine, and he was left hanging above the water. The view of the abyss
(*gouffre*) prepared him for the actual conversion of the night of 23 No-
vember (Muray, 181–82). As depicted here, however, Céline's conversion
was not to God but to style: "I had the same experience myself! . . .
exactly! . . . or just about . . . the same fright as Pascal! . . . the feeling of
the abyss! . . . but mine wasn't on the Pont de Neuilly . . . no! it happened
to me in the metro . . . facing the stairway into the métro . . . North-South
line! . . . you with me, Colonel? . . . North-South! . . . I owe the revelation
of my genius to the Pigalle station! . . ." (Y 535; 91). At first, he says, he
hesitated ("the dark metro? that reeking abyss, filthy and practical? . . ."
[Y 535; 92–93]), but then everything was swallowed up (*enfourné*) into
it. Céline frames his descent and conversion within a traditionally literary
model but establishes a clear contrast as well. The contrast is not mere
parody, though; the sights of Pigalle low life constitute a primary narrative
context of popular entertainment in the later novels.

These elements are nevertheless significantly cleaned up by their place-
ment within the slick modernity of the magic metro: in the postwar novels,
no matter how much Céline blackens himself by his associations, he remains unsullied within the genius of his style; he gives himself an alibi for
what he will show himself doing. A long process inheres within the apparently immediate and clean story of origin; Céline's Pascalian fear and his
mistrust of the filth, odor, and "practicality" of the metro date back to the
scenes of *Voyage.* "Bout bout" and Pascal both belong with the classics
and thinkers who merely described hell, those for whom one look down
was enough to convert. But the leap from the disenchanted veteran of
Voyage to the purely literary realm of style elides Céline's descent as it
actually occurred during the war. Just as the metro crushed the potentially
treacherous Mille-Pattes in *Guignol's band,* so Céline had made his style
into a weapon against the political treachery he suspected in the world
around him. The formal and fictionalized aggression of *Entretiens* draws
its power from that unavowed source condensed into the Pascalian myth
of its origin, the third rail of the *rame magique.* The aggression safely
contained, the autobiographical Céline of the war years could emerge,
figured as the victim by Charon's fatal *rame.* The narrator in *Féerie* and
the trilogy records his descent into hell as innocent victim, reconstructing
his experiences at our demand and for our benefit.

As *Féerie* opens, the Allies are approaching, and a visitor coming to
Céline in Montmartre is not yet able to take the route through Pigalle:

"She came in spite of the alerts, the metro breakdowns, the closed streets
. . . and from so far!" (*F1* 11). Instead of the metro, Céline introduces a
different *rame*, that of Charon, who turns the culprit into a repentant
victim:

> You always screw up the living . . . you don't understand the business
> of life very well . . . Oh, I have so many regrets! . . . Courtial . . . Follet
> . . . Elisabeth . . . Edith . . . Janine . . . that's something different than a
> hundred years in prison! . . . What a filth I am . . . (. . .) I deserve terrible
> treatment . . . what I've destroyed! my god! . . . Charon will see me from
> far far off: "Come on!" he'll tell me . . . and bam! . . . my mug . . . his
> oar! . . . wham! again! . . . getting me for my double-crossing! . . . Oh,
> I'd better hurry up, in the name of Styx! . . . I don't want to go with a
> rotten soul! . . . The carcass is nothing, ingratitude is everything! . . . I
> want to get back some esteem! . . . Self-esteem! . . . What's more, from
> my peers! . . . a place in the Academy! . . . At worst! . . . no matter
> which one! . . . consecration! . . . distinction! . . . so my dead can con-
> sole themselves a bit about my ways! . . . a bit of regard . . . my mother
> first of all! . . . I want my dead to reconsider me! . . . (*F1* 69)

Now, by all accounts the writings of Céline were far more collaborationist
than the actions of the doctor Destouches.[24] Yet the sins of this passage
are emphatically those of the biographical person: with the exception of
Courtial, the mad inventor and suicide of the pre-pamphlet *Mort*, all those
named are women from the life of Destouches. The writer takes no blame;
the "Battle of the Styx" is to convince us that Céline was simply a *sale
type*, a double-crosser but not a war criminal. Although constantly cast
into a hell of collaboration and war crimes, the postwar Céline will be-
smirch his fictional self only on personal, never on political, grounds.
Meanwhile, Céline the writer uses his *style émotif* not for the obvious
strategy of denying wrongdoing but to exaggerate it in such a way as
subtly to cloak its identity. He presents a persona dependent on our memory of Bardamu and Ferdinand from *Voyage* and *Mort*, but who, instead
of being a personally blackened outsider in a blackened world, is a personally blackened outsider not so bad as history has made him out to be, in a
world that is indeed *that* bad or worse.

When the "Battle of the Styx" continues in the trilogy, it inaugurates a

---

[24] The refrain of "some of his best friends were Jews" runs through the corpus of
Céline biographies, is fairly well documented by Gibault, and seems credible enough
given the oscillation in Céline's writing. See McCarthy 135; Gibault, vol. 2; and Vitoux.

full-blown descent into the war and authorizes a revision of the dangers
of the world below in place of the Vergilian rewriting of history to change
the world above.[25] In *Château*'s extended framing episode of Charon's
bateau-mouche, La Publique, we find the historical allegory of Céline's
relationship to his readers and critics to go with the stylistic-literary one
of *Entretiens.* Strongly suggesting Dante, Céline implicitly borrows both
the moral authority of his model and the authority of an exile looking
back at his native city without hope of return. The trajectory of the trilogy
will take him first to the Hohenzollern castle of Sigmaringen in southern
Germany, the final refuge of the Pétainists, then on a nightmare odyssey
across defeated Germany on his way to Denmark, where he had stashed
the gold from the royalties of his earlier novels.

   By recounting this part of his life, he is implicating himself as yet another collaborator who fled France for safety, but the prelude scene makes
it clear beforehand that all who will follow him as readers will be implicated in the same way he was. With Charon's *bateau-mouche,* we embark
on a pleasure boat on the Seine, an entertainment for the Parisian
"Publique," floating down the river while Céline the ferryman and crowd
pleaser turns his spotlight onto all manner of illicit activity being performed along the banks for our enjoyment from a safe distance. Céline's
gauntlet is that any Parisian who insists that beneath the tourist trappings
of the boat might lie the metro of their everyday commute, that Céline is
on the shore as well as in the boat, must also recognize his or her city as
the *collabo*'s hell.

   The context of the allusions in the opening sections of the prelude is
literary: wailing against his publishers' thefts from him, he prays, "Let me
meet them all in Charon's boat, enemies, friends, all with their guts around
their necks! . . . Charon smashing their faces in!"[26] In succession, Céline
attacks Gallimard ("Achille"), Jean Paulhan ("Norbert Loukoum"), and
a fair assortment of contemporary authors: Maurois, Mauriac, Thorez,
Sartre ("Tartre"), Claudel, Elsa Triolet and Aragon ("Mme Triolette and

---

[25] Erika Ostrovsky has noted the "frequent occurrence" of descents into hell in the
postwar trilogy, "represented by entry into subterranean labyrinths, tunnels, room no.
36 [*Château*], and bomb craters, or assemblies of monsters and demons" ("L.-F. Céline:
Creator and Destroyer of Myths," in *Critical Essays on L.-F. Céline,* ed. W. K. Buckley
[Boston, 1989], 94). Although these motifs are certainly present, they must be read in
context with the narrative strategy set up by Céline with the framing device of "La
Publique," and are not simply to be identified as part of the narrator's mythic role as
"shaman" (94).

[26] Céline, *D'un château l'autre,* in *Romans II,* ed. Henri Godard (1957; Paris, 1974),
15; trans. Ralph Manheim, *Castle to Castle* (New York, 1968), 15; hereafter cited
as *C.*

her gastritic Larengon"), and more (14–20; 14–21). Each group of names is punctuated by a blow of the oar: "The reception they'll get from Charon? *That's the question!* . . . *Wham! Bam!* Take it from me!" (19; 19). The first image of Charon places Céline in the role of a modern Dante, descending as narrator but also, as author, settling accounts by putting enemies in hell. The process is visible in the distortion of names: this may have served to avoid lawsuits, but the margin between reality and fiction had to remain narrow enough for the distortion to be identifiable.[27] We are in the allegorical framework of a *descensus:* the otherworldly punishments of Dante's hell have been condensed within the names themselves. Sartre is trivialized as "Tartar," the residue in wine casks or on poorly washed teeth; Aragon is rendered gastritic and equally trivialized (a *rengaine* is a banal or clichéd phrase); Claudel and Mauriac are presented ironically as in a *contrapasso*, "Ciboire et sa pharisienne."[28] Like Dante, Céline sometimes simply buries his enemies in excrement: Triolet becomes "Mme Lafente"; Duhamel, "Troudumel"; and Gallimard, Brottin.[29]

Céline's role as a modern Dante, dispensing punishments in the form of such insults, contextualizes the early pages of *Château* by urging us to imagine his journey through the inferno as one inspired by virtuous wrath. Similarly, when Céline first brings up his wartime experience, he does so in the ironic context of readers telling him not to feel sorry for himself ("That isn't so bad, you'll say . . . millions have died who weren't any guiltier than you!" [21; 22]). Accurate details of Céline's situation are represented in a perspective skewed so as to shift the reader's attention away from evaluation of them. The descent is autobiographical, but it is also allegorical: Céline rewrites history as he goes along. So, when the tables are turned, and Céline himself must confront Charon, the fear expressed earlier in *Féerie*, that Charon would soon be striking Céline himself over the head, is vitiated by the introductory *délire*. In other words, the image from *Féerie* of the unjustly accused Céline, rotting in the hell of a Danish prison (81) or fearing assassination in 1944 Montmartre (6–10), is supposed to remain in the back of our minds as the autobiography— Céline's Dantean exile—while we read *Château*.

Every descent authorizes itself by mortifying its predecessors; Céline

[27] For a chart of Céline's alteration of names, see Godard, 301–4.
[28] *F1* 149–61. *Féerie* includes a plethora of variations on the above. "Ciborium" is the sacred vase in which the hosts are stored; "pharisienne" has the figurative meaning of a religious hypocrite.
[29] Early version of *Château* (in *Romans II*, 1043); *Nord* (in *Romans II*, 506); *Château*, 11, passim. Brottin, from "crottin," animal (sheep or goat) droppings; often combined by Céline with Achille as Gallimard's given name.

bolsters his credentials over Dante by dirtying his hands on behalf of the realism of "taking us there." Having dispatched the Parisian literati, he proceeds to battle his own demons, the *collabos*. The doctor Destouches is summoned from his hilltop stronghold outside Paris to tend the aged and dying Mme Niçois in Lower Meudon. The descent is presented as a confrontation with his past: Céline describes himself as besieged in his house in Upper Meudon, surrounded and guarded by a pack of dogs (his Cerberus, in other words). His demons, however, can just as quickly turn against him as warders; for the dogs, besides scaring away prospective patients, remind him of his two years in prison in Denmark (57; 70).

Mme Niçois's house initiates a topographical allegorization of Céline's return from exile as a descent into Paris. After Körsor, Céline and Lucette flew first to her mother's in Nice to test the waters. The further distance of exile was safer but isolated and inhospitable; Mme Niçois's place has all Paris spread beneath it but is already getting dangerous: "So, I go down [*je descends*] to see Mme Niçois . . . But I'll repeat, I am on my guard . . . the people along the riverfront are hostile . . ." [61; 76]). Paris is inhabited by ghosts; there are souls waiting down at the quay to be ferried across the Seine by Charon, but waiting also to be brought back to life by Céline-author.

Having finished tending to Mme Niçois, Céline beholds the quay and its barges from her window. If the row of barges ("péniches") recalls the derivation of *rame* (subway train) from *rame* (ream of paper), we find a further affiliation with Céline's postwar definitions of the *style émotif* in the reaction to his first glimpse of *La Publique*: "Agar [his dog] would put me straight . . . ghosts or not ghosts? suffering from an illusion? or what? some effect of the water?" (68; 83). Agar does not bark at the boat, so it must be illusion; calling it "an effect of the water" identifies it with Céline's programmatic description of his own illusion-creating in the *Entretiens*:

> The reader of an emotive book . . . one of my works! . . . in emotive style! . . . (. . .) He seems to hear, would swear to it, that someone is reading to him inside his head! . . . (. . .) Not just in the ear! . . . no! . . . in the intimacy of his nerves! Right in the middle of his nervous system! inside his own head! (. . .) You dip a stick in the water . . . (. . .) and your stick looks broken! twisted! (. . .) [So] you break it yourself by God before dipping it in the water! What a trick! The whole secret of Impressionism (. . .) So you'll correct the effect (. . .) of refraction! Your stick will look completely straight! You just break it first! . . . before dipping it in the water! . . . (Y 545–46; 112–15)[30]

---

[30] Ellipses in the text are mainly of puzzled interpolations by the narrator's interlocutor, the Professor/Colonel.

Céline is describing the phenomenon of the tracks of his *rame magique:* the railings of classical style are straight, so the train crashes; those of his style look straight (appear like spoken language) but are really broken. Céline glosses the vision of the *bateau-mouche* with a definition of his style: "an effect of the water." The dog proves its illusory nature, but Céline still believes it, as if "someone is reading it to him inside his head."

Author and protagonist are clearly delineated through the play of the *rame:* we are in an allegory of conversion. Céline-protagonist, recalling his vision for us as prelude to the memories of the descent he is about to recount, shows himself taken in by the style. He is frightened by Charon, expecting the *rame* to smash him in the head just as that of the style already has. Céline-author displaces onto his protagonist as a question of fear all the consequences of the other misreading—the pamphlets—even though it had been historical in nature. The protagonist will lead us on a descent as an unconverted pilgrim, that is, a man ignorant of the implications of his actions. We, like him (although more than he), will be converted into a proper understanding of the history of the war. Céline's exculpation will arise from this understanding as a side effect of it, just as Dante's salvation was a side effect of his journey.

This phenomenon is common to the allegory of conversion: as part and parcel of the vocation received from God, the exile is vindicated. In Dante, it is less clear that this might be a principal reason for the elaborate framework of descent, conversion, and vision of the divine; in Céline, it is patently the motive of the entire structure. Céline makes no bones about his intentions of baiting us with a scandalous history of the war, although the motive of clearing his name remains unenunciated. This is an important difference in emphasis from the model evident in Augustine or Dante or in other twentieth-century reformulations, such as in Benjamin, Proust, Woolf, or the later Weiss, where the persuasive rhetorical structure of the allegory of conversion is explicitly placed in the service of some sort of transcendence.

The role of Charon, conversely, is displaced in the opposite manner: from the protagonist, where it had been in the earlier novels such as *Voyage* or *Mort,* it shifts to the author. The *rame* with which the pamphleteer had threatened the Jews is cleansed into the *rame* of pure style with which Céline-author is creating the masterful effects of this descent, in full knowledge of its fictionality insofar as concerns his own guilt. In other words, the polarization resolves the dialectic of aggressor/victim into two only partially realized poles. The biographical link to "hell" remains only in its "victim" half in the protagonist, whereas in the pamphlets and *Guignol's band* it had oscillated wildly from one to the other; the aggressor (Céline surrounded by his dogs, Céline placing all his enemies in hell)

remains only in the purely literary, stylistic context of the composition of
a novel.

The illusion of a dialectic remains—we have versions of both Céline-
victim and Céline-aggressor, of the one descending and the one already
there—but it is an "effet de l'eau": the incriminating moment of each has
been surreptitiously dropped out, and the dialectical relationship between
them is only faintly reproduced in the author/narrator interplay. In terms
of the allegory of conversion and in terms of responsibility to history, the
postwar trilogy is an enormous, brilliantly executed sleight of hand: as
magician, Céline pretends to saw himself in half. Like Aeneas's return
from the underworld through the ivory gate of dreams, the split is illusory,
but it did the trick nonetheless: Céline regained the open air of history,
redeeming his name as a preeminent modern stylist with the critical and
popular success of the trilogy.

The encounter with the boat itself is an amplification of the motifs
leading up to it. *La Publique* is ancient, pre-1900, Céline-protagonist tells
us, and it reminds him of his childhood trips, pre-1900, on similar
bateaux-mouches, punctuated by the same "Wham!" and "Slam!"
("vlang!" and "vlaac!") as Charon's oar; that is, slaps from the hands of
his parents (68–69; 84–85). This is no longer the child Ferdinand of a
similar voyage in *Mort,* however; the childhood is refigured into the faulty
dialectic of aggressor/victim: he was tortured then, and he is threatened
with the same torture again now. The first encounter stages the scene as a
mise-en-abîme of the novel as a whole: he is greeted at the riverfront by
Robert Le Vigan, the movie actor with whom he, his wife, and Bébert had
fled to Germany in 1944. Both are victims in the eyes of the protagonist
("Hunted to death like we've been" [73; 89]), but the different histories
explain the different status of each character vis-à-vis the boat and, thus,
vis-à-vis the story to come.

Le Vigan remained at Sigmaringen when the Célines left for Denmark
(they parted on bad terms, in fact) and was arrested while fleeing toward
Switzerland and in 1946 was sentenced in Paris to ten years' hard labor.
On parole after three years, he crossed the border to Spain and settled in
Argentina in 1950. Céline brings Le Vigan back to France as he would
have appeared in 1957, dressed in the gaucho outfit of his acting career,
ready to play the role of the one who stayed behind at Sigmaringen.[31] He
tells Céline that he collects money for Charon; those who pay enough
don't get their skulls bashed in. His friend Emile is the navigator and

---

[31] The biographical information is based on Godard's notes to *Romans II,* 1081–
82.

engineer. Le Vigan provides the relevant information about the mysterious *bateau-mouche*. It belongs to Charon; it is full of dead men; it is traveling down the Seine collecting the dead. Emile then tells his story. Victim of the postwar lynchings in Paris and buried in a mass grave, he followed the other corpses when they rose from their pit and headed down to the Seine ("dead-quiet pilgrimage," he calls it [79; 95]). They arrived at the boat, "And *wham! slam!* . . . his skull again . . . (. . .) who is it? 'I'm Charon, see!' " (79; 96). Emile concludes by assuring Céline in a menacing tone: " 'You'll see him . . . his oar in your face . . . you'll see him!' A promise . . . 'He splits their skulls with an oar . . .' " (80; 96). On board *La Publique* are those *collabos* who, unlike Céline, were not able to escape.

This *could* have been his fate: thus Céline sums up the threat he is staging, along with its historical background, to distract his reader from the more troubling and current proposition that this *should* have been his fate:

> Hanging around there, my curiosity would get me into trouble . . . (. . .) All this was fine and dandy, but suppose the monster with the oar caught me here? hanging around? (. . .) Oh, it was no time to fall asleep . . . think . . . sure . . . meditate . . . but get out of there . . . even reduced as I was . . . a wreck . . . practically out on my feet, I realized this was no place to be hanging around . . . in the first place . . . this *bateau-mouche*, *La Publique*, right at the bottom of our hill? and all these pilgrims with their smell? . . . And Le Vigan and the two others? . . . especially Le Vigan! . . . the admirable Le Vigan! . . . "Don't drag Ferdinand in the muck! . . . He's a bigger patriot than any of you!" His very words at the Supreme Court of Hate! . . . and him in handcuffs . . . standing right up front . . . not in the wings, not in a bistro, not in a milk bar, or at the Bal des Quatzarts! . . . he all alone . . . before the Council of the Inquisition . . . when they were trying to make him confess, to proclaim in a loud voice . . . that he accused me, that I had brought him to this . . . I and nobody else! . . . the rottenest mercenary traitor he's ever known! . . . the lousiest stinker of the whole Propagandastaffel . . . the radio, the newspapers . . . clandestine killers . . . me! I'm telling you what happened . . . the historical events . . . (85; 102)

This crucial passage compresses three time periods for Céline/Le Vigan into a single dynamic: their flight from Paris and time together at Sigmaringen (which is why neither suffered the fate of Emile); their fates at the hands of the postwar tribunal; and their present meeting, staged in 1957. The question raised here by the narrator is whether this meeting will replicate the first set of events or the second.

Céline raises the ghosts in present-day form because he believes it is still necessary to exorcise them. And he saves himself once more, fleeing back up the hill to his fortress. But Le Vigan has served to provide the bait of reminding the readers that Céline still has juicy wartime gossip to tell, at the same time displacing the guilt associated with such gossip. Emile has reminded the readers that they perhaps were not so innocent either in their postwar purge, that this Paris may not be so distant from their own. Céline has properly established himself as eyewitness while distancing himself from the events he will recount; he has also shown us the literary model he will follow in his chronicle. Consequently, once safe at home again, we see the shift from one *rame* to the other: as the speaking narrator thinks back over the events as frightened victim, Céline-author breaks in as the ferryman Charon, with his own *rame:*

> I know . . . I know . . . I missed Charon! . . . If I'd stayed a moment longer, I'd have seen him! . . . Le Vigan and the others must have seen him! . . . My excuse is . . . I felt the fever coming on . . . and I had another excuse . . . I'll tell you about it . . .
>
> To hell with all that! . . . I could also take you on an excursion with different people! . . . delirious wandering for its own sake! . . . a prettier place! . . . fever or no fever! . . . really a very picturesque place! . . . a tourist's paradise! . . . and better! . . . dreamy, historical and salubrious! . . . (102; 123)

The authorial voice appears to cut off the narrator in midsentence—"I'll tell you about it . . . / To hell with all that!" (Je vous raconterai . . . Là zut!). The author takes over the otherworldly vision to promise even better things; he will outdo Charon with the spectacle of *collabos* and Germans together in Sigmaringen.

But we should recall once more the motivation behind the framing device: the passengers on Charon's boat differ from the readers in that they are dead—after all, the blows of the *rame* crack open the skull. Céline's *rame*, in contrast, merely puts emotion inside our heads as the style overwhelms us, but we remain alive and our subjugation is only in our heads. Tarrying in his pages, soaking up the proffered entertainment of atrocities, we implicate ourselves and accept the terms of a false choice: either to reject Céline's books as sullied by his past or to assent to their absolute autonomy; either to reflect from without or to be carried off thoughtlessly into the house of horrors. The illusory separation between *collabo* and stylist converts the reader into an expurgated version of Céline's own past. In the postwar novels Céline restages his trial in absentia;

luring us in with promises of the "true story" and seducing us with the genius of his style and rhetoric, he makes the decision to read his fiction into an acquittal of his history.

Insomuch as they duplicate the constructions of Céline's poetics as critical categories, the traditional divisions of Céline's reception between the pure stylist whose life was repellent (or appeared so) and the would-be stylist irrevocably soiled by his politics are exemplary of a modernism of reading. They can account neither for the power of Céline's style nor for the autobiographical transformations of the narrative voice, nor can they accurately describe the interplay between the two that structures the oeuvre from *Voyage* to *Rigodon*. Readings of modernism must recognize and move beyond the conversionary poetics of the period that would channel modes of reading into damnation or salvation, allowing no common ground for interpretation. Moreover, because we have uncritically inherited such critical patterns from our modernist past, we continue to apply the hagiographical modes of reading attributed by them to their own past; hence our literary historical and theoretical categories remain in many ways determined by those of modernism. Céline can sharpen our awareness of the fault lines negotiated by the autobiographical voice, the hidden stakes of the allegory of conversion, and the sleight of hand that would make language the vehicle of truth and biography the province of fiction. At the same time, we require new means of distinguishing between the dubious results of Céline's descent to the underworld and the more palatable visions of, for example, Woolf or Benjamin.

A first step is to reevaluate the sources of the structures used in modernism. Once we take full account of the stakes of the fraught medieval dichotomy between poetic fiction and religious truth, we find a signifying structure, tagged by motifs of the descent to the underworld, that generates meaning out of the interplay between pagan and Christian, descent and return. Consequently, the postmodern Peter Weiss can help read the premodern *Commedia*, not in terms of the modernist choice between sovereign poet or plodding Christian but as a staging of the stakes involved in either choice, an exploration of how the past is rewritten whenever preserved and the reader coerced whenever convinced. Céline's insinuation of a collaborationist past into the dynamics of his poetics raises the question, If art is neither autonomous from life nor wholly subject to it, how can the relationship between the two be understood and evaluated? The answer, as we shall see, lies not in the choice but in the movement between the two, in the tense reciprocity between medieval and modern, and between descending to the underworld and rousing the world below.

3

The Conversion of Dante

It is with fiction as with religion: it should present another
world, and yet one to which we feel the tie.
—Herman Melville, *The Confidence-Man*

The War is such a tremendous landmark that it imposes
itself upon our computations of time like the birth of
Christ. We say "pre-war" and "post-war," rather as we
say B.C. or A.D. . . . You will be astonished to find out
how like art is to war, I mean "modernist" art.
—Wyndham Lewis, *Blasting and Bombardiering*

AUGUSTINE'S EXPLOITATION of the tension between Aeneas and Paul,
between poetry and Scripture, in order to authorize a prophetic voice left
Bernard Silvestris exploring the impossibility of basing authority on poetic
creation: these are the poles of the allegory of conversion. Dante incorporated that model into the two voices of the *Commedia;* the moderns recu-
perated his summa of that tension into a wholly secularized concept of
hell as the world we now inhabit. During modernism, Dante underwent a
conversion, or, as Borges might have put it, a *renovación,* from dead
allegory to living myth, from prophet to poet. The Aenean Dante was
pushed to the fore, and it was now the Pauline visionary who slipped in
through the coincidences and accidents of the dialectic. This mythified
Dante provided the model for a high-modernist incorporation of contemporary philosophies, theories, and psychologies into fictional frames, and
for the reception of the modernist descent to the underworld as a timeless,
archetypal journey. Dante's unification of Aeneas and Paul resulted in a
modern model for generating extratextual authority out of a putatively
autonomous poetic text. As such, no overt consideration of the grounds

of prophetic authority was possible any longer: Dante must be either allegorical or poetic, either religious or secular, either medieval or modern.

Now, in Céline's use of the modern cliché of war as hell, we saw that a conversionary structure was still entailed by that image. There is an underlying common ground to the symptomatic dichotomies in each; modern warfare renovates Augustine's religio-historical analogy; it is seen as the Christ-event of a modern allegory of conversion, structuring a newly authorized politico-historical narrative. Peter Weiss's work draws out the ramifications of this heuristic, proposing the post-World War II necessity of refiguring modernism as a crux to be imitated: we must now descend to it as a past to be rewritten. So, in order to grasp Dante outside the polarized reading he received from and imparted to modernism, we have to conceptualize the terms of that reading. As we see in this chapter, Weiss's monumental project for a postwar *Commedia* creates the space for a renewed look at the tensions within the *Commedia* itself.

Descent into Modernity:
Peter Weiss's *Welttheater*

Peter Weiss documented two experiences of the modern in his postwar writings: the one that he had and the one that he ought to have had. Born in Berlin in 1916 to a Hungarian Jewish father with Czechoslovakian citizenship and a Swiss mother, Weiss grew up in Bremen before returning to Berlin in 1929 and moving on to London five years later. The family then relocated to Czechoslovakia, where Weiss studied painting at the Academy of Fine Arts in Prague. At the start of the war, they settled in Sweden, where Weiss lived until his death in 1982. The first, the actual experience of the *entre-deux-guerres* was thus as a painter, a Jew, and an exile. When Weiss next visited Germany, it was as a Swedish correspondent surveying the ruins of Berlin in 1947; when he switched from painting to writing in the late fifties, his first work was not in German but in Swedish. The writing falls into three roughly chronological but overlapping groups: the autobiographical texts and the experimental prose fiction of the late fifties and early sixties; the increasingly radicalized theater, from *Marat/Sade* (1964) to *Trotski im Exil* (1970) and *Hölderlin* (1971); and the monumental novelization of the *entre-deux-guerres* through a first-person narrator who *ought to have been* Peter Weiss, *Die Ästhetik des Widerstands* (The aesthetics of resistance, 1975–81).

Where Céline based his postwar oeuvre on a total reconstruction of his past, Weiss constantly wavered between on the one hand an exilic past of missed encounters and vanished forms (the discarded métier of painter) and a present built out of direct engagement with politics, and on the other hand sorties into the myriad modernisms that could have been. A 1963 visit to the site of Auschwitz described in "Meine Ortschaft" (My Place), emblematized the tension of this wavering as a descent into hell: "Only this place, which I knew about for a long time, but first saw only recently, lies completely on its own. It is a place for which I was intended and from which I escaped. I myself experienced nothing in this place. I have no other relation to it than that my name stood on the lists of those who were to have been moved there permanently. I saw this place twenty years afterward. It is immutable." [1] As the site where he was supposed to have died, Auschwitz marked a *Nullpunkt,* a zero point between death and life, between past and present, between pre-and postwar. Weiss spent the last two decades speaking with the dead, excavating possible worlds of modernism, possible lives for the very different world he now inhabited.

If Auschwitz was the vanishing point of the historical vision, its constant referent was Dante. Structurally, in his use of the Dantean model of descent as a means of affiliating past with present, and thematically, in the motifs of exile, political engagement, and conversion, Weiss both delineated for himself the modernist contours of the *Commedia* and recreated a *Commedia* fraught with the antinomies of the *après-guerre.* [2] The centrality to Weiss's oeuvre of writing a *"Commedia* for our time" first became

---

[1] "Meine Ortschaft," 1965, rpt. in *Rapporte* (Frankfurt, 1968), 113–24; this citation, 114; hereafter cited as *R.*

[2] The relationship between Weiss and Dante has been much worked on by German critics. There are two primary emphases: the relation of the *Divina Commedia* Project to *Die Ermittlung* (*The Investigation,* Weiss's play about Auschwitz) and other dramatic works, and the relation of one or both to the *Ästhetik.* For the former, see Manfred Haiduk, *Der Dramatiker Peter Weiss* (Berlin, 1977), 119–24; Erika Salloch, *Peter Weiss' "Die Ermittlung"* (Frankfurt, 1972), 47–72, trans. "The *Divina Commedia* as Model and Anti-Model for *The Investigation* by Peter Weiss," *Modern Drama* 14 (1971): 1–12; Rolf Krause, *Faschismus als Theorie und Erfahrung: "Die Ermittlung" und ihr Autor Peter Weiss,* EH, 1st ser., 541 (Frankfurt, 1982), 30–146; Hans-Peter Burmeister, *Kunst als Protest und Widerstand: Untersuchungen zum Kunstbegriff bei Peter Weiss und Alexander Kluge,* EH, 1st ser., 824 (Frankfurt, 1985), 32–42; and Alfons Söllner, *Peter Weiss und die Deutschen* (Opladen, 1988), 161–69. For the second group, see Klaus Scherpe, "Die *Ästhetik des Widerstands* als *Divina Commedia:* Peter Weiss' künstlerische Vergegenständlichung der Geschichte," in *Peter Weiss: Wirk und Wirkung,* ed. Rudolf Wolff (Bonn, 1987), 88–99; Burmeister, 133–35; and Kurt Oesterle, "Dante und das Mega-Ich: Literarische Formen politischer und ästhetischer Subjektivität bei Peter Weiss," in *Widerstand der Ästhetik? Im Anschluß an Peter Weiss,* ed. Martin Lüdke and Delf Schmidt, *Literaturmagazin* 27 (Reinbek bei Ham-

apparent in his *Notizbücher,* the eighteen-hundred-page documentation of a twenty-year career as a writer in the German language, from 1960 to 1980.[3] The very gesture of publishing the *Notizbücher* was predicated on the canonical authority of the oeuvre, and the unhappy coincidence of Weiss's death in the same year sealed the *Notizbücher* and the published oeuvre into a perfectly bounded relationship between two narratives of his career.[4] The literary works pushed the possibility of a politicized aesthetic as far as the forms permitted; the *Notizbücher* let stand the politicization while raising a new series of questions on its means and consequences.

The raw material of the *Notizbücher* is the comprehensive coverage of the events of the twenty years of Weiss's literary production and the obsessive collection of historical material for use in that production. The mass of detail coheres around a pair of structural motifs that cast the endeavor in terms of a modern *descensus.* First, there is the presence of Dante's *Commedia* as an epistemological system, the great code through which Weiss gave meaning and structure to his life and work.[5] The *"Divina*

---

burg, 1991), 45–72. Although Scherpe's and Oesterle's essays are more sophisticated, all these studies are based on a fairly limited reading of Dante and thus restrict themselves to an interpretation of the relationship solely on the explicit terms of Weiss's own reading. Within these limits the relationship has been well documented; beyond them there remains much ground still to cover.

[3] *Notizbücher, 1960–1971,* 2 vols. (Frankfurt, 1982); *Notizbücher, 1971–1980,* 2 vols. (Frankfurt, 1981), hereafter cited as *NB1* and *NB2,* respectively. *"Notizbuch"* can be translated as either "notebook" or "diary."

[4] Such canonization may be easily verified with a glimpse at any bibliography of Weiss criticism in Germany, especially since the appearance of the *Ästhetik.* For a general bibliography, see Jochen Vogt, *Peter Weiss* (Reinbek bei Hamburg, 1987), 147–54; for an annotated bibliography of criticism of the *Ästhetik,* see Robert Cohen, *Bio-Bibliographisches Handbuch zu Peter Weiss' "Ästhetik des Widerstands"* (Hamburg, 1989), 165–86. In addition to more than thirty book-length studies and essay collections on his early work, there have appeared at least eleven special issues of journals and collections of essays and at least ten book-length monographs on the *Ästhetik* in the decade and a half since the appearance of the final volume in 1981.

[5] At least, that is, insofar as they can be said to represent his life and work. Weiss claimed to have published the notebooks without any editing except to correct spelling and to remove shopping lists and phone numbers, as well as material used directly elsewhere (in interview with Burkhardt Lindner, "Zwischen Pergamon und Plötzensee oder Die andere Darstellung der Verläufe," in *"Die Ästhetik des Widerstands" lesen,* ed. Karl-Heinz Götze and Klaus Scherpe [Berlin, 1981], 158–59; further references from this volume are cited as Götze/Scherpe; trans. Christian Rogowski, "Between Pergamon and Plötzensee: Another Way of Depicting the Course of Events: An Interview with Peter Weiss," *NGC* 30 [Fall 1983]: 107–26). It appears that one may take the notebooks as a fairly good indication of Weiss's articulation of his life.

Commedia-Projekt" ranges from draft fragments in prose and verse to Weiss's organization and interpretation of his life according to the sigla *INF, PURG,* and *PAR.* The second structural thread emerges during the seventies as we bear witness not only to the researching and composition of the *Ästhetik* but also to Weiss's reenactment of the novel in his own life.

The point of conjuncture between the two threads is the autobiographical voice. Here is an example from early in the *Notizbücher:*

> A few words about myself—the narrator. I'm European, if not to say citizen of the world, belonging to no nation, but at home in many. This, because at one time driven from my native town & return forbidden on penalty of death by burning. Learned how to get along in exile, how to find my way around anywhere. Death sentence revoked, can come & go.
> Battle now intensified—
> even harder to approach & to represent—
> don't have much time to choose words, must struggle to see what is right. Can't use classical poetry, only daily press at my disposal— for fleeting comparison, for discarding. (*NB1,* 474; 3 Jan. 1966)

At first glance, we find a recapitulation of Dante's life, historicizing the figure for his new role as Weiss's narrator: a European adapting to permanent exile from Florence under threat of execution. "Death sentence revoked" signals a shift to Dante as metonymy for the *Commedia* and its reception, the writer living on in his poem. At the same time, however, Weiss's life is even more closely paralleled: exiled to Sweden, the threat of burning that of the concentration camps for a half-Jew whose name appeared on the death lists, the revocation signaled by the end of the war.

What follows then reads as a description of Weiss's life as a writer: the difficulty of representation, the sense of urgency, the choice of daily events over classical literature—here we find the figure of the late sixties and seventies, the radical convert to Socialism. And yet, we may still retrieve from it the image of a Dante who showed himself struggling over representation in composing his *Commedia* and who participated in and depicted Florentine politics. Weiss elegantly blurs the lines between possible referents for the "narrator": the assumed one of Dante and the no less assumed one of Weiss as reteller of the *Commedia.*

Ambivalence toward the Dantean tradition of descent runs through his oeuvre, for Weiss was keenly aware both of the contradictions involved in the claim to prophetic authority and of the possibility nonetheless of converting that authority to the service of revolution. As a postwar writer, Weiss planted the Dante project firmly within the *entre-deux-guerres* context of modernist uses of the topos: the autobiographical inferno remains the Second World War; the literary descent takes up Dante as he was read within that same period. Just as Benjamin's Dante had come through Baudelaire and the Second Empire, Weiss's came by way of the *entre-deux-guerres*. I examine this reading in detail in the discussion of the *Ästhetik* and the later *Notizbücher* below. First, however, it is necessary to trace the threads of autobiographical and literary descent as Weiss defined them through the early prose and the *Notizbücher:* once we see how he cast his life as the *Commedia,* we can interpret how the *Ästhetik* cast the *Commedia* as his life.

Just as in Dante's *Commedia* the setting of the journey in 1300 forms a *Nullpunkt,* a new Christ-event toward which everything prior has led and from which everything afterward originates, so is there a moment of recognition in Weiss's oeuvre that functions as a fixed date, the allegorical nadir toward which everything converges and from which everything returns.[6] The visit to Auschwitz in 1963 has its antecedents in an autobiographically voiced memory of Sweden in 1945.

Then, in the spring of 1945, I saw the end of the development in which I had grown up. On the dazzlingly bright screen I saw the places for which I had been destined, the figures with whom I was supposed to have belonged. We sat in the seclusion of a dark room and saw what had up to this moment been inconceivable. We saw it in its full proportions, which were so vast we would never be able to comprehend it in our own lifetimes. A sobbing could be heard and a voice called out: Never forget this. It was a miserable senseless cry, for there were no longer any words, there was .nothing more to be said, there were no declarations, no more admonitions, all values had been destroyed. There in front of us, among the mountains of corpses, cowered the shapes of utter humiliation in their striped rags. Their movements were intermina-

---

[6] Weiss gave an autobiographical resonance to the postwar commonplace of the *Null-Punkt* or "Zero Hour." For a similarly thoughtful consideration of the concept, see Alexander Kluge and Oskar Negt, "1945 is an unusable time, the unexpected gap in the system that prints experience; life stories [*Lebensläufe*] turn and collective movements fall into old forms. Without the window of this *Null-Punkt* opened 'into itself' [*an sich*] and not 'for us' [*für uns*], however, German history cannot be known" (*Geschichte und Eigensinn* [Frankfurt, 1981], 379). Like Benjamin's and Woolf's (see Chapters 5 and 4, below), Weiss's autobiographical allegory carries a generational meaning.

bly slow, they reeled around, bundles of bones, blind to one another in their world of shadows. These eyes in the skeletal skulls did not seem to grasp that the gates had been opened. Where was the Styx, where was the Inferno, where was Orpheus in his underworld, surrounded by the rippling trills of flutes, where were the great visions of art, the paintings, sculptures, temples, songs and epics. Everything was reduced to dust and we could never think again of looking for new comparisons, for points of departure in the face of these ultimate pictures. This was no kingdom of the dead. These were human beings whose hearts were still beating. This was a world that had been constructed by human beings. And then we saw them, the guardians of this world: they had no horns, no tails, they wore uniforms and they huddled together in fear and had to carry the dead to the mass graves. With whom did I now belong, as a living person, as a survivor. Did I really belong with those who stared at me with their immense eyes, whom I had long since betrayed, or did I belong with the murderers and executioners. Had I not tolerated this world, had I not turned away from Peter Kien and Lucie Weisberger, and given them up and forgotten them. It no longer seemed possible to go on living with these inextinguishable pictures before my eyes. It no longer seemed possible ever to go out again, into the streets, and up into my room.[7]

Weiss introduces in this passage the same moment of insight that he would later reproduce in the draft prologue to the *Divina Commedia* cited above. We find, in particular, the same opposition between "the great visions of art"—here prominently represented by Dante's *Inferno*—and the pictures of the daily press—here a newsreel of the concentration camps. Most notably, we also find a date for the insight, 1945.

Now, the novel in which this episode appears was not entitled *Nullpunkt* but, rather, *Fluchtpunkt,* or *Vanishing Point.* Two nuances of the title are especially apt at this juncture. First, Weiss entitled the novel with a hallmark of modern theory of Western art, the vanishing point with which figurative painting from the Renaissance onward constructed the

---

[7] *Fluchtpunkt* (Frankfurt, 1962), 210–11; trans. E. B. Garside, Alastair Hamilton, and Christopher Levenson, *Vanishing Point,* in *Exile* (New York, 1968), 194–95; hereafter cited as *F. Exile* also contains *Leavetaking,* a translation of *Abschied von den Eltern* (Frankfurt, 1961). The latter fictionalizes Weiss's life from birth to his arrival as exile in Sweden in 1939; *Fluchtpunkt* novelizes the years 1939 to 1947. For Weiss on this period of his life, see also the interview with P. Roos, "Der Kampf um mein Existenz als Maler," in *Der Maler Peter Weiss* (Exhibition Catalog, Bochum Museum, 1980), 5–37. For a critical biography, see Vogt.

illusion of real perspective, with the spectator granted the privileged line of sight, thus being enclosed and, as it were, sealed into the painting. This nuance is made ironic in the passage above. The newsreel pictures refuse perspective, refuse "the great visions of art," and the narrator responds by sealing himself up: "It no longer seemed possible to go on living with these inextinguishable pictures before my eyes. It no longer seemed possible ever to go out again, into the streets, and up into my room." Unable either to abandon art or to face the total revolution of it necessary to deal with these new facts, the narrator closes himself into his individuality, making of himself the vanishing point into which everything converges and from which *nothing* escapes.

In this early incarnation, the narrator recovers from the moment of shock and returns to the street: "I had breathed, had spoken once again and laughed, had read books once again and contemplated artworks" (*F* 212; 195). But the images remained and made a mockery of all attempts to create. The narrator's guilt at surviving is analogous to later doubts in the *Notizbücher* as to the complicity of Dante vis-á-vis the ruling class and the Catholic religion. Like Vergil before him, Dante's political position as propagandist could never be ignored; each had made it an integral part of his creation. The conclusion of *Fluchtpunkt* elided this contradiction; the *Ästhetik* would confront it head on. When asked much later to distinguish the first-person narration of *Abschied von den Eltern (Leavetaking)* and *Fluchtpunkt* from that of the *Ästhetik*, Weiss said that whereas the latter was intended "to take hold of the entire epoch around this *I*," the former expressed the individual's self-liberation.[8] "That evening, in the spring of 1947, on the embankment of the Seine in Paris, at the age of thirty, I saw that it was possible to live and work in the world, and that I could participate in the exchange of ideas that was taking place all around, bound to no country" (*F* 307; 245). The narrator of Weiss's *Divina Commedia* emerges here for the first time, if bereft thus far of the social conscience, the awareness of contradictions that his later incarnations would possess.

Dante's *Vita nuova* ends similarly, giving in hindsight a hint of the *Commedia* to come: "After I wrote this sonnet there came to me a miraculous vision in which I saw things that made me resolve to say no more about this blessed one until I would be capable of writing about her in a

---

[8] "Peter Weiss im Gespräch mit H.-L. Arnold," in *Die Ästhetik des Widerstands*, ed. Alexander Stephan (Frankfurt, 1983), 32–33. See also *Peter Weiss im Gespräch*, ed. Rainer Gerlach and Matthias Richter (Frankfurt, 1986), 244–45; hereafter cited as Gerlach/Richter.

nobler way."[9] The *Vita nuova* offered an autobiographical reading of
Dante's lyrics as an allegory of a failed love affair with Beatrice; the
Commedia reread that affair as an allegory of conversion. Weiss applied
the same model to the Auschwitz *Nullpunkt*. Crux of the moment of
individual crisis leading to liberation in *Fluchtpunkt*, the figure of Lucie
Weisberger is explicitly identified with Beatrice in a note from late 1964,
when Weiss was attending the Frankfurt trials. Weisberger dates back to
Weiss's youth in Prague. When he discovered while in Sweden that she
had been taken to Theresienstadt, he offered to marry her in an attempt
to save her, but nothing came of it (*F* 89–90). Weiss's Beatrice is a strong
misreading of Dante's: if the latter mourned the loss of a woman to whom
he had never even spoken a word, and who, in the *Commedia*, would
become the instigator of his salvation, Weiss, in contrast, felt responsibility
and guilt over someone whom he felt he had "deceived and deserted."
Weiss's muse was a dark one indeed, and the Auschwitz vision it inspired
would determine the subsequent understanding of both the Dantean and
the autobiographical past.

It is apparent that Auschwitz meant hell to Weiss in both a moral and
a literary sense. What had not yet fallen into place was the means of
combining the two. In that first representation of the moment, there was
no "kingdom of the dead," the guardians had no horns: Dante's means
were not deemed adequate to the new situation. *Fluchtpunkt*, like the *Vita
nuova*, proposed an apparently solipsistic reading. Auschwitz remained
the touchstone of the vision, but, from *Die Ermittlung (The Investigation)*
to the *Ästhetik*, Weiss would appropriate more and more of the *Commedia*'s model, finding ways in which it was still able to crystallize memories
and affects into a vision, and record that vision "in a nobler"—that is,
more public—"way."

The first stage of conscious formulations of the project grew out of the
desire to write a play about Auschwitz, to take on the task that was
inconceivable to the narrator of *Fluchtpunkt*. Some of the earlier uneasiness with Dante remains in the notes of 1964, but soon Weiss incorporated that uneasiness as a structural element instead of a structural
impediment. The framework of hell, purgatory, and paradise could be
retained, and specific analogues for characters and situations discovered;
even Dante's moral tone could remain, but in postwar images, "Inferno
with our contemporary perspective, with our imaginings of hell" (*NB1*
212).

[9] *Vita nuova*, ed. Domenico De Robertis, in *Opere minori*, vol. 1, pt. 1, 42.2; trans.
Mark Musa, *Dante's "Vita Nuova"* (Bloomington, 1973), 86.

The change in perspective is clearest in a revised scene of the newsreel footage in *Fluchtpunkt*. Here it is in Vergil's first words in the draft:

> The poet Dante painted us a picture
> of a place which appeared to him in fruitfulness
> Where we requite our sins with days
> This picture however cannot help us much . . .
> The great art it was concerned with is false . . .

And the chorus of shades answers him:

> There is only one space for all our deeds
> and that is here here we are at work unpunished
> Nothing yet has turned out badly for us in this place
> And we are ceaselessly honored for it
>   (*NB1* 477–78)

Weiss's research into the *Commedia* rendered dialectical the earlier insight that Dante's world does not exist and that great art is false; Weiss now planned to take the modern cliché that this world and the people in it constitute hell and make the cliché ring true as a comprehensive reading of modernism.[10]

Not only would the Auschwitz-Inferno document the survival in this world of all those who in Dante's hell had been subjected to endless punishment, but Weiss would heighten the cruelty by staging it as a farce: "Inferno: to make a farce out of the persecution of the Jews: the imprisonment, the tortures, in the end the murders—laughter about these things. Party game" (*NB1* 265). To be sure, Dante's *Inferno* had its fair share of farce—in particular the scenes with the demons in Malebolge (cantos 21–22)—but always with demons and shades of sinners as butts of the joke, not the innocent victims as intended here.

---

[10] Weiss was no amateur Dantist: he read criticism and history of the poem and the epoch and had an understanding of the context and the working of the poetics in the *Commedia* to rank with romance philologist modernists such as Pound and Eliot; more, then, than those whose Dante was more on the level of cultural patrimony, such as Benjamin, Céline, Proust, or Woolf. This does not make his Dante any more or less "correct" than any other; it does mean that his particular misreading, and its particularly postwar traits, can and should be sounded to greater depth. Weiss listed references in the notebooks; see esp. *NB1* 217. Krause studies the depth of Weiss's debt to Olaf Lagercrantz's work on Dante (62 ff.; see also *R*, 169), but his pointless attack against Weiss's readings of history and politics undermines the soundness of his critical insights.

This apparently cynical concept incorporates an angry charge of irony, the full meaning of which becomes evident in the suggestion for the inscription on the gates to *Paradiso:* "Entrance to Paradise: Arbeit macht Frei" (*NB1* 227). The idea for an Auschwitz farce is grounded in the sick irony of the camp's administration, which had placed the phrase over the entrance. But employing it as the entrance to paradise underlines the new scheme for a *Commedia* and recasts the term altogether. Weiss's Paradiso is where the victims suffer:

> Then after their death they step forward into the fields
> which promise them eternal happiness
> so they find nothing but their pain
> Pain once suffered is never gone
>
> (*NB1* 477)

Inferno and Paradiso are mirror images more so here than in Dante, for they share even the location—at this point Auschwitz, later simply the world from the time of Auschwitz onward. The only shift from one to the other is the double meaning inherent in "Arbeit macht frei." For Marx, too, the workplace was in the image of Dante's hell; the worker's salvation lay not in resignation but in the refunctioning of the oppressor's own tools: "Freedom through labor." Behind the slogan of the horrors of Auschwitz lies a kernel of Marxist truth, and that kernel is all that distinguishes hell from paradise.

Weiss's early conceptions of the *Commedia,* saturated in the Frankfurt trials and the composition of the *Ermittlung,* remained resolutely negative. The *Ermittlung* served as a means toward knowledge, to disenchant what seemed incomprehensible by demonstrating its function within the development of capitalism.[11] The next stage of the project's conception came to grips with the problem of the figure of Dante and a more dynamic depiction of the world situation. Auschwitz was reestablished as the *Nullpunkt,* the point of reference and of imitation, the point at which hell and paradise are revealed in their baldest connection to each other. A vision of the world derived from them guided Weiss's new plan for a *theatrum mundi,* a *Welttheater* encompassing the state of the postwar world.

---

[11] *Die Ermittlung,* in *Stücke I* (Frankfurt, 1976), 257–449; trans. Jon Swan and Ulu Grosbard, *The Investigation* (New York, 1966). The play is divided into eleven "Gesänge," or cantos, each subdivided into three parts, for a Dantesque total of thirty-three. The detailing of the relationship between the camps and German industry forms one of the basic thematic motives of the play.

Weiss's subsequent sigla *INF* and *PAR* are conceptually straightforward, and the detailing of their inhabitants was clearly an object of diversion for him. The problem areas were the characters of Dante and Vergil and of *PURG*, the dynamic components of the *Commedia*. Two motifs dominate the later notes (1967–69): the necessity of optimism in *Paradiso* and the nature of the Dante/Vergil figures as first-person narrators. *Purgatorio* is seen as the stage in which the narrator prepares us for *Paradiso:* "Insurrections, Struggles for Liberation, Revolution"; meetings with Marx, Lenin, Trotsky, Fanon, Che Guevara; nothing absolute, everything in movement, "Pol-Gegenpol"; "the meaningful emergence of the necessity for a socialist social order"; it had to end optimistically (*NB1* 594). Along with the development of a political alternative out of oppression, pillaging, and alienation, there is equally the discussion "if 'Art' is still possible" (596). *Purgatorio* mediates between the otherwise identical *Inferno* and *Paradiso:* everything in the one has been prepared for in the other; all those exploited by the ones seen in hell and the same complaints as in hell, but "illuminated by the experiences in PURGATORIO" (600).

The illuminator of *Paradiso,* then, would be Dante. After a biographical description similar to the entry of 3 January 1966, Weiss continues: " His manner: terse, at first often in doubt, unsure, given to depression (this serves him well in the world of INFERNO), also blackouts, lapses, even total mental breakdown—then he sets up optimism as a working thesis and masters himself" (*NB1* 601). By the end of *Purgatorio,* then, this Dante would have a "firm political conviction (without belonging to a party)" (*NB1* 593). As Weiss remarks, however, he would also be inclined consitutionally toward the dwellers in hell. This refers both to the discussions in *Abschied* and *Fluchtpunkt* of a sense of belonging by nature more to the oppressors than to the oppressed, and to the enduring suspicion of the worldliness of "great art."

Both questions arise in Weiss's sketch of Vergil as the conformist, at least partly corrupted, who tries to persuade Dante to become a member of hell. Vergil is the spokesman of the esoteric, of the philosophic, and of "art" and is full of ambition (*NB1* 600). Although this might appear a clean break from the idolized mentor of Dante's *Commedia*, the conclusion of the sketch makes it clear that Weiss continued to bear that model firmly in mind: "Then in PURGATORIO he will gradually be dethroned, until in the 27th [canto] he is got rid of, because in no way still needed" (600). In Dante's scheme, Vergil is an inhabitant of hell, unable to conceive of precisely the faith (analogue to Weiss's "optimism") that will save Dante when Beatrice takes over in *Purgatorio* 27. Weiss's socialist reading draws out the tension in Dante's use of Vergil to characterize the achievements and limits of the classical tradition and its pagan poetry. By updating the *Commedia* with strict analogues to its allegorical framework, Weiss also polemically rewrote a modernist Dante. His Vergil takes on the added symbolic weight of a "great art" inextricably implicated in the oppression of the ruling class that runs from antiquity through to high-modernist claims of autonomy.

The Dante-character, on the other hand, remains, as in the *Commedia*, a utopian figure: subject to all the pressures and temptations of a Vergil, he is able nevertheless to move beyond him. Weiss imagines *Paradiso:* "Here must Dante now step forth, changed since INFERNO, politically conscious and now himself active and engaged" (600). With the last comprehensive set of notes to this stage of the project, Weiss had found a guide for his audience, a Dante who was looking more and more like the narrator of the *Ästhetik*. A few pages later, we find that next stage emerging: "DIVINA COMMEDIA started over. Now prose version" (665).

There remained a further hurdle to be jumped in the transition from theater piece to novel. Unlike those of the Dante-character above, the political views of the narrator of the *Ästhetik* do not change during the course of the novel; born in the month of the Russian Revolution, he is politically conscious and committed from birth. Where, then, is the expected conversion? We find a clue in an early formulation of what would become one of the central bones of critical contention around the *Ästhetik*, the form of the so-called *Wunschautobiographie* ("wish-autobiography").[12]

As a child I was already a "Socialist"
as a child was already in the independence movements
in school was already an "Agitator"
in school already belonged to the "Proletariat"
nothing new under the sun
                                          (NB1 521)

The scare quotes and the ironic conclusion appear to denote Weiss's mockery of his own conception. He wrote during the same period about a

---

[12] Weiss coined the term in an interview with Rolf Michaelis in late 1975, following the publication of the first volume, and it became the center of polemics against the novel (Gerlach/Richter 216–23). For a summary, see Stephan, " 'Ein großer Entwurf gegen den Zeitgeist': Zur Aufnahme von Peter Weiss' *Ästhetik des Widerstands*," in Stephan, 346–66; and Ingeborg Gerlach, *Die Ferne Utopie: Studien zu Peter Weiss' "Ästhetik des Widerstands"* (Aachen, 1991), 167–82.

play on the subject of his own life. He also noted that "Dante must experience everything in his own body / Everything happens to me" (551).

The gloss must come first from the *Commedia*.There are two elements to the Dante-character's conversion, both in Dante's and in Weiss's versions: a religio-political one and the attainment of the means to represent it. Weiss's indecision over how to combine or whether to separate the two elements is related to uneasiness over Dante's dissolution of the political into the individual, what I have described in Céline and Augustine as the rhetorical totalitarianism of the autobiographical voice. Weiss was comfortable neither with the content of the politics nor with the means of persuasion. By the time he was planning the *Ästhetik*, he had decided that the narrator would no longer be tempted by Vergil and would not be politically co-opted. The narrator's conversion in the *Ästhetik* was to be solely literary: "to recount according to the understanding attained" (*NB2* 817).

But what of the other facet of conversion? Contrary to the arguments of critics of the term *Wunschautobiographie*, Weiss did not simply take the political for granted. Rather, he used the project not only to organize his documentary theater and his projected *Welttheater* but also to categorize his own life.[13] The political conversion was truly personal and as authentically autobiographical and textually indisputable as the religious conversion recounted in the *Commedia*. As we have found, Weiss traced it back to the vision of 1945 related in *Fluchtpunkt,* but we do not see its resolution, the realization of its significance, until the *Notizbücher* and Weiss's 1965 conversion to Marxism. It is thus coextensive with the Dante project.

The *Wunschautobiographie* expresses the projection of this actual conversion back into the prehistory of its occurrence. It is *Wunsch* only in its dating, not in its substance; and the shift in time is the allegory created by Weiss through the splitting of his autobiographical voice. The full significance of the *Notizbücher* becomes legible—or, rather, is rewritten —in the retrospect of the *Ästhetik*. The novel retells the achievement of the means of representation; the *Notizbücher* recounts the actual conversion and as such is both pretext and appendix to the *Ästhetik*. Weiss has disentangled the two strands of the Dantean allegory of conversion: the

---

[13] See especially the identification of intimate relations with *PURG* (wife, friends, children, parents; *NB1* 495, 500). See also the reception of his English friend Ayschmann by Charon as the "Jew of renown" (*NB1* 274), and the recasting of Friederle, the future Nazi of the narrator's childhood in *Abschied*, as the haughty Ghibelline leader Farinata of *Inf.* 10 (*NB1* 299).

Figure 1. The Great Altar, Pergamon Museum, Staatliche Museen, Berlin. (Foto Marburg/Art Resource)

political, religious, and historical development are recounted in the *Notizbücher,* and the development of the ability to represent that change in the *Ästhetik.* A close look at how he achieves and indicates this separation in the novel on the one hand and in the late *Notizbücher* on the other can elucidate the structure of Weiss's rereading of the *entre-deux-guerres;* it subsequently allows the strands of the allegory of conversion to be disentangled more easily out of the *Commedia* inherited by contemporary criticism from modernism.

THE *Ästhetik* is begun and framed within an *ekphrasis:* the description, reception, and study of the relief sculptures of the altar to Zeus in the Pergamon Museum, Berlin. This initial episode is programmatically emblematic of the process of the reception of art through which Weiss proposes an "aesthetics of resistance." As a painter, he had tended to trust the immediacy of pictorial image over printed word; with the *ekphrasis* here, Weiss signals a more complex relationship: the *Ästhetik* will be about using one art form to represent another, one form of experience in order to bring forth another. As products of the same *entre-deux-guerres,* the techniques of surrealism and of Brechtian epic theater can collaborate in the task of representing the historical experience of the time in a new light.

In the first eight sections of the first volume, Weiss sets out the terms

Figure 2. East frieze: Lion's claw of Heracles, Zeus, Porphyrion and two other giants. (Foto Marburg/Art Resource)

in which he plans to recontextualize the modernist dichotomy between aesthetics and politics in a fictional skein that extends from the neoclassicism of the Pergamon altar, through the two allegories of the *Commedia*, the allegory-versus-symbol debate, and up to socialist realism and postmodernism. This theoretical skein is held together by the complex interplay Weiss establishes among currently accepted history, the history he is rewriting, and the history he is newly creating; and within a constellation of forms, tenets, and attitudes formerly thought compatible by virtue only of their having cohabited the same thirty-year period in the first half of the century. It is a pattern as tightly woven as the densest high-modernist icons but shot through with the historical avant-garde's critique of art as such.

The first scene not only begins with words painting sculpture but continues by representing a heightened form of reception by the three young friends, Coppi, Heilmann, and the narrator. The viewers are shown being lured into the force field of the artwork in a moment of ahistorical, affective, and mythic empathy. Such moments are, as in this first scene, followed by or interspersed with moments of lucid criticism and analysis,

where the artwork is then brushed against the grain (as Benjamin might
have put it) through research and study.[14] Other examples are the narrator's experience with Géricault's *Raft of the Medusa* in the Louvre at the
beginning of volume 2 (7–33) and Stahlmann's account of a visit to
Angkor in volume 3 (93–108). Weiss uses ekphrastic accounts symbolically: that is, in the meaning of their reception, the artworks receive a
fixed significance reflecting the overall thematic structure of the novel. At
the same time, they play an allegorical role within the narrative, dynamically representing the process whereby such fixed symbols are created.

    As the key symbol, Pergamon is received by Coppi, Heilmann, and the
narrator as an almost overwhelming figure of oppression: they feel the
threat intended for the rebellious slaves of Eumenes in the second century
B.C.E. by the pro-imperial allegory of the Olympian gods' defeat of the
giants' rebellion. They do not question this first shock of recognition;
rather, it is the ground on which the research and discussion in the following pages of the novel are constituted. At the same time, Weiss in the
narration seeks to cause us to feel the same affect. The novel begins in
medias res with a tour de force description of the *gigantomachia* (battle of
the giants, 7).[15] On the following page, the narrator draws a step back to
include the viewers in the picture ("we")—Coppi, Heilmann, and the
anonymous narrator (8). A few pages later, another step back provides a
glimpse of their brown-shirted compatriots on 9 September 1937. The
reception of the Pergamon frieze continues sporadically over the next fifty
pages, using a dialogue between Coppi (working-class agitator with little
respect for art) and Heilmann ("our Rimbaud," privileged background,
secret agent for socialism) to bring out the central tenets of the novel's
proposed "aesthetics of resistance."

    Based on this episode, the "aesthetics of resistance" would describe the
means by which things in general, and especially art, may be grasped as

---

[14] Burkhardt Lindner suggests that the privileging of images establishes a kind of
"hallucinatory realism," which results in the moment of "subjective projection" on the
part of the viewer, followed by the process of "materialistic interest" ("Halluzinatorischer Realismus: *Die Ästhetik des Widerstands*, die *Notizbücher* und die Todeszonen
der Kunst," in Stephan, 164–204; trans. Luke Springman and Amy Kepple, "Hallucinatory Realism: Peter Weiss' *Aesthetics of Resistance, Notebooks*, and the Death Zones
of Art," *NGC* 30 [Fall 1983]: 127–56). Lindner's essay is a valuable introduction to
the central textual concerns of both novel and *Notizbücher*.

[15] That Weiss understood this particular interpretation as the fixed symbol of the
first part is evident in a sketch where he entitles it "GIGANTOMACHIE" and the second
(Spanish) part "TAUROMACHIE" (Bullfight, *NB2* 401), Picasso's *Guernica* being the
exemplary artwork of the second part.

symbols of one's historical, political, and/or economic situation, how they can continue to have relevance beyond the time and place of their production. Weiss's *ekphrases* are symbolic because one makes them identical with one's self; through identification, one makes an artwork into a symbol. The purpose of the Pergamon episode, and of the novel as a whole, is to demonstrate how the process of identification can be made revolutionary and consciousness-raising.

Now, the analysis I have just given of Weiss's use of *ekphrasis* and symbols is a bit unfair; it suggests Weiss is giving a slightly hipper version of Georg Lukács's arguments in favor of realism. The resemblance is not accidental: the episode following the Pergamon reception records a discussion at Coppi's apartment among himself, Heilmann, Coppi's mother, and the narrator which covers precisely the ground of the *entre-deux-guerres* debate over expressionism in which Lukács's views figured so prominently.[16] As Andreas Huyssen has shown, however, Weiss subtly shifts the terms of the debate.[17] Whereas for Lukács a socially progressive art working through identification was possible only in the so-called totality of the nineteenth-century realist novel, Weiss suggests that such identification was in fact to be found in certain artists of the avant-garde so vehemently rejected by Lukács: "We distinguished between attacks against what was exhausted and dying out, and simple lack of respect, which in the final analysis still supported the market" (1:57).

The reception described here is certainly one of identification with artworks as they speak directly to one's situation; what is striking is the sleight of hand Weiss pulls off in the middle of it. By basing the possibility of any aesthetic evaluation on content and identification, he sidesteps the major modernist arguments about art and politics: anything goes so long as it gives the correct shock to the system. Thus does the discussion conclude: "We insisted that Joyce and Kafka, Schoenberg and Stravinsky, Klee and Picasso belonged in the same ranks in which was also to be found Dante, with whose *Inferno* we had been occupied now for some time" (1:79). The concluding clause, characteristic of the *Ästhetik*'s technique of transition, segues into the seventh section of volume 1, the three friends' reading of Dante. It thereby introduces the *Commedia* in precisely the context in which Weiss had conceived of it for his project: a Dante for

---

[16] For a collection of the pertinent documents, see *Aesthetics and Politics,* ed. and trans. Rodney Livingstone (London, 1977); hereafter cited as *A&P.*

[17] "Memory, Myth, and the Dream of Reason: Peter Weiss' *Die Ästhetik des Widerstands,*" in *After the Great Divide: Modernism, Mass Culture, Postmodernism* (Bloomington, 1986), 115–38; this reference, 123–26.

our time, which would retain all the traces of Dante's own time and which would grow out of and respond to the concerns of reading the modernist past.

If we have seen the aesthetics of resistance in operation in the trio's reception of the Pergamon altar and the historical avant-garde through identification, research, and discussion, the *Commedia* gives the beginning of a different model: the production of one's own work of art, the allegorical frame within which it becomes possible to interpret the ekphrastic symbolism. I suggested above that the political conversion of the narrator was shifted into the *Notizbücher*. One could argue, in fact, that the narrator's political commitment is static and symbolic in the *Ästhetik*, just as the *ekphrases* are. With the reading of the *Commedia*, in contrast, the allegory of artistic conversion enters the novel, as it does in Eleanor Pargiter's reading of it in Woolf's novel *The Years*. For it is in the section directly following that of the reading of the *Commedia* that Weiss's narrator first employs the first-person singular and first discusses himself and his relation to art, one that, unlike the political commitment of his character or of Heilmann and Coppi, will indeed change throughout the novel.

In the *Commedia*, the entire afterlife is eternal and fixed by God as if in an *allegoria in facto;* Dante merely reports it ("Dante der Reporter," as Weiss would have it [*NB2* 85]). This parallels the historical data of the *Ästhetik*, the fruit of Weiss's years of research: "Everything that is said has taken place, at any event according to the dates; the names are authentic, as are the places where the figures stayed" (Götze/Scherpe, 155). But, as Lindner has noted, there are certain discussions and situations that cannot be authenticated and probably did not occur, in particular the receptions of artworks and discussions about art by Coppi and Heilmann.[18] Lindner does not attempt to gloss these exceptions, but they require it, for they are consequently part of Weiss's—and not, that is, God's or history's—allegory; they are *allegoria in verbis* and not *in facto*. Hence, they must partake of the same code of interpretation as the other major fictionalization, the *Wunschautobiographie* of the narrator's working-class, politically conscious background.

The first indication of such an allegory appears in a level of the Pergamon episode that is not explicitly enunciated in the reception by the three viewers. For the shock of their reaction, their empathy with the propagandistic oppression of the slaves through the crushing of the giants' rebellion,

----

[18] In Stephan, 192. Moreover, as Lindner points out, the only visit to the Pergamon altar documented by Weiss is his own with a companion, Uli, at some point, it seems, around 1937 (*F* 13–15).

is shown to the readers as analogous to the present example of National Socialism. Eumenes' regime, in its privileging of neoclassic art and its outcry against other races and "barbarians" (1:47), is evidently analogous to Hitler's. We are not dealing here with an art that the narrator or his friends would wish to produce; however, even such a reactionary art, we discover, when rubbed against the grain, may produce the utopian image of a Heracles, the crucial figure who if present would have fought on the side of the gods but who endures only through his mythological emblems, which remain in the frieze as sign of the fact that he would also have been able to shift the balance of the battle in the other direction.

Weiss has fictionalized an allegory of immediacy, of the possibility of a radical symbolization of artworks. Here, too, Heracles is emblematic. The central symbolic figure of the novel, he is the missing piece of the artworks described by Weiss, the dynamic part that of necessity is always left out when the artwork is hypostasized into symbol. Heracles is present only as an allegory—the lion's claw that is his traditional emblem—and as such is never present in unmediated form. He too is made a symbol, but a symbol of his own mediatedness. Hence, the open air—for Heracles in the novel symbolizes the utopian step from resistance to revolution—cannot be received symbolically. Heracles symbolizes for Coppi, Heilmann, and the narrator what the allegory of their reception of art is to symbolize for us. The episode of reception is emblematic but not immediate; their resistance is factual and we can thus easily symbolize it for ourselves by identifying with it, but the utopian moment of a revolution in the way we read art remains mediated, allegorical.

Now, Weiss is still not finished with this episode. Simply because Heracles remains allegorical does not mean that he does not exist, that he is a mere fictional device. After the Pergamon episode, the discussion with Coppi's mother about the historical avant-garde, and the reading of the *Commedia*, Coppi and Heilmann disappear from the narrative. The narrator thinks back on them at several moments during the novel, but they do not reappear until the first pages of the second part of volume 3. The text begins in medias res with what appears to be a recapitulation of the Pergamon scene and debate (3:169–71). The date is belatedly revealed now to be 1944, however, and the third-party companion of Coppi and Heilmann is no longer the first-person narrator but Lotte Bischoff, who has entered Germany illegally, stowed away in a freighter, and serves as Weiss's narrator and witness of the final annihilation of the communist resistance in Berlin while the first-person narrator remains in Sweden. The first and emblematic scene of resistance is recapitulated here as prelude for the long account of executions to come.

The scene has a further effect. We must recall that the three volumes of the *Ästhetik* were published separately in 1975, 1978, and 1981, and the *Notizbücher* not until 1981; consequently, the majority of Weiss's first readers were still unaware of the extent to which the novel was grounded in fact. To be sure, Weiss had made his work habits fairly clear in earlier interviews (see Gerlach/Richter, 208–51), but few seem to have taken him at his word until presented with the overwhelming evidence of the *Notizbücher*. Heinrich Vormweg recounts reaching this episode in the third volume and suddenly realizing that Coppi and Heilmann must be historical figures like all the rest.[19] What had been thought to be a purely fictional and symbolic introductory framing device turned out in retrospect to be an emblematic mix of myth and history, symbol and allegory.

Just what the shift signifies is made apparent in the long concluding sentence of the novel, in which Weiss returns once again to the Pergamon frieze, but this time with Coppi and Heilmann as figures sculpted within it: "I would go up to the frieze where the sons and daughters of the earth rose up against the might which always strove to take back from them what they had won fighting, I would see Coppi's parents and my parents in the rubble . . . and Heilmann would quote Rimbaud, and Coppi recite the Manifesto, and a place in the fray would be free, the lion's claw would hang there for anyone to take, and so long as they did not leave off from one another, they would not see the claw of the lion's skin" (3:267–68). The novel begins anew, but it is now ourselves and the narrator who are standing before the frieze. The narrator has become a writer, and we have become capable first of identifying and then of analyzing the frieze that is Weiss's novel. The *Ästhetik* is a representation of the *gigantomachia;* its substance is the history of the resistance; its lion's claw, the fictionalized moments of Coppi and Heilmann before the frieze, allegorizes the hard return from the descent into hell.

How have we learned to read in this manner by the end of the novel? Let us return to Vormweg's moment of recognition. Why had Vormweg not considered the possibility of Coppi and Heilmann's historicity, especially given Weiss's various pronouncements to that effect? There are two interrelated explanations. The first, as Vormweg is led to confess, is that Germans (not to mention non-Germans) were by and large simply unaware of the history of the antifascist resistance (111). The second is that we are naive readers: the intentionally planted recapitulation scene, in which, in a technique dear to Weiss, it is a few pages before we are able to decide if it is a retelling of the same, 1937 scene with the narrator, or a new, 1944 scene with him (which seems implausible, since he is in Swe-

---

[19] Heinrich Vormweg, *Peter Weiss* (Munich, 1981), 111.

den), or, as we finally discover, a new, 1944 scene with Lotte Bischoff standing in the place of the narrator—this scene intentionally foregrounds its shaking of our traditional assumptions of reading fiction. It further leads us to question how we have previously been reading those scenes in which the fictional narrator has interacted with figures of whose existence we were aware, such as Brecht in the second volume.

Our identification, in other words, has been of the wrong kind. Just as the standard, programmed response to the Pergamon frieze would be to identify with the victorious gods, so we have assumed that characters in a symbolic situation must be fictional, and that a mythic figure such as Heracles will never appear to claim his lion's claw. We have accepted the new symbolism of the first scene through identification with the three viewers but have forgotten the research and study, the decoding of the historical (Pergamon; resistance) and allegorical (consolidating power; creating a novel) frame in which this symbolism is embedded; we have subsumed history into myth.

The narrator is the vehicle for progressing from one form of identification to the other: Weiss plants the groundwork of the shift in the seventh section, the reading of the *Commedia*, but does not give the final shock until that late moment in part 2 of volume 3. The first sentence of this seventh section introduces the *Commedia* as a rebus of the genre of Joyce's *Ulysses*, an allegory to be analyzed and deciphered. The ensuing sentence describes it as a topography to be entered into, one that "lays claim to a lifespan," leading all the way to the heights that lie "beyond the imaginable [*vorstellbar*]" (1:79). We find both the moment of research and interpretation and the moment of identification in the first instances of the reading. The third sentence specifies the role of the *Commedia* in the *Ästhetik*, for it indicates the point Coppi, Heilmann, and the narrator have reached in it: "we had read only as far as Francesca da Rimini and Paolo Malatesta" (79).

The episode of Paolo and Francesca, the first shades in hell proper with whom Dante-protagonist converses, is emblematic of the mechanism of the allegory of conversion in the *Commedia*. Francesca recounts her tragic story of adultery, justifying her actions by reference to the seductive power of the book the two were reading, *Lancelot*, which becomes, in her words, their go-between. Dante-protagonist's reaction, like that of many of his readers in identification with him, especially in the nineteenth century, is to faint, overcome with sympathy for the betrayed couple. Now, it becomes abundantly clear as the poem progresses that within the Christian system of punishment and reward there can be no justification for such sympathy. We have, instead, been led into the first trap of the naive reader: immediate, emotional identification with whatever one reads. Just as Paolo and Francesca have been damned for what they did in imitation of a work of fiction, so is Dante-protagonist at this point under risk of damnation for his identification with Francesca's own self-justificatory story.

The *Commedia* does not simply record God's system of punishment and reward from a retrospective point of view; it interposes the immediate reactions of the not-yet-converted protagonist as he learns to overcome his sins, which are emblematized as a failure to read properly. As readers, we too must learn to distinguish between the Dante who knows and is narrating in retrospect and the Dante who learns only gradually and whose reactions are unreliable. In Weiss's version, however, the aesthetic has been provisionally separated from the political: neither the three friends' commitment nor that of the reader is directly at stake; rather, we are at risk of falling into a trap of naive aesthetic interpretation by underestimating the veracity of the characters. Weiss recoils from the ideological authority of the Dantean structure of conversion—as Bernard did, faced with Augustine's version—but also seeks to confront his readers with its power as a tool for representation.

The allegory of conversion is present in the *Ästhetik* not on a political level—the characters already know how to read reality—but only on an aesthetic one—the narrator must learn how to write. This is the sense of the tripartite scheme Weiss applied to the novel in retrospect in 1979:

> Volume I the collective battle over the production of culture, the conquest of the means of expression
> with which the experiences of the wronged, the oppressed can take shape
> Volume II process of individuation
> attempt to change aesthetics from a tool for apprehending cultural events into an instrument of engagement
> Volume III to recount according to the understanding attained
> (*NB2* 817)

The *Ästhetik* follows this structure in terms of the narrator's artistic development but not in the historical plot. Each volume recounts a descent into the underworld; the characters discuss, argue, act, but they do not develop or evolve in a novelistic sense. This is not to say that they have no psychology, but that their lives are fixed, emblematizing a crucial moment, just as Dante's shades remain realistic while being already dead.[20] Rather, it is

---

[20] For a convincing demonstration of Weiss's rendering of psychologically complex characters without psychologizing them, that is, without making their psychology into the explanation for their actions, see Robert Cohen, *Versuch über Weiss' "Ästhetik des Widerstands"* (Bern, 1989), 111–52.

only the narrator who follows the structure, and, just as the Pergamon episode frames the political history, so do the Dante reading and the subsequent encounter with the father frame the allegory of conversion, the narrator's accession to writing and our learning how to read through his example.

The crucial moment of the Dante reading comes in the shift from reception to production, from reading against the grain to creating revolutionary art. "Until now we had encountered art only in terms of reception"; but the *Commedia* first gives the trio the idea of "producing a book" (1:81). The function of this production is set up through their understanding of Dante. Weiss renders this reading as a subtle allegoresis of Dante's poem that reframes the representational issues of the Auschwitz *Nullpunkt* within the problematics of an aesthetics of resistance. Hell becomes the very real terror of death that can be confronted, made material, and overcome only through the mediation of art. The threat is mediated through the personifications encountered in hell; Vergil represents memory, the continuity of tradition that gives the ability to summon all the past to the boundary point between life and death (1:81–82).

The allegoresis of the *Commedia* just presented is put to the test of three distinct responses: Coppi complains of the distance retained by Dante's artistic consciousness; Heilmann defends the necessity of anesthesia in order to react to the "Ursachen des Alpdrucks" (the origins of the nightmare [83]). Both respond to Dante as to the Pergamon frieze on the novel's symbolic level. The narrator's reaction—and I believe this to be his first recorded reaction as an individual—is in a different register: "I found myself at a turning point, in transition to a new part of life" (87). The calque of "ritrovai" from the first verse of the *Inferno* suggests that we have come to the first descent of the novel, with the *Commedia* as its impetus: the narrator steps out for the first time as an individual in imitation of the pilgrim and of the pilgrim's past.

The eighth section translates this analysis of the *Commedia* into plot as the narrator descends into the past in order to be reunited with his father. This is not only the first section in which the narrator is alone; it is also the first moment of subjective, individual vision, and the first moment of surrealistic distortion of reality in the novel. We begin with the narrator seated on a box in the deserted room where he (and at one time also his parents) lived until the present moment, as he is leaving for Spain to fight in the civil war. The central question of the passage is embedded in this setting: "whether all occupation with books and pictures had been only running away [*eine Flucht*], far from practical, overwhelming problems?" The sentence concludes with a succinct and concrete image of those prob-

lems, "the cold, emptied-out room" (1:88). The word *Flucht* should remind us of the ur-expression of the question of art in *Fluchtpunkt:* the
Nullpunkt of Auschwitz may have been extended back into the antifascist
resistance, but the point remains the same. The hard realities of this first
focus on the narrator set the stakes of the autobiographical voice within
the novel itself: is Weiss justified in portraying himself as a working-class
revolutionary? Is this fiction a flight from reality or a necessary distancing?

Before continuing with the narrator's descent, we should follow up the
thread of the question, for Weiss gives it a direct answer later in volume
1, referring back to the positions of Heilmann and Coppi and privileging
that of the former. Near the end of this volume, in Spain, the narrator and
his English companion Ayschmann discover and study a reproduction of
Picasso's *Guernica,* which for them shows "that there is no split between
the social and political materialization of art and its being" (1:337).[21] The
key image for them in the painting is the remnant of a Medusa figure:
Picasso becomes like Perseus, slaying the Medusa by viewing it through a
mirror. To make the connection to the previous Dante discussion clearer,
Weiss's narrator corrects Coppi's earlier criticism of Dante's distance from
his subject: "Any attempt unmediatedly to expose the subject of the picture would lead to the extinction of the work" (1:339). The way of
avoiding the danger of being petrified by the horror of one's object of
representation, the way to confront one's own death, is by the indirection
of allegory.

The "great visions of art," blotted out by Auschwitz, return as models
for the mirror in which the Medusa can be glimpsed in order to be overcome. Weiss filters Dante's Medusa scene through *Guernica* and renovates
its meaning. Freccero has convincingly glossed the threat of the Medusa
in *Inferno* 9 as an allegorization of Paul's two types of interpretation: the
Old Testament attention to the letter that kills and the New Testament
focus on the spirit that gives life (119–35). Excessive identification, too
much attention to the surface without interpretation, leads to petrification,
death, or, as Weiss puts it, extinction. The danger, in other words, is of
naive readings like those of Dante's identification with Paolo and Francesca, of the young Augustine's with Dido and Aeneas, or of ours with

---

[21] The constellation is complexly embedded within questions of autobiography and
the production of art. Ayschmann was a friend of Weiss's youth; their brief friendship
is recounted in *Abschied* (107–15). Weiss met him while his family was in England on
their way to Sweden, and the intense relationship culminated in Weiss's first exhibition
of paintings. Shortly thereafter, Ayschmann disappeared, apparently off to fight in the
Spanish Civil War.

Coppi and Heilmann. Our identification may allow us to faint from empathy with the resistance, but that resistance will thereby be irredeemably destroyed and the novel thus extinguished *(erloschen);* it will not remain in our memory, it will not overcome death. No descent without a return.

The narrator's descent in the eighth section presents itself as a direct response to the threat of extinction. It takes place in the context both of Weiss's own past as a writer and of the narrator's individual past and fear of death. The vision begins with the perception of someone buried under the linoleum of the kitchen floor. His father's body rises up out of the floor, but the face will not assume the father's features, for the narrator is unable to speak, unable to imagine, unable to make anything comprehensible, much less representable (1:92). Petrified with fear, faced with death because unable to mediate, to get distance from it and make it comprehensible *(begreifbar)*, the narrator takes what the trio had found to be Dante's solution: the concrete description that builds up piece by piece a reality that words and pictures cannot achieve (1:80).

He loses his body, flies out the window and over Berlin, finds solace in its reality and in his distance from it, and then returns: "Only in this way, feet first, backward once again through the window, was I able to get into the kitchen, and it was the same kitchen that I had just left, the kitchen in which the electric bulb burned over the floorboards where my father lay between the broken-open planks. . . . And because every doubt had now disappeared, the lump of clay was able to take on the facial features intended for him [*ihm zugedachten Gesichtszüge*]. My father raised himself up" (1:95). All is the same, but it is now mediated through the "ihm zugedachten Gesichtszüge": death is countered by remembrance; the path to the future will be shown by the return to the past. It should be noted that the narrator's father in fact outlives the trajectory of the narrative; at this point in the diegesis, he is with the mother in Czechoslovakia. The episode is wholly subjective and wholly allegorical: the narrator enacts the process of composition just attributed to Dante—he even gives it the inverted biblical resonance of the son creating the father in his image out of clay. He overcomes the effect of muteness suffered from attempting to stare directly at death by mediating it through his flight over Berlin.

Thus does Weiss identify his stylistic technique: the subjectivizing instances of surrealism, of allegory, of dreams partake of the fictional thread of the novel along with the scenes of art reception and the *Wunschautobiographie*. The speech that eventually comes out of the mouth of father Anchises, Weiss's analogue to the *Aeneid*'s prophecy of future deeds, is a history of the Communist and Socialist parties in Germany, and their internecine disputes and eventual failure at revolution, centered on the father's role in the 1919 revolt in Bremen. This is the first hard lump of history thrown out at the reader by the novel; significantly, it is mediated through the fiction of the dead father. Weiss's family was indeed living in Bremen during the revolt, but as prosperous members of the middle class. This then is the task of the first volume, "the collective battle over the production of culture, the conquest of the means of expression with which the experiences of the wronged, the oppressed can take shape" (*NB2* 817); it is framed by and formulated through the narrator's personal experience.

As frame both for the novel and for the first part, the descent of volume 1 is most important for understanding the relation between history and myth, allegory and symbol in the *Ästhetik*. The descents of the other two volumes recapitulate the historical movement: just as the narrator's conversion is a priori and static, so the situation of oppression does not significantly change in the timespan of the *entre-deux-guerres*. The repetition of a movement that ought to result in conversion and change serves instead to stress the failure of the resistance. At the same time, as with the figure of Heracles, there remains movement on the aesthetic and literary front, in the allegory of the writing of the novel. We examine the latter below. As for the descent of volume 2, it is documented by Weiss's reference to volume 2, part 1, in the *Notizbücher* as "KATABASIS" and is centered on the narrator's thoughts in exile in Sweden about Coppi, Heilmann, and Paris (2:122–24).[22]

The volume begins with the narrator's stopover in Paris, washed away from the collapse of Spain like the shipwrecked sailors in the *Raft of the Medusa*. Paris has already been marked as prelude to the descent by the father's recollection of his own Paris visit during the talk with the narrator discussed above. One descent leads to the next. The first showed the means of mediating the gaze onto death through remembrance of the past in order to represent it, as prelude to the task of reporting the collapse of the Spanish Civil War that occupied the remainder of volume 1. The second descent is performed to show the effects of this collapse on the individual: volume 2, part 1, takes up the *Raft of the Medusa*, the missed convergence of avant-garde (Dada) and revolution (Lenin) on the Spiegelgasse in Zurich during World War I, and the nervous breakdown of the narrator's friend Rosalinde Ossietsky in Sweden. The moment of descent occurs in the narrator's room and outside on the Fleminggata in Stockholm, as the narrator recapitulates motifs from *Inferno* 1–2 to depict the state of his doubt, lamenting his exile and the absence of Coppi and Heilmann, unable

[22] See discussions of the episode by Scherpe (in Wolff, 94) and Oesterle (62–69).

to remember their discussion of the second and third cantos of the *Inferno* (2:122).[23]

The second descent is figured in a primarily metaphorical manner: it is connected with memory and interpretation. In the third volume, in contrast, we find a physical, realistic, and historically documented descent on the narrative level in Lotte Bischoff's illegal entry into Germany as a stowaway. The metaphor remains, of course, to describe the "Hadeswanderung" (NB2 761) through wartime Germany, but Bischoff is depicted at this point as a chronicler descending into hell with no return trip possible.[24] On the level of the historical chronicle, then, there is no three-part structure like that of Weiss's original conception; rather, hell repeats itself three times; we have only the image of descent to the underworld and attempt at return, but apparently no *PURG* and no *PAR*.

Change does occur, however, in the relation of the narrator to each descent: here is where the tripartite structure can still be applied. We studied the moment of the first descent in detail: the narrator's emergence as an individual voice out of the reading of Dante, and his learning to represent by distancing himself from the figure of his father. Seen in Weiss's earlier terms, this depicts the narrator's ability to represent the past, but still passively, as if suited to hell. The second volume records the transformation of the passive ability gained through the first descent into one of *engagement* (*das Eingreifen*), the process of individuation, the start of the journey back into representation. The narrator's descent here is one of doubt over the memory he had recovered in the first volume, one of doubt over his ability as an individual in the absence of his friends and in exile; in Dante's terms, his inability immediately to climb the mountain of purgatory without first journeying through hell (*Inf.* 1); in Weiss's terms, the doubt of purgatory.

The descent on the historical level consists in his becoming again active politically (the work for the journalist Rosner paralleling joining the army in Spain in volume 1); the purgatorial moment appears in the doubts over

---

[23] Oesterle suggests the Dante motif here is left over from an earlier draft where the episode would have been near the beginning of the first formulation of the novel as "DER WIDERSTAND" (*NB2* 103), to have taken place only in Sweden (65). This seems a plausible etiology; as with Lindner's note on the lack of documentation for the reception and discussion of art, however, we must bow to the care with which Weiss composed and hence interpret the choice not to excise it as something other than mere oversight.

[24] Bischoff survived to be interviewed by Weiss for her memories of the whole business. This comes up in the *Notizbücher* and is treated below.

writing. Here, he first becomes a chronicler, first works on a writing project with Brecht, first sets words on the page (see esp. 2:306–10). Weiss
called part 2 of the volume "ANABASIS": the ascent and battle following
the *katabasis* of the first part. The narrator joins the resistance—both
political and aesthetic (with Brecht's figure in the center)—at its height in
Sweden before it recollapses symbolically in Brecht's flight for London
and the narrator's cataloging of his library as an inventory of the past
threatened with disappearance (2:312–19).

The third volume documents the analogous political collapse in great
detail; as the outline cited above has it, it "recounts according to the
understanding attained." Weiss's *Purgatorio* was to end with the utopia of
socialism and a politically committed Dante; *Paradiso,* to be that Dante's
recapitulation of *Inferno* as the story of the victims, with hope always in
the background. Certainly, the narrator is not converted at the end of
volume 2; he does, however, emerge as a writer and an individual. Consequently, he can recede to the background: in volume 3, as Weiss told
Lindner, "the big events push to the foreground; they were so overwhelming and monstrous that everything autobiographical must step back"
(Götze/Scherpe, 154). The third descent, Lotte Bischoff's, frames the extended execution of the resistance members that occupies much of the
second part of the volume, as putatively from her point of view as being
in Berlin but in fact from that of an omniscient narrator. Our first-person
narrator has revealed himself as the accomplished author; he has mastered
the means of production, and so, like Dante before him, he effaces himself
before the task at hand, that of representing the unrepresentable and the
unimaginable.

Although Dante-protagonist nearly vanishes in *Paradiso,* the voice of
the converted Dante-poet remains, punctuating his text with the celebrated
asides about his inability to achieve what he is about to achieve. As for
Weiss, he depicts the inexpressible within the novel in two ways: first, by
replacing the many *ekphrases* with descriptions of experiences instead
of artworks, in particular the beginning in medias res of the mother's
dumbstruck vision of horror and the terrible experiences of Lotte Bischoff
and Karin Boye, and also in alternate forms of writing, such as Heilmann's
"Brief an Unbekannt" (letter to an unknown person, 3:199–210).[25] Second, Weiss radically alters the traditional time scheme by casting the final
pages, the summary of what happened after 1945 and up to the present,

[25] The irony in the conceit of an open letter by a man about to be executed is that
the "Unbekannt" (Unknown person) can also be the anonymous narrator, to whom
the letter by its tone *is* apparently addressed.

in the future subjunctive, thus positing a present-day narrator but refusing grammatically to concede his existence. It is the effect of this gesture at the end of the novel, and the converse presence of numerous "asides to the reader" in the notebooks—complaints, that is, over the difficulty of writing the third volume—that I turn to at this juncture.

THE FINAL THREE sections of the third volume of the *Ästhetik* run as follows: Lotte Bischoff's report (220–39) of the executions recounted in the previous section (210–20), rendered in third-person *erlebte Rede,* or *style indirect libre;* Hodann's dilemma, his conclusion that a German culture can no longer exist and that a culture in exile is unable to accomplish anything, also given in *erlebte Rede,* but with the narrator present (239–57);[26] and last, the narrator's first-person (mostly plural) account of the years since the war (257–68, with the future subjunctive beginning in earnest after the preterit form of "fragten wir" on 260).[27] The first two sections take place at the end of the war, although the report by Bischoff also contains a passage in the future subjunctive in which she imagines herself teaching the history of the resistance (3:236–37). Like Hodann's repudiation of the ability of culture directly to bridge political gaps, this is important in setting up the final passage. If Hodann in the second volume bore traces of Vergil in his role as guide and mentor in Sweden (Oesterle, 64), it is logical (if also biographically accurate) that his death fall within the sphere of the war; like Vergil, he remains bounded by its limits. Bischoff, on the other hand, is likened to Mnemosyne, the goddess of memory under whose aegis the work was undertaken and who becomes central to the third volume (3:222–24).[28]

Memory, as we saw in the Dante reading of volume 1, was personified

---

[26] Max Hodann, psychiatrist and high-ranking member of the Communist Party, plays an important role in the novel, both historically and as mentor of the narrator. He is commander of the forces in Spain with which the narrator serves; he is one of the narrator's best friends and support in Sweden; his pessimistic conclusions in discussion with the narrator introduce the concluding episode. In fact, Weiss originally planned to end with Hodann's suicide; instead, he transferred the episode to the *Notizbücher,* for reasons discussed below.

[27] Following Lindner's account, "Ich Konjunctiv Futur I oder die Wiederkehr des Exils," in Götze/Scherpe, 89. Any reading of this passage begins with Lindner's seminal essay.

[28] "Total art [*die Gesamtkunst*], he [Heilmann] continued, or total literature [*die Gesamtliteratur*] is available to us under the protection of a goddess, Mnemosyne, whom we are still able to validate. She, the mother of art, is called Remembrance" (1:77).

for the three readers by Vergil, and gave continuity beyond life and death and the ability to recall the entire past to the border point (*am Grenzpunkt*). On the one hand, it freed the individual to face his or her past without fear of death; on the other, it showed that loss of the fear of death constitutes the posterity of the work of art, a posterity that consists in bringing others face to face with the thought of their own deaths. This is the role Bischoff takes over from Hodann in the third volume; she is the narrator's guide through the *Paradiso,* she mediates the petrifying visions of Berlin. And, in the end, she, like Beatrice, takes her place in the heavenly rose, canonized as a saint of the resistance (3:267).

Now, a principal reason for the role Bischoff plays in the *Ästhetik* was the fact that she was still alive in the seventies and Weiss was thus able to spend long hours interviewing her.[29] Weiss said that he focused primarily on either those characters he had known personally (Ayschmann, Hodann) or those he was able to interview (such as Bischoff and Wehner): "If possible for me at all today, thirty-five years later, then I could imagine to myself how I had once spoken with them" (Götze/Scherpe, 157). We may, then, add the living figures to our earlier list of Weiss's allegorizations, the list of retrojections around the constellation of the *Wunschautobiographie.*

All these elements are cast back as they would have been in the past, but fully formed as they could only have been with the point of view and labor of a Peter Weiss in the 1970s: "Everything that is brought to speech was represented first in myself, discovered in part only from the stifling experience of exile. Only thirty-five years after the events portrayed here did the understanding and perceptions lie before me that made it possible for me to write about that time of the antifascist struggle" (Gerlach/Richter, 244). The events are authentic in the sense that things *could have been* this way; indeed, the factual structure of dates, places, and meetings is generally completely authentic, as Weiss has stressed, but even the less factual elements, such as the reception of artworks and the autobiographically based narrator's working-class background, are historically plausible, if simultaneously allegorical, requiring interpretation. Weiss's defense against attacks on his *Wunschautobiographie* points toward such an interpretation: his status in Sweden as an exile and artist was proletarian for all intents and purposes (Gerlach/Richter, 231–32). I do not intend here to take issue with the tenability of such a stance but rather want to point out that, once again, what Weiss would hypostasize in the figure of the narrator he also represented as a bona fide process in his own life.

[29] See *NB2,* 92, 99, 172–73, 602–3, 712–13.

In the final pages of the *Ästhetik*, the same hypostasization determines the use of the future subjunctive. As Lindner has observed, it is only in this passage that we are made aware of a narrating presence behind that of the first-person narrator and in which the relationship between the "Ich-Erzähler" and the "erzählten-Ich," between the "Erzählzeit und erzählte Zeit," becomes a theme of the novel (first-person narrator/narrated narrator; time of narration/time being narrated [Götze/Scherpe, 89]). This astute analysis of the dynamics of the passage remains, however, overly formalist, for Lindner interprets the use of the future subjunctive solely as a stylistic device and the Pergamon recapitulation solely as a thematic one, both signaling the author's sinking in high-modernist fashion back into his own work as into a "second exile" (93). As I have demonstrated with the Pergamon recapitulation, and as I now show with the use of tenses, the stylistic and thematic devices demand allegorical interpretation in the same manner as other elements of the allegorical frame of the novel: they have both aesthetic and political effect.

Quite simply, the future subjunctive signals and caps off the same hypostasization of the political/historical aspect of the autobiographical allegory that was outlined above. The novel is constructed around the *Nullpunkt* of the end of the war, with its meaning derived from the Auschwitz *Nullpunkt* of Weiss's earlier novel. After this point, representation became impossible; so Weiss simply retrojects all his material to its proper place in memory before that moment. Everything that comes afterward, including his own moment of writing in the seventies, depends on and is unable to escape that moment. This, again, is analogous to Dante's 1300 eschatology and to the eschatology of the Christ-event for Augustine. Even though the *Commedia* depends on Dante's existing beyond 1300 in order to write it, the narrative, what is depicted, is shown as hypostasized in 1300, and all the shades recount the cruces of their lives with reference to that date, knowing nothing about what might come afterward except in terms of prophecy.

Weiss was able to find stylistic analogues to the personal significance of 1945: his German, he claimed, was that of another generation; writing it was a struggle: "For me it is not a naturally flowing language. I don't have unmediated contact with it" (Götze/Scherpe, 167). We should recall his explanation for the great blocks of text out of which the novel is constructed (there are no paragraphs, only section breaks every ten or so pages denoted by a space of one line) and the elision of vowels as a means of concentrating the language and as a technique that is found often in earlier German: to give a sense of breathlessness and urgency to things past (Gerlach/Richter, 220). These are the things we as readers must learn to notice and to decipher; these are the things over which the narrator must gain control in order to represent what he has seen.

The final recapitulation of the Pergamon frieze places Heilmann and Coppi within it, analogues to the emblematic lion's claw of Heracles, allegories of return for us as he was for them. As Lindner suggested, on a formal level this return is the journey back into the novel; we begin again at the beginning, but this time rereading with a new understanding of what we are looking for. But it goes further than that: in our emulation of the narrator, whose allegory of conversion we have followed and experienced, we become authors of the novel. The utopian allegory of this transformation, the part that cannot be symbolized in the frieze, is twofold: that the hope for return is not lost, the postwar debacle not permanent, not reality; and that it may be changed simply by the way in which it is depicted—the descent into the past has the power to reimagine the future by rewriting the past.

The *Ästhetik* thus presents itself here as a high-modernist novel; its model is Proust's *Recherche*. Its allegory of conversion is intended as a model we can follow to descend into our memories and return with the ability to read the present correctly; it functions as a model for the author by sending him back into his novel, for as finally converted pilgrim he is ready to begin the work that as already converted author he has just finished depicting himself getting ready to write. Putting aside the question of Proust's political allegory, we have already seen how Weiss hypostasized his own. The process, the allegorical frame of that hypostasization, is not only in the final pages of the *Ästhetik*, or in the return to the opening pages, but in the writing to which Weiss sends the figure of his narrator at the end of the allegory of conversion—that is, in the *Notizbücher*.

In the *Notizbücher*, published directly after he could have expected his readers to have finished their first reading of the *Ästhetik*, and thus to have undergone the process of conversion through which they were led by the narrator, Weiss refused to permit either a simple formalist reading of his novel or a political rejection of it as a *Wunschautobiographie*. Instead, he unfolds another narrative before our eyes, the allegory of the political conversion, the process by which the apparently static *Wunschautobiographie* came into being. We should remark how fitting it is that the formal model of the *Ästhetik* be the high-modernist novel, for that form reached its height during the thirty-odd years covered by Weiss's novel and did not, by common critical consensus, extend beyond the war. Moreover, critical evaluation of the high-modernist novel during the fifties performed the same hypostasization to which, without the political allegory, Weiss's novel is also susceptible: the autobiographical voice within the allegories of conversion of Proust, Joyce, Mann, or Broch was frozen into a formal and hermetically sealed meditation on language. As the newly contextualized readings of Céline in Chapter 2 and of Woolf and Benjamin in Chapter 4 and 5 suggest, this is not the only possible reading of high modernism any more than it is the only reading of the *Ästhetik*, even if it has continued to dominate accounts of these writers at least through the vogue of poststructuralism.

Weiss descended into modernism to recover its dialectical potential: the *Ästhetik* is a novel that brings the meaning of high modernism and the avant-garde to life while recreating out of them a new, postwar form. Both in its formal debt to high modernism *and* in its direct political engagement, the *Ästhetik* deliberately presents itself as wholly anachronistic. The allegorical frame serves to place Weiss's untimely political and historical meditations, and even the style of his German, in their proper context as equally anachronistic, but at the same time to provide us with the tools for making contemporary sense of that very anachronism. In other words, all the elements of the novel that impart the formal qualities of a high-modernist novel, a self-contained work of art, and that thus open it up for criticism as anachronistic in this day and age of postmodernism, are coded so that their anachronism, their formal success, are not simply static symbols but function dynamically as allegory.

Lindner has gestured toward the meaning of this allegorical code: "If the author masks himself in the first-person narrator for the sake of the representability of his research, so is the present the place from which he writes. Instead of letting ourselves be blinded by the phantasm of authenticity, we must track down the construction of the present in the novel" (in Stephan, 184). The construction of the present to be tracked down, I would argue, is the allegorical frame, the constellation of fictionalization that becomes most apparent in the final passage of the novel and is glossed by the *Notizbücher*, which present Weiss's construction of the novel in its context of the past twenty years.

There is neither space nor, I think, need at this point to give an exhaustive account of the *Notizbücher*. Recall my earlier argument that the notebooks too are dominated by the epistemological framework of the *Commedia*. If in the *Ästhetik* the *Commedia* is the means by which the narrator achieves the ability to represent the past and we the ability to interpret it—the allegory of conversion in its artistic sense—then in the *Notizbücher* we see the *Commedia* from the first Dante notes of 1964 onward as an allegory of conversion in the historical and political sense, as the way in which Weiss organized in the present the history that in the *Ästhetik* he would retroject into the past as an already fixed quantity.

Only through the *Notizbücher* is it possible to realize the scope and depth of Weiss's investigation, the obsessiveness with which every last detail of his reconstruction is plotted; the sheer weight of concrete details, which, as his narrator, Coppi, and Heilmann discovered of Dante, is the only way, piece by piece, of making real what cannot be represented directly (1:80). The *Notizbücher* ignore the historical barrier of 1945 in other ways as well: they conclude, except for a final page of framing notes on the completion of the novel and on the necessary anonymity of the narrator, with the thirty-page epilogue of Hodann's suicide in 1947 that was originally intended as the novel's conclusion (*NB2* 898–925). We cited Weiss's reasons for the exclusion above: history in the *Notizbücher* is fluid; in the *Ästhetik* it is constructed absolutely around the *Nullpunkt* of 1945.

There are many ways of evaluating Weiss's monumental achievement. Since through the *Notizbücher* Weiss reveals all his secrets and disenchants the aura, the notebooks allow him to get away with the pure anachronism of an immensely long, difficult, complex, and successful high-modernist novel. If we put this back in the perspective of Dante, however, we may be able also to gloss the sheer difficulty of the novel. Through the structure of descent and return, the autobiographical voice fuses myth and history, individual and social; Dante's rewriting of history, his interventions into Florentine, Italian, and European politics, are grounded and authenticated by the success of his artistic mission. He welds our acceptance of them to our acceptance of his success in depicting his vision of the afterlife. Thus his addresses to the reader: he stakes his historical return on the artistic conversion. This duplicity is the referent of the allegorical frame of Weiss's novel. Weiss presents the political agenda already symbolized, objectified, hypostasized, just as we see Coppi and Heilmann understand the Pergamon altar. Again, this is not to say that within the symbolization things are any less dynamic than the movement of the gods and giants in their battle, only that their discourse, in all its movement and complexity, is fixed: Heilmann is "our Rimbaud" from the first page to the last. Nothing in the novel attempts to persuade us to accept these meanings; they are simply given.

Persuasion is, however, at the center of questions of representation and of the production of art. For what we do have to be persuaded of is that the symbols of this novel are, indeed, authentic and not simply novelizations. This is the mistake of identification that the allegorical frame, beginning with Coppi and Heilmann at the museum, seeks to correct. The identification, the point Weiss (like Dante before him) must convince us of, is that everything in the novel is authentic, as a dream is, that all the elements are real and can be termed unreal only in the manner of their construction (as in a dream). As in a dream, we will perceive the aesthetic construction of real elements as if it were actually happening, even if at various times we remind ourselves as part of that construction that we are, indeed, dreaming. The constellation of the narrator, of the autobiographical voice, constitutes this construction; it is what permits everything to be authentic. "I have been everywhere where I place my *I* in the book; I have spoken with every person whom I name; know all the streets & locales—I depict my own life, I can no longer distinguish btw. what is invented and what authentic—it is all authentic (as in dreams everything is authentic)—" (*NB2* 872–73). The allegory of conversion within the novel, the tripartite structure delineated by Weiss, teaches us how to recognize the dream structure, the allegory that frames the symbolic pieces.

The *Notizbücher*, in contrast, recapitulating step by step, document how the dream authenticity was achieved, where the pieces came from, and, more important, what they mean in the present. The pressure of the present is not hidden in bad conscience behind the face of the novel's *Wunsch*-narrator; rather, it is represented by the allegorical gesture of fictionalization, by the events and stylistic and thematic devices that did not but could have occurred. In other words, it is the emblem of an artwork that cannot be symbolized, that existed only in mediation, as a sign of its absence. To be formalistic about it, the notebooks are the Heracles of the *Ästhetik;* their lion's claw in the novel is the constellation of the *Wunschautobiographie.* If present, they would still fight on the side of the gods: they would guide us through a past inevitably leading to the present we now live in; the conditional history of the novel's conclusion would be reality; the past dead and buried; the frieze a triumphant monument over the ruins of another failed revolt. By emblematizing his process of writing and identification within the novel, Weiss allegorizes a utopian connection to the past: if—and only if—mediated, the remembered history of catastrophe might outlast its death and write a different history after it.

At the same time, by objectifying the political agenda of the novel, Weiss separates it from the aura of his authorial voice. Augustine, Dante, Proust, and Céline channel the political through the personal allegory of conversion. The success of their artwork *is* the success of their political agenda. Weiss allows his novel the success of learning to read it, of receiving it, but his narrator does not give us the analysis and research; the return, the success of the work as a political gesture remain contingent on our return. He will not deny that he is implicated in that return, however; instead of predicating the political on the imitation of his success as a

writer, he predicates it on our imitation of his labor as a writer: the
construction of the political *ekphrasis* documented in the *Notizbücher*.
Hence, Weiss renovates the sense of return from the descent to the underworld. "The lion's claw would hang there, waiting to be seized" (3:268):
the authentic return lies not so much in the *Ästhetik* but in the *Notizbücher*. For if the notebooks are the lion's claw—what remains absent
from the artwork when it is symbolized into an object—then they express
the moment of utopia, the possibility of change.

Weiss was not satisfied with the formalistic solution to return that the
modernist Dante and Proust in the common postwar reading of them
would give: the book as allegory and utopia of the world, the means of
rereading it. Or, better, he put forth that that solution was no longer valid
in a postwar world. Instead, he sends us back to the work in progress, not
so much as a postmodern allegory of the impossibility of closure (as the
eighties would have it) but as a monument to his own labor. What he
could have, what he should have done in the years from 1917 to 1945,
Weiss instead had to do thirty-five years later. It should not be overlooked
that in so doing he unearthed a neglected and important moment of history, a renewed and vital reading of the *entre-deux-guerres*. The *Ästhetik*
records what indeed was for history and what *might have been* for Peter
Weiss; the *Notizbücher* record what indeed *was* for Peter Weiss and what
might have been for history.

Storming the Gates of Paradise: Dante's *descensus ad superos*

Weiss's implicit distinction between a modernist and a postwar Dante
goes a long way toward delineating the fault lines of the *Commedia*'s
descent: where its antinomies lie, how they have set the terms for modernist readings of the poem, and how they might be reread in a postwar
setting. The great divide in modern Dante studies has been the necessity of
choosing between a *Commedia* as poetic artifact and a *Commedia* as
inspired prophecy, and this has polarized what is actually a dialectic
wrought within the text through the dynamics of the descent. We saw the
same dialectic manifested in the *Odyssey* on the level of textual unity and
in the *Aeneid* on the level of thematic unity; in criticism of the *Commedia*,
we find it on the level of doctrinal unity, labeled and dichotomized as the
"allegory of poets" and the "allegory of the theologians."

Since the time of Coleridge and Goethe, judgment of the *Commedia*
has redounded to whether or not it can be considered "medieval," that is,
whether or not it participates in the debased genre of "poetic fictions." If
we recall Augustine and Bernard, we can recognize here a new polariza-

tion of the old question of authority raised by the Christian descent. For Dante's poem to retain its status as classic in a modern canon, it must first be asserted as unique, and it must then be shown to succeed where it shows its predecessors to have failed. The success of the *Commedia* on these terms has been critically registered in two primary ways in the past two centuries: first—and this is the mode of modernism proper—it surpasses any medieval antecedents by its freedom both from medieval superstitions and from medieval genres, either wholly or in chosen episodes such as Paolo and Francesca or Ugolino; second—and this is the modernizing critical reading of the postwar period—it succeeds by virtue of its divine authority. The latter is the Frecceran model of the allegory of conversion: the poem would unify the Augustinian model within a narrative descent modeled on biblical exegesis and not on poetic fictions.[30]

Such holistic readings result from total identification with the text—either by assimilating it to the present (Goethe, Coleridge, Croce, Eliot) or by giving in to a modernist reading of the medieval (Freccero, Hollander, Mazzotta).[31] We must now reread the poem for what it can tell us, both about the means of creating a signifying structure of authority powerful enough to generate such critical identification and about the uses to which such a structure can be put. This is possible from a vantage point that sees the *descensus* functioning not only through assertion of originality on the surface but also through latent acknowledgment and working-through of its debts.

The *Commedia* does not propose a choice between artifact and doctrine; rather, it uses the mechanism of descent to create a discursive space

---

[30] See the discussion in Chapter 1, pp. 20–27.

[31] See, for example, Johann Wolfgang von Goethe, "Dante," in *Kunst und Literatur*, ed. Werner Weber and Hans-Joachim Schrimpf, vol. 12 of *Werke*, ed. Erich Trunz, 14 vols., Hamburg ed. (Munich, 1978), 339–42; Goethe, "Dante," in *Essays on Art and Literature*, ed. John Gearey, trans. Ellen von Nardroff and Ernest H. von Nardroff, vol. 3 of *Goethe's Collected Works*, 12 vols. (Princeton, 1994), 180–82; Goethe, "Dante," in *Schriften zur Weltliteratur*, ed. Horst Günther (Frankfurt, 1987), 234–43; Samuel Taylor Coleridge, "Lecture 5, 1819," in *Lectures 1808–1819 on Literature*, ed. R. A. Foakes, 2 vols., vol. 5 of *The Collected Works of Samuel Taylor Coleridge*, ed. Kathleen Coburn, 16 vols. (Princeton, 1987) 2,397–403; Benedetto Croce, *La Poesia di Dante*, 2d ed. (Bari, 1921), trans. Douglas Ainslie, *The Poetry of Dante* (1922; rpt. Mamaroneck, 1971); T. S. Eliot, "Dante," 1929, rpt. in *Selected Essays* (New York, 1950), 199–237; Eliot, "A Talk on Dante," 1950, rpt. in *Dante in America: The First Two Centuries*, ed. A. Bartlett Giamatti (Binghamton, 1983), 219–27. See also Robert Hollander, *Allegory in Dante's "Commedia"* (Princeton, 1969), and the essays collected in *Studies in Dante* (Ravenna, 1980); Giuseppe Mazzotta, *Dante, Poet of the Desert: History and Allegory in the "Divine Comedy"* (Princeton, 1979).

in which newly to explore the affiliation between them as myth and history. The figures of Vergil and Paul delineate the contours of that space. As we saw in the first chapter, Vergil functioned for the allegorical tradition from Augustine and Macrobius through to Dante both as a source of tension between classical pagan poetics and Christian Scripture and as a model for representing that tension. At the same time, at the Christian pole of the problematic, standing simultaneously for the possibility and the difficulty of its resolution, we find the Apostle Paul. Augustine appealed to him to authorize a narrative *allegoria in facto* in the *City of God* and to complete his conversion in the *Confessions*. Paul also makes a significant cameo appearance in Bernard's commentary, in the gloss of *Aeneid* 6.126–31 as the unattainable *other* means of return from the underworld—the route by way of paradise. Christine de Pizan will use Pauline language in the *Mutacion de Fortune* and *Chemin de long estude* to describe the visionary state she is unsuited to attain. In the *Commedia*, Dante-protagonist's famous words to Vergil, "Io non Enëa, io non Paulo sono," signal that Dante intends, like Augustine, to use *both* the classical pagan and the Christian scriptural traditions as models for his poem.[32]

Vergil and Paul appear as personifications of the two modes of allegory —*in verbis* and *in facto*—in allegorical literature and in critical discussions of allegory in this period.[33] The locus classicus is the *descensus ad*

---

[32] *Inferno* 2.33. Dante Alighieri, *La Commedia secondo l'antica vulgata*, ed. Giorgio Petrocchi, 4 vols. (Mondadori, 1966–68); trans. and comm. Charles S. Singleton, *The Divine Comedy*, 6 vols. (Princeton, 1980–82).

[33] I use the term "personification" here to encompass the range of literary shorthand whereby the figures of Vergil and Paul—whether evoked by name, by citation, or by allusion—raise issues of classical pagan versus Christian scriptural authority. By calling them personifications, I am distinguishing between two degrees of *auctoritas:* a simple appeal to a prior authority and an appeal that is simultaneously a problematizing gesture serving to create for the current author an autobiographical voice. Whether the "simple" appeal is ever really "simple" is a moot point; it designates the least degree of complexity involved in an appeal to *auctoritas*. Furthermore, the use of "personification" stresses the allegorical mode of the gesture of *auctoritas:* just as a personification renders in a single figure one or a constellation of abstract concepts and concrete phenomena in such a way as to permit it to interact within a narrative structure, so here do the figures of Vergil and Paul participate in the construction of an autobiographical voice within the allegorical narrative of the *descensus ad inferos*. On the centrality of *auctoritas* to allegorical interpretation, see A. J. Minnis, *Medieval Theory of Authorship*, 2d ed. (Philadelphia, 1988), 63–72. For an insightful discussion of words and deeds in the etymology of *authority*, see Jacqueline T. Miller, *Poetic License: Authority and Authorship in Medieval and Renaissance Contexts* (New York, 1986), 29–33.

inferos; the *Commedia* codifies the scheme and extends it to the limits of its figurative potential. Specifically, the weight of the poem's elaborate devices of self-authorization is divided between the two personifications: Virgil accompanies Dante-protagonist on an autobiographical journey of conversion cast as an *allegoria in verbis* that will provide the means for interpreting the tripartite otherworldly system attributed to the *auctoritas* of God (Dante's *Ästhetik*); Paul generally lingers in the background as marker for the poet of both the possibility of such a representation and the prohibition of it (Dante's *Notizbücher*).

Dante uses the poetic model of Vergil to navigate between the extremes of the Pauline tradition to which he seeks access, to express the paradox of the *auctor*'s prohibition of the endeavor and the unauthorized, apocryphal approval of it.[34] He aims to unite the two modes of vision, at the same time making it clear that their different narrative and theological exigencies dictate different compositional strategies. In particular, each mode of vision requires and is granted a particular mode of allegory. The protagonist's Aenean journey is an autobiographical and allegorical narrative of conversion along the lines of Augustine; the poet's Pauline journey is a representation of the vision as if it were an allegorical exegesis of the text of God's system of life after death. In other words, Dante acknowledges the fictionality of the Aenean journey as a way of shifting onto it questions of authority that are in fact relevant only to the other, Pauline journey.

Just as Augustine used the autobiography of conversion in the *Confessions* to transform his life rhetorically into a text of God that as a side effect he was authorized to interpret with prophetic authority, so Dante used an autobiographical allegory of the protagonist's conversion to furnish the key to interpretation of what would thereby be authorized as God's, not Dante's, text. Both construct a chain of mediation: God to protagonist, protagonist to poet, poet to reader. The first link is rendered as *allegoria in facto*, the vision of God's truth; the second is the convert's interpretation of that vision for himself; the third is the poetic reconstruction of the process of interpretation as an *allegoria in verbis*. This is the ground for the *Commedia*'s radical rewriting of past history: Vergil personifies a complex vision of classical and medieval poetics to be sur-

---

[34] "Quoniam raptus est in paradisum: et audivit arcana verba, quae non licet homini loqui" (How that he was caught up into paradise, and heard unspeakable words, which it is not lawful for a man to utter [2 Cor. 12:4]). For the relevant texts and a history of the Apocalypse of Paul, see Theodore Silverstein, ed., *Visio Sancti Pauli* (London, 1935); ed. Eileen Gardiner, *Visions of Heaven and Hell before Dante* (New York, 1989), 13–46.

passed by Dante; Pauline allegory is given a forbidden allure whose prophetic Christian component authorizes the Dantean rewriting and pulls it beyond the orbit of its predecessors.

Starting from the schematization of the two modes in Vergil and Paul, I focus on two cantos, *Inferno* 14 and *Purgatorio* 1, as significant loci in the *Commedia* for the convergence of classical/scriptural issues. As with the Pergamon altar in the *Ästhetik*, the tensions mustered by a paradigmatic scene of reception and reading are embedded within an intricate skein of narrative, intertextual, and intratextual threads woven together by the allegorical structure. My reading seeks to draw out the consequences of that pattern for the modern descent and at the same time to contribute to the ongoing discussion within Dante studies of where and how Dante's *allegoria in verbis* and *in facto* intersect and interact within the *Commedia*.[35] For the polarization of this discussion, as with those on Homer and Vergil, has tended to close off a contextualization of Dante within modernism—within what has been, after all, the twentieth-century context of the discussion. As Weiss's postwar dramatization of such a contextualization has demonstrated, affiliating a modernist reception of Dante with modernist literature as such can provide a contemporary perspective on both.

Inferno 14 finds Dante and Vergil leaving the wood of the suicides to enter the third ring of the seventh circle, the burning plain on which the violent against God are punished. With its allusions to Cato and the Latin epic tradition, its encounter with the blasphemer Capaneus, the famous crux of Vergil's extended description of the *veglio* of Crete and its allusions to the journeys of both Aeneas and Paul to Rome, the canto provides imagery of conversion—pagan to Christian, East to West, past to present, sin to redemption, descent to return—that is both more densely packed and farther-reaching than has generally been noted.[36] The allegorical force of the canto's negative typology of pride is clarified when recapitulated in

---

[35] The literature on Dante's use of allegory is long, convoluted, and hard-fought, and I cannot do justice here to the intricacies of its history. The modern beginnings arise from Auerbach's "Figura" and Charles S. Singleton's *Dante's "Commedia": Elements of Structure* (1954; Baltimore, 1977). Pépin's *Dante et la tradition de l'allégorie* is exceptionally lucid in summarizing the debate up to 1970 and in distinguishing different modes of allegory. For scholarship since 1970 in the United States, see esp. the essays reprinted in Freccero, as well as Hollander and Mazzotta. More recently, see Teodolinda Barolini's ground-breaking study, *The Undivine Comedy: Detheologizing Dante* (Princeton, 1992).

[36] For an overview of interpretations of Capaneus and the *veglio* of Crete, see the articles by Umberto Bosco and Giovanni Reggio in *ED*. See also Ettore Paratore, "Il

a positive light in *Purgatorio* 1–2: it is simultaneously a narrative meditation on pagan and Christian pride and a metanarrative meditation on pagan and Christian modes of allegory, a dramatization of what is entailed by conversion and by the recapitulatory representation of that conversion. *Inferno* 14 provides a point of entry into an interpretation of the central paradox of Dante's poem: the *Commedia* claims to be a *menzogna vera,* a true lie, an Aenean *descensus ad inferos,* which is simultaneously— and not, that is, only *sequentially*—a Pauline *ascensus ad superos,* an unmediated vision of divine truth.

We can begin with Capaneus, famous for his proud blasphemy of Jupiter, and a figure who has traditionally been read as the precise analogue of a Christian blasphemer, a prime example of medieval syncretism. But as the first figure of classical, pagan literature to play a dramatic role as a soul punished in Dante's hell, Capaneus also suggests a conscious conflation of pagan and Christian whose purpose is to thematize the issue of transgression. Presumption against God is tagged as classical and pagan; the answering necessity for the convert to accept without further inquiry is equally tagged by contrast as Christian and Pauline.

The pagan blasphemer's first words, "Qual io fui vivo, tal son morto" (What I was alive, such am I dead), precisely summarize the condition of hell, the reification of its souls into an eternal present that merely reflects the absolute past of their failed lives.[37] This is the state of the art of God's justice: it eternally freezes the poses of the damned into the essence of what they were. The narrative of Dante's journey, conversely, acts in the opposite direction: that which Dante was, he is no longer; there where he was, he is no longer; he has made the journey and returned. As Walter Benjamin has argued, reification is the state of the allegorical object: only

canto XIV dell'*Inferno,*" in *Lectura Dantis romana* (Turin, 1959); Claudio Varese, "Canto XIV," in *Letture dantesche: "Inferno,"* ed. Giovanni Getto (Florence, 1955), 251–66; Mario Apollonio, "Il canto XIV dell'*Inferno,*" in *Lectura Dantis Scaligera* 1 (Florence, 1967–68), 451–78; Umberto Bosco, "Il canto XIV dell'*Inferno,*" in *Nuove Lettere* 2 (Florence, 1968), 47–74; and especially Mazzotta, 14–65. Mazzotta is the first critic to have made an extended comparison of what he calls "the figurative pattern surrounding the Old Man, the dramatic significance of the island of Crete, the rationale for allusions to Ovid's and Virgil's texts, and . . . the cracks in the statue" (15), connecting *Inf.* 14 with *Purg.* 1. As instructive and innovative as it is, Mazzotta's reading remains overly extrinsic for my purposes, concerned more with Dante's position vis-à-vis medieval theologies of history than with the textual dynamics informing Dante's manipulation of that along with many other medieval traditions.
[37] I am indebted to Barolini's interpretation of this phrase as a summary of the condition of hell.

by thus being mortified, by being broken out of the continuity of time, does a person or object become legible as allegory.[38] The shade's defiant cry is his self-identification as *figura:* just as the continuum of world history was fixed by the birth, crucifixion, and resurrection of Christ, so is the continuum of Capaneus's life fixed irrevocably by his death and the punishment received thereafter.

Canto 14 itself, however, is constructed as a space of transitional figures and borderline topography proper to the poetic concerns of the narrative *allegoria in verbis.* Emblematic of the transitional movement is Cato, who is introduced as if coincidentally in a descriptive simile as a classical novelty, symbol of fortitude in Lucan's *Pharsalia,* the only man able to withstand the horrors and torments of the Libyan desert.[39] But he appears in flux and as a question: topographically, the system of Dante's otherworld that has fixed Capaneus ought to place Cato either in the wood (*Inf.* 13) or on the plain (*Inf.* 14), but that system sets him instead as the blessed guardian of purgatory.[40] The early allusion suggests a spatial tension between a Vergil hovering on the edge of the desert and a Cato striding

---

[38] *Ursprung des deutschen Trauerspiel;* see the discussion in Chapter 5, pp. 210–14.

[39] "Lo spazzo era una rena arida e spessa, / non d'altra foggia fatta che colei / che fu da' piè di Caton già soppressa" (The ground was a dry deep sand, not different in its fashion from that which once was trodden by the feet of Cato [14.13–15]). The episode of Cato in the Libyan desert is related in 9.365–950 of Lucan's *Pharsalia* (trans. J. D. Duff [Cambridge, Mass., 1928]).

[40] That Dante intended the salvation of Cato as a shock is testified by the trouble he has given readers since the earliest commentators. Two general explanations are proffered: either Cato is an *integumentum,* thus having no significance as a suicide or a pagan (Benvenuto, Landino), or Dante was simply carried away by his admiration of Vergil and Lucan (Daniello, Muratori, Bettinelli, Tommaseo; see Mario Fubini, "Catone l'Uticense," in *ED*). Auerbach introduced the possibility of considering the shock of Cato's appearance as a conscious choice on Dante's part in "Figura" (64–67). Mazzotta goes more fully into the purpose of Cato's position at the beginning of *Purgatorio* and possible connections with *Inf.* 14 (14–65). Joan M. Ferrante also suggests such a structural role, in connection with the *veglio,* with Matelda, and with Dante's personal identification with the Roman as a political martyr (*The Political Vision of the "Divine Comedy"* [Princeton, 1984], 205–9, 246–48). On medieval views of Cato's status as a suicide, see Ferrante, 206–7, and Ernst Kantorowicz, *The King's Two Bodies: A Study in Medieval Political Theology* (Princeton, 1957), 484–92. Marco Praderio has pointed out to me that Cato's refusal to lend credence to the oracle of Jupiter in the desert ("That one, full with the god whom he bore hidden in his mind, poured forth from his breast words worthy of the oracle itself"; *Pharsalia* 9.564–65), which has traditionally been used to support the portrayal of Cato as a proto-Christian, can equally be seen as a form of presumptuous self-reliance bordering on the blasphemous.

across it that develops into the narrative crux of the damnation of one
virtuous pagan and the salvation of another that frames the *Purgatorio*.
The spatial dynamics are underpinned by a lexical web tying the issue of
salvation together with issues of poetics which, once untangled, also helps
resolve the local, static cruces of Capaneus and the *veglio.*

The language remains topographical, for the poetics are interrelated
through the scripturally derived imagery of plants: salvation as the bringing of life to the desert is troped as the poetic translation of the desert
into the garden, another transaction between pagan and Christian that
is far from mere syncretism. Canto 14 begins with the protagonist "con-
strained" by "the love [*carità*] of my native place" to gather up the "scattered twigs" *(le fronde sparte)* broken from the bush/soul of the anonymous Florentine suicide of the wood of the suicides (1–3). These are the
results of the exposition in Canto 13 of Florentine self-destruction; the
next canto is centered on analogous examples of buffeted, helpless, and
self-destructive souls: the blasphemer Capaneus, lying supine, exposed to
the rain of fire on the burning plain; and the *veglio,* the Old Man of
Crete, weeping for mankind through the fissure in his body, allegorizing
irrevocable decline.

The Florentine's request to gather *fronde* will be repeated on the shore
of purgatory by Cato himself, another suicide, another victim of civil war,
and another lover of his "natio loco."[41] The pliant reed with which the
protagonist is commanded to gird himself in *Purgatorio* 1, however, is in
stark contrast to the strikingly fragile bush of *Inferno* 13, torn apart by
damned souls and pursuing hounds. It is the only plant able to grow on
those distant shores, "però ch'a le percosse non seconda" (because it yields
not to the buffetings), and rather than being destroyed, it is "marvelously"
reborn each time it is plucked (*Purg.* 1.103–5, 134–36). The shattered
suicide and the staunch Pharsalian Cato are recapitulated through the
pliant reed set on a "lito deserto / che mai non vide navicar sue acque /
omo, che di tornar sia poscia esperto" (desert shore, that never saw any
man navigate its waters who afterward had experience of return [*Purg.*
1.130–32]).

The distinction in natural landscape develops a moral distinction between pride and humility; it sets out as well a poetic distinction between

[41] On Cato as patriot, see *Convivio*, ed. Cesare Vasoli, in *Opere minori*, vol. 1, p.
2; vol. 5 of *La letteratura italiana: Storia e testi* (Milan, 1979), 4.27.3; trans. W. W.
Jackson, *Dante's "Convivio"* (Oxford, 1909), 287. The image of Cato as "severissimus
verae libertatis auctor" (the severest model of true liberty) also figures prominently in
the *Monarchia* (ed. Bruno Nardi, in *Opere minori*, vol. 2, 2.5.128–70).

two types of novelty. For the purgatorial novelty of "mai non vide" finds
a different nuance in the infernal description of the burning plain: "A ben
manifestar le cose nove, / dico che arrivammo ad una landa / che dal suo
letto ogne pianta rimove" (To make these new things clear, I say we
reached a plain which rejects all plants from its bed [*Inf.* 14.7–9]).[42]
Novelty in hell is different from that in purgatory: the phrase "le cose
nove" stresses the protagonist's transition from the novelty of the Florentine suicide to the new sight of the plain of fire; but novelty on the deserted
shores of the mountain is presented from an opposite point of view. That
is to say, if both the Florentine and the burning plain are novelties for
Dante-protagonist and subsequently left behind by the forward progress
of his journey, it is Dante-protagonist himself who is the true novelty seen
by the mountain of purgatory.

   This is a crucial distinction, for the poet has switched modes: infernal
novelty is seen from the point of view of the protagonist's narrative of a
journey; novelty in *Purgatorio* is given as if from the point of view of
God's creation witnessing the man who will first represent it and interpret
it for readers back on earth. The plant, "reborn" *(rinata)* for each soul
who plucks it, girding each soul—including the protagonist—with an
emblem of purgatorial humility, ought not to find anything new in the
protagonist per se. The shift in point of view has identified the novelty as
appertaining instead to the poet, but the moral register remains constant:
the novelty resides in the *superbia* of the poet among the universally humble souls otherwise seen by these shores.

   The distinction is underlined by Cato's challenge to the protagonist and
his guide, the first words of dialogue of the canticle: "Chi siete voi che
contro al cieco fiume / fuggita avete la pregione etterna?" (Who are you
that, against the blind stream, have fled the eternal prison? [*Purg.* 1.40–
41]). Dante and Vergil have certainly "fled the eternal prison" in escaping
from hell, but the rivulet they followed flows from Satan to the mountain
of purgatory (*Inf.* 34.130–32), and so they have in fact traveled with, and
not against, its current.[43] Dante-protagonist, journeying through hell only

---

[42] Barolini has established the "the poetics of the new" as a determinant feature of
the *Commedia*'s poetics, a way of marking differentiation in the representation of the
afterlife. See *Undivine Comedy*, 21–46 and passim.

[43] Whether the *ruscelletto* of *Inf.* 34 flows away or toward Satan is left ambiguous in
the text, dependent as it is on the "quivi" of the narrator's "d'un ruscelletto che quivi
discende" (34.130), which comes directly following the total disorientation resulting
from Vergil and Dante's crossing the center of the earth. The early commentators Buti
and Landino interpreted the direction as I do here; "from Benvenuto on," as Pazzamuto

so as to reach purgatory, is topographically with the current of this "blind stream," descending ever further into sin but against its moral description of the condition of hell, since he is on a journey of conversion.[44]

Cato's surprise, analogous to the novelty witnessed by the desert shore, comes from the sight of one who has taken a novel route. Once purgatory has been attained, however, that novelty for the most part disappears; Dante follows the same path as the other souls, moving with the current both topographically and morally. Hence, Cato's remark and the point of view of the desert shore stress the particular novelty and also potential sin that does persist: the poetic project, the pride inherent in depicting what only God can depict, the pride paradoxically signaled by the narrator's taking on the point of view of the humble reed to describe his arrival.

The gap between protagonist and poet is subtly but clearly delineated: the protagonist's journey, with proper authorization from on high, follows a correct if novel path from hell; but the poet's journey is novel not in where it has escaped from but in where it is going (damnation being a less sacrosanct subject for representation than salvation). This is the gist of the particular form in which the novelty is expressed ("che mai non vide navicar sue acque / omo, che di tornar sia poscia esperto"): the poem is novel not in what it has done—the descent into hell—but in what it has yet to do—that is, the return.

One of the most striking examples of a descent rewriting its predecessors, Dante's rendering of Ulysses' journey as a *folle volo*, a mad flight, is remembered here in all its *superbia* and daring. In the account of his final voyage in *Inferno* 26, the poet's Ulysses shows that he did manage to reach what appears to be the mountain of purgatory of his own volition, sailing beyond the known ends of the earth, but not that he was "esperto di tornar" (expert in returning), for his ship plunged in a whirlwind straight to the bottom of the sea.[45] The poet surpasses the daring attrib-

---

puts it, the direction has been glossed as coming from purgatory, possibly descending from the river Lethe in the earthly paradise ("Fiume," *ED*). The only basis, however, for the latter conclusion is to avoid contradicting Cato's words in *Purg.* 1.40. My point is that Dante may have meant to do just that, and at the very least meant to retain an ambiguity in the rivulet's origin as either in the tears of the *veglio di Creta* or in the river Lethe. I take up the issue more fully in the final section of the chapter.

[44] The gloss is paralleled within the poem as well, in Guido del Duca's description of the Arno in *Purg.* 14.16–66. The Arno is given as the blind stream degenerating as it falls through Tuscany, reaching its nadir in the "trista selva" of Florence.

[45] Barolini's recent addition to the long tradition of readings of the Ulysses canto stresses the extent to which Ulysses is "fundamental to the *Commedia*" in his reflection

uted by him to his predecessor, stressing, especially at the beginning of *Purgatorio*, the greater novelty, greater danger—and greater moral and poetic authority—of the goal of his "voyage": the poem's conceit of rendering God's text of the saved souls.

Vergil and medieval lore had provided backing for visions of hell; the nether world was after all seen as better suited to the earthly and corrupt medium of poetry. In contrast, Paul's silence about the heavens—the return—set the tone both for the relative scarcity of literature on purgatory before Dante (not to mention its obvious absence from classical sources) and for the theological dangers implicit in writing about it.[46] The problem of paradise, finally, was of a different order, since both Christian and classical pagan models existed. As we have seen, however, the literary models, especially *Aeneid* 6, were fundamentally problematic because they placed the Elysian Fields in the underworld. This became, in fact, a potent symbol both of the mechanism of conversion and of the paradox of the literary representation of paradise: that a classical paradise could appear only in hell came to mean not only that conversion occurs through contemplation of the infernal nature of this life but equally that God can be made manifest only through the corrupt medium of language.

The tension between Christian and pagan *auctores* is evident on the intertextual level. Paratore has gone so far as to suggest that there are more classical references in *Inferno* 14 than in any other canto of the *Commedia* (29).[47] Nevertheless, although we find here the Dantean pantheon of classical *auctores* (Vergil, Ovid, Lucan, Statius, in descending order of frequency cited), it is God who is the *artifex* first alluded to in the canto, as the author on behalf of whose representation Dante is mustering the corps of poets. The transition from second to third ring, from wood to plain, is made with reference to God's *art:* "dove / si vede di giustizia

---

of "the poet's transgressing of the boundary between life and death, between God and man" and of Dante's awareness of the danger in what he was doing (58). Ulysses is Dante's take on the medieval topos of poetry writing as sailing, which I discuss in detail in the following chapter, for Christine de Pizan would adapt the same topos of transgressive poetry and shipwreck leading to hell in the autobiographical passages of the *Chemin de long estude* and *Mutacion de Fortune;* Woolf would also employ the motif of the sea voyage in terms of artistic creation in both *The Waves* and *Orlando*.

[46] On concepts of purgatory before Dante, see Jacques Le Goff, *La Naissance du purgatoire* (Paris, 1981); trans. Arthur Goldhammer, *The Birth of Purgatory* (Chicago, 1984); and Morgan, *Dante and the Medieval Other World*.

[47] In addition to the allusion to Lucan's *Pharsalia* in the Cato simile, some others are the figure of Capaneus from Statius's *Thebaid*, the descriptions of Crete from the *Aeneid*, and motifs of the *veglio* from Ovid's *Metamorphoses*.

orribil arte" (where a horrible mode of justice is seen [14.6]). The implicit distinction is made abundantly clear in the apostrophe immediately following the reference to Cato: "O vendetta di Dio, quanto tu dei / esser temuta da ciascun che legge / ciò che fu manifesto a li occhi mei!" (O vengeance of God, how much should you be feared by all who read what was revealed to my eyes! [14.16–18]). Dante figures a chain of mediation from God to the protagonist to the poet to us, his readers: between God and the protagonist's vision stands the text of the afterlife ("O vendetta di Dio"—the system of hell); between that vision and the reader stands the poet's manifestation of it to us, the recapitulation of his vision as a journey of conversion, as the *Commedia*. The difference in usage again raises the question of the two modes of allegory—*in verbis* and *in facto*—used in constructing the *Commedia*.

The shift between modes is expressed through the double usage of *manifestar* in the first eighteen verses of the canto, once to express the poet's *arte* ("A ben manifestar le cose nove") and once to express God's. As poet reconstructing his experience as protagonist, Dante speaks to us in the active voice, telling how he will describe in order to "ben manifestar" the novelty he is seeing. As protagonist recalling his vision of God's *arte*, he reverts to a passive construction, "ciò che fu manifesto a li occhi mei." The narrative of the journey stands between us and the text of God both in terms of the conceit that the poet has chosen what to represent to us from what he saw and in terms of the dynamics of conversion narrative —the double point of view that forces us to interpret in the temporal space between pre-and postconversion, between protagonist and poet.

It is apparent from the central verse of the tercet that the two modes of poesis are figured distinctly by Dante: between the text of God's vengeance and the poet's vision of it we find the impetus to conversion: "quanto tu dei / esser temuta da ciascun che legge." The impending description of the plain of fire is framed by an apostrophe characterizing it as God's text for us to read and consequently as God's text for us to interpret. The poet clues us in as to what the correct interpretation would be with the word *temuta*: as the opening verses of the *Commedia* stress, "paura," fear (*Inf.* 1.6), is the first step toward conversion, the most basic lesson of hell.

At the same time, we should note what has occurred between the first and the second use of *manifestar*. In the mode of narrator of the journey, the poet places us as readers very differently than he does in the mode of reporter of God's justice. The classical reference to Cato both mirrors our possible question as to that justice (where is the suicide/blasphemer Cato?) and situates us in a different chain, that of classical, pagan, epic narrative, the *arte* of representation. The insertion of the allusion to Cato between the two modes of *manifestar* establishes the canto as one that is particularly concerned with the dynamic of classical pagan versus Christian scriptural in the context of narrative of conversion versus exegesis of God's text—that is, the problematic of *allegoria in verbis* versus *in facto*. The principal figures of the canto, Capaneus and the *veglio,* pointedly raise the conflict between classical pagan and Christian scriptural; the connections with *Purgatorio* 1 situate the conflict within the context of the two allegories.

If we consider Dante to be presenting the text of the afterlife as that made by God, and as distinct from the recapitulation of the journey by which he allegorically presents his interpretation of God's text, then its status as *allegoria in facto* becomes self-evident. For the poet's primary conceit is *not* that he is composing an *allegoria in facto* but that he is interpreting such an allegory already composed by God for our edification as readers. Consequently, it is not necessary to prove—as has always been a sticking point in discussions of Dante's allegory—that the narrative of conversion, the means by which Dante structures his representation of God's *arte,* is intended as an *allegoria in facto,* as literally historical and true. Rather, it functions as an *allegoria in verbis,* modeled on the descent of Aeneas received in the Middle Ages as a journey of the soul to God, and patterned as a "menzogna vera."

In these two cantos we find the journeys of Aeneas and Paul, the Vergilian and Christian models of descent, invoked at crucial transitional moments in the unfolding of Dante's conception of the two modes of allegory. I examine below how Dante took the strategies and problems implicit in the invocation of Aeneas and Paul in *Inferno* 2 to develop them more fully as the model for a *"descensus ad superos"* later evoked in modernist descents. It is necessary first to clarify more broadly the theoretical framework within which Dante uses the narrative interaction with Vergil as a personification of the classical, pagan derivation of *allegoria in verbis* both to create his autobiographical voice and to distinguish it from that of Vergil, leaving him behind as he moves into the Pauline territory of the *Paradiso.*

THE CONCERNS evident in *Inferno* 14 and *Purgatorio* 1—the tension between classical pagan and Christian scriptural, between narrative and interpretation—figure prominently in the theorization of allegory in *Convivio* 2.1, the unfinished prose work between the *Vita nuova* and the *Commedia* where Dante once again glossed his lyric poems, this time as allegories about Lady Philosophy. The distinction is between two modes of reading: poets take the first two of the four levels of meaning as a "bella menzogna" that leads to the truth beneath, whereas theologians understand them as one historical event fulfilled as *figura* by another. This distinction has given rise to the critical terminology of "allegory of poets" and "allegory of theologians," but not enough attention has been paid to Dante's stress, like Augustine's, on the literal as the necessary path to the other three meanings and as the necessary first step in interpretation, whichever mode is being used, before any thought is turned to the allegorical.[48]

The stress on similitude, along with certain indications as to the relationship between the two allegories in the *Commedia*, is evident in the *Convivio*'s definition of poets' understanding of allegory, for the example given is of a poet who used his art and knowledge to descend to the underworld:

And to make this intelligible, it should be known that writings can be understood and ought to be expounded chiefly in four senses. The first is called literal, [and this is the sense which does not go beyond the strict limits of the letter; the second is called allegorical,] and this is disguised under the cloak of such stories, and is a truth hidden under a beautiful lie.[49] Thus Ovid says that Orpheus with his lyre made beasts tame, and trees and stones to move toward him; that is to say that the wise man

[48] "And in demonstrating this, the literal must always go in front, in such a way that the others are contained [*inchiusi*] within its meaning [*sentenza*], without which it would be impossible and irrational to understand the others, and in particular the allegorical" (2.1.8; 74). Dante's emphasis on the importance of the literal increases the possibility of his use of Aquinas's unusual location of *allegoria in verbis* within the literal level (see Pépin 1970, 76–77). As Antonio Pagliaro has pointed out, "in no other medieval text except Saint Thomas's is the precedence of the literal over the allegorical affirmed with so much vigor and so much insistence as in this Dantean postulate" ("Simbolo e allegoria," in *Ulisse: Ricerche semantiche sulla "Divina Commedia,"* vol. 2 [Messina-Florence, 1967], 467–527; this quotation, 472). For Augustine, see *De doctrina Christiana*, CCSL 32, iv.i, 3.10.14–16, 22.32–27.38; trans. D. W. Robertson, Jr., *On Christian Doctrine* (Indianapolis, 1958). For a more extensive consideration of the allegory issue within Dante studies in Italy and the United States, and the status of the *Convivio* and the Epistle to Can Grande therein, see Pike, 137–51.

[49] The brackets indicate a celebrated lacuna. We need only lend it as much weight as many have in the past if we continue to consider it necessary to discard the "allegory of poets" in favor of that of "the theologians." If, as I am suggesting, Dante makes clear his different use of both senses through his examples later in the passage, in the Epistle to Can Grande, and, most important, in the *Commedia*, then the authenticity of the words filling the lacuna becomes a moot point. For the textual history, see the editors' note to the passage. G. R. Sarolli summarizes the discussion and pronounces his acceptance of the above-cited text, *Prolegomena alla "Divina Commedia,"* (Florence, 1971), 42–50.

by the instrument of his voice makes cruel hearts grow mild and humble,
and those who have not the life of Science and of Art move to his will,
while they who have no rational life are as it were like stones. . . .
Theologians indeed do not apprehend this sense in the same fashion as
poets; but, inasmuch as my intention is to follow the custom of poets, I
will take the allegorical sense after the manner which poets use. (2.1.3–
4; 73)

It is a mistake, I believe, to deny Dante in his interpretations of allegorical
tradition the subtlety and daring we are willing to grant him elsewhere.
What I see him doing in the *Commedia* is adapting this definition of
allegory as the poets use it—which is already unusual in its insistence on
four levels—to represent a figural exegesis of God's book of the otherworld. We have already seen the self-consciousness with which medieval
allegorists approached classical texts and the acute awareness of a Bernard
Silvestris both of the limits of poetic fictions and of the haziness of the
boundary between *integumentum* and *allegoria*. In the passage above,
Dante shows a similar awareness by using the opportunity of a supposedly
neutral example to bridge the two modes, allegorizing the conversion of
his audience by the power of the poet's words.

Orpheus is both a locus classicus for definitions of *integumentum*, of
allegoria in verbis, and a medieval type for Christ; in other words, he is
an important bridge between the two modes of allegory.[50] Dante's stress
on the literal asks that we restore the sense of wonder to events that
Aquinas had rationalized into an allegory of rhetoric moving men with
hearts of stone, but at the same time that we retain the allegorical sense.[51]
With his poetry, Orpheus affects not only the standard human audience
but wild beasts; he controls the world of words and the world of things,
causing trees and rocks to move. At the same time, on the allegorical level,
Dante extends this control beyond Aquinas's "proper" use of rhetoric and
into conversion: the descending poet provides "scienza e arte" and teaches
reasoning to those who were as stone. Not only does Dante render his
allegoria in verbis as an allegory describing the poet's conversion of his
audience, but he maintains strict similitude between literal and figurative
levels while doing so. If the literal level is mythic, each element in that

---

[50] For Orpheus in examples of *integumenta* in Bernard and the other Chartrians, see
Pike 83–104. See also Pépin 1970, 109–10, where it is suggested that Dante may have
taken the example from Bernard, or from Cicero by way of Brunetto Latini. For the
typological identification of Orpheus with Christ, see Sarolli, 31–32.

[51] See Aquinas, *In Aristotelis Librum De Animo Commentarium*, 1, lect. 12 (*ad* 1,
5, 410*b* 28); quoted in Pépin 1970, 110.

myth nevertheless corresponds to a complex degree with each element of the allegorical level; it is equally possible, as Dante goes on to demonstrate, to draw out the meaning of the moral and the anagogic levels.

We can conclude that the Dantean distinction between allegory of poets and of theologians is more one of genre than of hierarchy. The former is composed of personifications acting out a narrative of conversion; the latter is composed of *figurae* in a fixed vision of history. The truth or falsity attributed to the literal level follows from the generic division and characterizes not so much the degree of separation between letter and allegory as the qualities of a connection based in one case on the analogies of a mythic narrative structure and in the other case on the temporal relationships in a figural and historical structure between past, Christ-event, present, and future. The "menzogna vera," the fiction of the *Commedia,* lies in the mediation implicit in the recapitulation of "what was" as "what I saw," in the act of representing and introducing a reader's guide to the absolutely true things of God's otherworld.

It is a wholly different issue that, formally, Dante is the author of God's text as well; as in the *Confessions,* a hidden effect of the allegory of conversion is to generate the authority necessary for that conceit to be taken as true, to focus all suspicion on the means of generating that authority and none on what the authority generated might then accomplish. This is the effect adapted by modernism and received on an exclusively formal level as the aesthetic work's representation of its self-creation. It is the effect Peter Weiss confronts within modernism when he separates full-fledged authority from the means of generating it, rendering the former in the *Notizbücher* and the latter in the *Ästhetik.*

It requires the descent through hell to teach the protagonist allegorical interpretation—for what else is it to teach an animal humility than to learn the act of glossing it allegorically and thus to take on the poet's role as the *Convivio* defined it? Humility appears in the *Commedia* as the reed with which the protagonist girds himself in *Purgatorio* 1; it is a basic lesson of the *Inferno.* As Freccero has noted, the *Inferno*'s first canto prefigures the same paradox of the *descensus,* and we see that Dante has defined it through the figure of Orpheus: it is a descent of humility and debasement but achieved through the pride of poetry. The canto begins with the moment of the protagonist's conversion as he climbs out of the dark wood, but it shows him unable to proceed further; he has not yet, as Orpheus had, learned how to sing humility into the leopard, lion, and wolf, the three beasts that block a direct ascent of the mountain. Hence the need for Vergil to appear and to teach him the science and art of wise men.

Vergil's lesson is paradoxical, for the protagonist learns how to read Vergil and the Vergilian tradition against the grain; that is, Dante sets up Vergil as the past against which his (hereby) newly constituted vision of the underworld can take form. My contention is that the fiction of Dante's poem is not so much—as Singleton famously suggested—that it is not a fiction, that Dante indeed saw God's afterlife in a vision, but rather, as with any descent to the underworld, that he died. The terms of the descent and the terms of the polarities with which Dante will thereby be playing are set by the interaction with and between the predecessors Vergil and Paul, pagan *katabases* and Christian otherworld visions.

The fault line is not, however, concerned with whether Odysseus descended or simply spoke with the dead from the border of Hades, or whether Aeneas's vision glorifies or critiques its imperial context. Here, the conversionary nadir of the descent can take on figural significance because the *Commedia*'s fiction is that the poet is speaking to us as a beatified soul, able to prophesy and render an *allegoria in facto* by virtue of knowing the mind of God, of existing with him outside temporality. As in the *Confessions*, if conversion can imitate the life of Christ, the meaning of one's life is revealed, fulfilled, because one has imitated his very death, resurrection, and ascension to God. This is the generic mechanism of the journey to the underworld as autobiographical allegory of conversion, the paradox whereby the autobiographical voice is authorized—and Dante's is perhaps its most ambitious and successful expression.

The complicated part of the fiction is that his death is not figured until Dante *leaves* hell and enters purgatory. This is the residue of *Aeneid* 6 as disseminated from Augustine through the Chartrians: hell is this life, imprisonment in the body. Dante may have a more dialectical view of the body, but hell remains the only realm to which he does not expect to return: he narrates a descent through it only to illuminate its figural meaning for us, so that we also may learn from it *without* having to experience it literally in the afterlife, that is, anagogically. This is one of the primary points of transference to the modernist descent: if still within a Christian framework, Dante's representation of the contemporary world as hell remains convincingly secular. Descent and conversion are thereby graspable as ontological categories; as predecessor, Dante makes his *Commedia* accessible enough to be rewritten as the religious model surpassed by the secular modernist.

Once we separate the narrative model of education in reading the underworld from the visionary and apocalyptic model of what is actually signified by the things that are there, we may both clarify the interaction of classical and Christian within the poem and observe more precisely those elements that were explicitly taken over by modernism as a model for education in aesthetic vision. On the one hand, we have the doctrinal (according to Dante) interpretation of the souls encountered and their punishments, penances, or rewards: here the literal sense inheres solely in the historicity of the souls (as Dante, as God, chooses to present it); their sense as fulfilled *figurae* retains that same plastic historicity. They are a living text, like world history in Augustine's model, like God's book of creation: there is a fixed meaning attributable to each in the "divine" scheme of the afterlife, and that scheme is glossable according to the traditional four levels of the medieval distich traditionally attributed to Augustine of Dacia "Littera gesta docet, quid credas allegoria, / moralis quid agas, quo tendas anagogia [The letter teaches the deed, allegory what to believe, the moral how you must act, anagogy where it will lead]."

The exegesis of that text, however, is not presented discursively; rather, it is narrativized as the learning process undergone by Dante-protagonist in a personification allegory. The cruces of poesis of *Inferno* all refer to the poet's recapitulation of the journey and not to the text of the afterlife. The prologue scene, Medusa, Geryon—these, like all the staged *drama* in hell, are to be glossed not in a figural but in a poetic manner. That is, following the *Convivio,* we are not to concern ourselves with their literal veracity so much as with the similitude of that literal sense with the allegorical sense of interpretation: the spirit-and-letter problem derives from the iconography of the Medusa, the question of the fraudulence of poetic language from Geryon's construction out of images and texts of fraud. This need in no way be a reductive form of interpretation: what it does do —and this is its fictivity, its *menzogna*—is to collapse a wildly incompatible range of literal senses into a single level of narrative.

On the literal level "Geryon," with its face of a just man, body of a serpent, paws of a beast, and tail of a scorpion, is not a historical "monster"; it is simultaneously a fantasy (a fraudulent "invention") *and* an amalgam of textual references to the "poetic fictions" of Vergil and Ovid; it is a mythological beast, composed of parts each of which is susceptible to a moralizing allegory of Fraud but also emblem of the problematics of classical poetry in a representation of God's creation of the afterlife. Geryon, like Medusa, like the three beasts of the first canto, conflates classical myth, Christian doctrine, literary criticism, and exegetical terminology as literal meanings of creatures whose encounters with the protagonist stage a set of simultaneously interpretive and narrative conflicts. What might elsewhere be spun out as a series of possible interpretations in a discursive exegesis is instead concentrated into a volatile and tension-ridden personification that must before all else be interpreted according to its role in the dynamics of the journey narrative.

If we extend this distinction to personages from the historical or mythic

past such as Vergil, we find that, contrary to Auerbach's influential reading, the historical Vergil, revealed in his significance as *figura* in the scheme
of God's justice, is clearly present only when the character Vergil takes his
place with the great poets of antiquity in *Inferno* 4.[52] In the allegory of
conversion, Vergil's role is a far more complex amalgam of the knowledge
that was attributed to the historical Vergil, from Stoic philosophy and
cosmology to the contents of his and his predecessors' poetry; of the Vergil
of medieval legend famed for his powers of magic and prophecy; and of a
more autobiographical Vergil, a figure in whom Dante invests a meditation on the allure, the heights, and the restrictions of classical pagan poetry
and poetic fictions within the framework of a representation of sacred
history.[53] Vergil's importance to the narrative of the first two canticles
testifies to the centrality of these issues (as compared to what is rendered
thereby as the rather more straightforward role of Paul). But this is not
a static emblem: it dramatizes the constellation through the narrative
conflicts it confronts within the Christian framework of the poem's
conception.

To call Vergil Reason in this allegory of conversion would not be incorrect; it is time, however, to acknowledge that Dante displays in his conception of Vergil a far more fluid and complex conception of Reason than
many allegorical readings of the *Commedia* have attested. Barolini has
demonstrated the subtlety and suppleness of the characterization of Vergil
and what he may signify; I propose that we also consider how that subtlety
was incorporated by Dante within the literal level of a personification of
Reason within a narrative allegory.[54] The relation is distinct from the use
Dante makes of Vergil as an author; after all, he uses sources such as
Ovid, Statius, or Lucan with nearly as much frequency as Vergil, but they
do not enter into the narrative allegory the same way.[55] There is a literary

[52] Needless to say, the fact that the pilgrim joins the five is not part of God's justice
of hell, since we are told at various times he has been saved. This episode belongs,
fittingly, to the allegory of poets and is to be interpreted along those lines. On this level,
the poets are equal in the use Dante makes of them textually.

[53] As Domenico Comparetti has documented, Vergil's medieval attributes ranged
from being the model of poetic and rhetorical skill to being the prophet of Christ and
fount of all wisdom to being a skilled magician (*Virgilio nel medio evo* [Florence,
1896]; trans. E. F. M. Beinecke, *Vergil in the Middle Ages*, 2d ed. [1903; rpt. Hamden,
1966]).

[54] Teodolinda Barolini, *Dante's Poets: Textuality and Truth in the "Comedy"*
(Princeton, 1984).

[55] The cases of Lucan and Ovid are clearcut; Statius, in his status as a saved pagan
convert, enters the narrative explicitly as a subsidiary of the Vergil-Paul problematic
and thus is himself a personification, and is dealt with below.

polemic woven into the allegory here analogous to the one staged in encounters with poets of the vernacular tradition Dante reconstructed by virtue of his descent into hell.[56] The classical tradition is being redefined through the selection of Vergil as its embodiment, as well as through the qualities attributed to Vergil by Dante.

As we have seen, the selection goes with the choice to render a narrative *descensus ad inferos*. The ongoing crux of Vergil places his figure within a field of tensions newly redefined by the descent of the *Commedia*. This is the flexibility of personification allegory: Vergil as medieval summa of knowledge and the resonances of the *Aeneid* as text are conflated within a single, concrete, and plastically rendered figure, able to act dynamically within a narrative structure. It is an effect impossible to any other literary device. The protagonist's growing attachment to the Vergil of the *Commedia* thus has nothing to do with the historical character of the Roman poet, as figural readings from Auerbach onward maintain. Rather, it implicates this personification as an integral element of conversion; it posits an inseparability of Vergil and Paul that is simultaneously an act of literary criticism and an assertion of life experience.

This is not, again, a historically true Vergil; in that it is a concrete rendering of diverse phenomena, experiences, texts, and abstract concepts as a single, dynamic character, it must be a fiction. Nevertheless, the literal meaning remains vital to the interpretation; for, in terms of similitude—its resemblance to the allegorical meaning this constellation has for the character of Dante and for our interpretation of it—it *is indeed* perfectly true. As Weiss would put it, it is authentic as dreams are authentic. We are in the province of personification allegory, the allegory poets use; it does not directly represent history and so its literal sense is not "true." It translates abstract concepts and moments lacking evident temporality into dramatic narrative. The most central of these concepts is the dyad of Vergil and Paul, classical pagan and doctrinal Christian; the dramatic narrative is the descent to the underworld, and the difficult return. We find it epitomized in key moments of each text: Vergil's twin gates of sleep and the Pauline *raptus* into paradise:

> Twin gates of Sleep there are, whereof the one is made of horn, and thereby an easy outlet is given to true shades; the other gleaming with the sheen of polished ivory, but false are the dreams sent by the spirits to the world above. There then with these words Anchises attends both his son and the Sibyl, and dismisses them by the ivory gate. (*Aen.* 6.893–98)

---

[56] See Barolini 1984, 85–187, for the effects of staged encounters with Dante's lyric predecessors on the subsequent construction of the literary canon.

It is not expedient for me doubtless to glory. I will come to visions and
revelations of the Lord. . . . And I knew such a man (whether in the
body or out of the body, I cannot tell: God knoweth;) How that he was
caught up into paradise, and heard unspeakable words, which it is not
lawful for a man to utter. Of such an one will I glory: yet of myself will
I not glory, but in mine infirmities. (2 Cor. 12:1–5)

Through the ivory gate comes the mythic Dante dear to secular modernists, the one so crucial to the many attempts to incorporate contemporary
philosophies, theories, and psychologies into fictional frames. Hence the
preponderance of Dantean imagery and infernal journeys from the romantics to Dostoyevsky, Rilke, Pound, Eliot, Proust, Broch, and Mann, to
name some of the more canonical.[57] This Dante is inseparable from the
Pauline vision of the Christian Dante, but the two are not necessarily
indistinguishable; modernism and its reception have tended to distinguish
falsely and to separate accordingly. Céline, Woolf, and Benjamin suggest
possible means of tracing and accounting for the effects of such distinctions; Weiss has shown the necessity of such a shift in modes of reading
for a postwar writer. He raises as well the desirability of attempting anew
to observe the distinction and inseparability of the two strands in the
Commedia itself, both to demonstrate the power of such a structure and
to dramatize its drawbacks.

I WANT NOW to return to the cantos under discussion, *Inferno* 14 and
Purgatorio 1, in order to show what can be gained from viewing the
Commedia as structured around two distinct modes of allegory, both in
terms of the poem's cruces of interpretation, the poles of Vergil and Paul,
and in terms of its modern reception. It is now possible to take full account
of the constellation of issues Dante incorporates into the narrative crux of
Vergil's damnation and Cato's salvation. Not only do we find an analysis
of the place of Reason, classical culture, and poetry within a Christian
sphere, but we discover an implicit argument for the necessity to consider
them of a piece. That is, any element that comes within the aegis of
Vergil's character must consequently be included within the thematic interpretation of his damnation.

   We can observe this principle at work as we consider the key figures of
Inferno 14, Capaneus and the Old Man of Crete, in relation to the Vergil-
Paul tension. If Capaneus is fixed by his fulfillment as *figura*, he remains
fluid insomuch as he participates in the narrative of Dante's journey. Any

---

[57] See also Menocal's reading of Eliot's and Pound's dance with Dante (89–129),
and Knowles's study of purgatorial imagery in literature of World War II.

complete separation of the two strands is, of course, impossible; the absolute *figura* of Capaneus exists only in the ideal, not in the represented form of Dante's creation of God's afterlife. It is rather like reading a text of exegesis of a part of Scripture of which we can have no other knowledge. The Capaneus episode may theoretically be divided along these lines into the two parts of his presentation: 46–66 and 67–72. Even the manner in which Capaneus breaks into the conversation of Dante and Vergil, however, as well as the uncharacteristic forcefulness of the guide's response, may be interpreted as part of the allegory of conversion.[58] Insofar as it gestures to the reading of the sacred text, Vergil's admonishment of Capaneus serves to gloss the sin of blasphemy as pride (we may also read into it a classical parallel to Lucifer, something the pagan Vergil does not seem to notice). Vergil's subsequent explanation to the protagonist (68–72) also has elements of the exegesis in it, giving more background on the "historical" Capaneus, revealed in the moment of his blasphemy and death on the ramparts of Thebes as a figure of Lucifer.

At the same time, Vergil's interaction with Capaneus sets up a dialogue on classical pagan poetry within the narrative allegory of conversion, laying the groundwork for questions of classical versus Christian that will be raised more directly in *Purgatorio*. One of Vergil's functions in the *Commedia* is to voice reasonable doubts and to give reasonable explanations for them; bringing to our attention Capaneus's identity as a king out of classical myth (drawn by Dante from Statius's *Thebaid*), Vergil's explanation provides the opportunity to remark that in fact Capaneus is the first such soul with which they have interacted. The focus of the novelty, the blasphemy at Jove translated into blasphemy toward God, is contextualized with the questions of poetic tradition raised by Vergil's gloss of Capaneus through his successor Statius. Vergil's mode, the allegory of conversion, addresses theological questions raised by Capaneus's appearance in the afterlife by first subtly underlining and then translating them into questions of poetry.

Blasphemy, especially understood as pride, is shown to be a sin endemic to classical poetry, particularly, as we will see, that of the Golden Age: Vergil and Ovid. Vergil-guide's pride lies in the extent of his knowledge,

---

[58] "E quel medesmo, che si fu accorto / ch'io domandava il mio duca di lui, / gridò: 'Qual io fui vivo, tal son morto. . . .' / Allora il duca mio parlò di forza / tanto, ch'i' non l'avea sì forte udito: / 'O Capaneo, in ciò che non s'ammorza / la tua superbia, se' tu più punito' " (And that same one, who had perceived that I was asking my leader about him, cried out, "What I was living, that am I dead. . . ." Then my leader spoke with such force as I had not heard him use before. "O Capaneus! in that your pride remains unquenched you are punished the more" [14.49–51, 61–64]).

the status of his *Aeneid* as a source book not only for the history of the
Roman empire but for philosophy, theology, and even destiny.[59] In the
end, however, Dante's condemnation of Vergil is neither more nor less
categorical than Augustine's in the *Confessions*. Both condemn as rational
Christians only to redeem and incorporate irrationally: Dante allegorizes
into the narrative of the *Commedia* (in the form of the tension between
God's justice and his difficulty in accepting it) the same movement
whereby Augustine was able to bring the structure of the *Aeneid* into
the Christian autobiography of conversion while still dismissing it out of
hand.

The limits of vision of Dante's Vergil are those of reason and those of a
pagan, unable to encompass God's vision. In a tour de force of narrative
allegory, each of Vergil's failures also works to trope each moment when
Dante's imagination exceeds what is acceptable—including all of *Paradiso*
—as a moment in which any saved person would be able to follow. In
other words, Dante tropes his assumption of divine authority as a test not
of *his* status (and authority) but of ours: if we are converted, we will be
able to follow (i.e., we will accept the conceit); if not, like Vergil, we will
remain behind.

It is important to remember here that the allegory is concerned not with
the damnation of the historical Vergil but with the role of Reason—and
more specifically the role of classical culture as embodied by Vergil and as
the pinnacle attained by Reason—in the conversion experience and the
vision of the ineffable. Vergil's speeches are our source for nearly all
the data of Dante's cosmos: it is Vergil who outlines the geography, the
topography, the astronomy, and the physics of hell and purgatory (although he needs more assistance in the latter realm). It is significant that
Dante places this information under the aegis of the allegorical figure of
Vergil, not necessarily because he wants thereby to cast it into doubt but
because it is that part of the afterlife which may be known unproblematically (i.e., without danger and without salvation) by the uninitiated, even by
a virtuous pagan, by Reason, by classical culture. When Dante addresses
the ones in "piccioletta barca, / desiderosi d'ascoltar" (in little barks, eager
to hear [*Par.* 2.1–2]) at the beginning of his ascent to the heavens, he is
addressing not only his readers but his Reason, his Vergil. Desire, as Vergil
almost bitterly expresses it in *Purgatorio* 3, is the condition of the virtuous
pagans damned in Limbo; it is the condition of rationality, the condition

[59] See Comparetti's discussion of the *sortes Vergilianae* (47–49), also discussed by
Augustine in the *Confessions* (4.3.5) and adapted by him to Scripture in the "tolle lege"
scene (8.12).

of life on this earth. Hence, the poet tells us, it is not those "desiderosi d'ascoltar" who will be able to follow, but those already converted, those who have moved from desire to faith, who are dead to this world.

This is also the substance of the lesson of humility given so sharply by Cato to Vergil in *Purgatorio* 1, the lesson of one virtuous pagan to another. Indeed, the reaction of Cato may strike the reader as nearly as irrational as so many have taken Dante's salvation of him in the first place to have been. It is clear from *Inferno* 14, however, that Vergil could never take Cato's place: after glossing Capaneus, he warns the protagonist to follow behind and not to set foot on the burning sand but to trace the edge of the woods (14.73–75). It is Cato's uprightness crossing the desert that carried him out of Dante's wood of the suicides, an uprightness that is the righteous equivalent of the superhuman pride of Capaneus (and of the Giants to whom he refers) and serves Dante to underline the extra-rationality of God's justice and mercy. If one of Vergil's roles is to dramatize the rationally permitted limits of Dante's art, then Cato demarcates the boundaries of this reading in *Inferno* 14 and *Purgatorio* 1.

Certainly, Vergil's instructions read as an injunction to steer clear of pride and blasphemy, yet his words seem unwittingly to imply that the poet nevertheless, like Cato, will have to pass through the desert, to descend to the underworld and return. In good *descensus* tradition, Vergil is the predecessor who is mortified into the mythic symbol of everything the current poet will surpass as history. Vergil's descent is no longer a viable model, as we discover when the souls arrive on the shore of Mount Purgatory, singing the psalm of survival in the desert, "In exitu Israel." Dante uses Vergil and *allegoria in verbis* to signify his transcendence of that model: "In exitu Israel" is the example in the *Convivio* and the Epistle to Can Grande of the mode of *allegoria in facto*. Quilligan has noted that Dante makes the literal sense of these souls equivalent to the anagogical: both signify entering into a state of grace (1992, 102–3). I would go further: they sing of their transition from literal to figural, of their revelation as *figurae*; in the drama of Dante's allegory of conversion *in verbis*, they personify the *allegoria in facto*.

The angel guiding the boat is the first of many purgatorial agents of God's *arte*; his journey and means of propulsion are those to which Dante aspires but is (according to his conceit and according to tradition) unable to achieve:

> Vedi che sdegna li argomenti umani,
> sì che remo non vuol, né altro velo
> che l'ali sue, tra liti sì lontani.

> Vedi come l'ha dritte verso 'l cielo,
> trattando l'aere con l'etterne penne.
>
> (2.31–35)

Look how he scorns all human instruments, and will have no oar, nor other sail than his own wings between such distant shores; see how he holds them straight toward heaven, fanning the air with his eternal feathers.

The wings/oars imagery goes directly back to the counterimage of Ulysses (not to mention the impotent flapping of Lucifer's wings in *Inf.* 34), but I focus here on the posture of the angel: it disdains human "argomenti"— and the double meaning of words and things could not be stronger here— and it stands, holding its wings "dritte verso 'l cielo." This is the lexicon of *Inferno* 14, of Cato and Capaneus: the translation of souls from history to *figurae* may only, it seems, be achieved by disdain for human means, by transgressing the desert.[60]

It is Vergil who describes the purgatorial scene to the protagonist: he is perfectly aware and rationally acceptant of the limits he may not transgress; he is unaware that Dante-poet will indeed have to go beyond them. It is Vergil also who in *Inferno* 14 tells the protagonist of yet another desert, the one on which stands the *veglio* of Crete.

> In mezzo mar siede un paese guasto
> . . . che s'appella Creta,
> sotto 'l cui rege fu già 'l mondo casto.
>   Una montagna v'è che già fu lieta
> d'acqua e di fronde, che si chiamò Ida;
> or è diserta come cosa vieta.
>
> (94–99)

[60] Although I accept Mazzotta's reading of exilic resonance in the Dantean image of the desert ("The desert marks our estrangement from the world and is the perspective from which we can question the very language we use, the falsifications and ambiguities that language harbors" [12]), I prefer to stress not Dante's consciousness of the ambiguity of language but his manipulation of its transgressive qualities, his play on the literal sense: desert is exile not less from meaning than in this life, and in *allegoria in verbis*. Like Augustine, Dante chooses to descend into the classics and exudes confidence in his ability to control the transgressive status of that descent. He seems less worried about whether he is able to control his poetic means than whether he is permitted to, and indeed less worried about permission than about manipulating the imagery of transgression itself as a poetic device.

In the middle of the sea there lies a wasted country that is named Crete, under whose king the world once was chaste. A mountain is there, called Ida, which once was glad with waters and with foliage; now it is deserted like a thing outworn.

This is another Mount Purgatory, but *in malo,* without the angel's wings, without the *fronde* of the reed and the "miglior acque" (better waters). It contains its image in the memory of the lost earthly paradise, when the world was once chaste. It is the birthplace of Jupiter, the god blasphemed by Capaneus and the god who signaled the end of the Golden Age by usurping his father's place. But if the shores of purgatory are deserted because they have not seen any man navigate them who had hope of return, the shores of Crete are deserted because they have: both Aeneas and Paul passed through here.

For the classical pagan and for the Christian voyager, Crete was a midpoint, a transitional stage in their journeys from old world to new: from Troy and Jerusalem, respectively, to the common goal of Rome.[61] The meaning for each was different, however. For Aeneas—and it is from *Aeneid* 3 that much of the geography of the description above is taken— Crete was the intended destination because of Anchises' misreading of Apollo's prophecy, "Long-suffering sons of Dardanus, the land which bare you first from your parent stock shall welcome you back to her fruitful bosom. Seek out your ancient mother. There the house of Aeneas shall lord it over all lands, even his children's children and their race that shall be born of them" (3.94–98). Crete, greeted with joy, and the new city quickly built and nostalgically called Pergamum, returns only plague to the Trojans; they discover belatedly that they have misread the oracle and must seek their *other* ancient mother, the one in Latium.[62] The false start and false journey arise from failure to detect an ambiguity in reference and from eagerness to be on one's way. For Paul, in contrast, Crete was simply a stopping point directly along his divine mission to Rome. God would preserve him and his men from the storms, although the ship would be lost: "For there stood by me this night the angel of God, whose I am, and whom I serve, Saying, Fear not, Paul: thou must be brought

---

[61] Charles Grandgent outlines the reading of the missed meeting of Empire and Cross in his edition of the *Commedia* (1933, rev. ed. Singleton, Cambridge, Mass., 1972), 126.

[62] The imagery of the plague (*Aen.* 3.137–39) finds its way into Dante's conception of a ruined Crete in the imagery of the "paese guasto" (Singleton 1980–82, 1.2.240).

before Caesar: and, lo, God hath given thee all them that sail with thee" (Acts 27:23–24). The question is not one of interpretation but one of the necessity of faith and obedience: woe to the centurion, who "believed the master and the owner of the ship, more than those things which were spoken by Paul" (Acts 27:11). The Apostle's destination, ability to reach it, and even the safety of those with him are never in doubt.

Needless to say, neither of these is the journey for which Dante borrows the names of Aeneas and Paul in *Inferno* 2; both are at earlier stages along the way to their becoming figures of empire and church, respectively. The poet's reminder of Aeneas and Paul in *Inferno* 14 finds him also at a crossroads in the consideration of pagan and Christian models of the *Commedia,* although the implicit distinction between Aeneas's cul-de-sac of misinterpretation and Paul's teleological path is already evident. But, still in transition, Dante has not brought his allegory of conversion to the hybrid synthesis evident in *Purgatorio* and consummated in the transition from Vergil to Beatrice.[63]

The crossing of narrative paths on the blasted Mount Ida gives a context for the other figure of *Inferno* 14, the "gran veglio," who stands "dritto" within it, his back turned toward Damietta, his gaze fixed on Rome as if in "süo speglio" (103–5). William Anderson has noted the situation of Crete midway on pilgrimage routes between Rome and Sinai and passing through Damietta.[64] Weighed down by his clay foot, the *veglio* is stalled midway on pilgrimage, his gaze fixed on his goal of the "eternal Rome":

[63] Evidence of the synthesis can be seen in the final return of Aenean imagery when the converted pilgrim's reunion with his ancestor Cacciaguida in the sphere of Mars is compared with Aeneas's reunion with his father in the Elysian Fields: "Sì pïa l'ombra d'Anchise si porse, / se fede merta nostra maggior musa, / quando in Eliso del figlio s'accorse" (With like affection did the shade of Anchises stretch forward (if our greatest Muse merits belief), when in Elysium he perceived his son [*Par.* 15.25–27]). Dante figures precisely the meeting with the father in paradise that Bernard would not permit himself in his commentary. Paul, in contrast, returns in name for the first time since *Inf.* 2, in four references (18.131, 21.127, 24.62, 28.138), twice as an early convert, twice explicitly as an author, the dual character of voice of God and limit case of expression resolved into one of licit expression of divine knowledge: in the "orals" the converted pilgrim takes in *Par.* 24, he refers his examiners to Paul (24.61–63); Beatrice concludes her list of the angels of the Primum Mobile by referring to the *raptus* of Paul to which Dante alluded to begin the canticle (1.73–75; 28.136–39).

[64] William Anderson, *Dante the Maker* (London, 1980), 290–94.

La sua testa è di fin oro formata,
e puro argento son le braccia e 'l petto,
poi è di rame infino a la forcata;
    da indi in giuso è tutto ferro eletto,
salvo che 'l destro piede è terra cotta;
e sta 'n su quel, più che 'n su l'altro, eretto.
    Ciascuna parte, fuor che l'oro, è rotta
d'una fessura che lagrime goccia,
le quali, accolte, fóran quella grotta.

(106–14)

His head is fashioned of fine gold, his arms and breast are pure silver, then down to the fork he is of brass, and down from there all is of choice iron, except that the right foot is baked clay, and he rests more on this than on the other. Each part except the gold is cracked with a fissure down which drip tears, which, when gathered, pierce through that cavern.

Just as it stands at the crossing of the paths of Aeneas and Paul, so is the *veglio* composed of classical and biblical sources—a hybrid of Ovid's four ages and Daniel's dream of Nebuchadnezzar (Dan. 2:31–35). The basic moral interpretation of the *veglio* as a symbol of human pride seems clear and is generally agreed on.[65] It provides the common ground for further interpretation.

We have three figures in the desert, all related to the problematic of pride and humility: the classical, pagan, upright, and redeemed Cato (pres-

---

[65] See Mazzotta's discussion and bibliography (14–37). Mazzotta's analysis of the image and comparison of it with *Purg.* 1 are informative but suffer from a peculiar version of the secularization of Dante's poem. Mazzotta adapts the historiographic concept of figuralism to the region of literary history and transposes the methods of patristic hermeneutics into secular literature. In other words, he presents problems of secular literature from within the framework of Christian allegory, as, for example, in the conclusion to the chapter on Cato and the *veglio:* "The episode of Cato is, in effect, a rewriting, a revision of the same metaphors of nature and history in *Inferno* XIV. Literary revision, for Dante, attempts to give a mimetic representation of the redemption of history, and by what might be called the figural openness of Dante's poetic language attempts to disclose history's quest for an *eschaton,* the silence of the end where history's meaning comes into being. But ironically, at the very moment of the palinode the text fleetingly alludes to its own possible poetic snares" (65). By denying that literature and theology—*allegoria in verbis* and *in facto*—can coexist, interact, and yet remain distinct within the poem, Mazzotta appears to me to elide the most important theological issues raised by Dante's poem—which are, without being identical or any less theological, the most important formal issues also.

ent by conspicuous absence); the classical, pagan, supine, and damned Capaneus; and the hybrid *veglio,* upright but split apart. Several points should be noted. First, the allegory of pride is derived solely from the Christian source of Daniel; Ovid's conception, as Grandgent and Anderson note, is cyclical. Second, we have a hybrid in terms of allegorical modes as well: whereas Vergil's descriptions of the mechanics of the otherworld are otherwise fairly discursive in form, we find here a full-fledged verbal allegory masquerading as an explanation of the hydraulics of God's system of hell. This is the third element of the hybrid: Dante combines classical and biblical images into a source of the rivers of hell. It is certainly the most poetical-sounding of the allegories that Dante will attempt to pass off as part of God's construction; moreover, it is perhaps unique in the *Inferno* in that he has Vergil locate it not in hell but on Crete—a Crete, however, which it seems difficult to imagine anyone believing existed in 1300. As an allegory of the state of Christendom, as an allegory of the state of Dante's poem—midway between East and West, pagan and Christian—it works perfectly as long as we do not attempt a figural interpretation.

But if we question the status of this image further, we find that no one claims to have seen it, not even Vergil. Indeed, Crete is the *Inferno*'s locus for sinful inventions and hybrids, for the transgressive *arte* of Daedalus— the bull of Pasiphae (12.12) and the flight of himself and Icarus (17.109–11)—not to mention the guardians Minos (whom Dante charges with the poetically central function of assigning each soul its proper circle) and the Minotaur. It would be unreasonable to accuse Vergil of sinful invention. We may, however, accuse him of passing on information dwelling solely in the realm of sinful invention: of Dante's fabrications, the *veglio* carries with it perhaps the least amount of rhetorical markers and the greatest amount of purely pre-Christian intertext. In other words, Vergil's reason is assimilated to the strand of sinful invention; at the same time, sinful invention thereby passes as a primary feature of God's construction of hell.

Needless to say, this is a key to understanding Dante's allegorization of the roles of God and man, *allegoria in facto* and *in verbis,* in the creation of hell. The dynamics of the narrative allegory guide us to an interpretation. The protagonist responds not in the slightest to his guide's elaborate allegory; he merely inquires logically where the other two rivers (Phlegethon and Lethe) might be. One, Vergil answers, is where the protagonist is at that moment, and the other, "Letè vedrai, ma fuor di questa fossa, / là dove vanno l'anime a lavarsi / quando la colpa pentuta è rimossa" (Lethe you shall see, but out of this abyss, there where the souls go to wash themselves, when the fault repented of has been removed [136–38]). This is intriguing: directly after he has recounted an utterly fanciful

allegory, Vergil apparently shows himself to be prophet of the protagonist's salvation and to know the entire layout of purgatory.

Where does he obtain such information? Speculation in search of "the
truth" is evidently pointless; nevertheless, Dante has chosen to create a
situation in which the question logically arises. We should then assume
that a clue to the answer lies within the province of reason, within, that is,
the text of the poem before us. We are being reminded, I think, first of all,
of how close classical pagan literature was to Christian cosmology (and to
Dante's conception of it); indeed, the description of Lethe, and even a
certain conception of purgatory, are drawn from *Aeneid* 6. Vergil does
not mention where in purgatory Lethe is; he simply knows (or *his* poem
does) that it is in the Elysian Fields and not in Tartarus. He also knows
that "Lethaei ad fluminis undam / securos latices et longa oblivia potant"
(At the waters of Lethe's streams they drink the soothing draught and long
forgetfulness [*Aen.* 6.714–15]), and that it is part of the process whereby
souls not damned to the other parts of the underworld are cleansed of
their sins and sent back up to earth (6.741–42).

In other words, *Aeneid* 6 is the likeliest source for Vergil's explanation
to Dante about Lethe—in the sense of what Vergil represents in Dante's
autobiographical allegory of conversion—and hence also a major source
of the eventual representation of Lethe in the earthly paradise. But between Vergil's version and the conception Dante will give in *Purgatorio*
28, the cyclical conception of the afterlife, part also of the hybrid nature
of the *veglio*, will be left behind. Just as the *veglio*'s faulty pre-Christian
hybridity will be eclipsed by the prophetic chariot hybrid of Ezekiel and
John, old and new, so will Vergil be eclipsed by Beatrice while his underworld conceptions remain, but within a purely eschatological structure.

I do not recall cantos 28 and 29 of *Purgatorio* gratuitously here; Vergil
remains on the scene there just long enough to hear his conception of the
river corrected by Matelda. Our and the protagonist's penultimate view of
the poet is a final reminder both of his achievements and of his principal
failure: to conceptualize paradise.[66] Matelda tells Vergil, Statius, and Dante:

---

[66] The final view stresses only his incomprehension, his "stupor." After the first
appearance of the procession of the books of the Bible in the earthly paradise, "Io mi
rivolsi d'ammirazion pieno / al buon Virgilio, ed esso mi rispuose / con vista carca di
stupor non meno" (I turned round full of wonder to the good Vergil, and he answered
me with a look no less charged with amazement [29.55–57]). Reason, paganism, and
classical culture have been completely overwhelmed. See the readings of the complex
series of intertextual references to Vergil in the essays by Michael C. J. Putnam, Peter
S. Hawkins, Rachel Jacoff, and Jeffrey T. Schnapp in *The Poetry of Allusion: Virgil
and Ovid in Dante's "Commedia,"* ed. Jacoff and Schnapp (Stanford, 1991), 94–156.

"Quelli ch'anticamente poetaro
l'età de l'oro e suo stato felice,
forse in Parnaso esto loco sognaro.
    Qui fu innocente l'umana radice. . . ."
    Io mi rivolsi 'n dietro allora tutto
a' miei poeti, e vidi che con riso
udito avëan l'ultimo costrutto;
    poi a la bella donna torna' il viso.
                    (28.139–48)

"They who in olden times sang of the Age of Gold and its happy state
perhaps in Parnassus dreamed of this place. Here the root of mankind
was innocent. . . ." I turned then right round to my poets, and saw that
with a smile they had heard those last words; then to the fair lady I
turned my face.

The affective Vergil remains to be missed after the procession and to be
immortalized as such in the *Commedia;* the poet Vergil is given his leave
here; reason is abandoned and preserved simultaneously. The final irony
perhaps is that it is the poets who sang of the Golden Age—Vergil and
Ovid—who remain forever in Dante's limbo, and the one who sang of
Capaneus and the Theban war who is saved. Like the *veglio* of Crete, they
are fixed and fallen even though their golden heads may remain intact.

   Inferno 14 thus runs through *Purgatorio* as far as the trajectory of
Vergil goes, as far as the allegory of conversion or the allegory of poets
remains an explicit issue. Dante begins the canto by alluding to his having
removed Cato, who would belong there; he concludes it by having Vergil
describe the removal of Lethe, which is in the underworld of *Aeneid* 6, to
the top of Mount Purgatory, where Vergil will never see it except as a
bitterly ironic token of his own destiny to return again to limbo without
drinking of it, damned thus to remember and to desire what he could
not explain. Lethe figures the moment of the protagonist's baptism, his
fulfillment as *figura;* Cato marks the moment the process begins: *Inferno*
14 brackets the entire narrative movement of *Purgatorio.* Dante plants
the trajectory of ascent within the narrative and imagery of descent; the
recognition of infernal transgression encodes the means of paradisal transgression.

   The double movement is encoded topographically as well, for the canto
takes place solely at the edge of the wood of the suicides: as it ends, Vergil expresses the same restriction evident at the start and midpoint of
the canto, telling the protagonist not to transgress: "Omai è tempo da
scostarsi / dal bosco; fa che di retro a me vegne: / li margini fan via, che

non son arsi, / e sopra loro ogne vapor si spegne" (Now it is time to quit
the wood; see that you come behind me: the margins, which are not
burning, form a path, and over them every flame is quenched [139–42]).
Wholly in transition between the wood and the burning plain, between
the violent against themselves and the violent against God, the canto is
itself bracketed by references to *Purgatorio* mirroring the protagonist's
entire climb, his progress out of the desert.

The canto equally encodes double movement onto the topographies of
hell and of purgatory: whereas the geography of the latter arose in response to the creation of hell—the mountain of earth repelled by the fall
of Lucifer's pride, excavating the abyss—the water systems are seen to be
disconnected. The origin of the infernal rivers in the *veglio*'s tears must be
regarded as a poetic allegory of mankind's response to the fall: the *veglio*
can only be a man in transition, a protagonist converted in mind but not
yet in body. It is an allegory Vergil can narrate but cannot see himself in
and whose significance he cannot fully comprehend: he synthesizes pre-
Christian myths into a novel allegory, but he lacks the *facta*, the Christian
perspective of *figura*.

A further analysis of Vergil's *veglio* reveals, within the context of the
poem as a whole, what he missed. First, if he were fixed in his pride like
Capaneus, the *veglio* would not weep, however blasted he might be; he is
instead fixed in the desert, eyes turned to Rome but his feet unable to
move him there, as the protagonist's feet support him unevenly in his
first attempt to approach the image of purgatory in canto 1. Unlike the
protagonist, who limps most in the left foot, the *affectus* or will, the *veglio*
rests more heavily on its most flawed limb, the right foot of terra-cotta,
or, following Freccero's gloss of *Inferno* 1, that of the intellect, which
suffered the wound of ignorance. The *veglio*'s physical state, representative of ignorance, and his mental state, weeping because desirous of what
he has lost, are also those of limbo, in which the souls of the virtuous
pagans are "sospesi," suspended by a *contrapasso* fashioned of their own
desire (*Inf.* 4.40–42).

Vergil's description precludes direct interpretation of the paradox of
being fixed in a transitional state, so Dante does not question it: the tears
are there to give rise to the rivers of hell. Dante's question does cause
Vergil explicitly to point out that the only pure river, Lethe, is not part of
the system of tears. The *veglio* is in a state of constant desire; otherwise it
would not weep. It is not a conscious weeping; the language stresses only
that the tears drip through the fissure. The head does not weep—it is
golden and pure; the weeping is thus an instinctual or bodily desire, and
an eternal one. We have seen that the *veglio* finds its fulfillment in the

other *veglio* of the poem, the figure of Cato on the shores of purgatory; it equally finds a parallel in its narrator (and apparent inventor), Vergil. Product of the Golden Age of Latin poetry—Ovid and Vergil—and of a prophet of the Old Testament, the *veglio* mourns the fall of the old while ignorant of the new: he gazes at the image of it as if in a mirror. The cleft, certainly, begins in the Silver Age, but it is from this age that Dante's saved Cato (out of Lucan) and saved poet Statius come: those who crossed the desert into purgatory, those whose poems are of civil war, of endings instead of beginnings.

Vergil displays his ignorance of this crossing in a minor slip that nevertheless will make all the difference. There is a curious omission in the description of the hydraulic system of hell: he makes it into a stagnant, clogged-up pool: "Infin, là dove più non si dismonta, / fanno Cocito; e qual sia quello stagno / tu lo vedrai, però non si conta" (Then their way is down by this narrow channel until, there where there is no more descending, they form Cocytus—and what that pool is, you shall see; here therefore I do not describe it [14.118–20]). This is as far as Vergil goes; as far as he knows, the tears have no further effect. Dante gives us no hint as to whether or not Vergil is aware of the opening at the base of Cocytus; he certainly does not mention it here where it would make sense to do so. Nor does he describe it once they have passed over Lucifer's torso; it is the narrator who tells us about the rivulet that has created a passage from the center of the earth—the depths to which mankind may descend— to the other side and the mountain of purgatory:

> Luogo è là giù da Belzebù remoto
> tanto quanto la tomba si distende,
> che non per vista, ma per suono è noto
> d'un ruscelleto che quivi discende
> per la buca d'un sasso, ch'elli ha roso,
> col corso ch'elli avvolge, e poco pende.
> (34.127–32)

Down there, from Beelzebub as far removed as his tomb extends, is a space not known by sight, but by the sound of a rivulet descending in it along the hollow of the rock which it has eaten out in its winding and gently sloping course.[67]

---

[67] There has been a modicum of critical discussion in the past over this element of the geography of hell. The main question is whether to read the "tomba" as a space extending from Beelzebub to just beneath the earth's crust (Grandgent, 308) or as a smaller space surrounding the Devil's feet (Michele Barbi, *Problemi di critica dantesca:*

Another and a truly liminal region: beyond Lucifer, beyond the place to which he has fallen ("tomba"), but not yet in purgatory; known not to sight but only by the sound of the stream trickling through it: this is the geographical equivalent of the sleight of hand whereby Dante reverses directions and gains twelve hours by crossing the center of gravity. Yet such sleight of hand and leap of the imagination are precisely what are lacking in Vergil's allegory of the *veglio* and explanation of the hydraulic system. We must pass beyond it and assume that, somehow, Lucifer's wings are not able to freeze every last tear of the *veglio* and that over the years this infinitesimal amount, trickling down his body just as Dante and Vergil will, has eroded a passage from hell to purgatory. This is the passage through which a soul that should be damned may yet escape beyond all reasonable assumptions; thus Cato characterizes it when he confronts Dante and Vergil in antepurgatory.

The damned certainly cannot escape this way; they have been fulfilled as figures already, they are fixed like Capaneus. The gloss must be sought in the narrative of conversion: it is the protagonist for whom the journey through hell is a reading of God's book, a conflation of texts and figures in his mind, who is able to use this exit. It is the way around God's restrictions, the way of escaping from hell, of reaching purgatory while still alive; unforeseen by Vergil, it is a way outside reasonable limits.[68] Vergil seems unaware: reasonably, there is no hope for him to be saved,

---

Prima serie (1893–1918) [Florence, 1934], 244–46; and Singleton, 1.2.643–44). The point of contention appears to miss the point of Dante's language: no matter the size of the *tomba*, there is a certain stretch of rock they are able to penetrate only because of the erosion caused by the rivulet. Singleton's attempt to dismiss the crux—"No allegory or symbolism seems to be implied in this; all is strictly within the literal dimension of the narrative. This is simply the way which they found, and which they took" (644)—merely indicates that a sufficient gloss has not yet been found. As for the question of the direction of the rivulet's descent discussed above (note 43), my argument depends not on proof but on the ambiguity of the sleight of hand that dominates the end of *Inf.* 34. That it cannot be decided if the rivulet descends from Lethe in the earthly paradise, sign of the end of purgatory, or if it descends from the erosion of the tears of the *veglio* is a fitting symbol of the nature of Christ (man/God) and of Dante's synthesis of allegory.

[68] It is in the lowest circle of hell, in Ptolomea, that Dante had stressed the other end of this irrationality by refusing the grace of repentance to Fra Alberigo and Branco d'Oria, damning them years before their deaths (33.118–47). He will do the opposite at the beginning of *Purgatorio*, saving Manfred, for example, because of last-minute repentance after a life of "horrible" sins (3.121–23). This is the context bracketing the transition from utter damnation to perfect grace, the apparent irrationality of God's justice and the instantaneous granting of his mercy.

nor for any fallen soul, a belief to which the *veglio*'s tears attest. But, as Dante shows at the end of this canticle and the beginning of the next, even the image of the *veglio* presented by Vergil as eternally fixed in its fallen state can be redeemed by the journey of conversion. Cato, unlike Vergil, seems perfectly aware of the route; it makes up his first words to the protagonist and his guide: "Chi siete voi che contro al cieco fiume / fuggita avete la pregione etterna?" (Who are you that, against the blind stream, have fled the eternal prison? [*Purg.* 1.40–41]).

Thus is a poetic allegory of the fallen state of man transformed into a blind stream leading directly to a state of grace. The *allegoria in verbis* converts itself into a figure of the *allegoria in facto*. There are two ways of reaching purgatory, as Cato knows well in his role in Dante's journey narrative. One is by the *arte* of God, directly to grace, as with Paul; the other is through the underworld, the *arte* of men, so fraught with paradox that only an *un*reasonable man would attempt it. One reason Cato is standing at the foot of the mountain of purgatory is to testify to this second route; he is the fulfillment of the figure of the *veglio* as an emblem of Dante's poem, transforming itself from mourning, fallen pride into rebuking, upright pride.

Dante's autobiography of conversion takes the embrace of paradox and irrationality (or faith) at the core of Augustine's *Confessions* and allegorizes his adaptation of it as the structural principle of a poetic allegory used to conjure into being the divine text of God's afterlife. The principle of conversion—accepting an authority greater than one's own, beyond reason, time, and conception, a mystery—is made one of narrative as well. If we are to be converted to God, we must be converted to belief in Dante's ability to represent him (and thus belief in the *facta* of the *Commedia*). A literary conversion, then, can storm the gates of paradise only by imagining such an action as movement in the opposite direction: only by descending into the underworld of classical pagan poetry are Augustine and Dante able to return at the same time to the heavens. The authority of the endeavor is figured solely by the mechanism of conversion: we believe them because they are with God; they are with God because we believe them. Dante's Vergil personifies in the end the doubting rationalist who would never believe it; consequently, we must leave Vergil (along with all the predecessors he embodies) behind and follow only Dante if we want to return to see the stars.

There is a modernist Dante—the *descensus ad superos*—but there is also a Dantean text that incorporates that modernist reading while simultaneously revealing its fault lines, staging an autocritique of its methods through the same autobiographical voice that generates its extratextual authority. The former, the embrace of irrationality in terms of a structure of descent so as to return, is recognizable in much of modernist theory and literature from Marx's embrace of crisis to Freud's method of free association and Proust's *mémoire involuntaire*. And if we step outside our modernist habits of reading, we can also begin to see the framework that stages the autocritique: it identifies itself with the descent, by its incorporation of the Dantean text and by its incorporation of the autobiographical voice. This is the reading of modernism and of Dante suggested by Peter Weiss; it is equally the position Christine de Pizan allegorizes for herself in the role of a poet constructing a post-Dantean descent; and it is also the position Christine makes visible in the purportedly high-modernist poetics of a writer such as Virginia Woolf.

4

The Gender of Descent

[Christine de Pizan] aspires to the upper regions where
the highest minds soar, but no sooner does she try to take
flight than she is dragged down by the heavy weight of
the barbarism and pedantry of her age.
—Arturo Farinelli, *Dante e la Francia* (1908)

She is merely the victim of her extraordinary gift of fancy
(not imagination). . . . Whereas a woman cannot walk
through a meadow in June without wandering all over
the place to pick attractive blossoms, a man can. Virginia
Woolf cannot resist the floral enticement.
—Arnold Bennett, "Queen of the High-Brows" (1929)

THE COINCIDENCES and accidents that connect Christine de Pizan and
Virginia Woolf, two writers unaware of each other's works, are of a
different order from those that convert Aeneas to a Christian and Dante
to a modernist, but perhaps even more striking. Both allegorize as a
change of sex the woman writer's difficulty in gaining authority and participating in a literary tradition; both stage seminal framing scenes around
the reading of misogynist texts. Both, moreover, structure their allegories
through the *descensus ad inferos*. The focus here, however, is not on the
hard return and accession to prophetic authority but on the impossibility
of any descent to start with. Christine and Woolf exploit the mechanism
of descent to explore the reasons for which they are excluded from it.
Christine exposes the *Commedia*'s tensions by polarizing the poem as the
monolithic authority she will then claim to be unable to equal. Woolf
performs a similar operation on a tradition she traces from Dante through
Shakespeare to her contemporaries Joyce and Eliot. The fortuitous affiliation between medieval and modern indeed demonstrates the synchronicity

of two women writers, but in a Marxian sense: both avail themselves of the autobiographical voice in the structure of the descent to dramatize metanarrative and metatextual questions. Just as they generate authority by claiming exclusion from it, so do they reveal the rhetorical status of self-deflating gestures in the past texts they have constructed as monolithic. The radical transformatory gesture—male to female or female to male— with which the descent is framed uncovers the radical conversion of the past rendered by every descent, whether figured as traditional or not; conversely, the Dantean antithesis should remind us that any overturning of tradition in such a context equally sets itself up as a rewritten alternative.

"O voi che siete in piccioletta barca": Christine de Pizan and the Topoi of Descent

O voi che siete in piccioletta barca,
desiderosi d'ascoltar, seguiti
dietro al mio legno ché cantando varca,
　　tornate a riveder li vostri liti:
non vi mettete in pelago, che forse,
perdendo me, rimarreste smarriti.
　　　　　　(*Paradiso* 2.1–6)

O you that are in your little bark, eager to hear, following behind my ship that singing makes her way, turn back to see again your shores. Do not commit yourselves to the open sea, for perchance, if you lost me, you would remain astray.

Writing approximately one hundred years after Dante, Christine de Pizan responded to his work in two ways. First, she constructed her oeuvre and its claim to authority around an autobiographical voice predicated on the experience of being left behind in a *piccioletta barca*. Like Bernard before her, she explicitly refused the authority to be derived from claiming divine inspiration. Second, whereas Bernard's rejection was philosophically motivated, Christine literalized the traditional topoi of authority. By grounding her experience not in her intellectual identity but in her physical being, Christine reworked the antinomies of the *descensus* as essentialism versus education, nature versus nurture. She was thereby able to use the discursive space of the *descensus* both to explore the social constraints of a professional woman writer and to generate a paradoxical authority out of those constraints.

The first experience of being left behind recorded by Christine is the reaction to the death of her husband, court notary under Charles VI, in 1390, when she was twenty-five. Her poetic vocation is shown to derive from an emotional as opposed to an intellectual stimulus: the first twenty poems of her first collection, *Cent Ballades,* are written in the persona of a mourning widow driven to poetry as a means of expressing her sorrow.[1] While always grounding her voice in experience, Christine uses the rhetorical force derived from it to support motifs of a different order altogether. Now, there is a clear analogy here with the impetus of Beatrice's death behind Dante's *Vita nuova;* etiological sorrow over loss is a common topos in lyric poetry. Christine, however, grounds the sorrow materialistically: certainly she *was* sorrowful, but it became ever more apparent that she was driven to express herself in poetry at least as much for economic reasons—she had an extended family to support and little fixed income—as for emotional ones. Widowhood could easily be adapted to the courtly lyric and was an important element of the novelty of Christine as a female poet to which she partly attributed the early success that helped keep her family solvent.

The connection between the literary representation and the material reality of widowhood remained fairly submerged as long as Christine stayed within the courtly tradition of her lyric poetry. It was when she moved into the more rarefied and restricted genres of allegory and historiography that she began exploring the connection through the themes of education, tradition, and literary authority. Not surprisingly, it is at this point also that the topoi of widowhood, poetry, and authority converge in imagery of descent. Counterposing her *piccioletta barca* to what she would figure as Dante's soaring authority to represent divine vision and to prophesy history, she generated a new and influential voice by stressing its very insufficiency.

Christine was a prolific writer; she tells Lady Philosophy in the *Avision-Christine* that between 1399 and 1405, the height of her career, she compiled fifteen principal volumes and seventy quires of minor works.[2] Her writings continued to incorporate moments figured as autobiographical; I focus here on her allegories, each of which is wholly framed by autobiographically voiced episodes.[3] Her husband's death continued to accrete

---

[1] *Oeuvres poétiques de Christine de Pisan,* ed. Maurice Roy, vol. 1 (Paris, 1886–96); hereafter cited by page number.

[2] *L'Avision-Christine,* ed. Mary Louise Towner (Washington, D.C., 1932), 164.

[3] I do not include the works of allegoresis, such as the *Epistre Othea,* which also address questions of interpretation, but not directly from within the compositional framework of descent. For a persuasive analysis of Christine's strategies in this work, see Sandra Hindman, *Christine de Pizan's "Epistre Othéa": Painting and Politics at the Court of Charles VI* (Toronto, 1985).

meaning as, in Weiss's terms, a *Nullpunkt,* a moment of conversion that both placed Christine within a Dantean tradition and problematized her affiliation with that tradition. The verse allegories, *Le Livre du Chemin de long estude* (The book of the path of long study) and *Le Livre de la Mutacion de Fortune* (both ca. 1403), which I discuss first, dramatize Christine's self-transformation into a figure of authority on both counts: widowhood fixed her identity as a woman by nature and experience but also forced (and freed) her to write as a man in a male *translatio studii,* or "transfer of authority."[4] Of the three prose allegories, *Le Livre de la Cité des Dames* (*The Book of the City of Ladies*), *Le Livre des Trois Vertus* (The Book of the Three Virtues), sometimes called *Le Trésor de la Cité des Dames*), and *L'Avision-Christine* (ca. 1405), I limit my analysis to the first.[5] The *Cité des Dames* provides a theoretical framework for the voice generated out of the *Chemin* and the *Mutacion,* manipulating the authority of the *translatio studii* and questioning its validity by recourse to a revised authority of experience.[6]

---

[4] *Translatio studii,* as Earl Jeffrey Richards succinctly puts it, is "the theme of the historical transfer of literary culture from Athens to Rome to France" (intro. to *The Book of the City of Ladies,* trans. Earl Jeffrey Richards [New York, 1982], xxvii). See Michelle Freeman, "Problems in Romance Composition: Ovid, Chrétien de Troyes, and the *Romance of the Rose,*" *Romance Philology* 30 (1976–77): 158–68. It is paralleled in the political sphere by the *translatio imperii,* the derivation of political authority from Rome (Ernst Robert Curtius, *European Literature in the Latin Middle Ages,* 1948, trans. Willard R. Trask [Princeton, 1973], 29) or from various Trojan ancestors to various medieval European nations (Hindman, 35). My understanding of it here, as of similar topoi of *auctoritas,* translation, and commentary seen in earlier chapters, is as a dynamic site where abstract concepts of genealogy, authority, and tradition are dramatized allegorically through extended metaphors of sailing a ship, descending to the underworld, or founding a city. As we shall see, *translatio* in Christine's hands functions like Dante's *Commedia,* dealing with textual and metaliterary issues inseparably from narrative ones.

[5] For an illuminating discussion of the use of allegory in the *Avision,* see Christine Reno's transcription and commentary of a glossatory preface to it ("The Preface to the *Avision-Christine* in ex-Phillips 128," in *Reinterpreting Christine de Pizan,* ed. Earl Jeffrey Richards [Athens, 1992], 207–27). Reno notes the broad influence of religious exegesis on the three levels of interpretation Christine suggests for the "parole couverte" of her book, while also stressing the political, as opposed to solely spiritual, thrust behind the allegory (220–21). As the following discussion of the development of Christine's authority through allegorical writing should demonstrate, the relation between the political intervention of historical allegory and the spiritual values of medieval exegesis is plotted through and mediated by the autobiographical voice.

[6] On various possibilities of dating the works, see Suzanne Solente's introduction to the *Mutacion de Fortune,* Maureen Curnow's to her edition of the *Cité des Dames* (1–

Christine derives three central topoi from the *translatio studii* in these texts: the ship, the descent, and the city. Although differently stressed in different texts, they are interconnected in the Vergilian tradition: Aeneas's voyage to Italy to found Rome. The sea voyage leads to the descent to the underworld, which results in the founding of a new city; each topos establishes the metaphorics of literary creation of the previous one. Like Dante and other medieval allegorists, Christine uses the topoi within an allegorical setting to translate metaliterary and metanarrative discussions into narrative structures. The topos of voyage matches generic issues to the story of her widowhood, especially the shift from lyric to epic poetry; the topos of descent affiliates the necessary authority for the venture with the issue of Christine's creation as an *auctor* through the writing of history; the topos of founding a city figures the goal of what is to be represented by positing the exemplary status of her achievement. Although Christine does not move through them in a strictly chronological fashion, each topos characterizes a particular grouping of her oeuvre, from the courtly lyrics to the verse allegories to the prose allegories.

When Christine introduces the image of the ship on the open sea in Ballade 13, it seems to be a simple metaphor for her widowhood:

C'est fort chose qu'une nef se conduise,
Es fortunes de mer, a tout par elle,
Sanz maronnier ou patron qui la duise,
Et le voile soit au vent qui ventelle;
Se sauvement a bon port tourne celle,
En verité c'est chose aventureuse;
Car trop griefment est la mer perilleuse.

(14)

It's quite something when a ship steers itself through the hazards of the sea, all on its own, without a sailor or captain to guide it, and when the sails are opened to the blowing wind; if it return safely to a good port that truly is an unusual occurrence; for the sea is too terribly perilous.

As in the other ballades of mourning, she presents herself here as desolate and without resources; the primary strength she allows herself is the depth of her grief, through which nothing can reach her. The persona, then, is

61), and Richards's to the translation (xxi-xxvi). The immediate question is less one of dating than of precedence. For my purposes, it is enough to group the *Chemin* and the *Mutacion* together on the one hand and the *Cité des Dames, Trois Vertus,* and *Avision* on the other.

one that is no match for the trials of fortune: "Car trop griefment est la mer perilleuse."

Later, in the *Avision* in 1405, Christine glosses the image in autobiographical terms: "Now it was necessary for me . . . to guide the boat left on a stormy sea and without a captain. That is to say the forsaken household far from its home and country" (154). Indeed, the practical way in which Christine took control of the ship on the open sea was by means of the ballades she began writing on the subject of that inability. Any tentativeness in her newly chosen profession was perfectly matched by the generic expectations of the lyric: as Ernst Robert Curtius has documented, the nautical metaphor was a commonplace for the composition of a work, and "the epic poet voyages over the open sea in a great ship, the lyric poet on a river in a small boat" (128). As a lyric poet, Christine could not portray herself in control of a ship on the open sea; as a woman, she *had* to be out of her depth.

Whether or not Christine was conscious in the ballade of the tradition of the metaphor, she certainly lends it such significance in retrospect: when she moves into allegory, she quite explicitly rewrites the meaning of her widowhood and of the sailing ship, shifting them to the context of gaining authority—the *descensus ad inferos*. In the lengthy autobiographical introduction to the allegorical description of the castle of Fortune that frames the twenty-three-thousand-verse world history of the *Mutacion*, Christine inverts the relationship between literary and autobiographical voice.[7] In the ballades the generic metaphorics underpinned the autobiographical; here, the experience (the firsthand knowledge of Fortune gained through the shipwreck it nearly drove her into) grounds the allegory of her authorization as historian. In other words, Christine justifies telling her story because it is through her experience that she has arrived at Fortune's court, but the intention is thereby to authorize her voice through literary, and not simply experiential, means.

Consequently, we find her life retold in allegorical terms. Her father, Tommaso di Benvenuto da Pizzano, who left Venice to become court astrologer to Charles V, represents learning; he brings it with him from Italy as the *translatio studii* Christine will inherit. He had wished for a son to carry on the tradition, but Christine's mother, Nature, prevailed in-

---

[7] *Le Livre de la Mutacion de Fortune*, ed. Suzanne Solente, 4 vols. (Paris, 1959–66); hereafter cited by verse number. The first 1,400 lines recount the transformation autobiographically; the next 2,800 describe the castle of Fortune from within the same context; in the subsequent 18,000 lines, the frame recedes to the background as Christine recounts world history from within its vantage point.

stead, and she was born a girl. Christine presents the dual form of her autobiographical voice, but paradoxically rendered: the historical figure of the father serves as an allegory of learning; the personification of Nature represents historical experience.[8] The female experience determines the course of the autobiographical narrative as personification allegory: Nature sends Christine by boat to the court of Hymeneus. Here she lives happily for thirteen years in a courtly setting of "the honourable company of men and women." The court being near the sea, sailing on it was often necessary; her husband, "par son sens soubtil," knew all the secrets of navigation. The metaphorics of the earlier ballade are taken up again, growing out of the same experiential setting of marriage and subsequent widowhood: sailing the ship signifies supporting the household.

This is what Christine means when she introduces her account as a truthful fiction: "Verité est ce que je dis; / Mais, je diray, par ficcion, / Le fait de la mutacion, / Comment de femme devins homme" (What I say is the truth, but I will tell the facts of the transformation, how I changed from a woman to a man, through a fiction [150–53]). The events, the experience, are true; the allegory of the ship is a "ficcion." Hence, when, describing the metamorphosis itself, Christine reiterates her claim to truth ("Et si n'est menconge, ne fable, / A parler selon methafore"), she is again referring to the experience being described and the allegorical language used to describe it. She falls asleep; Fortune changes her into a man; the ship strikes a rock; she wakes up and takes hammer and nail to repair the vessel. In the context as described above, hammer and nail become the pen and paper of her new career as lyric poet. It is not surprising, then, that she prefaces the description of the transformation with several stories out of Ovid: the content, the substance of the transformation is her change into a breadwinner, but the form, the structure of it is her change into a poet. The former she authorizes with the claim to truth; the latter with a *translatio*.

The scene of widowhood settles into a topos of writing: "Or fus je vrays homs, n'est pas fable, / De nefs mener entremettable" (Now I was a real man—this is not a *fable*—capable of sailing ships [1391–92]). She

---

[8] Jeanette Beer discusses a large number of the "truth assertions" of the first part of the *Mutacion*, showing how Christine mixes "autobiography . . . with allegory, history with mythology" to give the *Mutacion* "the advantages of both fact and fiction" ("Stylistic Conventions in *Le Livre de la Mutacion de Fortune*," in Richards, 124–36; this citation, 125). The discussion focuses on the topic of her title; Beer does not seek further meaning or pattern in Christine's unusual combination of conventions.

steers the ship toward the island of Fortune and finishes off an extended *auctoritas* by bringing the ship safely into the port of her stated subject: "A celle heure que homme devins, / Et certes par leur vertu vins / A port, et a cognoistre appris / Gouverner nefs et le pourpris" (At that hour I became a man and surely by their virtue came into port and learned the knowledge of sailing ships and of harbors [1445–48]; cf. Curtius, 128– 29). It is important to note the double *translatio* employed here. On the one hand, Christine brings back the metaphorics of widowhood to recall both her earlier fame and her earlier generic identity as lyric poet. On the other hand, however, she draws out the poetic topos implicit within these metaphorics: as a man, she is now empowered to take on the wholly new task of composing what amounts to a world history.[9]

And, again, the genealogical allegory sets out the two strands: the per-sonification, the "ficcion" of the ship at sea presents her autobiographical experience; the topos, the "verité" of the passage, presents the *translatio* derived from her father. She is authorized to write about Fortune because, as a woman, she has suffered from it and thus knows about it from experience; she is authorized to write about Fortune because, as a man, she has read what she needs in order to assemble and set down the mate-rial and because she possesses the artistic ability to see the task through.

Christine's autobiography thus complements the narrative strategy: the recapitulation of her life, along with the elaborate, allegorical *auctoritas,* brings her out of the sea of "Grant Peril" to the castle of Fortune sus-pended above it. Once there, she gives in the second part a long description of the castle and its four gates (Richece, Esperance, Povreté, Attropos [Fate]) which, once again, is composed at the same time out of experiential and authorial allegory. There are four paths for ascending to the top of the castle: Grant Orgueil (Pride) and Grant Barat (Malice), which are both slippery means; Grant Science and Juste Vie, which are sure. Both the latter paths, Christine tells us, are secure against "Mesure" (Ill Fortune); Grant Science she characterizes with the image of Cadmus and the snake at the fountain of learning—it leads to "paradis terrestre";[10] Juste Vie leads directly to the highest heaven, "Si hault qu'il voit Dieu face à face": "Mais estroit le fist tout de gré / Jhesus, qui meismes y monta / Et toutes

---

[9] Joël Blanchard remarks on this shift from a courtly voice to that of a "male" historian ("Christine de Pizan: les raisons de l'histoire," *Le Moyen Age* 92 [1986]: 420).

[10] This image is examined in the discussion below on the earthly paradise in the *Chemin,* where it also appears and receives its proper gloss.

choses surmonta" (But it was quite intentionally made narrow by Jesus, who ascended it himself and overcame all things [3264–67]) The source of the metaphorics should be apparent: the division is once again between classical pagan literature and Christian Scripture, *allegoria in verbis* and *in facto*.

Christine's transformation, couched as it is in the terms of the first half of the division, is an attempt to cross over to the second by means of the first, to take on a prophetic voice through the path of "Grant Science." In other words, Christine uses the personification allegory of her life to recount a conversion to the *translatio studii* of her father: Vergil, Augustine, and Dante. We should thus expect to find at this point an image of the *descensus ad inferos,* and, indeed, it occurs in conjunction with the metaphorics of shipwreck:

> La est le Gouffre Perilleux
> De mer, qui tant est merveilleux
> Qu'il s'angloute tout le navire,
> Qui vers celles parties vire;
> Tout y perist, tout y affonde
> Et tout y chiet en mer perfonde
> Qui de cellui gouffre s'aproche,
> Ou tout froisse par dure roche
> D'aymant, qui atrait le fer,
> Et puise jusques en Enfer.
>   (3965–74)

There is the Perilous Abyss of the sea, which is so marvelous that it swallows up all vessels that make their way toward these parts; everything that approaches this abyss perishes, sinks, and falls into the deep sea, which crushes everything with hard magnetic rock (that attracts iron), and draws it all the way to Hell.

Christine places her proper experience within the universal thematics of the sea of "Grant Peril"; the underworld is an ambiguous image of both damnation and knowledge.

The primary signification is that shipwreck on the way to the castle of Fortune leads straight to hell. But there is a continuation of the literary topos of sailing as well: the locution "puiser aux sources" (to consult the original authors) precisely describes the means by which Christine as compilator saves her ship from disaster. Experientially, she was headed for shipwreck when widowed, but shifting her descent to a metaphoric level saved her from disaster on a biographical one. Like Peter Weiss, but in a different manner, Christine separates the historical from the aesthetic descent. She does so by means of generic distinctions: the allegory remains the narrative *integumentum* of the journey to the castle of Fortune; the descent occurs solely in the metaphorical realm of the *translatio*. She lays no claim to the path of "Juste Vie," attempting instead to chart a new way to a prophetic voice by means of her "experience" as widow.[11]

The separation is clear in a further passage from the description of the oceans surrounding the castle:

> Ne sçay que vous en die plus?
> Tout ne deviseroie en plus
> Ne que j'eusse peu puis yer
> Toute l'eaue de mer puisier.
> La sont les Merveilles du monde,
> Et, qui lira la *Mapemonde*,
> La en trouvera grant partie;
> Et comme la mer est partie
> Par le lieu moult diversement,
> Et des fleuves le versement
> Et les naiscences et les sources,
> Dont toutes rivières sont sources.
> (4017–23)

Could I not tell you more? I could not show it all any more than I could draw out all the water from the sea. There are Wonders of the world there, and if you read the *Mappa Mundi* you will find a great deal of it there; how the sea is divided by land in many ways, and the paths of rivers and the origins and sources from which all streams are born.

The metaphorics are carefully and elegantly interwoven in this example of the results of the near-shipwreck. As a captain fit to sail the open seas, she has knowledge of all the waterways of the world; she expresses that knowledge to us in the language of *auctoritas*, citing the authority of the *Mapemonde* and punning on the word *source* as simultaneously geograph-

[11] Hence, where Beer sees Christine claiming that "metaphorical discourse brought even poets and historians together" in the use of *integumenta* (125–26), she elides the other, literal truth of *allegoria*. Beer remarks that Christine has Ovid *(Ovide Moralisé)* and the *Histoire ancienne jusqu'à César* agreeing on the "allegorical truth" of Hercules' descent into the underworld as prefiguring Christ's descent into hell: "Christian and pagan truth blended in the labors of a classical hero" (126–27). Christine's poetics make it clear that such a blend remains distinct from the figural poetics of Scripture, "Juste Vie," and Dante's *Commedia*.

ical and literary. Furthermore, the use of *source* as a rhyme word in the passage highlights the ambiguity in the previous image of "puiser jusques en Enfer"; descent for Christine paradoxically signified salvation from descent.

The *Mutacion* alludes to the topos of descent while expounding an autobiographical allegory of sailing the sea; the *Chemin* alludes to the latter as topos while expounding a version of the autobiographical allegory of descent. As Kevin Brownlee has noted, the *Chemin* is explicitly structured to parallel Dante's *Commedia*.[12] In the form of a dream vision ("Ce ne fus pas illusion, / Ains fu demonstrance certaine / De chose tres vraie et certaine" [This was no illusion but the certain demonstration of a quite true and certain matter; 454–56]), the *Chemin* traces the ascent of the path of "Grant Science" described by Christine in the *Mutacion*. Her guide for the journey is the Sibyl Almathea, who in introducing herself tells about the prophecies of Christ made by herself and the other Sibyls, then describes her service as guide to Aeneas—whom she led through hell, informed about his future, and told of the founding of Rome ("Ce lui prophetisay de bouche" [595–612])—and, finally, her partial burning of the books of prophecy of the future of Rome.[13] All this was remembered by Vergil, she says, who wrote of her in his works. The Sibyl then gives her reasons for coming to Christine: "Or me suis je manifestee / a toy que je voy apprestee / A concevoir, s'en toy ne tient / Ce que grant estude contient" (Now I have appeared to you whom I see ready to discover if within you might be that which accommodates great learning [635–38]).

The Sibyl represents two things subsequently glossed by Christine's translation of her into "grant estude": the *descensus ad inferos* and the resultant power of prophecy. The response of Christine-protagonist makes clear the importance of the gloss: she first recapitulates the Sibyl's credentials as guide to hell with reference to Aeneas and then continues: "Quant ainsi vous me voulez duire / En contree mains rioteuse / Que n'est ceste et plus deliteuse, / Si vous merci de cest honneur" (When thus you want to guide me in a less riotous and more pleasing land than this one, then I thank you for the honor [686–89]). The topos of modesty retains its literary quality in the calque of Dante's "Io non Enëa, io non Paulo sono" and is humorously literalized at the same time into the modest refusal

[12] *Le Livre du Chemin de long estude*, ed. Robert Püschel (Berlin, 1881). Brownlee has called the *Chemin* "the first serious reading of the *Divina Commedia* in French literature" ("Literary Genealogy and the Problem of the Father: Christine de Pizan and Dante," Robert Branner Forum for Medieval Art, Columbia University, 27 Oct. 1991).

[13] All this information returns in the *Cité des Dames,* as is seen later in this chapter.

required of a widow with pretensions to moral rectitude.[14] Christine both contrasts her courtly credentials to those of Dante and Vergil and genders the motif of her inability to take such a journey.

The sense of her refusal is strengthened by the subsequent verses, in which Christine again literalizes the topos of modesty: she calls herself the Sibyl's "humble chamberiere" (697) and proceeds to dress herself for the journey as just such a figure ("Si m'atournay d'un atour simple, / Touret de nes je mis et guimple" [701–2]). They set out in the October cold, but the *chemin* (710) quickly brings them to a "biau lieu frais et entier" (727) such as one sees "ou mois de may" (721); the courtly shift of season signifies a switch in tone from a "male"-gendered to a "female"-gendered allegory, another motif that will be echoed in Woolf's writings.[15] Christine's learning has taken her not into the underworld of tradition but to the *locus amoenus* of courtly love.

The different route has, however, achieved much the same purpose and leads to much the same poetics. They find themselves in the "terrestre paradis" (762), at the summit of a mountain, where she sees a "fontaine clere et vive" (799) in which nine ladies are bathing who "Moult sembloient d'auctorité / Et de grant valour et savoir" (816–17). And, like Dante with Vergil, Christine asks the Sibyl, "Le nom et la signifiance / Me vueilliez tout manifester, / En alant sanz nous arrester" (Please make clear to me all the names and meanings while we go along without stopping [868–70]). Christine's courtly way and womanly attire have led her as far as Vergil led Dante, but they will not take her any further.

It is at this moment that Almathea takes over the role of Dante's Beatrice and at the same time explains to Christine what she has lost by taking the path of *long estude;* the gloss of the *locus amoenus* also serves to gloss the autobiographical allegory. The Sibyl grants Christine's request to gloss the paradise by pointing out the two paths ("sanz plus, non trois") that lead to heaven:

Le chemin que tu vois plus drois;
Plus estroit et plus verdoiant,

[14] For examples of Christine's use of humor to underscore points of literary polemic, see Thelma Fenster, "Did Christine Have a Sense of Humor? The Evidence of the *Epistre au Dieu d'Amours,*" in Richards, 23–36.

[15] Woolf uses the change of season to indicate allegorically a change of mode in *A Room of One's Own:* following the denial of a male *descensus ad inferos,* the narrator sneaks into the magical garden of the women's college at Fernham and slips briefly from the October dusk to a spring evening (*A Room of One's Own* [1929; New York, n.d.], 16–17; hereafter cited as *ROO).*

La face de Dieu est voiant
Cil qui le suit jusqu'a la fin.
Le chemin de plus courte fin
Qui est de celui au delez,
Que tu vois plus large en tous lez,
Cil, je te creant fermement,
Conduit jusques au firmament. . . .
Mais ceste voie est plus certaine,
Car par science et ordenee,
Mais celle autre est ymaginee
Par celle nous fault toutevoie
Passer, car ceste estroite voie
Te seroit trop fort a suivir.
(902–19)

The path that you see to be straighter, narrower, and greener—the one who follows it to the end sees the face of God. The path whose end is nearer, which is the one to the side, which you see wider on all sides—that one, I firmly assure you, leads up to the firmament. . . . But this path is more sure, because ordered and through knowledge—but the other is imagined—and through this one we must nevertheless pass, for that narrow path would be too narrow for you to follow.

The distinction between paths and the limit set to her journey are the same as in the *Mutacion:* she is permitted to glimpse the heavens but not to see the face of God directly. The two paths will be specifically gendered later on by the Sibyl; for the moment, she gives a more ontological explanation: the path of "long estude" is safer.

As the Sibyl expands on the gloss of the path as "study," the *descensus ad inferos* is manifested as the specific danger of the "narrow path":

Mais cestui plus que parchemin
Ouvert, ou nous sommes entrez,
Si est reservé aux lettrez
Qui veulent aler par le monde,
Sanz querir voie trop parfonde:
Car qui en trop parfonde mare
Se met, souvent noie ou s'esgare.
(932–38)

But this one [path] into which we have entered, which is open more widely than parchment, is thus reserved to the lettered who want to go through the world without seeking an overly profound path; for the one who sets out onto an overly deep sea often drowns or loses his way.

We rediscover the topos of sailing the seas strictly within the metaphorical register of letters, with the addition of the dazzling wordplay of *parchemin* as both "parchment" and "by this path" (the preceding rhyme word is "chemin" [931]). This is the prohibition seen in Bernard: the scholar of "fictions" is not permitted to aspire toward representing truth. The warning here is more explicit than in the *Mutacion*, and its Dantean resonance established by the concluding verb, "s'esgarer" (*Dict. Littré:* "perdre son chemin"), thus drawing out the image of Ulysses' mad, disastrous, and—like Christine's—alternate route to the mountain of purgatory in *Inferno* 26.

The Dantean imagery, combined with the intertext of the *Mutacion*, provides a reading of the Sibyl's extension of her warning to include within it the "mal chemin";

> Des voies a cy forvoians
> Et a mal chemin avoians
> Regardes loings la voie ombreuse!
> La vois tu noire et tenebreuse?
> En enfer celle conduiroit
> Sanz revenir qui s'y duiroit.
>
> (949–52)

Look carefully at the shadowy way of the paths branching out from here and leading to evil paths! Do you see it black and full of shadows? That one leads the one who takes himself down it into hell without return.

The irony of the verses is patent: the Sibyl who had introduced herself as the one who led Aeneas through the underworld and out again ("Parmi enfer le convoiay, / Puis en Ytale l'avoiay" [599–600]) tells Christine there is no return by this route. The interpretation is apparent: both the Dantean resonance and the fact that the "Gouffre Perilleux" in *Mutacion* is said to draw all the way down to hell lead us to identify this path with the narrow path leading to a vision "face to face" with God, and thus with Dante's vision and with the *descensus ad inferos* as the only path to divine authority and a truly prophetic voice.

The full ramification of the division of the two paths, and the autobiographical allegory behind it, becomes evident at the climax of the introductory scenario of *auctoritas*. Following the long gloss of the fountain as wisdom ("Sapience"), its relation to her father, who also drank from it, and Cadmus's encounter there with a serpent, which discourages many from drinking there (whence the image in the *Mutacion*), the Sibyl calls the path "long estude" (1103). Like the path in the *Mutacion* briefly, this path is fully identified with the mythographical tradition of *integumentum* through the Sibyl's language: "Pour les gentilz est reservé, / Et pour les soubtilz fu trouvé" (It is reserved for the gentlefolk and was found by the subtle [1107–8]). In the lexicon of medieval allegoresis, it is the "subtle" who are able to discover hidden meaning beneath the surface veil of fiction.

In her response, in contrast, Christine subtly distinguishes her use of Dante and Vergil as *auctores* for her *chemin* from their role in the other *chemin,* the one to which she has no access; the key term is the image of descent.

> Mais le nom du plaisant pourpris
> Oncques mais ne me fu apris,
> Fors en tant que bien me recorde
> Que Dant de Florence el recorde
> En son livre qu'il composa
> Ou il moult biau stile posa:
> Quant en la silve fu entrez
> Ou tout de paour yert oultrez,
> Lors que Virgille s'apparu
> A lui dont il fu secouru,
> Adont lui dist par grant estude
> Ce mot: Vaille moy long estude
> Qui m'a fait cerchier tes volumes
> Par qui ensemble acointance eusmes.
> Or congnois a celle parole
> Qui ne fu nice ne frivole
> Que le vaillant poete Dant,
> Qui a long estude ot la dent,
> Estoit en ce chemin entrez,
> Quant Virgille y fu encontrez
> Qui le mena parmy enfer,
> Ou plus durs liens vit que fer.
>   (1125–46)

But the name of the pleasant haven never was taught to me except insomuch as I well remember that Dante of Florence recorded it in the book that he composed, where he laid out a very beautiful style: when he had entered the wood into which all because of fear he had strayed, when Vergil, by whom he was rescued, appeared to him, to whom he spoke these words from great learning: avail me now long study, which has led me to search through your volumes through which together we became acquainted. Now I, who was neither foolish nor frivolous, knew from these words that the worthy poet Dante, who had a taste for long

study, had entered upon this path, when he met Vergil there, who led
him through hell, where he saw harsher things [or "stronger bonds"]
than iron.

More explicitly than in the *Mutacion*, Christine distinguishes her descent
as a purely *authorial* maneuver, a *translatio studii* that, following (or
rather, reencountering) her father, will lead her to Italy. As she makes
equally clear, however, this will not be an *allegoria in facto* like Dante's,
an actual journey through hell. She is following the path of his reading,
not that of his vision.

The subtlety of Christine's reading of Dante is apparent from her choice
of allusion. As Brownlee (1991) has observed, the calque of Dante's recognition of Vergil, "Vaille moy long estude" is made to serve as Christine's
"verbal golden bough," the talisman of her journey, which she will pro-
nounce at key moments in the poem. In other words, she has joined two
crucial Dantean themes in this passage: the use of Vergil's character as an
allegory of "lungo studio" and the Christian rewriting of Vergil's golden
bough into the divine authorization for his descent. The conjuncture
underlines the fact that *long estude* is her only authorization; she has no
mandate from heaven to match Dante's or Vergil's: "Si dis que je
n'oublieroie / Celle parole, ains la diroie / En lieu d'ewangille ou de crois /
Au passer de divers destrois" (And I say that I did not forget these words,
for I would speak them in place of the gospels or the cross when passing
through various straits [1147–50]).

Thus does Christine find herself led beyond the *terrestre paradis* and on
a tour of the East, its ruined cities of the past and its sites of pilgrimage;
the Sibyl finally brings her to a ladder to the heavens, where she is to
receive her mission from the court of Wisdom to relay to the princes of
France—a secular and immediate endeavor, not a prophecy of the future.
If the difference in missions is apparent from the conclusion of the *Chemin*
(although such a mission certainly remains in the political tradition of
much of Dante's poem), it is the clear focus of the scene of ascent itself.
On reaching the ladder, which Almathea glosses as Speculation, Christine
finally receives from her a summary and an explanation of her limitations.
She is qualified by her study, the path she has taken, to climb the ladder
leading up to the firmament, but not to go further:

Monter ou firmament te fault,
Combien qu'autres montent plus hault,
Mais tu n'as mie le corsage
Abille a ce: toutefois say je
Que de toy ne vient le deffault,

Mais la force qui te deffault
Est pour ce que tart a m'escole
Es venue. Fille, or acole
Celle eschiele, et devant iray.
                    (1673–81)

It is necessary for you to ascend to the firmament, even though others
climb higher, but you don't at all have the body fit for that: nevertheless,
I know the fault is not yours; the strength you lack is due to your
entering late into my school. Daughter, now grab this ladder, and I will
go in front.

Two uses of enjambment and caesura punctuate the speech. "Es venue.
Fille, or acole" emphasizes the gendered nature of the fault; as she would
explain in her later works, Christine came late to school because she was
born a girl. The distinction is equally developed through the wordplay of
the first enjambment and caesura: her lack is expressed physically (*corsage, force*) where we would expect moral qualities like *courage;* there is
a further reference to her feminine apparel in the pun of *abille* as both the
adjective "habile" (fit, clever) and the past participle "habillé" (dressed).
In other words, it is her experience that has excluded her from the narrower path.

This experience is given full narrative play in the action that follows:
fearful of climbing the ladder, Christine compares herself to Icarus, who
climbed too high and perished in the sea (1723–32). The Sibyl responds
by telling her that she is acting true to her sex ("Femenin sexe par droi-
ture / Craint et tousdis est paoureux" (The feminine sex as a rule fears and
always is afraid [1736–37]) and that she will not fall like Icarus because
she is not climbing the ladder out of presumption. By combining an ironic
allusion to the limitations of her sex with a pointed allusion to Dante
faced with a journey on the back of Geryon, Christine makes it clear that
the female experience with which she is playing remains a crucial feature
of her allegory.[16] Her lack of presumption lies in knowing her place as a
woman.

[16] Christine shows her close acquaintance with the Geryon episode in the *Avision,*
where she encounters the vice Fraud and inquires whether she might not have seen her
in the form of Geryon when Dante was led through hell by Vergil (90). The episode in
question is *Inf.* 17. Richards cites the *Avision* passage as evidence of Christine's awareness of the Dantean distinction between the allegories of the poets and of the theologians in "Christine de Pizan and Dante: A Reexamination," *Archiv für das Studium
der neueren Sprachen und Literaturen* 137 (1985): 107.

That this knowledge is fully implicated in the limitations placed on her authority as writer is apparent from the borrowing of Dante's questioning of his authority in the *Inferno*. What she also borrows is the slipperiness that goes with such a questioning; for what these two allegorical works are about is the way Christine shows simultaneously the courtly tradition she is allowed to have, the clerkly tradition from which she is excluded, and the *translatio studii* that permits her to be within both at once. Dante used Icarus to express reservations about what he was about to do regardless of any reservations; Christine uses Dante's Icarus (like his Ulysses above) to express her awareness of what she is not allowed to do and will not do.

After taking Christine up to the tenth heaven, the Sibyl turns around and tells her it is time to descend: "Car cy dessus n'iras tu pas, / Il ne te loit passer un pas / Oultre ce ciel; tant que tu portes / Ce corps, closes te sont les portes" (For you will not go higher than here; it is not permitted you to go a step beyond this heaven; so long as you carry this body, the doors are closed to you [2031–34]). We have already been given ample evidence that the Sibyl's explanation is inadequate as a general rule, but it is perfectly true of Christine as woman writer. The enjambment and wordplay in the third verse again emphasize both the generic split of the exclusion (*allegoria*/*integumentum*) and its gendered grounds; the equivocal rhyme of "portes" links the closed gates on the one hand, in a learned Neoplatonic topos, to the body with which she is burdened, and on the other, in the gendered sense previously seen, to the body she is dressed in. Her thoughts express her frustration: "Ainsi de la m'estut partir, / Dont il me desplut, sanz mentir" (Thus I had to depart from there; a thing which, I will not deny, displeased me [2045–46]); they return to a "biau lieu . . . / Non si noble ni si luisant / Comme est l'autre, trop s'en falloit" (beautiful place . . . not by any means so noble or so splendid as the other [2059–61]). They return, that is, to Wisdom's court, where Christine will be given a message by a series of familiar personifications of virtues and vices: excluded from Dantean *allegoria*, we remain in an *integumentum*.

Although the earnestness of Christine's political allegory at the court of Wisdom is not in question, the tone of the frame calls for further analysis, for it appears to tell us: I would like to prophesy like Dante, with divine authority, but cannot; I would like to write the third book of the Bible but must settle for a psychomachia. Instead of God, Christine sees the "influences et destinees" corresponding to the will of heaven above. Instead of the perfect celestial rose, she sees Nature complaining that her children are destroying each other, more distressed than when Pluto kidnapped Proserpine or Phaeton drove the chariots of the sun. The final note of self-parody is sounded by the poem's conclusion, in which Christine does not have time to make her farewells to the Sibyl because she is awakened by her mother telling her that she has overslept.

Several elements of the poem, then, are overdetermined; the mother provides the first.[17] In the ballades, Christine had already gendered the courtly, lyric tradition as female in contrast to the exclusively male epic. She now sets off the mythographic, personification tradition in the same way against the Christian, figural one. Neither "female" form had been seen in the past as suited for the open sea or the highest heaven. Christine had proven her dexterity within the former traditions; the lyric in her ballades, as seen above; personification in the poems on the *Rose* and in the *Epistre Othea*. In both cases, her primary aim was an immediate intervention, be it literary or political.[18] The two traditions were gendered female precisely because Christine had already established herself within them.[19]

At the same time, paradoxically, they represent what she allegorizes in the *Mutacion* as her transformation into a man; they *are* her *long estude*. In the *Chemin*, I would argue, we find Christine-protagonist coming to terms with the limitations that Christine-poet expresses her gender as having placed on her. The poem is powerfully structured after a model held up frequently by her as superior to the traditions above, while at every step it asserts its own inability to translate itself up to the same level.

---

[17] It is also most likely a parody itself of the conclusion of Jean de Meun's continuation of the *Roman de la Rose*. In that poem, the dream is cut off abruptly as Amant, having taken his pleasure from the rose, awakes. Christine's ends just as abruptly, but with the intrusion of her everyday reality. This underlines the self-consciousness of Christine's tone: the parody serves both to bring out the gendered ending of Amant's fantasy and to distinguish hers from it even while partaking of the same generic construction.

[18] On the former, see Charity Cannon Willard, *Christine de Pizan: Her Life and Works* (New York, 1984), 73–89; Kevin Brownlee, "Discourses of the Self: Christine de Pizan and the *Rose*," *Romanic Review* 79:1 (Jan. 1988): 199–221; Lori Walters, "The Woman Writer and Literary History: Christine de Pizan's Redefinition of the Poetic *Translatio* in the *Epistre au Dieu d'Amours*," *French Literature Series* 16 (1989): 1–16; and Walters, "Fathers and Daughters: Christine de Pizan as Reader of the Male Tradition of *Clergie* in the *Dit de la Rose*," in Richards, 63–76. See Hindman's study of manuscripts of *Othea* for the political intent of that work.

[19] As is readily apparent, Christine's strategies need have no bearing on the fact that both the courtly and clerkly traditions were overwhelmingly male-gendered anyway, especially in her focusing in both cases on the central role of the *Rose* in each of them. That there was more precedent for her in the lyric tradition does not then mean that it was a normal, thus experiential, occurrence.

In the end, then, Christine genders the Italian past in the poem as female, for her father is said also to have followed this same *chemin de long estude*.

I suggest that we can read this move as a translation of Dante back into *integumenta*. The *Mutacion*, especially in the play of its images with those of the *Chemin*, presents Christine's rewriting of the allegory of conversion as a metamorphosis into a man. If in Ovid the gods perform their transformations only as the last resort to avoid a tragic end (and sometimes too late to avoid one), so for Christine transformation occurs when she has painted her voice into a corner; the *Mutacion* shows her translating the *Chemin* into a truly "male" voice as she has so gendered it in that work. The division of the *Chemin* still holds, but her reworking of the autobiographical allegory into the topos of sailing a ship provides her with a means of descending without divine authority; as suggested above, Christine descends purely through her sources.

In the *Mutacion*, Dante appears not as the poet of hell but as the political exile, victim of Fortune (4644–70); if the two roles may not converge in terms of authority, they do so in terms of autobiography. In other words, Christine has replaced Dante's divine authority with that of her experience; her conversion midway through her life's journey matches his. Dante's *allegoria in verbis* is his conversion through God, however, whereas hers is the conversion through Nature: in both, the truth is told according to metaphor. Dante's *allegoria in facto* is the divinely inspired truth of his vision; hers is the literal reading of the sources left to her through her father, the *translatio studii* of Vergil-Augustine-Dante, the same order of study and research as seen in Weiss's *Notizbücher*.

Her humor remains in evidence: not permitted or not permitting herself the descent into Dante's divinely ordained hell, she instead sends herself as woman through the equally alien (if all too close) hell of the misogynistic tradition of clerkly letters. The now-authorized, hence converted, Christine recapitulates this descent as the starting point of the *Cité des Dames*. The substance of the autobiographical allegory—the mode of interpreting experience developed through her early works—lends her authority; the structure—the *translatio studii et imperii*—gives her the framework for recasting that interpretation into the prophetic and enduring form of the *Cité des Dames*.

REASON'S FIRST speech to Christine in the *Livre de la Cité des Dames* advises her on ways to withstand the onslaught of misogynistic *auctores* presented by her in the prologue:

One can interpret them according to the grammatical rule of *antiphrasis,* which means, as you know, that if you call something bad, in fact, it is good, and also vice versa.

You resemble the fool in the prank who was dressed in women's clothes while he was sleeping at the mill; when he woke up, because those who were making fun of him repeatedly told him he was a woman, he believed their false testimony more readily than the certainty of his own identity. Fair daughter, have you lost all sense? Have you forgotten that when fine gold is tested in the furnace, it does not change or vary in strength but becomes purer the more it is hammered and handled in different ways?[20]

Two different strategies of reading are proposed for Christine to follow in the allegorical project of constructing a City of Ladies with which Reason, Rectitude, and Justice are about to entrust her. The first, reading by *antiphrasis,* is a rhetorical technique and will be applied by Christine to the principal source of her compilation, Boccaccio's *De mulieribus claris (Concerning Famous Women):* she will generally preserve the content of his exempla of famous women but will reverse our reading of them.[21] The

---

[20] "The Livre de la Cité des Dames of Christine de Pizan: A Critical Edition," ed. Maureen Curnow (Ph. D. diss., Vanderbilt University, 1975), cited by page number; trans. and ed. Earl Jeffrey Richards, *The Book of the City of Ladies* (New York, 1982), hereafter cited by book, chapter, paragraph number, and page number; these quotations, 1.2.2, 624, 7; 1.2.2, 623, 6.

[21] Nearly three-quarters of the episodes of the *Cité des Dames* are based on Boccaccio's accounts in *Concerning Famous Women.* See Alfred Jeanroy, "Boccace et Christine de Pisan, le *De Claris Mulieribus,* principale source du *Livre de la Cité des Dames,*" *Romania* 48 (1922): 92–105; Curnow, 138–55; Richards 1982, xxxv-li, 259–71; Patricia A. Philippy, "Establishing Authority: Boccaccio's *De Claris Mulieribus* and Christine de Pizan's *Livre de la Cité des Dames,*" *Romanic Review* 77:3 (1986): 167–94; Maureen Quilligan, *The Allegory of Female Authority: Christine de Pizan's "Cité des Dames"* (Ithaca, 1991). Until fairly recently, Christine's text was generally treated as a translation of Boccaccio (Jeanroy is representative). By now, however, the subtlety and complexity of Christine's use of her sources have been well established and her rewriting of Boccaccio well documented (see esp. Curnow's and Richards's notes, Philippy, Quilligan, and Eleni Stecopoulos and Karl D. Uitti, "Christine de Pizan's *Livre de la Cité des Dames:* The Reconstruction of Myth," in Richards, 48–62). In this chapter, I focus only on those aspects of Christine's use that pertain to my particular argument. Boccaccio's text was available to Christine both in the original Latin and in Laurent de Premierfait's 1401 translation, *De cleres et nobles femmes* (Richards 1982, xxxv). Since Laurent's translation does not exist in a modern edition, I follow Richards (xlix) in citing from Zaccaria's critical edition of the Latin text (vol. 10 of *Opere,* ed. Vittore

second strategy is structural and metaphorical and centers on Christine's definition of her own authority and authorial voice. Here, Christine will take a different tradition, a *translatio studii* running from Vergil to Dante by way of Augustine, whence she will derive the allegory of the founding and building of a city that is simultaneously a rereading and rewriting of her literary and historical tradition.[22]

As part of the alteration and recontextualization of her Boccaccian source, Christine emphasizes the themes of the destruction and founding of cities, particularly Troy and Rome, and of the creation and practice of language, reading, and prophecy. At the same time, through the focus on her respective *translatio imperii* and *translatio studii,* Christine opposes what she represents as the misogynistic tradition of Boccaccio and of Jean de Meun's *Roman de la Rose,* simultaneously proposing an alternative that she will figure as both preexistent (Vergil to Dante) and particular to women.[23] These images pertain directly to the autobiographical allegory

---

Branca [Verona, 1967]), hereafter cited by chapter and page number; trans. Guido Guarino, *Concerning Famous Women* (New Brunswick, 1963).

[22] This part of Christine's writing strategy in the *Cité des Dames*—the frame allegory of the city—has been less fully and less clearly documented in the critical literature. Curnow (1037), Richards (1982, xxvix), Christine Reno ("Virginity as an Ideal in Christine de Pizan's *Cité des Dames,*" in *Ideals for Women in the Works of Christine de Pizan,* ed. Diane Bornstein [Detroit, 1981], 80–82), and Quilligan (1991, 95–103) have duly noted the presence of the *City of God* in the title; Reno compares it with the fragility of the fortress in the *Rose;* Quilligan suggests an anti- or counter-Roman tradition. Richards and Quilligan focus on anti-Vergil-Augustine-Dante motifs, which seem to me to be balanced by the positive *translatio studii* I discuss below. Glenda McLeod's argument that the image of the city was to be read on four levels ranging from "the female gender . . . to the end point of history in the Augustinian City of God" is more evenhanded but does not develop any relation between the levels of interpretation ("Poetics and Antimisogynist Polemics in Christine de Pizan's *Le Livre de la Cité des Dames,*" in Richards, 37–47; this citation, 44). Joël Blanchard emphasizes the "metonymic" relation between Christine's writing of a *compilatio* and the construction of the city ("Compilation and Legitimation in the Fifteenth Century: *Le Livre de la Cité des Dames,*" in Richards, 228–49, this citation, 229).

[23] Nearly all recent studies of the *Cité des Dames* note the focus of the antimisogynist polemic against Jean de Meun; some discuss its connection to Christine's use of Boccaccio. I am indebted to Sylvia Huot, "Seduction and Sublimation: Christine de Pizan, Jean de Meun, and Dante," *Romance Notes* 25 (1985): 361–73, for suggesting Christine's presentation of separate and opposed *translationes studii* in the *Cité des Dames* and for her characterization of that opposition along the lines of Jean de Meun vs. Dante. Earl Jeffrey Richards has written extensively on the subject in terms of the generic distinctions between courtly lyric poetry and the "vision of poetic continuity" of *Inf.* 4, *locus amoenus* and earthly paradise. See *Dante and the "Roman de la rose": An Investigation*

worked out in detail in the *Chemin* and *Mutacion* through the topoi of sailing and descent, and precisely define the attitude Christine intends to take toward the conclusions drawn from those works. Reason's strategy of *antiphrasis* deals explicitly with the question of literary tradition and *auctoritas;* the passage establishes the principles for what amounts to Christine's translation of Boccaccio, alerting us that it will be not a literal but a corrective rendering of the original. The second passage retells once more the story of Christine's transformation, her conversion to a man, while reversing the terms, treating it, that is, as an *antiphrasis.*

Given the context of the *Chemin* and *Mutacion,* however, the image of gender transformation is more complex than it appears at first glance. According to the *Mutacion,* and with the sense of *auctoritas* that goes along with it, Christine at this point would remain a man. Indeed, the three women appear to her as in the anecdote, "as if I had been awakened from sleep" (622); and Christine, like the fool, imagines on waking that she is a woman simply because of the clothes in which she is dressed—hence her despair. So we have a paradox similar to the ones in the earlier allegories: her experience, the clothes she wears, are presented as an appearance obscuring the true identity underneath.

The primary meaning refers to the works of the misogynistic, clerkly tradition, which have obscured the truth of the female experience. Christine deals with these texts by simple reversal: the misogynist appraisal of women is incorrect. The meaning recovered through reversal then changes the terms of the debate, for the truth of her literary identity is that she is an *auctor* and thus male. As reader and translator of Boccaccio, Christine may read by experience—as a woman—and also as a rhetorician (practicing *antiphrasis*) and compiler, for she has already affiliated these topics through gender. At the same time, as an *auctor,* as the composer of an allegory, and as prophet and founder of a new city, she is a man dressed as a woman; that is, she is a convert to the male-gendered *translatio studii* of Vergil, Augustine, and Dante, one who has set forth across their ocean, descended to their hell, and returned from it.[24]

The dual identity embedded within the image of gold used by Reason

---

into the Vernacular Narrative Context of the *"Commedia"* (Tübingen, 1981), 85–88, and "Christine de Pizan, the Conventions of Courtly Diction, and Italian Humanism," in Richards, 250–71. The influence of Huot's and Richards's readings is also evident in the contributions by McLeod, Stecopoulos and Uitti, and Walters to the Richards volume.

[24] Blanchard's insightful essay "Compilation and Legitimation" suggests the potentiality for these strategies of Christine within the generic "constraints" of the *compilatio.*

is apparent in its double allusions. The first reference is to Dido, whose story as founder of Carthage is recounted in the first part of the *Cité des Dames*. Dido escaped with the gold of Phoenicia by disguising it as worthless objects (1.46), using it to purchase the land of Carthage. This is the interpretation by *antiphrasis:* Boccaccio is the gold with which Christine is escaping from the clerkly tradition, disguised as the misogynist dreck of her source and the dull veneer of the translator. This is reading as a woman, as Susan Schibanoff has put it in the same context, but it is not the whole story, for, as Quilligan has remarked, Dido takes the gold into Africa, a significant movement away from Rome in Christine's city-founding imagery (1991, 72–73).[25]

At the same time, if we also take into account Augustine's celebrated use of the Old Testament image of the Israelites taking the gold out of Egypt, we find a potent interpretive image moving in the opposite direction—toward Rome. As we have seen, Augustine moves metaphorically in the direction of Rome as the model for the *City of God,* the model from which Christine also borrows her title and central metaphor. Augustine's use of the incident concerns not experience, as in Dido's story, but interpretation: just as the Israelites took the gold out of Egypt to use in the Promised Land, so may we use whatever of the pagans serves us, as long as we do it within a Christian context. Hereby, as we saw, Augustine preserved the structure of Vergil's *Aeneid* while dismissing its substance. The gold in this sense in the context of the passage above would stand for the core of Christine's conversion, the transformation into a man by virtue of her descent and return via a *translatio studii* of Vergil, Augustine, and Dante. Hence, her metaphorics move in both directions; for, like Augustine before her, Christine will structure her movement away from the antithetical, Roman, pagan, (she adds male) tradition by means of that same tradition. She will found Carthage with the gold she will have taken from Rome—with, that is, the very misogynistic tradition she wishes to extirpate by the founding of her new city.

---

[25] Susan Schibanoff, "Taking the Gold Out of Egypt: The Art of Reading as a Woman," in *Gender and Reading: Essays on Readers, Texts, and Contexts,* ed. Elizabeth A. Flynn and Patrocino P. Schweikart (Baltimore, 1986), 83–106. Quilligan's context is the discussion of Semiramis as the sign of Christine's rewrite of Dante (69–85). Although Quilligan's argument for Christine's redemption of Semiramis as a female authority is persuasive, her rehearsal of the *translatio* of Vergil-Augustine-Dante and its significance for Christine is not, as it posits a facile and unproblematic transference of polar opposites from one author to the next. The genealogy of city imagery is certainly essential to an understanding of the *Cité des Dames,* but only if that genealogy is understood as being conflicted and dialectical at each stage.

The introductory scene of the *Cité des Dames* plants the elements necessary for the interpretation of the allegory and its strategies in terms both of the various traditions with which Christine is working and of the relationship to those traditions developed in her earlier works.[26] Consequently, the allusion to "Io non Enëa, io non Paulo sono" with which she responds to the mission of founding a city also recalls her dilemma in the *Chemin:*

> I am not Saint Thomas the Apostle who through divine grace built a rich palace in Heaven for the King of India, and my feeble sense does not know the craft, or the measures, or the study, or the science, or the practice of construction [*de maçonner*]. And if, thanks to learning [*science*], these things were within my ken, where would I find enough physical strength [*force suffisante*] in my weak feminine body to realize such an enormous task? But nevertheless, my most respected ladies . . . I know well that nothing is impossible for God. Nor do I doubt that anything undertaken with your counsel and help will not be completed well. . . . Behold your handmaiden [*chamberiere*] ready to serve. (1.7.1; 638–39; 15–16)

The passage is particularly rich in allusive force. First of all, we find the crucial elements that led the Sibyl in the *Chemin* to accept Christine's *modestia* at face value and not take her through hell or to the highest heaven: the lack of "force" and her quality as "chamberiere." The gendered metaphorics are adapted here for the new context through the physical description of the endeavor: she knows nothing of the art or practice of "maçonnage."

At the same time, however, she immediately accepts the mission, and with the same pagan/Christian split as did Dante: she claims authorization by both God *and* the Sibyls. The Dantean intertext also establishes the mission as descent, but descent in the particular meaning we have learned to give it from the earlier writings: she is authorized as a man, and thus the transformation does hold; she will descend, however, as a woman—"par Nature," as she says. The new topos introduced in the title of the *Cité des Dames* establishes a new metaphorical field: Christine will be digging for gold. The reality of Dante's journey receives a new twist: if in

[26] Quilligan remarks on the importance of this "threshold scene" for establishing the terms of Christine's allegory and cites the allusive presence of the *Mutacion* and the *Chemin*, the former negatively in Christine's insistence on her "femaleness" ("the transformation . . . is specifically disallowed" [52]), the latter in a new allusion to Dante's "Io non Enëa, io non Paulo sono" (58).

the *Mutacion* she glossed the reality as experience and the allegory of conversion as study, here the allegory remains study, but the historical ground, the *allegoria in facto*, becomes an archaeological excavation.

That is to say, as possessor of the field of letters, she is going to rebuild the Vergilian-Augustinian-Dantean Rome as a City of Ladies by means of the gold stolen from Boccaccio and Jean de Meun, gold she will bring back with her from the hell to which she will descend, gold dug from the same fields of letters to which she now belongs as a male *auctor*. She is not merely dismissing or rewriting the misogynist tradition; she is digging it out, melting it down, and recasting it within the mold of a foundational structure equally derived from another part of that tradition. The crucial figures Nicostrata, Almathea, and Proba exemplify the procedure: through her representation of them in the new context of the allegorical frame of the *Cité des Dames*, Christine makes each one into a personification of her project.

As with the introductory figure of *antiphrasis*, Christine's rendering of Boccaccio's Nicostrata/Carmentis (1.33.1, 37.1, 38.4; 2.5.1) simultaneously undermines his *auctoritas* and heightens it by stressing the combination of the Arcadian woman's prophecy of the future city of Rome and invention of the Latin alphabet. Christine avails herself of Boccaccio's authority to strengthen her point ("And let no one say that I am telling you these things just to be pleasant: they are Boccaccio's own words, the truth of which is well known and evident" [1.37.1; 748; 78]), while the substance of the point is that Boccaccio's authority itself derives from the language invented by a Carmentis grounded by Christine in his authority. By describing Carmentis teaching the scholars "like a school-mistress . . . the lesson thanks to which they consider themselves so lofty and honored, that is, she taught them the Latin alphabet!" [1.38.4; 751; 80]), Christine reveals the subtlety of her dependence on male *auctores:* their tradition is in fact hers, as she is in the process of defining it.

As she has parodied herself through depicting gender limitations in terms of her dress, Christine parodies herself here in the figure of Nicostrata/Carmentis as a schoolmarm ("leur maistrece a l'escolle"). This should not disguise from us the seriousness of the endeavor, however; rather, it should alert us to the care Christine takes in the use of gender pronouns. This is apparent in another of Reason's summaries of the deeds of Nicostrata, where the connection between language and prophecy is made explicit and the project of the City of Ladies predicated on its use of both not only as the endpoint but as the origin of the *auctores* of which the book is ostensibly a compilation: "The benefits realized by this woman are infinite, for, thanks to her, men have been brought out of ignorance and led to knowledge, even if they do not recognize it; thanks to her, they possess the means . . . to know the past, present, and future" (1.37.1; 748; 78).

Christine will do the same thing with Boccaccio's brief account of the prophecy of the founding of Rome, told in the section of part 2 of the *Cité des Dames* on woman prophets. Boccaccio introduced the story of the invention of language by mentioning that Nicostrata's son Evander founded Rome; Christine brings out the crucial imagery of her city by making the prophetess herself into the founder of her city, writing and city-founding evidently being analogous for her: "This Nicostrata . . . was also a woman prophet: for as soon as she had crossed the River Tiber and had climbed the Palatine Hill with her son Evander, frequently mentioned in histories, she prophesied that a city would be built upon this hill, the most famous city in the world ever, which would rule over all worldly dominions. In order to be the first to lay a stone there, she built a fortified castle on that site where, just as was said earlier, Rome was founded and built" (2.5.1; 798; 106).[27] The addition of the final sentence to Boccaccio's version renders Nicostrata as a *mise-en-abyme* of Christine in the frame allegory, down to the laying of the first stone of the foundation: language and city are the two myths of origin Christine has brought back with her from her descent.

She is building her *Cité des Dames* both physically and literarily, underneath and up through Western cultural tradition—the fortified castle already built in the place where Rome was said to have been the first— rewriting its history as she recasts its foundations, claiming all the riches and authority of Rome as her own and redefining them in the process. The mechanism of creating the future by recreating the past is that of the *descensus ad inferos;* this is the heritage Christine borrows from the tradition she is recreating in her own image. Boccaccio, however, is only the substance being recast within the structure she defines through her alterations of his text. Nicostrata's founding of Rome points toward the Vergilian authority of the model; the episodes of Almathea and Proba further develop the *translatio studii* through Dante familiar from the *Mutacion* and the *Chemin.*

---

[27] Cf. Boccaccio: "Coming from the Peloponnese to the mouth of the Tiber, likewise led by his mother, he named the Palatine Hill (after either his father Pallas or his son) where afterwards mighty Rome was built. Here with his people and his mother he settled, and built the city of Pallanteum" (27, 114; 52). There is no mention of a prophecy here, less emphasis on Nicostrata's leading role over her son, and no mention of her desire to be "la premiere qui pierre y asseyst" (the first to lay a stone there).

Christine gives Almathea pride of place in the catalog of the Sibyls at the start of the second part, turning Boccaccio's brief account of a prophetess into a meditation on her use of *Aeneid* 6. Having emphasized the continuing analogy of language and building by changing Boccaccio's topography of a ruined temple into the "vers rimés" of a book of prophecies,[28] Christine then continues by citing the Sibyl's other claim to fame: "Several fictions [*aucunes ficcions*] say that she led Aeneas into hell and brought him back again" (2.3.1; 793; 103). The rendering of Boccaccio's "preterea" as "aucunes ficcions" demonstrates again the subtlety of Christine's use of citation. Apparently stressing the fictionality as a way of dismissing the account, she turns it into a discussion of the need of a "ficcion" to structure any such account.[29]

Having discussed the nine books eventually bought by King Tarquin, which "declared in full the things [*faiz*] that were to happen to Rome in the future" (ibid.), Christine asks rhetorically, once again stressing the gender of the noun in the question, "So I ask you then to tell me, was there ever a man who did this?" (2.3.2; 794; 104). A few lines later, she concludes with the answer: "Vergil speaks in verse about this Sibyl in his book" (2.3.3; 794; 104). For it was indeed Vergil who had declared what was to happen to the Romans; this was the goal of the *descensus ad inferos* on which Almathea led Aeneas. As with Nicostrata, the context of prophecy is language: Christine precisely valorizes the claim of "aucunes ficcions" of Vergil and Dante over the purported facts of Boccaccio. The latter is useful for surface authority; the others are necessary for appropriating and rewriting that authority.

Christine allegorizes the distinction between the ways she uses the *auctores* in her rendering of Boccaccio's account of Proba the Roman, who

---

[28] "They say moreover that on the Baian shore near Lake Avernus she had a marvelous temple, which I myself have seen, and I have heard that it has retained its name up to this time; for even if it is in decay because of its antiquity and half destroyed by negligence, it retains its ancient majesty even in ruins and offers the visitor its grandeur to admire" (26, 110; 50). Christine uses the ambiguity of "oraculum" to render the ruins of a temple as a book of prophecy: "Moreover it is written that while standing on the Baian shore of the lake of Hell [*le lac d'Enffer*], she received a noble and wonderful response and divine revelation, written and preserved in her name and composed in rhymed verses. And although this example is extremely old, it still elicits admiration for this woman's grandeur and excellence from all who consider and examine her" (2.3.1; 792–93; 103).

[29] Both Richards ("Christine relegates Virgil to the literary scrap-heap without even bothering to name him" [1982, 263n]) and Quilligan, who cites Richards approvingly (1991, 113), uncharacteristically take Christine at face value here.

composed a fourth-century Vergilian cento of the life of Christ. She cites Boccaccio's account of Proba's writing techniques fairly closely; in this case, the new context is enough to change the meaning. On one level, the cento form accurately renders the cutting and pasting Christine is doing to *De claris mulieribus;* at the same time, it describes the possibilities inherent in a pastiche of recreating Vergil within a Christian context as Vergil and yet also something else entirely. In its new context, Boccaccio's account again reads like an autobiographical allegory of Christine: "Proba the Roman . . . was of equal excellence and was a Christian. She had such a noble mind and so loved and devoted herself to study that she mastered the seven liberal arts and was a masterful poet and brought such great labor of studying to the books of the poets and especially Vergil's *dittiez,* that she knew them all by heart. . . . It occurred to her that one could completely describe the Scriptures and the stories found in the Old and New Testaments with pleasant verses filled with substance taken from these same books" (1.29.1; 725–26; 65). To transform the pagan into the Christian, the misogynistic into the City of Ladies, adding nothing, but signifying solely through the new context in which the words were placed: Proba's brainstorm is also Christine's.[30] Before continuing by citing Boccaccio's detailed description of the technique, Christine identifies his role in her account by again citing his condescension: " 'Which certainly in itself,' remarks the author Boccaccio, 'is not undeserving of admiration, that such a noble idea could come into a woman's brain, but it was even more marvelous that she could actually execute it' " (1.29.1; 726; 65–66).

The "chose plus merveilleuse" Christine is about to "mettre a execucion" on Boccaccio is that, given the right context, even such condescension can be gloriously ironized: his words can be made to mean things Boccaccio could never have thought they would.

> For then this woman, quite desirous to bring her thinking to fruition, set her hand to it and now this woman would run through the *Eclogues* and then the *Georgics* or the *Aeneid . . .* that is, she would skim as she read, and now in one part she would take several entire verses unchanged and in another borrow small snatches and, through marvelous craftsmanship and conceptual subtlety, she was able to construct entire lines of orderly verse. She would put small pieces together, coupling and joining them, all the while respecting the metrical rules, art, and measure

---

[30] See Blanchard's discussion of the story of Proba as a *mise-en-abyme* of Christine's work of compilation (in Richards, 239–40).

in the individual feet, as well as in the conjoining of verses, and without making any mistakes she arranged her verses so masterfully that no man could do better.[31] In this way, starting from the creation of the world, she composed the opening of her book, and following all the stories of the Old and New Testaments she came as far as the sending of the Holy Spirit to the Apostles, adapting Vergil's works to fit all this in so orderly a way that someone who only knew this work would have thought that Vergil had been both a prophet and evangelist. (1.29.1; 726–27; 66)

We saw Christine in the *Mutacion* turn herself into a man in order to authorize a *compilatio* of world history; here she takes the *auctores* and dresses them in women's clothing, a Christian retelling pagan history as if it had always been Christian.

Certainly, the Christian identification of the City of Ladies is evident in the contents of the third part, the collection of martyred female saints who provide the "haulx combles des tours" (high pinnacles of the towers [974; 217]). At the same time, as we have seen, Christian also functions in analogy with "feminist" as opposed to the misogynistic, "pagan" tradition of Christine's Boccaccio.[32] When Christine places herself in the genealogy of Nicostrata, Almathea, and Proba, founders of Rome and creators of language, she equally places herself in the Christian genealogy of Vergilian *descensi ad inferos* and foundings of the new Rome from Augustine to Dante. By means of pointed references and more subtle allusions, Christine shows how from the failed attempts of the earlier allegories, she has now acceded to the authority of the Vergilian *translatio*. Moreover, she suggests how the writing strategies dictated by this *translatio* structure her ongoing willful misappropriation of the other, misogynistic *translatio* leading from Ovid through Jean de Meun to Boccaccio, which she had begun addressing early in her career in the *querelle des femmes*.

The ramifications of the two models are played out in a contrast between Vergil and Ovid in the second part of the book, where an attack on the misogyny of the latter is followed by a reworking of the story of Dido and Aeneas into a further image of Christine's endeavor. Rhetorically, the

---

[31] Adding the customarily refigured gender hyperbole is the only significant departure from Boccaccio, who has here, "She observed the metrical rules, and preserved the dignity of the poetry, so that no one except an expert could have discerned the joinings" (97, 392–94; 219).

[32] Indeed, as Stecopoulos and Uitti have argued, the third book can be seen as a response to Boccaccio's exclusion of contemporary women from his book and the related argument that "womanly fame is to be construed as a function of the individual woman's *overcoming* her 'nature' " (49; their emphasis).

attack on Ovid restates the arguments of part 1.[33] Christine cites Ovid's defense of his discussion of the deceitfulness of women in the *Ars amatoria* as necessary to warn men. She then has Droitture cite Christine in response: "As for the charge that women are deceitful, I really do not know what more I can say to you, for you yourself have adequately handled the subject, answering Ovid and the others in your *Epistre au Dieu d'Amours* and your *Epistres sur le Roman de la Rose*" (2.54.1; 927–28; 187). Having explicitly carried the *translatio* from Ovid to Jean, she continues by discarding Ovid's argument about the common good: "The common good of a city or land or any community of people is nothing other than the profit or general good in which all members, women as well as men, participate and take part" (2.54.1; 928; 187). Ovid portrays the wrong version of a city and the wrong concept of the commonweal; rewriting Boccaccio's story of Dido immediately following the passages above, Christine splits up Boccaccio by reintroducing Vergil's version in order to propose Carthage as another Rome and a proper city.

Dido's story is recounted in two parts: the widow's flight from Phoenicia with her murdered husband's gold and the founding of Carthage, and her constant but tragic love for Aeneas. My contention is that one reason for the split is to deal with each of the two *translationes:* they are linked in that both pertain to the same character, the same text, the same writer, but they are distinct in theme and structure. The first story comes from Boccaccio and reads as another version of Christine's literary autobiography. Placing her stress on the account of the founding of Carthage, Christine adds the attribute of prudence to Boccaccio's version of the name change from Elissa to Dido: "For her outstanding strength, courage, and bold undertaking as well as for her very prudent government, they changed her name and called her Dido, which is the equivalent of saying *virago* in Latin, which means 'the woman who has the strength and force of a man' " (1.46.3; 775; 95).[34] The identification with Elissa's "transmu-

---

[33] See in particular Reason's "biography" of Ovid in 1.9.

[34] In Boccaccio's text, the etymology comes near the beginning of the tale, directly following the death of Dido (or Elissa, at this point), introducing her reactions to her brother Pygmalion's tormenting of her: "Having consumed much time in weeping and having often called in vain upon her beloved Acerbo, and also assailed her brother with all manner of curses, she decided to flee, whether forewarned in sleep—as some would have it—or taking counsel from herself, lest perhaps her brother's avarice draw her into death as well. So, having put aside feminine weakness and hardened her spirit into virile toughness, whence later she earned the name of Dido, meaning in the Phoenician tongue the same as *virago* in Latin, and bringing others from among the leaders of the

tation" into the *virago* Dido broadens the scope of Christine as author: not only is she capable of founding a city by "entreprise" but she is capable of governing it prudently. This is the usage to which she submits Boccaccio's *translatio:* his gold is sneaked out of Phoenicia and used to found a City of Ladies, recast *in bono,* just as Medea first appears in Christine's text solely as a woman of learning (1.32; 732–34).

What of the other *translatio?* It enters into the Dido story directly following the later attack on Ovid, as Christine's supplement to Boccaccio, who does not speak of the affair with Aeneas. Taking her version probably from the *Histoire ancienne,* Christine eliminates any references to the effects of the affair on the city; this part of the story is concerned exclusively with Dido's personal life (2.55; 929–31). Christine stresses Dido's hospitality and generosity and Aeneas's ingratitude and treachery. Dido's suicide is the first in a series of stories given in response to the Ovidian accusation of inconstancy; a glance at their contents helps explain the substance of the response. First comes the second part of Medea's story, also in purely personal terms: Medea is cast as another victim of a treacherous lover, with all mention of her children (and murder of them) excised (2.56; 931–33).[35] The fates of Thisbe and Hero are then recounted: both die (or believe they do) alongside a constant lover (2.57–58; 933–37). The stories of Guismonda and Lisabetta follow (*Decameron,* Day 4, 1st and 5th stories), each deceived by a relative (father and brothers, respectively [2.59–60; 938–51]).

Treachery by men is one theme, but the common thread is the Christian virtue of tolerance and piety epitomized in the rendering of Griselda's story (2.50; 900–910), which Christine takes from Petrarch's overtly moralizing version in order to empathize with the piety of the victim's stoicism and constancy (Richards 1982, 266n; 1992, 261). Griselda represents one extreme—marriage—of the moral code of conduct endorsed by Christine in positive opposition to what she sees as Jean's immoral stance. The other option, sainthood, is documented at length in the endless succession of gruesome martyrings of joyfully suffering women saints of the third part.

---

city, who for various reasons bore hostility to Pygmalion, she led them to her intention" (42, 168–70; 87). Although one might have expected Christine to preserve the parallel of emphasis on the reaction to the death of the husband, she nevertheless saw fit to emphasize the parallel instead in the act of founding the city—privileging the active, creative role over the reactive.

[35] Stecopoulos and Uitti argue that the rewriting of Medea turns on the personal quality of "feminine fidelity" in a context of Christian morality (54–55).

In Huot's terms, Christine opposes sublimation to seduction, giving a traditionally Christian choice of marriage either to a mortal man or to Christ.

The counterattack against Ovid, Jean, and Boccaccio comes not on the narrative level but in the alternative structure of the work, in Carthage as a new Rome. New contextualization provides a new moral order. Dante's morality suits Christine; her Dido gives no snubs to Aeneas in the underworld.[36] This is not to say that she does not find the *translatio* of Dante to be also misogynistic; she finds it so in its textuality, however, not in its narrative. Consequently, it is on the textual level that she snubs it. In her renderings, Dido, like Almathea, Nicostrata, Proba, and many others, takes Vergil's model and transforms it textually while conforming to it on the surface.

In her earlier works, Christine showed herself excluded from the structure Dante used, left behind as he continued on to found Rome. Unlike Bernard Silvestris, who represented the denial of authority out of philosophical rigor, Christine represented it as deriving from necessity. As Bernard used philosophy to chart the limits of the structure, so Christine made a virtue out of necessity, dressing up a radical recasting of Western tradition as conformity to it. The Christian poetics of Augustine and Dante structure her surface melting-down of the substance of Ovid, Jean, and Boccaccio, reversing their misogyny by *antiphrasis*. At the same time, beneath the disguise of the constructive authority of the voyage, the descent, and the founding of the city, Christine reconstructs her own tradition within, up, and through that of Vergil-Augustine-Dante. She takes the structure of the Vergil-Augustine-Dante tradition and dresses it up in the clothing of the women's tradition it had recounted. She ends up con-

---

[36] On Christine's "universalist ideal," see Earl Jeffrey Richards, "French Cultural Nationalism and Christian Universalism in the Works of Christine de Pizan," in *Politics, Gender, and Genre: The Political Thought of Christine de Pizan*, ed. Margaret Brabant (Boulder, 1992), 75–94; and Brabant and Michael Brint, "Identity and Difference in Christine de Pizan's *Cité des Dames*," in ibid., 207–22. Both essays, along with the contribution by Sheila Delany, "History, Politics, and Christine Studies: A Polemical Reply," 193–206, and Delany's earlier polemic, "Mothers to Think Back Through: Who Are They? The Ambiguous Example of Christine de Pizan," in *Medieval Texts and Contemporary Readers*, ed. Laurie A. Finke and Martin B. Shichtman (Ithaca, 1987), 177–97, explore the tensions in the model of society suggested by the *Cité des Dames*. My aim here has been less to enter that debate than once again to outline a set of fault lines on which a writer has used the motif of descent to generate meanings to be debated. But it is necessary first to see that debate as internal to Christine's poetics.

vincing it that its Troy, its City of God, and its New Rome were founded, built, and created by women, and are being ruled by them as well.

As a result of its reception of Dante no less than of its reception of Christine de Pizan, scholarship of the early twentieth century saw in her echoes of Dante a genuflection by rote that betokened at best a vague familiarity, at worst the ignorant repetition of a name overheard among her betters.[37] Readings of the modernist appropriation of Dante and the descent into hell have stood for a long time in something of the same situation. The remarkable analogous form in which Woolf simultaneously mythified and transformed a tradition from which she maintained to have been excluded allows us to distinguish between the synchronic and diachronic components of the *descensus ad inferos*. The attitude toward the past may have altered somewhat—founding the city is no longer the central issue, excavating it is—but the metaphorical garb remains strikingly similar to the transformation undergone by Christine. Read in the context of Christine's manipulation of topoi and *translationes* and of a dialectically construed Dante, Woolf's oeuvre reveals an alternate modernist strain intertwined with the reading Woolf has traditionally received as a high-modernist stylist. But as we have seen above, it is not in this alternative that a new reading of modernist and medieval literature lies, but in the possibility it creates of grasping the tension and interaction in the force field created between the one and the other.

"Romps of Fancy": Virginia Woolf, Turf Battles, and the Metaphorics of Descent

Cowan, Erasmus Cowan, sipped his port alone, or with one rosy little man, whose memory held precisely the same span of time; sipped his port, and told his stories, and without book before him intoned Latin, Virgil and Catullus, as if language were wine upon his lips. Only— sometimes it will come over one—what if the poet strode in? *"This* my image?" he might ask, pointing to the chubby man, whose brain is, after all, Virgil's representation among us, though the body gluttonize, and as

---

[37] See, for example, Arturo Farinelli, "She is not able to offer in her oeuvre more than an extremely pale reflection of the human and divine drama that unrolls in the *Commedia*" (*Dante e la Francia dall'età media al secolo di Voltaire* [Milan, 1908], 156); and Henri Hauvette, "These reminiscences of the *Divine Comedy* should not surprise us coming from the pen of an Italian woman who remained . . . very devoted to the great poet of Italy" (*Etudes sur la "Divine Comédie"* [Paris, 1922], 153).

for arms, bees, or even the plough, Cowan takes his trips abroad with a French novel in his pocket, a rug about his knees, and is thankful to be home again in his place, in his line, holding up in his snug little mirror the image of Virgil, all rayed round with good stories of the dons of Trinity and red beams of port. But language is wine upon his lips. Nowhere else would Virgil hear the like. And though, as she goes sauntering along the Backs, old Miss Umphelby sings him melodiously enough, accurately too, she is always brought up by this question as she reaches Clare Bridge: "But if I meet him, what should I wear?"—and then, taking her way up the avenue towards Newnham, she lets her fancy play upon other details of men's meeting with women which have never got into print. Her lectures, therefore, are not half so well attended as those of Cowan, and the thing she might have said in elucidation of the text for ever left out.[38]

Within a brief description of two relationships to Vergil and his tradition, Virginia Woolf defines the antinomies of gender that frame her oeuvre and continue to structure its reception. It is immediately apparent that she is presenting not only two modes of reading but two ways of writing: Cowan, distorted by overindulgence yet possessed of the connoisseur's expertise, wanders through the western European tradition, always secure because he has Vergil tucked away at home in his snug little mirror; he is complacent, but the unbroken heritage of two thousand years remains undeniably dazzling. Miss Umphelby, in contrast, indeed has the classics on her lips, but they do not seem to serve her or to suit her quite so well; when she lets her fancy wander, it always takes her away from those verses and into "other details . . . which have never got into print."

Now, when Virginia Woolf went herself to the women's colleges of Newnham and Girton in October 1928, she lectured on the same problematic. In the published version, *A Room of One's Own,* Woolf addressed the woman writer's lack of a tradition allegorically, in the more tragic myth of Shakespeare and his sister. The former, she says, "very probably [went] . . . to the grammar school, where he may have learnt Latin—Ovid, Virgil, and Horace—and the elements of grammar and logic" (*ROO* 48). Judith, however, receives only the scraps of her brother's learning ("no chance of learning grammar and logic, let alone of reading Horace and Virgil" [*ROO* 49]) and no encouragement; she has no tradition to think back through and no possible profession, and suffers accordingly, seduced and abandoned by actor-manager Nick Greene.

[38] *Jacob's Room* (1922; New York, 1978), 41–42. Hereafter cited by page number as *JR*.

Although Woolf wrote herself into the brief sibling allegory—her first image of the classics was through smatterings of older brother Thoby's education—she did not have quite the same difficulties as Judith.[39] She learned Greek and Latin from tutors Clara Pater and Janet Case and would eventually read Vergil as well as many of the Greeks in the original languages.[40] In other words, her relationship to Vergil approximated the description of Miss Umphelby in *Jacob's Room*. Knowledge of Vergil provides an allusive connection between autobiographical figures of past and present: Judith is proposed as the tragic past of youth, a mother to think back through; Miss Umphelby as the present-day scholar/writer, immersed in but not fulfilled by the sought-after education.

Woolf would map the new path from a rethought Judith to a reread Miss Umphelby in her two most resolutely nontraditional works: *Orlando* and *A Room of One's Own*. In them, she wove autobiographical motifs of her own (lack of) education within larger social allegories in ways extremely similar to what we saw Christine de Pizan doing above.[41] Synchronically related, as we shall see below, the historical contexts of the two differ considerably. Christine's allegories of learning and experience grew out of the disdain expressed in the *querelle des femmes* and elsewhere for the *Roman de la Rose* and its antecedents, and the awe expressed for the *Commedia* and its antecedents; Christine developed a counterattack

[39] On Woolf and Thoby, see Quentin Bell, *Virginia Woolf: A Biography*, 2 vols. (New York, 1972), 27, 68–69.

[40] William Herman, "Virginia Woolf and the Classics," in *Virginia Woolf: Centennial Essays*, ed. Elaine Ginsberg and Laura Moss Gottlieb (Troy, 1983), 260.

[41] There is no evidence that Woolf had any familiarity with or even awareness of Christine's writings. The original text of the *Cité des Dames* has not been republished (Richards's translation being the first modern edition); Woolf could have encountered the lyric poetry, and there exists a sixteenth-century English translation by Brian Anslay (*The Boke of the Cyte of Ladyes* [London, 1521], rpt. in *Distaves and Dames: Renaissance Treatises for and about Women*, ed. Diane Bornstein [Delmar, 1978]), but I have found no sign that she was aware of or had read these or any of the other prose works of Christine translated during the Renaissance. In addition to the structural use of the topos of descent and of transformation discussed below, certain similarities, especially between the *Cité des Dames* and *A Room of One's Own*, are quite striking: the scenes of reading at the start of the former and in the British Library in the latter book, for example (see Sheila Delany, "A city, a room: The scene of writing in Christine de Pisan and Virginia Woolf," in *Writing Woman: Women Writers and Women in Literature Medieval to Modern* [New York, 1983], 181–97). See also Earl Jeffrey Richards, "Sexual Metamorphosis, Gender Differences, and the Republic of Letters: Or, Androgyny as a Feminist Plea for Universalism in Christine de Pizan and Virginia Woolf," *Romance Languages Annual* 2 (1990): 146–52.

against the former through the structural armature of the latter. Woolf's *querelle* stands out most clearly against the backdrop of her literary feud with the Edwardian novelist and critic Arnold Bennett. He attempted to turn her language against her by excluding her from the metaphorics of descent; her "counterblast" appropriated the metaphorics to allegorize a poetics of gender. We find "Bennett" and "Woolf" squaring off on the turf of writing in the figures of Cowan and Umphelby, Mr. Bennett and Mrs. Brown, Judith Shakespeare and Nick Greene.

Beginning in medias res with Bennett's review of *A Room of One's Own*, we discover him fully immersed in the metaphorics. Apparently responding to the portrait of himself and his fellow Edwardians in Cowan, he finds Woolf to be the spit and image of Miss Umphelby: "She is merely the victim of her extraordinary gift of fancy (not imagination) . . . whereas a woman cannot walk through a meadow in June without wandering all over the place to pick attractive blossoms, a man can. Virginia Woolf cannot resist the floral enticement." [42] Bennett thus permits—indeed, he limits Woolf to—a female wandering of fancy, "the floral enticement." Woolf used the same imagery in the essay in order, like Christine, to make a virtue of necessity: she constructed *A Room of One's Own* around the denial of access, so eloquently expressed subsequently by Bennett, to the

[42] Arnold Bennett, "Queen of the High-Brows," *Evening Standard*, 28 Nov. 1929; rpt. in *Arnold Bennett: The "Evening Standard" Years: "Books and Persons," 1926–1931*, ed. Andrew Mylett (Hamden, 1974), 326–28; rpt. in part in Robin Majumdar and Allen McLaurin, eds., *Virginia Woolf: The Critical Heritage* (London, 1975), 258–60 (hereafter cited as *M&M*). Bennett was lampooned by name in the ninth chapter of *Jacob's Room*, the scene at the British Museum: "Youth, youth—something savage— something pedantic. For example, there is Mr. Masefield, there is Mr. Bennett. Stuff them into the flame of Marlowe and burn them to cinders. Let not a shred remain. Don't palter with the second rate. Detest your own age. Build a better one. And to set that on foot read incredibly dull essays upon Marlowe to your friends. To which purpose one must collate editions in the British Museum. One must do the thing oneself. Useless to trust to the Victorians, who disembowel, or to the living, who are mere publicists. The flesh and blood of the future depends entirely upon six young men. And as Jacob was one of them, no doubt he looked a little regal and pompous as he turned the page, and Julia Hedge disliked him naturally enough" (107). Andrew McNeillie touches on this moment in the Woolf-Bennett feud (*The Essays of Virginia Woolf*, ed. McNeillie, 6 vols. [New York, 1987-], 3:xiii; hereafter cited by volume and page number as *Essays*) but without noting that Woolf embeds the satirical jab at Bennett within the larger context of an oedipal genealogy of male scholars and the subsequent exclusion by the young Jacob of his contemporary, Julia Hedges. The three-way dynamic, evident in *JR* as well as in the later writings, is analogous to the one in Benjamin's criticism, with the addition of the component of gender. In both cases, it is a focal point of the autobiographical voice.

male wandering of "imagination." After all, the first of the three setbacks the narrator suffers at Oxbridge is nothing else than losing the "little fish" of her thought when she is *forbidden* to wander off the gravel path onto the green turf, for such wandering is the exclusive preserve of Fellows and Scholars.

From the pagan *error* of the "poetic fictions" of Miss Umphelby's Vergil, we have moved to the Christian allegory of Dante: unlike the dons of Oxbridge, Woolf will not be allowed to err from the straight and narrow path to follow the rite of passage into the authority of literary tradition; neither the Beadle nor Bennett will permit her a descent in order to accede to the arcane knowledge of the arts and sciences, to a past of fathers to think back through. Thus is the *descensus ad inferos* generally manifested in modernist literature. Neither Woolf nor Bennett was necessarily playing consciously on the topos of descent to the underworld, but the metaphorics appear nonetheless at the heart of the matter, dramatizing the abstract issues of poetics and ideology in terms of allegorical narrative.

I want to read their debate for the ways it helped generate and structure Woolf's writings of the 1920s. Her expression of strategies of rereading and rewriting in terms of the participation in or exclusion from the *descensus* suggests that *A Room of One's Own* and *Orlando* constitute a structural alternative to the other novels. This means expanding our sense of the topos from a metaphorical definition of the exclusive male tradition into the concomitant structuring of narrative therefrom. The *imitatio Christi*, with conversion at midpoint, ascension at the end, and prophetic authority between, is a consistent structural component of Woolf's fiction. The framework within which each of her novels would continue to be evaluated as "modernist" remained in fact the Christian polarity of Augustine and Dante: was it a model descent for high-modernist authority or an aimlessly Vergilian wandering?

The pagan/Christian tensions seen in medieval narratives of conversion continue to affect the modernist structures descended from (and returning to) them. We need only recall modernist medievalism from William Morris through Yeats, Pound, Joyce, and Eliot, and the Christian allegories of Oxford medievalists such as C. S. Lewis, Tolkien, and Charles Williams, to realize that Woolf's use of Vergil and Dante as symbolic representatives of the gendered power structure epitomized by Oxbridge is a gesture more symptomatic than idiosyncratic. What is most interesting about her position is that she manipulated medievalist motifs to negotiate not only the direct attacks of culturally conservative Edwardians such as Bennett but also the more complex and closer-to-home pressures of her high-modernist contemporaries.

As Beth C. Schwartz has noted in another context, the distinction of

Christian versus pagan was an important element of Woolf's conceptual-
ization of the role of gender in reading and writing.[43] Because Woolf's
"medievalism" stressed the difficulty of access to the past and the consequent need to rewrite it, it can suggest a framework for getting at the more
hidden—since less overtly polemical—rewritings of the past in the authors
mentioned above. Woolf's oblique and conflicted appropriation of medievalist poetics points the way toward a clearer understanding of modernism's complex and multivocal use of the classical and medieval traditions
to ground its contemporary projects. Not surprisingly, it is the overtly
polemical *Room of One's Own* that provides the interpretive means, on
the one hand, of perceiving the construction of Woolf's novels of the
period around the Christian and eschatological narrative of death as the
central determining figure of meaning; and, on the other hand, of reading
Orlando as a full-blown allegorical parody of this structure through the
failure of its protagonist to die at the proper moment.

In the allegorical and comic mode of *Orlando* and *A Room of One's
Own*, Woolf depicted herself and the woman writer as resolutely excluded
from and outside the male tradition as she had defined it; in the narratives
where the mode is primarily serious, she sought to define herself, her
problematics, and her tradition from within it.[44] Hence, in *A Room of*

---

[43] "Thinking Back through Our Mothers: Virginia Woolf Reads Shakespeare," *ELH*
58:3 (Fall 1991): 744 n. 11.

[44] I use the term "serious" or "traditional" narrative to signify that, whatever the
formal innovation involved, the psychological realism of the characters remains what
is at stake and is motivated and determined by the effect of death on these characters;
I use "comic" to signify that the narrative is not motivated by death. Finally, I use
"allegorical" here to signify that the characters are *not* drawn primarily for the sake of
psychological realism: they serve structural, social, autobiographical, and/or polemical
purposes and are constructed more through allusion and caricature than through observation and description. Evidently, "traditional" or "serious" literature in other periods
(the Middle Ages, for example) would be defined precisely as "allegorical." Indeed,
Dante's *Commedia* may mark a shift, since it is both "traditional," motivated by
death and structured around it allegorically, and "comic," since predicated on the final
avoidance of death: it begins badly and ends well. In terms of the first part of this
century, the "allegorical" mode, because of its nongenerational attitude toward rereading and rewriting tradition, is proposed to suggest Woolf's alternative to the direct,
generational confrontation of both Bennett's "Edwardian" and the more avant-garde
"Georgian" schools with the nineteenth-century realist tradition. At this point, a brief
chronology of the writings of Woolf referred to below may be helpful: *The Voyage Out*
(1915), *Night and Day* (1919), *Jacob's Room* (1922), "Mr. Bennett and Mrs. Brown"
(1924), *The Common Reader*, 1st series (1925), *Mrs. Dalloway* (1925), *To the Lighthouse* (1927), *Orlando* (1928), *A Room of One's Own* (1929), *The Waves* (1931), *The
Years* (1937), *Between the Acts* (1941).

One's Own, Woolf presented the reality of her situation—unable to descend as a man, she does so as a woman; whence *Orlando* allegorically reveals the goal of her fiction—to descend as a man but return as a woman.

FOR OUR CONCERNS in this chapter, the feud with Bennett began in September 1920, with the publication of *Our Women: Chapters in the Sex Discord.*[45] Bennett's basic conclusion there was twofold: men are inherently superior in all areas of intellectual and creative production; men and women view the world in essentially different ways (this was illustrated with a series of sketches about Jack and Jill). Woolf recorded her dismay in a diary entry of the time:

> For somehow Jacob has come to a stop, in the middle of that party too, which I enjoyed so much. Eliot coming on the heel of a long stretch of writing fiction (2 months without a break) made me listless, cast shade upon me; & the mind when engaged upon fiction wants all its boldness & self-confidence. He said nothing—but I reflected how what I'm doing is probably being better done by Mr Joyce. Then I began to wonder what it is that I am doing. . . . But I think my 2 months of work are the cause of it, seeing that I now find myself veering round to [John] Evelyn, & even making up a paper upon Women, as a counterblast to Mr Bennett's adverse views reported in the papers.[46]

She had apparently not read the book and apparently did not write the article, at least not in article form; Bennett's meaning for her was and

---

[45] *Our Women: Chapters in the Sex Discord* (London, 1920). In addition to the notes and introductions to *M&M*, Mylett, and *The Author's Craft and Other Critical Writings by Arnold Bennett*, ed. Samuel Hynes (Lincoln, 1968), and to Woolf's diaries and correspondence, two articles on this well-documented topic are particularly helpful: Edwin J. Kenney, Jr., "The Moment, 1910: Virginia Woolf, Arnold Bennett, and Turn of the Century Consciousness," *Colby Library Quarterly* 13 (1977): 42–66; and Beth Rigel Daugherty, "The Whole Contention between Mr. Bennett and Mrs. Woolf, Revisited," in Ginsberg and Gottlieb, 269–94. The exchange really began with Bennett's positive review in 1910 of the first Post-Impressionist Exhibition, curated by Roger Fry with Desmond MacCarthy and Leonard Woolf (Kenney, 46n). Virginia Woolf discussed the review in her 5 July 1917 *TLS* review of its reprint in *Books and Persons*. Although praising it (somewhat backhandedly) as the only proof in the book of Bennett's being "something more than an extremely competent, successful, businesslike producer of literature," she used the occasion to establish Bennett already as the figure of the passé Edwardian novelist (*Essays* 2:130).

[46] *The Diary of Virginia Woolf*, ed. Anne Olivier Bell, asst. McNeillie, 5 vols. (New York, 1977–84), 2:68–69; hereafter cited in text by volume and page number as *Diary*.

would remain symbolic, involving social, literary, and personal levels.[47] Bennett's book emerges in this passage as a way for Woolf to assuage her insecurity at the stalling of *Jacob's Room,* due, it seems, to the thought of how it would compare with *Ulysses,* which Eliot had been describing to her and which she and her husband were considering publishing (*Diary* 2:68 and note). Worries about her contemporary, Joyce (and *his* evident command of and ability to diverge from his tradition), were intertwined with the reaction to the misogyny of the elder Bennett.

The party scene to which Woolf was most likely referring here is the Plumers' luncheon for undergraduates (*JR* 33–35), which directly precedes the description of Erasmus Cowan and Miss Umphelby. Although we cannot know conclusively, the latter passage reads quite closely as a response to the various concerns that had interrupted Woolf in the middle of her satire of the academic drawing room. Indeed, it is not difficult to see in Miss Umphelby's name an allusive reversal of the situation in which Woolf found herself in the diary entry. When Heracles was required by the oracle to go into slavery as atonement for the murder of Iphitus, he was sold to Omphale, queen of Lydia, and set to woman's work, while she, in turn, assumed the lion's skin and club of the demigod.[48] Just as

---

[47] The entry is dated 26 Sept. 1920; her friend Desmond MacCarthy (as "Affable Hawk") reviewed Bennett's book in the *New Statesman* on 2 Oct. 1920, generally agreeing with Bennett's estimation of women. Woolf responded in the *New Statesman* a week later (9 Oct. 1920, rpt. in *Diary* 2, app. 3, 339–40); MacCarthy's retort appeared in the same issue; Woolf replied the next week (*Diary* 2:340–42); MacCarthy capitulated. The significant terms of the argument have been well framed and analyzed by Alice Fox in "Literary Allusion as Feminist Criticism in *A Room of One's Own,*" *Philological Quarterly* 63:2 (Spring 1984): 145–46: Woolf defends Sappho as a prominent woman poet and gives the same argument of the lack of tradition as the reason for the lack of more woman writers before the eighteenth century that she would develop in *ROO.* Her rhetoric about "not knowing Greek" is worth noting, as it continues the Christian/pagan dichotomy mentioned above and discussed later in the chapter. In the first letter, she writes, "Naturally, I cannot claim to know Greek as Mr. Bennett and Affable Hawk know it, but I have often been told that Sappho was a woman, and that Plato and Aristotle placed her with Homer and Archilochus among the greatest of their poets" (*Diary* 2:340).

[48] It may also be noted that "omphal-," in addition to being the combinative form for referring to "navel," has the sense of "a central part; center; hub; a central point, as of the earth (Gr. myth.), or figuratively of a literary work" (*Webster's New International Dictionary,* 2d ed.). Miss Umphelby and Cowan would thus figure the navel point of *Jacob's Room,* the hub of its quality as literary. Moreover, as David Damrosch has brought to my attention, this is also the sense in which the word is used when it appears in the opening pages of *Ulysses,* describing Buck Mulligan's tower, and in

Cowan is personally belittled while also being made to stand for Vergil's heritage, the fun being poked at Miss Umphelby's wandering mind masked an allusively formulated elevation of her status to that of successful writer.

Significantly for the form of the debate, neither here nor ever would Bennett read between the lines of Woolf's writing. As in his later reception of *A Room of One's Own*, he took such descriptions in *Jacob's Room* at face value: the author had been "obsessed with details of originality and cleverness" to the point of not being able to create characters vital enough to merit the epithet of "big novelist" (*M&M* 113). With its polemical heading "Is the Novel Decaying?" Bennett's review article again touched a nerve in Woolf, leading, as Kenney has aptly observed (43–44), to a counterattack clearly motivated by more than this single paragraph in a review.[49] Already in the first version of "Mr. Bennett and Mrs. Brown," Woolf defined "Mrs. Brown" in the terms set forth above:

> For what, after all is character—the way that Mrs. Brown, for instance, reacts to her surroundings—when we cease to believe what we are told about her, and begin to search out her real meaning for ourselves? In the first place, her solidity disappears; her features crumble; the house in which she has lived so long (and a very substantial house it was)

order to distinguish it as Irish from its original construction by the Englishman William Pitt: "Billy Pitt had them built, Buck Mulligan said, when the French were on the sea [Napoleon, 1805]. But ours is the *omphalos*" (17).

[49] In fact, Woolf, as in the 1917 article, seems to have been preparing for an attack from Bennett on her new novel. In a letter of 21 May 1922 to Janet Case (her old tutor in the classics), Woolf had already framed the upcoming debate in the genealogical terms of dual traditions of *A Room of One's Own:* "But don't you agree with me that the Edwardians, from 1895 to 1914, made a pretty poor show. By the Edwardians, I mean Shaw, Wells, Galsworthy, the Webbs, Arnold Bennett. We Georgians have our work cut out for us, you see. There's not a single living writer (English) I respect: so you see, I have to read the Russians: but here I must stop. I just throw it out for you to think about, under the trees. How does one come by one's morality? Surely by reading the poets. And we've got no poets. Does that throw light upon anything? Consider the Webbs—that woman has the impertinence to say that I'm a-moral: the truth being that if Mrs. Webb had been a good woman, Mrs. Woolf would have been a better. Orphans is what I say we are—we Georgians—but I must stop" (*The Letters of Virginia Woolf,* ed. Nigel Nicolson and Joanne Trautmann, 6 vols. [New York, 1975–80], 2:529; hereafter cited in text by volume and page number as *Letters*). The list of Edwardians would later be honed, and the Georgians separated from the women without mothers, but the terms are already here; Woolf proleptically answers the moral tone of Bennett's upcoming attack on the New School ("Is the Novel Decaying?") by attacking his school as having been neglectful parents.

topples to the ground. She becomes a will-o'-the-wisp, a dancing light, an illumination gliding up the wall and out of the window, lighting now in freakish malice upon the nose of an archbishop, now in sudden splendour upon the mahogany of the wardrobe. The most solemn sights she turns to ridicule; the most ordinary she invests with beauty. She changes the shape, shifts the accent, of every scene in which she plays her part. (*Essays* 3:387–88)[50]

Tradition takes on the additional symbolic language of the house, but Bennett and Brown play the same role as before: she is not solid; she crumbles, changes into light, and ridicules his solemnity. Woolf took the very qualities for which Bennett had condemned her novel, conflated them with the image of women from his pamphlet, and presented the result as his projection as novelist onto his characters.

Woolf's double identification of herself as author and as Mrs. Brown is even more evident in the second published version of the essay.[51] The concluding passage quoted above reappears at the beginning of the essay as "some Brown," a charming and seductive will-o'-the-wisp who lures on the unsuspecting novelist Woolf in hope of finding her character (*Essays* 3:420–21). She cites Bennett as authority for this proposition and goes on to present the celebrated allegory of herself as passenger in a train compartment observing Mr. Smith harassing the poor Mrs. Brown, before he storms out, leaving the two women alone together. Woolf then continues, first by criticizing and satirizing the "Edwardians," especially Bennett, whom she quotes at length, then by presenting the noble but somehow failed efforts of the "Georgians," her own generation of Forster, Lawrence, Eliot, Joyce, and Strachey, and finally by "rashly predicting" that "one of the great ages of English literature is dawning" (436). She neatly left herself out of the dichotomy. At the beginning she had pictured herself

---

[50] This version appeared first, signed, in the "Literary Review" of the *New York Evening Post*, 17 Nov. 1923, and was reprinted in *Nation and Athenaeum*, 1 Dec. 1923, and *Living Age* (Boston), 2 Feb. 1924 (*Essays* 3:388). To judge from grumbling and defensive remarks in more recent Bennett scholarship, Woolf seems for the moment to have won the battle of posterity. See Irving Kreutz, "Mr. Bennett and Mrs. Woolf," *Modern Fiction Studies* 8 (Summer 1962): 103–15; Samuel Hynes, "The Whole Contention between Mr. Bennett and Mrs. Woolf," *Novel* (Fall 1967): 34–44; and the introductions and notes to Bennett 1974 and 1968.

[51] This version was first presented as a talk to the Cambridge Heretics Club, 18 May 1924, then published, with revisions, by Eliot in the *Criterion* in July, and later as a pamphlet by the Hogarth Press. All three versions are now in *Essays* 3, along with details of their evolution (384–89, 420–38, 502–17).

as a novelist on the hunt for Mrs. Brown; at the end we find her as character and novelist sitting in the railway car, tempted by but resisting the idea of writing about her fellow passenger.

Woolf slipped her own solution to the problem into the essay, but it appears allegorically, in the fictional anecdote, and not discursively, in the critical analysis that follows. Woolf the narrator fulfills the prediction of Woolf the writer. Her sketchy picture of Mrs. Brown as a war widow who has packed her bags to escape an unwanted proposal develops from the single line of dialogue pronounced out of the hostess's duty to make conversation: "Can you tell me if an oak-tree dies when the leaves have been eaten for two years in succession by caterpillars?" (424). The narrator of the allegory is left with a vivid impression of Mrs. Brown's story that precisely embodies the Umphelby style, "tragic, heroic, yet with a dash of the flighty, and fantastic. . . . The caterpillars and the oak-trees seemed to imply all that. . . . The story ends without any point to it" (425). Woolf has written herself into the allegory in a programmatic description of her theory of narrative; here is the "rashly" announced future glory of writing.

The description, however, is programmatic only in its allegorical significance; the surface meaning conforms to Mr. Bennett's image of the character and the woman writer. Like Miss Umphelby, Mrs. Brown follows tradition (one recites Vergil; one obeys convention), if not as well superficially as she might have (the thoughts of one wander; the other weeps and finally flees). The strategy Woolf follows is twofold: she lampoons Cowan and Smith and Bennett, and she shows herself apparently conforming to their estimation of her: she is flighty and cannot create character; as woman she is in the man's tradition but will never match him. At the same time, she reverses the parameters, turning the negative qualities into an allegory of her strategy of writing; the ways she valorizes Miss Umphelby and captures Mrs. Brown's character articulate their own mechanism. Mrs. Brown's single phrase would reappear as one of the central allegorical components of *Orlando:* the oak tree with the view of all England that metamorphoses into the prize winning poem of the Georgian Orlando. The female form of divagation leads to artistic success as the discursive writer Woolf has negatively defined it; writing as allegorical rereading is the strategy she personifies in her character.

BY WAY OF framing the later stages in the so-called Bennett-Woolf feud, I want to examine how Woolf, in *A Room of One's Own* and *Orlando,* further strengthened the ground for a reading such as the one given above, by herself returning to and reworking images, words, and episodes from earlier works. I have mentioned and will return to the Dantean episode on

the turf at Oxbridge. First, however, I look at some other instances of
Woolf's rereading as rewriting in *A Room of One's Own* with reference
to *Jacob's Room* (already suggested by the analogous titles) and then
examine how the feud itself was taken up by Woolf in her allegories of the
late twenties.

The caricatures of Cowan and the Plumers probably had their first
inspiration in Aldous Huxley's "Farcical History of Richard Greenow,"
published in *Limbo*, an early collection of short stories reviewed by Woolf
in the *Times Literary Supplement* of 5 February 1920.[52] Woolf records
being amused by the description of a dinner with the Headmaster of Aesop
and a Mrs. Crawister, "who talks to the bewildered boys now about
eschatology, now about Manx cats ('no tails, no tails, like men. How
symbolical everything is!')" (*Essays* 3:177). We know the Manx cat from
its appearance in a later luncheon scene, at Oxbridge, in *A Room of One's
Own*, where the narrator covers up for her outburst of laughter when
thinking of men and women humming poetry to each other at another,
prewar luncheon by pretending to laugh at the tailless cat outside the
window (*ROO* 13).[53] Like much else in *A Room of One's Own*, the
narrator's laughter may be taken allegorically, as applying to the problem
of writing; the path of allusion would seem to lead back to *Jacob's Room*
and to the review of *Limbo*. In the latter, we saw her laughing with Mrs.
Crawister at the symbolism of "men without tails"; in the former, we find
earlier versions of the humming of the poetry of Tennyson and Rossetti in
the somewhat less elegant but equally matched tandem of Cowan and
Umphelby, and also, directly before the luncheon scene, Jacob's rather
peculiar burst of misogyny, when he compares a woman's being in the
King's College Chapel to a dog's being there.

A closer look at this last episode brings out how Woolf exploited the
possible chain of allusion to deepen the resonance of episodes in the first
chapter of *A Room of One's Own:* "No one would think of bringing a

[52] Judy Little, *"Jacob's Room* as Comedy: Virginia Woolf's Parodic *Bildungsroman,"* in *New Feminist Essays on Virginia Woolf,* ed. Jane Marcus (Lincoln, 1981),
106.

[53] Discussing the origin of the Manx cat in *ROO*, Jane Marcus notes the allusion to
Huxley's story, citing it as another exploration of gender and writing in the setting of
two imaginary universities (*Virginia Woolf and the Languages of Patriarchy* [Blooming-
ton, 1987], 174). Fox adds Quentin Bell's mention that the tail was a sign in the
Stephens family of its literary tradition: "In the nursery it was believed that all Stephens
were born with little tails seven inches long. . . . They were all writers" (Bell, 1:18–19;
Fox, 148). See also Joanna Lipking, "The Manx Cat Again," *Virginia Woolf Miscellany*
23 (Fall 1984): 2–3.

dog into church. For though a dog is all very well on a gravel path, and shows no disrespect to flowers, the way he wanders down an aisle, looking, lifting a paw, and approaching a pillar with a purpose that makes the blood run cold with horror (should you be one of a congregation—alone, shyness is out of the question), a dog destroys the service completely. So do these women—though separately devout, distinguished, and vouched for by the theology, mathematics, Latin, and Greek of their husbands" (*JR* 33). No wonder the narrator in *A Room of One's Own* decides the second time around (*ROO* 8–9) not to venture into the King's College Chapel! The resulting combination of antinomies suggests those of the Bennett-Brown scenario, with the woman/dog as both polar opposite and twin of the man/Manx cat.[54] The former, although identified as female, is accused of an activity usually associated with male dogs, which makes it all the more likely that Jacob's repulsion arises from the perceived symbolic intent of marking territory.

The latter, though identified as male, lacks a tail; this recalls Jacob's mother and the cat given to her family by the Rev. Jaspar Floyd. Remembering Mr. Floyd's proposal, she has a pleased reaction similar to that of the narrator at the luncheon in *A Room of One's Own:* " 'Poor old Topaz,' said Mrs. Flanders, as he stretched himself out in the sun, and she smiled, thinking how she had had him gelded, and how she did not like red hair in men" (*JR* 23). Woolf's Jacob reversed the standard gender identification dog/man in order to exclude women from his territory; Woolf duplicated the reversal from another perspective in *A Room of One's Own*. The cat without a tail as woman writer superficially assuages convention while nevertheless retaining defiance of that convention—the image of Jacob's fear in the memory of the gelded Topaz.

The two creatures are further implicated in the gendered business of writing through their relationship to the turf and the gravel path of Oxbridge. A dog "on a gravel path" and showing "no disrespect for flowers" is acceptable to Jacob, but its "wandering down the aisle" to mark its territory in a quintessentially masculine fashion is not. In contrast, the

[54] For further evidence of the connection with "Mr. Bennett and Mrs. Brown" and of the gendered associations of cat and dog, see Wyndham Lewis's account of the quarrel: "Well then, when Mrs. Woolf, the orthodox 'idealist,' tremulously squares up to the big beefy brute, Bennett, plainly the very embodiment of commonplace *matter*— it is, in fact, a rather childish, that is to say an oversimple, encounter. It is a cat and dog match, right enough. . . . I doubt if, at bottom, it is very much more than a boy and girl quarrel (to change the metaphor from dog-and-cat)" (*Men without Art* [1934; Santa Rosa, 1987], 133). On Lewis's equally pointed and reductive evocation of the metaphorics in the context of *ROO*, see Marcus 1987, 136–62.

Manx cat "padding softly across the quadrangle" and pausing "in the middle of the lawn as if it too questioned the universe" (*ROO* 11) starts the narrator on the train of thought that leads to her inopportune laughter, which she can cover up only by pointing to the (male) figure of the cat on the turf. In a strategy similar to that seen in "Mr. Bennett and Mrs. Brown," the narrator uses the very image of her subterfuge as a means of dispelling the suspicions aroused by it in her traditional readers. Laughter in a sense at the memory of the fun she had reversing roles in *Jacob's Room* (and allegorically, then, thinking about a successful maneuver of women's writing), along with the ability to pass off the memory as the conformity of a lesser (Manx) male, become, in the narrative of *A Room of One's Own*, an allegory of a successful maneuver of woman's writing. And, again, the reception of Bennett gauges the success of the strategy: reviewing *A Room of One's Own*, he reacted anxiously but could accuse her only of what she was manifestly doing—being distracted at a luncheon —and not of the unperceived subterfuge.

The constellation of allusion coalesces around the question of turf, for Bennett's figure emerges along with Jacob's out of the first chapter of *A Room of One's Own*. On the trail of the little fish of her thought, the narrator sets off across a grass plot, only to be intercepted and turned back: "Instinct rather than reason came to my help; he was a Beadle; I was a woman. This was the turf; there was the path. Only the Fellows and Scholars are allowed here; the gravel is the place for me. . . . As I regained the path the arms of the Beadle sank, his face assumed its usual repose, and though turf is better walking than gravel, no very great harm was done" (*ROO* 6). The Dantean motif is evident, especially if we recall her final remark, that the protection of this turf, "which has been rolled for three hundred years in succession," had sent her "little fish" into hiding: her writing is suffering from being forbidden the privileged descent of error into conversion and revelation.

There is a further level of allegory at work, which duplicates that of the two images of Vergil above. In "Another Criticism of the New School" (2 December 1926), the first discussion of Woolf published by Bennett after the various versions of her essay bearing his name, he reviewed her books, confessing that he was "beaten" by her latest, *Mrs. Dalloway*. Bennett identified Woolf as the leader of the new school and faulted it through her with the absence of logical construction and the lack of concentration on the theme (if any), concluding that "interest is dissipated" and "material is wantonly or clumsily wasted" (1974, 5; *M&M* 190). He then conceded her some "exquisitely done" passages before going on to discuss "admirable specimens of narrative art and character-drawing" in other new novels. The examples of the latter cited by Bennett seem to have been calculated to strike close to home, for they were all three written by women, and all three, he wrote, "hold fast by tradition" and were not, therefore, "specimens of the new method." His final example was a work by a South African friend and protégée of his (he had written a preface to a volume of her stories), Pauline Smith: "And finally, I must mention *The Beadle* of Miss Pauline Smith. The reviews of *The Beadle*—seldom can a first novel have received such praise—do honour to the wakefulness and the insight of reviewers. This novel is simple; it is austere; its field is limited; it is without bravura or ornament of any kind. But its beautiful emotional quality is genuine and marvelously overcomes the reader. *The Beadle* is just about perfect and a masterpiece. The new school of fiction, however, can take no credit for the work, which is as old-fashioned as the moon" (1974, 6).[55] There is no more evidence that Woolf read Smith's novel than that she read *Our Women;* it can be assumed, however, that she read Bennett's review. The language of Bennett's description is well suited to his conception of the sexes—Smith's novel is "as old-fashioned as the moon," a time-honored symbol of feminine imitative dependence on and deference to the masculine sun—and to a contrast with his figure of Woolf —austere, simple, limited, without bravura or ornament, and so forth, a Mrs. Brown perfectly matched to Mr. Smith.

The Beadle, then, not only personifies the male's protection of his physical and intellectual turf; the allegory deepens through the allusive resonance of Bennett's image of a female dependent who does the work of protecting tradition for him. Just so, then, is the narrator next told by the fluttering "guardian angel" that she may not be admitted to the library at Oxbridge unless *accompanied* by a Fellow or furnished with a letter of introduction; as a writer, she remains orphaned. The Beadles, on the other hand, following the narrator's evening exit from the campus, are seen "fitting innumerable keys into well-oiled locks," as "the treasure house was being made secure for another night" (*ROO* 13); they are granted the keys to tradition, although only to protect and guard it, not to use it for themselves.[56]

The Beadle returns in the fourth chapter, where Woolf is discussing the

---

[55] The review is reproduced in *M&M* 189–90, but only as far as the criticism of the new school, and does not include Bennett's discussion of the other new novelists. Pauline Smith's novel was published in London in 1926 by Jonathan Cape.

[56] Compare with Orlando's vision of Victorian society: "In the old days, one would meet a boy trifling with a girl under a hawthorn hedge frequently enough. Orlando had flicked many a couple with the tip of her whip and laughed and passed on. Now, all that was changed. Couples trudged and plodded in the middle of the road indissolubly linked together" (*Orlando: A Biography,* 1928, ed. Brenda Lyons, notes Sandra Gilbert [Harmondsworth, 1993], 166; hereafter cited as *O*).

difficulty for a woman of writing when she had to "alter her values in deference to the opinion of others" (77). In keeping with the seriousness of this topic, Woolf heats up her rhetoric when she considers the advice of a pair of men who recommended in 1928 that prizes be given to "female novelists [who] aspire to excellence by courageously acknowledging the limitations of their sex" (78). At this point, she recalls the allegory of her opening chapter: "One must have been something of a firebrand to say to oneself, Oh but they can't buy literature too. Literature is open to everybody. I refuse to allow you, Beadle though you are, to turn me off the grass. Lock up your libraries if you like; but there is no gate, no lock, no bolt that you can set upon the freedom of my mind" (*ROO* 78–79).[57] Given the tone of Bennett's appraisal of *The Beadle* as an option to the "incoherent" *Mrs. Dalloway*, Woolf was able to have in mind here a specific as well as a social target for her defiance.

In fact, the answer Woolf gave to this dilemma is already present in the second part of the allegory of the first chapter: the dinner at Fernham. It will be recalled that it is en route to lecture at Newnham that Miss Umphelby is distracted from her recitations of Vergil in *Jacob's Room*. Here too, the narrator, still thinking about the pair of poets humming to each other, following in the footsteps of Miss Umphelby and her singing of Vergil, distractedly misses "the turning up" to Fernham (*ROO* 15). Unlike for Miss Umphelby, however,—and here we see a distinction between the aims of the two works—this missed turning proves the key (of a different sort) to the locks and gates of Oxbridge. Still following her thoughts (thus not being turned away from them), the narrator retraces her steps: "It was the time between the lights when colours undergo their intensification and purples and golds burn in window-panes like the beat of an excitable heart; when for some reason the beauty of the world revealed and yet soon to perish (here I pushed into the garden, for, unwisely, the door was left open and no beadles seemed about), the beauty of the world which is so soon to perish, has two edges, one of laughter, one of anguish, cutting the heart asunder" (*ROO* 16–17). She has missed her turning, but instead of continuing to descend, she goes back to the "turn up," and, never losing the thread of the "little fish" of the thought she has been following all day, she is, parenthetically, able to avoid the Beadle as well as the Bennett and to find her turf within the garden. Like Christine de Pizan before her,

[57] Bennett discussed Smith in two more *Evening Standard* articles in 1927 and 1928, focusing in both cases on her genius, the perfection of *The Beadle*, and on how "publishers . . . are now competing for her next book" (1974, 142; see also 21). Clearly, he was bent on providing her with the keys she needed.

Woolf uses the change of season from autumn to spring to signal a change of mode; she is now approaching the turf obliquely.

On the terrace appears an alternative to Miss Umphelby, J——H——, who is positively identified later in the essay as Jane Harrison, the feminist classicist.[58] If the surface tone of the description of the meager dinner at Fernham is dampening, the allusive tone shifts the balance back toward laughter: the entire passage has one of its sources in an episode Woolf removed from the duality of *Jacob's Room*. Originally intended to contrast "Angela's room" at Newnham to Jacob's at Cambridge, and published separately in *Atlanta's Garland* (of the Edinburgh University Women's Union) in 1926,[59] "A Woman's College from Outside" briefly presents a scene almost identical in tone to the one of the narrator's arrival at Newnham in *A Room of One's Own*.[60] A subtly different, enigmatic version of that arrival appears as part of a dialogue between the girls: " 'We're not eunuchs.' 'I saw her slipping in by the back gate with that old hat on. They don't want us to know' " (*Books and Portraits* 7). The related images of eunuch (as the gelded cat) and dog eventually slipped into *Jacob's Room;* the Manx cat ("we're not eunuchs"), which prowls the turf undetected by beadles, would have to wait until *A Room of One's Own* to make its official appearance.

In other words, Woolf made a practice of framing the rereading of her works; she took pains to point out the mythic past of Miss Umphelby and took pains to recover the Manx cat missing from *Jacob's Room*. The garden is not just a woman's alternative to the turf; to enter it is, surreptitiously, to sit as Manx cat in Oxbridge. The woman's tradition proposed in *A Room of One's Own* sets forth a strategy of allusive and allegorical rereading; that strategy is simultaneously demonstrated to be something else by Woolf in just such a rereading of her own, Georgian novels.

In a way, Bennett was one of her best readers. He saw that *Orlando* and *A Room of One's Own* belonged together and distinct from Woolf's other works: he attacked the latter as part of the "New School"; he dismissed the former two volumes for precisely those things Woolf was

---

[58] See Marcus's discussions of the significance of Jane Harrison to Woolf, and especially to *ROO* (1987, 180–81, 194–95n, and passim). Harrison had, in fact, died in April 1928 (the talks were given in October [*Diary* 3:179–81]). This may be one motivation behind the "spring twilight" of the scene in an October talk: the pressure of the present moment works differently in Fernham than at Oxbridge, where the Manx cat had sat in the "beautiful October day"; we are in an allegorical reality.

[59] E. L. Bishop, "The Shaping of *Jacob's Room:* Woolf's Manuscript Revisions," *Twentieth Century Literature* 32:1 (Spring 1986): 116.

[60] Rpt. in *Books and Portraits*, ed. Mary Lyon (New York, 1977), 6–9.

doing in them, linking them with paired titles: "A Woman's High-Brow Lark" and "Queen of the High-Brows":[61] "I surmise that Orlando is intended to be the incarnation of something or other—say, the mustang spirit of the joy of life, but this is not quite clear to me. . . . The succeeding chapters are still more tedious in their romp of fancy. . . . I shall no doubt be told that I have missed the magic of the work. The magic is precisely what I indeed have missed" (*M&M* 233).[62] One may add to these remarks

[61] It is perhaps not coincidental to note the role played by "high brows" in *Orlando* and *ROO:* Shakespeare is remembered by Orlando for his high forehead (79, 164), which the dome of St. Paul's recalls to her; in the passage discussed above, J—— H—— is described as having the same "great forehead" and "shabby dress" (*ROO* 17); and Judith Shakespeare has "the same grey eyes and rounded brows" as her brother (*ROO* 50). Again, *ROO* is telling us how to read *Orlando*, and Bennett unwittingly furnishes all the clues for the reading. (Bennett's titles, of course, also carry the weight of class connotation with them; Woolf is implicitly attacked for the imputed snobbery and lack of seriousness of the two works. Whether her conceptions of Harrison and Shakespeare retain remnants of that same class consciousness is another question.) For a more comprehensive reading of Shakespeare in *Orlando* and *ROO* as a "maternal muse" here implied by the imagery of the high brow, see Schwartz, 721–46. I would argue against Schwartz, however, that, as is also evident from the present imagery, Shakespeare occupies this maternal position *simultaneously* with the paternal one more traditionally argued for by Beverly Ann Schlack, "Fathers in General: The Patriarchy in Virginia Woolf's Fiction," in Marcus 1983, 54–56; and Maud Bodkin, *Archetypal Patterns in Poetry* (London, 1963), 301–2. I maintain that we have Shakespeare and his sister as twin and interrelated allegories of the two types generally opposed by critics.

[62] Another reader who received these two works as a set distinct from Woolf's other novels was Jorge Luis Borges, who translated both *Orlando* and *ROO* but nothing else by Woolf. (*ROO* was serialized in *Sur* in 1935–36; it and *Orlando* were then published in book form in 1937.) In October 1936 Borges published a capsule biography of Woolf in a book column for the society weekly *El Hogar* in which he lumps her other works together and then discusses *Orlando* and *ROO* as "musical pieces": "The hero of this extremely original novel—undoubtedly one of Virginia Woolf's most intense works and one of the most singular and maddening [*desesperantes*] of our age—lives for three hundred years and is, at times, a symbol of England and particularly of its poetry. Magic, bitterness, and delight collaborate in this book. It is, moreover, a musical book, not only for the euphonic virtues of its prose, but for the very form of its composition, made up of a limited number of themes that return and combine with one another. What we hear in *A Room of One's Own* is also a musical piece in which dreams and reality alternate and find their equilibrium" (*El Hogar*, 30 Oct. 1936; rpt. in *Textos cautivos* [Barcelona, 1986], 38–39; trans. in *Borges: A Reader*, ed. Emir Rodriguez Monegal and Alistair Reid [New York, 1981], 91–92). In characteristically eccentric fashion, Borges put his finger on the allegorical connection between the two works.

on *Orlando* Bennett's characterization of Woolf as author of *A Room of One's Own:* if the novels are personified in Miss Umphelby's sticking to Vergil with difficulty, these two texts let the Roman poet go altogether. They are romps of fancy indeed, but with the double edge of seriousness disguised allegorically underneath, as the Manx cat covered the serious laughter over the humming poets; such polemical humor is another feature shared with the earlier allegorical "romps" of Christine de Pizan.

THE ALLUSIVE constellation of a poetics of gender spun out above may be related to the narrative strategies of Woolf's novels through her use of Dante. The novels can be read as structured around a Christian and eschatological understanding of the significance of death: Christ died in the middle of his life (thirty-three years old); his death and resurrection provided the meaning and structure for a narrative of Christian history from the Creation to the Last Judgment. The opening words of Dante's *Inferno*—"Nel mezzo del cammin di nostra vita"—explain the significance of this structure for literature: a Christian life (and Christian allegory) is modeled on the life of Christ. Having descended and been converted, one can recapitulate his history. The true meaning is discovered —that is, reinvented—by retelling it from the vantage point of having ended.

We have seen already the rhetorical strategies necessary for this manner of mythifying history; we have seen Woolf's allegorization of her exclusion as woman writer from that possibility. Her fiction has generally been read as participating in a high-modernist search for ever-greater formal innovation, as an accepted part of that tradition. The double-edged valence of the eschatological structure itself and Woolf's ambivalence toward it, however, suggest that this may not be the only way of reading her use of it in the fiction. The comic and parodic reading suggested by *Orlando* and *A Room of One's Own* emerges as a second pole in the discursive space of the oeuvre if we reconsider the debt of Woolf's other fiction to Dante and the *imitatio Christi*.

Bennett's hostility betokened a wholehearted rejection of Woolf's writing for its failure to conform to the norms of Edwardian literature; the response of her Georgian contemporaries was rather more nuanced. It is the latter reception, based on high-modernist expectations of increased departure from, while remaining firmly within, an ongoing tradition of formal innovation, that has dominated Woolf criticism ever since. E. M. Forster's evaluation of the trajectory of Woolf's career is emblematic here: the first novel, *The Voyage Out* (1915), was a promising venture on the right path; *Night and Day* (1919) was disappointing because merely "a

novel of fact"; *Jacob's Room* then established the Woolf style, and all
went well until *The Years* (1937), when she deserted the poetry to which
she fortunately returned in her final work, *Between the Acts* (1941); her
nonfictional work was negligible.[63]

It is not coincidental that Woolf's use of the structure of the *imitatio
Christi* mirrors this trajectory: it is only partly present in *The Voyage Out,*
absent in *Night and Day,* and central from *Jacob's Room* through to *The
Waves.* The *Voyage Out* turns on the moment of greatest descent, Rachel
Vinrace and Terence Hewet's engagement at the native village in the jungle
interior, but it is undercut soon after by Rachel's unforeseen death. Conversely, in *Jacob's Room,* the first of Woolf's novels to be received as
properly modernist and experimental, we find the characteristic attempt
to reconstruct after the fact the meaning of the eponymous protagonist.
Our realization of Jacob's death in the First World War on the final
page of the book rewrites what we had been reading into the form of a
recapitulation and consequently demands a rereading under that assumption. The final page functions as both midpoint and endpoint of the narrative, repeating a pattern familiar to us from Augustine and Dante.

The eschatological structure continues through Woolf's "successfully"
high-modernist novels; the particular debt to Dante becomes manifest in
Mrs. Dalloway.[64] Woolf appears to have taken up the *Inferno* in response
to the war, and her reading was colored by it; she does not sound terribly
enthusiastic about the poem and seems to have left off somewhere in the
second half of *Purgatorio* (*Diary* 1:84).[65] This reaction carried over to the
use of Dante to delineate the character of Septimus. The shell-shocked
veteran is explicitly identified with the *Inferno* and the narrative of descent
to the underworld: his descent was the war, and he ends up a suicide,
unable to return, to escape the past.[66] The Dantean resonance in the story
of Septimus grounds the crucial final connection between himself and
Clarissa Dalloway, establishing coherence between the narrative threads

---

[63] E. M. Forster, "Virginia Woolf," in *Two Cheers for Democracy* (New York,
1942), 242–58. Rpt. in *Virginia Woolf: A Collection of Critical Essays,* ed. Claire
Sprague (Englewood Cliffs, 1971), 14–25.

[64] *Mrs. Dalloway* (1925; New York, 1953).

[65] "I cant open Dante or think of him without a shudder—the cause being I think
partly the enormous numbers of newspapers I've been reading in" (*Diary* 1:69).

[66] Beverly Ann Schlack has analyzed the use of Dante in Septimus's character, and
various motifs Woolf has taken from the grove of the suicides in the seventh circle of
hell, in *Continuing Presences: Virginia Woolf's Use of Literary Allusion* (University
Park, 1979), 69–70. Unfortunately, she restricts herself to a thematic reading of Dante
and seems to regard Woolf's use of allusion in general as a static and fixed instead of a
supple and highly motivated technique.

and within the apparently unmotivated and abrupt ending at Clarissa's soiree. To put it in narrative terms, her feeling of implication in Septimus's death on hearing of it at the dinner party causes her to recapitulate the day's events. Furthermore, it causes us as readers to reconsider the personal (in terms of suicide) and social (in terms of class) connections between the otherwise unconnected characters of the novel. Thus, we find ourselves in a modern but consistently Christian structure of the allegory of conversion: the characters are all related through the figural signifying power of Septimus's death.

The war also structures the narrative in *To the Lighthouse*, which is classically Vergilian as well as Christian: descent, prophecy, and return are laid out linearly. Hence, the descent into history of the second of the three parts, "Time Passes," parenthetically records the deaths of Mrs. Ramsay, Andrew, and Prue that structure our reading of the before and the after. It begins with Vergil's image: "One by one the lamps were extinguished, except that Mr. Carmichael, who liked to lie awake a little reading Virgil, kept his candle burning rather longer than the rest." [67] Like her contemporaries, Woolf was introducing patently non-naturalistic, allegorical schemas into the construction of her novels, a fact that Bennett seems, perceptively enough, to have sensed. Indeed, it was the only part that irritated him of a book that he regarded as her best: "Mrs. Ramsay almost amounts to a complete person. Unfortunately she goes and dies, and her decease cuts the book in two" (1974, 60; *M&M* 200). Once again, he hit the nail on the head.

Dante's name crops up again as someone Woolf felt like reading in the diary entry of 31 July 1926, which begins, "Here is a whole nervous breakdown in miniature" (*Diary* 3:103), and describes her condition following completion of *To the Lighthouse* at the end of May: "Read some Dante & Bridges without troubling to understand, but got pleasure from them" (103). But it is not until August 1930, when Woolf has rewritten her way to the hundredth page of *The Waves*, that we find Dante resurfacing on the same day in which her novel was "resolving itself . . . into a series of dramatic soliloquies": "This surpasses 'writing' as I say about Sh[akespea]re. I read the Inferno for half an hour at the end of my own page: & that is the place of honour" (*Diary* 3:312–13). She continued reading Dante regularly through 1940; his name constantly reappears in the "place of honour," interspersed with and implicated in the composition of *The Waves* and *The Years*.[68] These two novels are the most

---

[67] *To the Lighthouse* (1927; New York, 1955), 189; hereafter cited as *TTL*.

[68] See *Diary* 3:320, 326, 339n; *Diary* 4:5, 264, 274–75, 278, 283, 291–92, 295, 320; *Diary* 5:37, 90, 188, 329.

Dantean in structure of Woolf's books: the former modeled on the hours of the day and the ages of man, the latter citing the central canto of *Purgatorio* at its own midpoint.[69] A comparison of the use of the structure in them can also go a long way toward explaining their different reception by the Georgians and subsequently elucidate the role of the earlier *Orlando* and *A Room of One's Own* in guiding a reading based on that difference.

The Christ motif in the name Percival, the determining figure of *The Waves*, is evident, filtered through the medievalist romance of Arthurian legend. Moreover, the character dies at midday, the moment on which the various narratives of the characters all turn.[70] The mode of his death (falling off a horse) recalls traditional iconography of the conversion of Paul on the road to Damascus. Hence both the temporal and the thematic structures depend on the Christian narrative of conversion. This is set out for us by the conclusion of the novel in the voice of Bernard, the writer-figure among the siblings. In the final section ("Now to sum up . . . Now to explain to you the meaning of my life" [238]), at night, confronting death, Bernard recapitulates the concluded narrative for us, from beginning to end, with Percival's death in the center: "Soon, too, a maid came in with a note and as she [Jinny] turned to answer it and I felt my own curiosity to know what she was writing and to whom, I saw the first leaf fall on his grave. I saw us push beyond this moment, and leave it behind us for ever. And then sitting side by side on the sofa we remembered inevitably what had been said by others; 'the lily of the day is fairer far in May'; we compared Percival to a lily—Percival whom I wanted to lose his hair, to shock the authorities, to grow old with me; he was already covered over with lilies" (265). Bernard goes on to challenge death, riding against it in imitation of his brother, "with my spear couched and my hair flying back like a young man's, like Percival's, when he galloped in India. Against you I will fling myself, unvanquished and unyielding, O Death!" (297). The meaning is certainly not traditionally Christian, but the structure, symbolism, and resonance are.

As the reference to Percival suggests, Woolf's Christian borrowing is also resolutely literary in its provenance. In the margin of the diary entry discussing Bernard's final speech, Woolf copied the verses of *Inferno* 26.94–102: the speech of Ulysses to the protagonist Dante describing his final, mad voyage to the ends of the world, where his ship sank in sight of

---

[69] *Between the Acts* seems to be a different story; Knowles's chapter on the novel in *A Purgatorial Flame*, for example, does not turn up a single Dantean reference, basing its argument rather on contemporary references and general imagery of limbo (36–61).
[70] *The Waves* (1931; New York, 1978), 148–51; hereafter cited as *TW*.

the mountain of purgatory.[71] In the *Commedia,* the act was manifestly one of the pagan hero's damning folly, a contrast to the pilgrim Dante's correct path to the mount of purgatory, and also paralleled the danger involved in the pagan presumption of the poet Dante's endeavor. Woolf clearly identified herself here with Ulysses and with Bernard, in contrast to the pilgrim's piety; whether she regarded it as tragic folly or wild fancy depends on the tradition in which one chooses to read her, the interpretation one wishes to give the conclusion of *The Waves*—high-modernist drama or the "caricature value" of a "romp of fancy." After all, the passage comparing Percival to a lily continues by undercutting the seriousness of his death and its meaning: "So the sincerity of the moment passed; so it became symbolical; and that I could not stand. Let us commit any blasphemy of laughter and criticism rather than exude this lily-sweet glue, and cover him with phrases, I cried" (265).

In light of this passage it seems difficult not to see in the apparently deadly serious conclusion of *The Waves* a reflection of the conclusion of *Orlando,* where the modern heroine has a vision of her seafaring husband Marmaduke Bonthrop Shelmerdine,

There was her husband's brig, rising to the top of the wave! Up, it went, and up and up. The white arch of a thousand deaths rose before it. Oh rash, oh ridiculous man, always sailing, so uselessly, round Cape Horn in the teeth of a gale! But the brig was through the arch and out on the other side; it was safe at last!

"Ecstasy!" she cried, "ecstasy!" And then the wave sank, the waters grew calm; and she saw the waves rippling peacefully in the moonlight. (O 227)

[71] "Né dolcezza di figlio, né la pieta / del vecchio padre, né 'l debito amore / lo qual dovea Penelopè far lieta, / vincer potero dentro a me l'ardore / ch'i' ebbi a divenir del mondo esperto / e de li vizi umani e del valore; / ma misi me per l'alto mare aperto / sol con un legno e con quella compagna / picciola da la qual non fui diserto" (Neither fondness for my aged father, nor the due love that would have made Penelope glad, could conquer in me the longing that I had to gain experience of the world, and of human vice and worth. But I put forth on the deep open sea with one vessel only, and with that small company that had not deserted me). Woolf appears to have read the passage a few weeks afterward, 10 Jan. 1931: "Now those figures have driven away my stir & spirit of delight, whose wings were brushing me in spite of our solid middleclass household (servants again) & over cooked meat. I think a little Dante is indicated— Canto XXVI" (*Diary* 4:6). Whether she was returning to a favorite passage or just discovering it, the link to *The Waves* is apparent. Woolf clearly felt the ending of *The Waves* as closely as, although differently than, she did that of *Orlando.* On the significance of *Inf.* 26 in terms of the autobiographical allegory of conversion and the *descensus ad inferos,* see above, chapter 3, pp. 107–8.

Bernard's horror of the "immeasurable sea" (284) had its counterpart in Orlando's visionary ability to render it calm. Her husband neither sails beyond the Horn to Ulysses' doom at the South Pole nor follows Dante's poetic journey through purgatory; he flies straight back to Orlando with a wild goose. This does not necessarily cast the profundity of the conclusion of *The Waves* wholly into doubt, but it does suggest that its meaning rests on the contested ground between a high-modernist eschatology and a less privileged mode, one excluded from the previous tradition. In the language of Christine's use of the same topos of writing as sailing, the desire for epic voyage is counterbalanced by the strategy of rhetorical modesty of the *piccioletta barca*, Shelmerdine's brig by the toy boat on the Serpentine: "And repeating 'A toy boat on the Serpentine', and 'Ecstasy', alternately, for the thoughts were interchangeable and meant exactly the same thing, she hurried towards Park Lane" (*O* 199). The dilemma rendered more discursively in *A Room of One's Own*—writing within a tradition from which one is excluded—is also staged in the margins of the "successful" works as a tension between two possible readings.

The standard by which her works have generally been measured is the degree to which, as did her Miss Umphelby, Woolf appeared to take a traditional narrative and symbolic structure and apply them to the contemporary details of modern society. By this reading, in *Jacob's Room, Mrs. Dalloway, To the Lighthouse,* and *The Waves,* Woolf innovated within tradition in good high-modernist fashion. So, for Bennett and the elder generation, the ending of *Mrs. Dalloway,* for example, was unmotivated and abrupt (*M&M* 190); for her contemporaries, in contrast, it eloquently expressed the fragmentation of modern life. If the latter reception was more progressive in form, it was nevertheless no less rigid than the other in terms of its criteria for judgment.

We need only think of Bell's account of Leonard Woolf's reading of the manuscript of *The Years:* it was "a failure—but . . . not so disastrous a failure as Virginia had supposed," simply because it followed but diverged from *The Waves,* her most perfectly high-modernist work, which Leonard considered her masterpiece. Woolf found himself forced by his concern for his wife's health to stoop to the "duplicity" of telling her *The Years* was "extraordinarily good" (Bell 2:196). In other words, it did not meet the model of carrying forth the tradition that the "New School" expected of her; that is, it did not follow the steady forward march of progress expected of her by modernism (and by modernity).

As in the case of modern critical disputes over similar questions from Homer through Dante to the present, the reception has been structured around a modernist generational paradigm: the old guard's rejecting and the new guard's attacking the immediate predecessor and outflanking him by writing him out of the older tradition, while holding its own generation to the same model. This is the ideology of modernism, the language of its manifestoes. But a different critical paradigm suggests the possibility of shifting the terms of the debate. Just as the Homeric question is integral to the poem's internal dynamics, and Dante's allegory challenges us to accept its rhetorical power while remaining conscious of the sleight of hand by which it produces that acceptance, so Woolf's novels construct a high-modernist oeuvre while also problematizing such a construction.

The debate rages within her writings, and analysis of it should also be shifted within them, instead of remaining an external skirmish over a prized relic. The autobiographical voice in the descent helps pinpoint the loci of the internal debate, to specify its particular terms, context, and ideological weight. Woolf's subtle manipulation of the dynamics of literary creation suggests that we may read the apparent Bloomian anxiety of influence in terms of the tension between myth and history, between aesthetics and social conditions within the text.[72] The Edwardian rejection and the Georgian appropriation are symptomatic of the pressures thematized in the play of Woolf's novels between the expectations of the dominant modernist paradigm and the actual development of her oeuvre.

Read with attention to the stops and starts, detours, reversals, rewritings, and reevaluations of any oeuvre taken on its own terms, Woolf's certainly encompasses the traditionally construed high-modernism of *Jacob's Room* through *The Waves*. But it equally traces a commentary, a running set of glosses reminding us of the mythification of such a construc-

---

[72] I accept to a degree Gilbert and Gubar's definition of the woman writer's situation as a polar opposite of Bloom's "overwhelmingly male—or, more accurately, patriarchal" model of the anxiety of influence: "Thus the 'anxiety of influence' that a male poet experiences is felt by a female poet as an even more primary 'anxiety of authorship' —a radical fear that she cannot create, that because she can never become a 'precursor' the act of writing will isolate or destroy her" (1979, 49). Both their version of Bloom and their own model are arguably accurate depictions of modern literary dynamics (in *No Man's Land*, Gilbert and Gubar concede that both attitudes "often appear simultaneously in the texts of many major twentieth-century woman writers" [New Haven, 1988], 169). Yet, as the medieval example of Bernard suggests, this is not always exclusively a male/female split, nor is it necessarily a split between one set of texts and another. In its absolutist and static formulation, such a model disallows the possibility of the play, tension, and ambiguity within the transmission of authority we see in Bernard or Christine (and consequently in Augustine or Dante, Weiss or Benjamin); it discounts the ability to rewrite the past by simultaneously combating it *and* showing oneself victim of it (Céline, Woolf).

tion, of the sacrifice necessary for the return through tradition to the upper air of prophecy. My aim is not to reverse the paradigm and to privilege Woolf as the poet of postmodernism, indeterminacy, or social revolution; she was none of those things per se. Rather, I suggest the possibility of tracing the nuances of her particular imagination of the tensions between both projects, and reading her reception not as a question of either/or but as a record of reactions symptomatic to the issues set out from within the oeuvre itself.

LET US THEN see how this process might work, first in the "failed novel" *The Years* and then in that "something else entirely" *Orlando*. One sign of the shift in emphasis in *The Years* away from a purely high-modernist trajectory is the way Dante's figure actually enters the narrative as an act of reading by the protagonist: "the odd volume of Dante" that Eleanor picks up at her sister-in-law's family house:

> She opened the book that lay on the counterpane. She hoped it was *Ruff's Tour,* or *The Diary of a Nobody;* but it was Dante, and she was too lazy to change it. She read a few lines, here and there. But her Italian was rusty; the meaning escaped her. There was a meaning however; a hook seemed to scratch the surface of her mind. "chè per quanti si dice più lì nostro / tanto possiede più di ben ciascuno." What did that mean? She read the English translation. "For by so many more there are who say 'ours' / So much the more of good doth each possess." . . . The moths were dashing round the ceiling; the book slipped on to the floor. . . . Darkness reigned.[73]

This is the midpoint of the novel, and *Purgatorio* 15.55–56 the near-midpoint of the *Commedia;* from this point, however, *The Years* diverges from its model. If Woolf's gentle self-parody of her own reading of Dante corresponds to that of her knowledge of Vergil in Miss Umphelby, then here, too, it also allegorizes a moment of rereading. "The Moths" was the working title of *The Waves;* the defining moment of that novel was marked by Woolf with Dante in her diary; and the present Dantean citation can be glossed as a description of her narrative strategy of six distinct voices in it: "For by so many more there are who say 'ours' / So much the more of good doth each possess." Woolf has translated the dialogue carried on with Dante within her *Diary* during the composition of *The Waves* into an autobiographical voice in the novelistic form of *The Years. The*

---

[73] *The Years* (1937; New York, 1965), 212–13; hereafter cited as *TY.*

Years, then, will more manifestly thematize the tensions between Woolf's two projects than had the previous novels.

Indeed, as we discover, Eleanor is not only the protagonist but equally a personification of the critical issues of *A Room of One's Own.* We are told that she is the Pargiter without a memory (*TY* 157–58); she is also the Pargiter who perceives the existence of a pattern yet is unable to complete it (369). In the passage above, she hopes for "Ruff's Tour" or "Diary of a Nobody"; instead, she gets the tradition incarnate (Dante, that is).[74] The choice of volumes leads into the autobiographical allegory of the details of the nighttime scene. Woolf's remembrance of her last novel returns here in a new light and with a new choice: "If she left the window open much longer the room would be full of moths" (212). On the one hand, no memory means no light and no air; on the other hand, memory means Dante but also "The Moths" and what Woolf called the "pressure of the present moment," the demand to produce a modernist novelty. In other words, we are once again faced with the choices set out at the beginning of *A Room of One's Own* between bounteous luncheon at Oxbridge and meager supper at Fernham.

Such an allegorical reading is further motivated within the narrative of the novel. Eleanor's inability to remember is attributed in part to the Pargiters' childhood at Abercorn Terrace, portrayed in the first part of the novel and eventually revealed as a "hell" (321, 417). In a literal and figurative sense, to remember it means to rejoin Dante's tradition. So the reluctance to pick up Dante's book signals both the attempt to diverge from and the necessity to participate in it. If we trace the path taken by *The Years* following the midpoint scene, however, it becomes clear that by problematizing the moment of participation, Woolf has also turned the book away from a Dantean axis. The final third of *The Years* indeed

---

[74] I must note that the sole entry for "Ruff" in the *Oxford Companion to English Literature* is "Ruff's Guide to the Turf," an annual publication of the early nineteenth century devoted to horse racing. In a similar vein, Woolf may be alluding to the pun in Odysseus's trick on the Cyclops ("Odysseus" and "nobody" being near homonyms in Greek); the pagan Greek opposed to the Christian (or even Homer's Odysseus opposed to Dante's). It is important to remark that it is not so much the meaning that is contrasted—the verses out of *Purgatorio* express the paradox of Christian love; Odysseus's pun allows him to name himself, to express his individuality, at the same time remaining without a name by which to be identified when the Cyclops cries for help— as the structure in which it is to be expressed. So the guide to the "turf" or Odysseus's command of language within anonymity in a non-Christian format would have been welcome alternative constructions, but Woolf, like Eleanor, must make do with what is given her: the tradition of Dante.

presents a vision of paradise, but one that is off-kilter: the nonsense rhyme sung by the two children of the caretaker in the party scene (429–30) resembles nothing more than the Greek of Aristophanes' *Frogs* ("Breke-kekex ko-ax ko-ax").[75] Not knowing Greek, the Pargiters attribute their incomprehension to the cockney accents; the dawn approaches and the book concludes: "it is to the Greeks that we turn when we are sick of the vagueness, of the confusion, of the Christianity and its consolations, of our own age."[76]

Woolf's contrast of the otherness of Homer to the oppressive weight (as well as redemptive power) of Christian tradition is reflected in the novel's conclusion. As Josephine Schaefer argues (in a section entitled "The Vision Falters: *The Years:* 1937"), "Instead of enrichment, there is almost a parody, a belittlement of the great moments of stasis in her preceding novels. . . . At that party he [North] finds instead of Clarissa [Dalloway]'s carefully selected group, a motley assembly."[77] Schaefer's language reproduces the tension I have been describing, but I prefer to view it as an essential component of Woolf's oeuvre. Unlike in the earlier novels, we see the Christian trajectory here remain manifestly unfulfilled, mimicked but significantly altered: the characters receive no retrospective enlightenment; no death, but also no consolation. The move to parody betokens the affinity of *The Years* to *A Room of One's Own* and *Orlando*.

Jane Marcus has linked *The Years* to *A Room of One's Own* in terms of its antipatriarchal politics and has argued that the novel's phenomenal popularity with women and "common readers" sets it apart from contemporary works such as *The Waste Land* and *Ulysses* as "the female epic . . . another subversion of the patriarchal genealogical imperative of English fiction" (1987, 50, 74). If we read her analysis in conjunction with Schaefer's reaction to the novel as a self-parody, it becomes evident that Marcus is polemicizing from the opposite camp. Woolf's oeuvre is no more a monolithically constituted attack on the evils of patriarchal fiction

[75] Marcus suggests Aristophanes' *Birds* instead, which provides a connection with the fact that Woolf heard birds speaking in Greek during her madness (1987, 38; on the madness, see Bell, 1:90). *The Frogs*, in which Dionysus, wearing the lion skin of Heracles over the yellow silks of a woman's costume, descends to Hades to stage a contest of the tragic dramatists, presided over by the chorus of frogs, seems more fitting both to the sound and to the theme of *The Years'* divergence from Dante. Perhaps, of course, Woolf has merely combined allusions to both plays.

[76] "On Not Knowing Greek," in *The Common Reader: First Series*, ed. Andrew McNeillie, annot. ed. (1925; New York, 1984), 23–38; this citation, 38.

[77] *The Three-Fold Nature of Reality in the Novels of Virginia Woolf* (The Hague, 1966), 167–85; rpt. in Sprague, 130–44; this citation, 141.

and society than it is a self-limiting trajectory of successful and failed high-modernist masterpieces. Rather, it plots the difficulty of negotiating both irreconcilable aesthetic aims and conflicting social imperatives.

How then do we interpret this final vision of *The Years?* It can be seen, I think, as a response to the challenge Woolf set herself on finishing *Orlando,* one that also resulted in *A Room of One's Own* and that expresses elements of both Marcus's and Schaefer's views of Woolf's non-high-modernist writing: "I want fun. I want fantasy. I want (& this was serious) to give things their caricature value. And still this mood hangs about me. I want to write a history, say of Newnham or the womans movement, in the same vein" (Diary 3:203). We have already seen such a process at work where *A Room of One's Own* provides the "caricature value" of *Jacob's Room* and "Mr. Bennett and Mrs. Brown." It does not lampoon them but suggests a different reading of what is already there, the allegorical framework of the autobiographical voice that charts their intervention into the issues of Woolf's criticism, her feud with Bennett, her dispute with tradition. Woolf uses the allegorical voice created in *A Room of One's Own* and *Orlando* to provide the "caricature value" of *The Waves* and *The Years* as well.

The children's nonsense song suggests an alternative reading; it does so partly by providing another link to *A Room of One's Own.* The song takes the place of the peroration that Nicholas refuses to give (since there was no speech, he says; *TY* 431). We find the proper peroration to go with the children's cockney Greek, in fact, at the conclusion of *A Room of One's Own.* A peroration addressed to women requires something "particularly exalting and ennobling about it," Woolf remarks (*ROO* 114); she eventually provides it: "My own suggestion is a little fantastic, I admit; I prefer, therefore, to put it in the form of fiction" (*ROO* 117). Here she proposes that Judith Shakespeare did not, in fact, die but lives, as great poets do, as a "continuing presence." In other words, the fiction Woolf gives is of another tradition, one that spans the same three hundred years during which she has told us the turf of Oxbridge has been carefully rolled and tended.

It is not death, in other words, that gives meaning to her writings, she says here, for that is the work of the Nick Greenes (*Orlando*) and the Miltons (*ROO*), but rather the serious side of the caricature value. The work of the former tradition predominates in the "masterpieces"; and there is certainly also a Dantesque, Christian side to *The Years,* whence it derives the power of its emotion: that is the effect of the death that permeates it and makes Eleanor a tragic figure. But there is also another, Greek side: the trajectory of Edward's *Antigone,* which moves from Edward's reading in 1880 (51) to his translation that puts Sara to sleep in 1907 (135–37; as Dante had put Eleanor to sleep) and finally back to the Greek in the present day, when Edward refuses to translate for his nephew (413–14). When Eleanor recalls the play, Woolf cites it in the novel as the alien Greek script and gives no crib: the Greek of the scholarly pedant beckons to the infantile Greek of the children's song a few pages later as a second text to be deciphered. A different tradition frames Dante and his memory, encapsulating the same play and pedantry that combine so marvelously in *A Room of One's Own* and *Orlando*.

Eleanor's final, individual vision glosses the communal vision of the children's song. It is the same moment Woolf gives her narrator in the final chapter of *A Room of One's Own*: "the ordinary sight of two people getting into a cab" (*ROO* 100), but with a slight twist: Eleanor sees the couple get out of the cab, the woman following the man as he "fitted his latch-key to the door. . . . 'There,' Eleanor murmured. . . . Then she turned round into the room. 'And now?' she said," holding out her hands to her brother (*TY* 434). The different uses to which Woolf put the same scene express the difference between the predominant tones of her writing—serious and parodic—while also establishing a crucial link of meaning between them. *A Room of One's Own* uses the image to open up the possibility of androgyny, the "incandescent" writing of Shakespeare and his sister, within a contemporary setting, retrieving the lost little fish of thought from the first chapter; *The Years* uses the image to close the same couple back up into the locked ground of their turf, leaving Eleanor with possibility, but also forbidden and excluded. The accent in the novel remains, in other words, on the pressure of the present moment, the weight of history on the female subject and writer.

The Waves was equally framed by *A Room of One's Own* in serious caricatural form: we find the Pauline mode of Percival's death in a more material form, the narrator's liberating acquisition of "500 a year": "My aunt, Mary Beton, I must tell you, died by a fall from her horse when she was riding out to take the air in Bombay. The news of my legacy reached me one night about the same time that the act was passed that gave votes to women" (*ROO* 37). The traditionally modernist *Waves* gives Percival's fall a mystically Christian and profound meaning; its caricature value as allusively planted by Woolf gives it another, the now-familiar subterfuge that would make it allude to a simultaneously aesthetic (time and place to write) and political (suffrage) liberation.

The "aunt's legacy" further leads us into the material circumstances, the autobiographical context of *Orlando;* for the legacy of Mary Beton appears as well to allegorize Woolf's actual, sudden accession into self-sufficiency following the unexpected success of *Orlando*. It was *Orlando* that first made Woolf and her husband comfortably wealthy, and she took great pride in the fact. Going over the year's tally in her diary, Woolf notes with satisfaction about *Orlando:* "Its not scribbling; its keeping 7 people fed & housed: a great big man like Percy; a carrot-faced woman like Cartwright; they live on my words. They will be feeding off Women & Fiction [*ROO*] next year for which I predict some sale. It has considerable conviction. I think that the form, half talk, half soliloquy allows me to get more onto the page than anyhow else. It made itself up and forced itself upon me" (*Diary* 3:221). To revise Bennett's polarity, Woolf's fancies appear to be closer to reality than her imaginations are; *her* descent (the aunt's fall) is into economic facts and not into literary tradition.

Indeed, the allegory of Mary Beton in *A Room of One's Own* partakes in the economic facts as well. Drawn from the ballad of "Marie Hamilton," the sixteenth-century popular song of the queen's chambermaid who was hanged for drowning her child by the king,[78] the aunt's name of Mary Beton places Woolf's writing of *Orlando* at the origin of an independent, alternative tradition of women's writing. It is defined in relation to known tradition, as *A Room of One's Own* shows, but even if a "fancy," a caricature drawn from allegory (the mode of both books), a name from anonymous popular song, it remains rooted in economic and historical experience.

Orlando gives full narrative form to the tension in Woolf's works otherwise figured only allusively or in critical discourse. Orlando's fall reveals, in a bombastically allegorical masque, "The Truth and nothing but the Truth" (*O* 97), ending not in death ("Would that we might here take the pen and write Finis to our work!" [95]) but in the allegorical creation of a tradition of women's writing (historically based in the emergence of such a tradition in Restoration England), in the notification of the reader of a liberating legacy.[79] It also notifies the reader of Woolf's departure from her own novelistic tradition. In that tradition, a descent into the symbolic death for the acquisition of knowledge should occur around the age of thirty-three: vocation is received; works are created. But there is no death

---

[78] See Fox's perceptive analysis of the ballad's role in *ROO* (155–56).

[79] We may also recall the mystery of Orlando's first trance as parody of the mystery of Resurrection: "But now we come to an episode which lies right across our path, so that there is no ignoring it. Yet it is dark, mysterious, and undocumented; so that there is no explaining it. Volumes might be written in interpretation of it; whole religious systems founded upon the signification of it" (*O* 47). Elizabethan has given way to Jacobean.

in *Orlando;* there is no eschatology: transformed in *mezzo cammino,*
Orlando goes instead to live with the gypsies.

This, in a more traditionally high-modernist novel, would be the moment for another "Time Passes" episode, but earlier in *Orlando,* Woolf
had already made it clear that such a structure does not stand on its own.
Describing her youthful hero's profound thoughts under the oak tree at
his estate, she parodies the central chapter of *To the Lighthouse,* laying
on overtones of its place within a male tradition that she, "one old
woman," is sweeping up in half an hour: "How things remain much as
they are for two or three hundred years or so, except for a little dust and
a few cobwebs which one old woman can sweep up in half an hour; a
conclusion which, one cannot help feeling, might have been reached more
quickly by the simple statement that 'Time passed' (here the exact amount
could be indicated in brackets) and nothing whatever happened" (*O* 67–
68). In her notes to the 1993 Penguin edition of *Orlando,* Sandra Gilbert
glosses the passage in diametric opposition to *To the Lighthouse,* implicitly insisting on a separation between Woolf's styles: "*Time passed:* Woolf
here mocks the middle section, 'Time Passes,' of her previous novel. . . .
The meditation on time that follows gives light-hearted expression to a
serious artistic problem for the novelist" (244 n. 28). Gilbert reproduces
the Bennettian distinction between Woolf's serious novels and her "light-
hearted" romps. The external judgment has shifted from rejection to approval, but the terms of separation remain the same.

Why, however, could not Woolf have been using the less restricted
generic parameters of the mock biography to place the "serious artistic
problem" within a larger context? Not, that is, simply to poke fun at
herself but to elucidate the restrictions and compromises entailed by conforming strictly to the metaphysical concerns so dear to high modernism.
For the passage reconsiders not only the modernist formal obsession with
temporality but also the grandiose reflections on Time traditionally the
province of male scions such as the young Orlando. Furthermore, and
most important, it takes up again the figure of the old woman, kin of the
narrators of "Mrs. Bennett and Mr. Brown" and of *A Room of One's
Own,* who is also able to question, in terms of at least the past two to
three hundred years of literary turf, whether any time has passed at all.

The moment in which Orlando would have followed this pattern in one
of Woolf's serious novels, ordering the narrative in time-honored fashion,
becomes instead an allegorical enactment of the "half hour's sweeping" of
the old woman above. The rest of *Orlando* romps through the past three
hundred years, dramatizing the frequently dry seriousness of more recent
efforts to recuperate those "hidden from history" as a seriously caricatural
mélange of abstractions, texts come to life, authors, and love objects.

Orlando, seduced and abandoned by Nick Greene just as was Shakespeare's sister, and as was Mary Beton by the king, lives on through pulp orientalism, enlightened salons, and oppressive Victorian novels. In *A Room of One's Own,* Mary remained alive through the graces of Anonymous, and Judith through Woolf's "fantastic suggestion" of a "fiction"; for her part, Orlando avoids crucifixion by taking refuge in the caricature gypsy world of some forgotten romance of the Restoration.

A Room of One's Own and *Orlando* are structured identically in six chapters, with the return to England and a vision of Shakespeare at the midpoint (O 116–17; ROO 58–59).[80] Both books allegorically rewrite Woolf's inherited literary tradition as her own literary tradition: the pressure of the present (O 223) that would make her either an Edwardian Beadle or a Georgian creature of fancy gives way to a caricature version of both which simultaneously masks and realizes her true intent. The "phantasmagoria" as which *Orlando* was first received critically is closely linked to its identity for Woolf; it is both nearer to and further from reality than the actual "present."[81] In it, for example, poetry is never far from money: Nick Greene gets his pension; Addison, Pope et al. receive money under their plates; the two hundred guineas of Orlando's prize for "The Oak-Tree" seem to tickle her more than the honor of it. And so they should: the 11 October 1928 date of the musings in the novel is the same as the publication date for the book that would assuage Woolf's own fears that she was "a scribbling woman" by making her a wealthy one instead.

If Shakespeare and Nick Greene allegorize positive and negative aspects of male tradition within *Orlando,* the image of Knole House provides a third term, shifting the ground of possession.[82] Like Christine's City of

[80] We could identify the six sections roughly as heritage, writing, woman writer?, woman writers, books of the living, androgyny.

[81] For the reception, see *M&M* 222–26. The word "phantasmagoria," taken over from her negatively by the critics, is Woolf's own. She uses it in her diary to describe her envy over Vita Sackville-West's Hawthornden Prize for "The Land," which she cannot take seriously ("What then is the abiding truth in this phantasmagoria" [*Diary* 3:141; 23 June 1927]); she transforms both into Orlando's positive look at her life (and "The Oak-Tree"): thinking back on her poem and life, "What a phantasmagoria the mind is and meeting-place of dissemblables" (O 176). Furthermore, the word serves as an incontrovertible sign of *Orlando's* fictionality and phantasmagoric quality: Orlando uses it in the Augustan age of chap. 4; the word did not enter English until the early nineteenth century (*OED*). Like Benjamin, Woolf seeks to use the tradition to read what is excluded by it; "phantasmagoria" is the emblem of *Orlando's* relationship to Woolf's "serious" novels, related to them by reflecting them obliquely.

[82] On the role of Vita Sackville-West, her family, and her beloved Knole House in *Orlando,* see Frank Baldanza, "Orlando and the Sackvilles," *PMLA* 70 (1955): 274–79; Charles G. Hoffmann, "Fact and Fantasy in *Orlando:* Virginia Woolf's Manuscript

Ladies, Knole House does not replace the male tradition but reconstructs it from the ground up until it no longer recognizes itself. Woolf does not simply assert the beginning of a new tradition; she allegorically imagines its existence within Shakespeare and within the country house—within the bastions of the literary and sociopolitical establishments, respectively. It is now Orlando who is able to see all of England from the oak tree on the mound; it is his/her writing over the centuries that transforms that vision into the tradition of the "Oak-Tree"; and finally, it is from that mound that she recapitulates the history of the novel at its end, not, however, as Christian eschatology but as the Manx cat, sitting in the middle of her turf, seeing the entire past she has rewritten as the story of Judith Shakespeare (O 217–28).

Orlando gives novelistic form to the critical allegory of A Room of One's Own; the autobiographical voice restructures the allegory of conversion. This is the point made by the biographer/narrator when writing about the poetry prize (the "500 a year," that is, for the woman writer): "(. . . And we must here snatch space to remark how discomposing it is for her biographer that this culmination to which this whole book moved, this peroration with which the book was to end, should be dashed from us on a laugh casually like this; but the truth is that when we write of a woman, everything is out of place—culminations and perorations; the accent never falls where it does with a man.)" (O 215). The "peroration" that follows is the recapitulation recounted above; the extremes of fancy and reality (biography and allegory) in Woolf's oeuvre never cease to meet. The utterly fanciful "wild goose" is followed by the concrete datum, "the stroke of midnight, Thursday, the eleventh of October, Nineteen Hundred and Twenty Eight" (O 228).

Although the genre of autobiographical allegory created by Woolf in Orlando and A Room of One's Own is perhaps more "innovative" than that of her "serious" work, it does not ask us to dismiss the latter any more than to dismiss Shakespeare. Rather, it informs us, allusively, allegorically, and historically, that Woolf is not "aping" the tradition of the bard (cf. Fox 153–54) but recapitulating that of his sister. It is important that we contextualize properly her sense of Judith Shakespeare: she is allegory but also autobiography; she is caricature but also serious; she is fancy but also reality. She takes the same divergent path as her brother, and at the same ripe age; with his weight of tradition, however, he could die and resurrect and return with that learning; never having had a literary existence, Judith is unable, in fact, to die.[83] This is the common thread Woolf weaves by means of *Orlando* and *A Room of One's Own* through the seams of her traditionally modernist novels: every Umphelby is also an Omphale; every gelded cat a Manx; every Christian death a Greek metamorphosis.

The polarized reception of Woolf's writings that persists to this day suggests another way in which modernist antinomies of thought continue to structure postwar critical practice. As we observe in the next chapter in the open critical embrace of Benjamin's dialectical images either as a revolutionary form of political redemption or as a sign of the free-floating signifying form of allegory, the tendency to split Woolf into the serious, high-modernist formal experimenter or the subversive, parodic, Marxist feminist indicates the degree to which an inability to historicize critical practice inhibits a contextualized reading of past literature. Needless to say, the polarities I am constructing are polemical, but I think they are valid enough at least to suggest the need to rethink our attitude as postwar critics to a historical period no longer our own, and thus no longer defined by the same historical pressures as we are.

As I have argued, the terms of the critical polarities that define the tensions actually are present within the text, within modernism; one way their presence is signaled is by motifs of the underworld. The example of Céline affords a quite different set of polarities than Benjamin or Woolf, but once again it is divided along aesthetic and political lines. Moreover, as a contemporary of the latter two writers, but one that survived into the sixties, Céline straddled the modernist and postwar periods. His writing of the fifties was in fact constructed so as to take advantage of a continuing confusion between aesthetics and politics in order to recontextualize his earlier writings as already postwar in identity, thus erasing the effects of their implications in the cultural production of the war. As a starting point, Céline provides a historical bridge that can help explain both the

---

[83] Consequently, although I am in agreement with Gilbert and Gubar as to Judith's metaphorical centrality to Woolf's conception of a tradition of women's writing, I find the imagery of Christian martyrdom with which they connect her to represent only half the Woolfian narrative. Gilbert and Gubar stress the violence of the death and the need for resurrection by women poets (1979, 539–49); Woolf counterbalances this autobiographical intensity with the caricature value of the unmartyrable Orlando.

continuing desire today to view modernist writers such as Benjamin and Woolf as our contemporaries and the problems inherent in doing so. It is Benjamin who has best theorized the dialectics of myth and history performed by the descent; at the same time, his theorization is part and parcel of the *entre-deux-guerres*. A contextualized reading of Benjamin's use of the motif can help both to theorize the dialectic of medieval and modern within that period and to extend the insights of Weiss's oeuvre to a postwar reading of that theorization, the subject of the final chapter.

5

The Representation of Hell: Benjamin's Descent into the City of Light

> O poète, qui retournas l'oeuvre de Dante
> Et mis en haut Satan et descendis vers Dieu.
> [O poet who turned Dante's work upside-down
> And placed Satan on high and descended toward God.]
> —Emile Verhaeren, "To Charles Baudelaire"

> If Baudelaire is the first since Dante to be sovereignly
> focused, it is because he has always centered himself on
> inner life as Dante on dogma.
> —André Suarès, preface to Les Fleurs du mal

ONE OF THE guiding principles of Walter Benjamin's study of nineteenth-century Paris, the *Passagen-Werk* (Arcades project), is that the roots of modernism and modernity can be traced to the Christian Middle Ages and to classical antiquity. Like Woolf, Benjamin expressed this relationship in terms of a genealogical paradigm, as in the following conception of a historical narrative that would have both epochal scope and individual relevance: "Imagine that a man dies at the exact age of fifty on the birthday of his son, to whom the same thing occurs, etc.—this is the result: since the birth of Christ not even forty men have yet lived. Goal of this fiction: to apply to historical time a striking measure that would be adequate to human life."[1] Starting from the birth of Christ, Benjamin's anal-

---

[1] Benjamin, *GS* 5 (I°, 2). Further references to volume 5 of the *Gesammelte Schriften* (material pertaining to the *Passagen-Werk*) are given by the folder (*Konvolut*) notation of the passage (folder letter followed by folio number and note number per folio) when possible and by the page number when not. References to other volumes are given as volume number followed by page number.

ogy bears a strong resemblance to the Augustinian correlation of the stages of world history and the stages of human life.[2] This is the function of the allegory of conversion: to analogize between macrocosm and microcosm, to make history adequate to myth and myth adequate to history.

I argue in this chapter that the *Passagen-Werk* was intended to propose a version of this analogy adequate to the crises of the *entre-deux-guerres*.[3] There is an allegory of conversion wrought into the theoretical framework of the unfinished *Passagen-Werk*, for its armature is autobiographical and generational. In a note for the 1935 exposé of the project, Benjamin constructed a dialectical scheme that invokes both macrocosm and microcosm: "Thesis (bloom of the arcades under Louis-Philippe; panoramas, shops, love); Antithesis (decline of the arcades at the end of the 19th century; plush, wrecked mat[erial], the whore); Synthesis (discovery of the arcades, the unconscious knowledge of what has been becomes conscious; the doctrine of awakening; dialectic of persp[ective], dial[ectic] of fashion, dial[ectic] of sentim[entality]" (5:1216).[4] The chronology of the sketch is individual as well as historical: the first period marks the rise of the arcades but also the time of Baudelaire's youth; the second signals their decline but also the setting of Benjamin's childhood in Berlin; the third period begins with the rude awakening of his generation in the experience of modern warfare and also includes the "birth" of surrealism in Paris in

[2] See Pike, 32–38. For the medieval and Renaissance reception of Augustine's model, see J. A. Burrow, *The Ages of Man: A Study in Medieval Writing and Thought* (Oxford, 1986), 80–92.

[3] I examine the *Passagen-Werk* for its relation to the allegory of conversion and the Vergilian topos of *descensus ad inferos* within modernism. Although the *Passage*, or arcade, was essential to the project from the beginning, the title *Passagen-Werk* comes from Tiedemann, the editor of the collected writings, and has been criticized for implying an overly finished product. I use the term simply as the most widely disseminated title for the material contained in *GS* 5. For the concerns of this chapter, the degree of completion of the project is a red herring. For an excellent introduction to the project as a whole, see Susan Buck-Morss, *The Dialectics of Seeing: Walter Benjamin and the "Arcades Project"* (Cambridge, Mass., 1989), esp. 3–205; and the essays in *Walter Benjamin et Paris*, ed. Heinz Wismann (Paris, 1986); selected essays trans. in Irving Wohlfarth, ed., *NGC* 39 (Fall 1986). See also Pierre Missac's subtle and elegant *Passage de Walter Benjamin* (Paris, 1987), trans. Shierry Weber Nicholsen, *Walter Benjamin's Passages* (Cambridge, Mass., 1995).

[4] The note is diagrammed triangularly, with Thesis and Antithesis heading rectangularly diagrammed slogans above, Synthesis below, between the two, heading its own rectangularly diagrammed slogans. I have added punctuation and parentheses to give a sense of the ordering of the scheme. Brackets indicate my additions to Benjamin's shorthand.

the twenties and the historical situation of the project between the two wars. The structuring principle of the project's armature is the *descensus ad inferos*. In an early note, Benjamin wrote that "to fix the totality of the traits in which the 'modern' is expressed [*sich ausprägt*] would mean to represent hell" (S1,5). The representation of hell is a framing motif of the notes; it meant not only the creation of a series of images of the nineteenth century as hell but a narrative framework of descent and return grounding those images in the present-day experience of the city. Like Peter Weiss, Benjamin problematizes the links connecting the revolutionary change he desired to bring about in the present, his life as exile in Paris in the thirties, and the descent of research he documented in his notes and for which he took Baudelaire as his principal guide. We begin by reconstructing the endeavor to represent hell textually: the historical data Benjamin gleaned from the archives of the Bibliothèque Nationale converted nineteenth-century Paris into a *figura* of the disasters of the thirties. The Paris of the Second Empire would present the *Nullpunkt* of modernity from which Europe had never reemerged. Only the reorganization of reality based on the insights of descent to that static past could effect the necessary sea change in history.

The metaphor of descent to the underworld informs every register of the project, from the earliest formulations and gathering of material demonstrating his thesis, through the later focus on Baudelaire as possible guide to the descent, and, finally, to the autobiographical thread of his own descent as exile to Paris in the 1930s. Richard Sieburth has noted the resemblance here to "a number of romantic or modernist myths of descent"—Goethe's *Faust*, Pound's first Canto, the Hades chapter in Joyce's *Ulysses*, Eliot's *Waste Land*, and Rilke's tenth Duino Elegy—with the purpose of setting up Benjamin's "dialectical reversal of these myths of descent (or descents into myth)" in connection with a critique of the neoromanticism of the surrealists.[5] Sieburth's concentration on the ways Benjamin historicized myth while exposing history as mythopoesis (18) is representative of a widespread critical reluctance to examine the concomitant mythicization of history by means of which the materialist mythopoesis—the manifest critical aim of the project—is actually accomplished. This hearkens back to the supposedly irreconcilable poles of the reception of Dante: he is either a truth-telling prophet or a mythifying poet. By disregarding the full dynamics of the Vergilian topos of descent

    [5] "Benjamin the Scrivener," in *Benjamin: Philosophy, Aesthetics, History,* ed. Gary Smith (Chicago, 1989), 17; cf. GS 5 (N1, 9).

from which modern myths of descent are derived, modern critics cannot account either for the full dialectic in Benjamin's model or for the return to history involved in other modernist mythicizations, whether for good or for ill.

The modernist descent approaches the problematic of return more obliquely than its medieval predecessor, representing itself as interested only in hell. The allegorical significance of the descent comes to light only if we remember the problematic of return in the Vergilian topos, the ambiguities of the unstated conclusion to the Sibyl's warning: "But to recall your steps and pass back out to the upper air, this is the task, this the labor" (*Aen.* 6.128–29). The modernist interplay between fiction and metafiction is more pronounced, but the autobiographical voice continues to mediate. Hence the return implicit in Benjamin's generational autobiography; hence the feminist polemics in Woolf's *A Room of One's Own*, in her letters and essays, and in her fiction; hence Céline's manipulation of the shifting ground between fiction and autobiography from *Voyage* to *Rigodon* by way of the anti-Semitic pamphlets.

In each case, the voice is signaled by the allusory presence of the descent to the underworld. This is the subject of the second part of the chapter: to outline the autobiographical voice in Benjamin's notes, correspondence, reviews, and articles that creates the possibility of return; that is, the user's manual that would teach his contemporaries the skills necessary to decipher the figural images of hell uncovered in the project. The key here is the analogy between microcosm and macrocosm, as Benjamin personified the movement of history through figures from the surrealists to the right-wing intellectual and ideologue Ernst Jünger to the lyric poet and friend Friedrich Heinle, who killed himself in 1914 at the outbreak of the war. The representation of hell in the *Passagen-Werk* was to restore the individual to history; the interventions surrounding it supplied the countermovement, restoring history to the individual.

"Facilis descensus Averno" is a motto to *Konvolut* C, a set of notes on motifs of ancient Paris: catacombs, ruins, demolition.[6] In fact, the category

[6] *GS* 5:133–55. As each *Konvolut* is made up of a sometimes chaotic mixture of citations (and citations within citations), commentary, polemic, aphorisms, mottos like the one above, and even occasional dream protocols and autobiographical episodes, and as my methodology and intent are more critical than philosophical, I am not aspiring to any sort of faithfulness to the integrity of Benjamin's sources, except insofar as a comparison might better illuminate his strategy. One of the principal features of allegory is its amenity to the hidden allusion (often polemical), and Benjamin is a master at revealing his intent and agenda through symptomatic misreading, allusion, citation, and vocabulary (his systematic redefinition and reworking of key words). Discovering and analyzing these strategies is the guiding rule of this chapter.

of hell was one of the central elements of Benjamin's early formulation of his project, presented at Königstein in 1929; nearly all the explicit references to it date from that period.[7] Two distinct formulations of the category are discernible. The first was drawn out primarily by Theodor Adorno, who understood Benjamin's project to be based on the category of hell-on-earth as the dialectical negation of the capitalist myth of a golden age of prosperity.[8] Benjamin's strategy of citation and the focus of his analysis follow Adorno's model to a degree: consistently, an element of consumer culture labeling itself utopian and promising instant happiness will be read against the grain to reveal its infernal nature.

This is evident in the exemplary case of the arcades.[9] Benjamin traces their development as the embodiment of the myth of progress—purveyors of the most exclusive goods of capitalism, designed through the most advanced technology of iron and glass construction—at the same time revealing the arcades in his notes as literally deadly. An eighteenth-century incident is recorded in which a poison mixer and her two assistants, located in the Impasse Maubert, were found dead one morning of poisoned gas (E°,10). Similarly, Benjamin reads Zola's novel *Thérèse Raquin* (1868), which is set in an arcade, as a scientific development of "the dying

---

[7] That is, most of the notes can be found in the earliest collections, those entitled by the editor "Passagen I" and "Passagen II" in *GS* 5 and labeled by him ⟨A°, . . .⟩ and ⟨a°, . . .⟩, respectively; whence many of them were taken over by Benjamin into the later folders identified by him as [A, . . .] and then [a, . . .]. The Königstein talks brought together Benjamin, Adorno, Horkheimer, Gretel Karplus, and Asja Lacis, the Latvian woman who converted Benjamin to Marxism in the late twenties. Benjamin would later refer to the talks as historic and marking a turning point in his philosophical approach (cf. Buck-Morss, 24); they would equally have a decisive influence on the young Adorno (Buck-Morss speaks of his "conversion" in *The Origins of Negative Dialectics: Theodor W. Adorno, Walter Benjamin, and the Frankfurt Institute* [New York, 1977], 20–23).

[8] Adorno's presumption was based on the Königstein talks, where Benjamin had apparently presented, and the participants had apparently received, the planned *Passagen-Werk* as the embodiment of a shared philosophical project that was evidently outlined by them in a fair amount of detail (see Buck-Morss 1977, 22–23, 139–40). Whether or not Benjamin was in total agreement at that point as to the general understanding of his notes (for already in these early notes there is a clearly developed utopian element in his category of hell which Adorno may simply have chosen not to see), it can certainly be said that Adorno remained the consistent proponent of the project as outlined in 1929. Benjamin's thought is far more difficult to pin down: particularly under the growing influence of Brecht, it took on a more virulently materialistic strain than would ever be in line with what Adorno saw as their shared philosophical project.

[9] For an architectural and social history of the arcade form, see Johann Friedrich Geist, *Arcades: The History of a Building Type* (Cambridge, Mass., 1983).

out of the Parisian arcades, the decay of a type of architecture. . . . The book's atmosphere is pregnant with its poisons, and its characters die from them" (H1,3; also a°,4).

If the category of hell could be employed dialectically to negate the innumerable phantasmagoric illusions of heaven-on-earth produced within capitalism in the nineteenth century, it could serve in an analogous way as a philosophical category for the critical analysis of human activity under that same system. Benjamin defines time in modernity as the endless repetition of the same thing disguised by the illusion of its novelty. Such a perception of time had its hidden equivalent in the hell of antiquity; indeed, the punishment of a Sisyphus—ceaselessly rolling a rock up a hill only to see it invariably roll down again—or a Prometheus—whose liver is torn out by an eagle only invariably to grow back—would be the true image of nineteenth-century Paris (S1,5).[10] Revealing time in modernity as time in hell exposes the capitalist myth of progress as an infernal illusion. In the *Passagen-Werk,* Benjamin disenchanted such illusions by quite literally reconstructing Paris as hell. Each of Dante's *figurae* in the *Inferno* revealed the truth of his or her life as a fixed, emblematic moment of sin, but only to the reader trained to interpret beyond the illusion they retain of a full life. Just so does Benjamin's Janus-faced Paris reveal life under industrial capitalism as infernal repetition, but only once its inhabitants have learned to interpret its images and illusions correctly.

The strategy of disenchantment of the phantasmagoria of capitalism is most apparent in the notes presented by Benjamin at Königstein and in his final work, the theses "Über den Begriff der Geschichte" (On the concept of history), a frontal assault on the ideology of progress. And yet, despite Adorno's repeated efforts to convince Benjamin of the centrality of this form of ideology critique to the *Passagen-Werk,* his category of hell seldom if ever functions solely as such; rather, it is an internally dialectical concept and thus never wholly negative.[11] The distinction becomes clear

---

[10] Like most postmedieval writers, Benjamin held a syncretic conception of hell that included elements of both pagan Tartarus and Christian hell fairly indiscriminately. (To be sure, medieval writers were equally syncretic, but they remained acutely aware of being so.) At the same time, this does not mean that the tensions between them and the differing structures of signification to which the tensions gave rise do not remain, if somewhat dissociated from their original context. The distinctions between language and truth, poetry and nature, remain profoundly divided along pagan/Christian lines, just as the myth/history dialectic remains profoundly troped along the same lines, as becomes apparent in the discussion of the disputes between Benjamin and Adorno below.

[11] For Adorno, see the letters on the subject of the first exposé of the project, beginning with the so-called Hornberg letter of 8/2/35, in *Briefe,* ed. Adorno and

with reference to the topos of descent, which not only identifies the underworld as terrifying and dangerous (the negation of heaven-on-earth) but also proposes it as the only means to acquire knowledge of the future and the power of prophecy. Any critique equally involved the representation of the object of its critique; any representation meant a reversion out of history into myth. Benjamin was determined to convert the mythic element to his favor as the authority to prophesy the revolution to follow on the true vision of history. Consequently, he continued to insist that the most delusory objects of consumer culture would reveal utopian moments once their illusive promises had been seen through.

He found an exemplary model of the category of hell in fashion (B2,4). In its capacity as a force of negation, fashion brings the false illusion of its novelty to bear on modernity in general. Constructing an allegory based on the eponymous personifications of Giacomo Leopardi's "Dialogue of Fashion and Death," Benjamin suggests the power derived by fashion from promising eternal youth through nothing but endless novelty. Because of the proliferation of commodities in the nineteenth century, the renewal of fashion occurred so quickly that the source of its fascination—the denial of death—is lost to sight. This is patent in the inorganic nature of the commodities through which it was expressed. Thus Benjamin reads fashion against the grain to negate its illusion of eternal youth and novelty.

He then focuses the attention of his allegory onto the image of the fashion model, who is able to simulate eternal youth only by virtue of her replaceability, her status as commodity.[12] The contradiction embodied by the model—an organic body selling itself as an inorganic commodity—found explicit expression in the figure of the prostitute. Unlike the model, the prostitute remains resolutely corporeal (organic) in the very process of making herself into a commodity (inorganic) by selling herself. The fact that the arcades were a frequent setting for prostitution leads to the allegorical expansion of Leopardi's dialogue: "He [death] bestows the armature of the whore as a trophy on the banks of a new Lethe which rolls its asphalt-stream through the arcades" (B1,4; also ⟨f°,1⟩). Whereas the phantasmagoria of Fashion bestows forgetfulness like the river of the underworld, the prostitute shows herself to be already, like all under capital-

---

Gerschom Scholem (Frankfurt, 1978), 673–82; trans. Manfred R. Jacobson and Evelyn M. Jackson, *Correspondence* (Chicago, 1994), 494–503; hereafter cited as *B;* see also the letters on the first Baudelaire essay, beginning 11/10/38 (*B* 782–90, 579–92).

[12] Benjamin uses the word *Mannequin,* which, with the same double meaning as in English of organic or inorganic, begs the question being raised here.

ism, an inhabitant of that underworld; she reveals the face of death within the promise of eternal life.

Just as the prostitute belies the promise of eternal life, so is gambling "the hellish counterpart of the music of the heavenly legions" (O10a,6). Benjamin discusses both phenomena in terms of "die sündigste Wonne" (most sinful bliss) and superstition, analyzing their appeal as the opportunity of placing one's fate under the control of pleasure. Besides supplying a moral and economic critique of life under capitalism, Benjamin's Parisian figures strongly recall the corrupt but prophetic figure of the baroque allegorist in his *Trauerspiel* book. The gambler presents a critical image of financial speculation in nineteenth-century Paris, while he equally proposes a debased but still recognizable portrait of the baroque allegorist, piling ruin on ruin in the effort to redeem meaning: "The ideal of experience in the form of a shock is the catastrophe. This is quite clear in gambling: by means of ever higher bets, meant to redeem what has been lost, the gambler steers toward absolute ruin" (O14,4).

At this point, the category of hell shows itself to be more than dialectical negation; it presents a type of prophetic knowledge along with the capacity to negate. When read correctly, Benjamin claimed, fashion can also be demonstrated to predict future social developments.[13] The gamblers' and the prostitutes' taint of sin is morally ambiguous: like the baroque allegorist, these figures are fallen, damned, while also able to create images that reveal the truth of their state. A closer look at the rewriting of the *Trauerspiel* in the *Passagen-Werk* demonstrates the ambiguity at the heart of Benjamin's category of hell which proposes both descent and return.

Benjamin suggests the connection in an early note to the *Passagen-Werk:* "Parallelism between this work and the Trauerspiel book: both in common the theme: theology of hell. Allegory Advertisement. Types: Mar-

---

[13] This dialectical moment is implicit in his reading of Grandville's caricatures (the second section of the exposé places Grandville and fashion together, along with world expositions and advertising) and in his dubbing fashion the "Forerunner, nay, the eternal placemarker of Surrealism" (B1a,2), whereby he simultaneously critiques the surrealists for their dependence on surface phenomena and credits them with the discovery of the fruitfulness of those phenomena for cultural criticism. Benjamin explicitly discusses fashion as the presage *(Flaggensignal)* of things to come in another note: "The one who could understand how to read them would know in advance not only about new currents of art, but about new statute books, wars, and revolutions," although he recognizes that such reading is normally possible only in retrospect, as he is doing: "Herein doubtless lies the greatest attraction of fashion, but also the difficulty in making it fruitful" (B1a,1).

tyr, Tyrant—Whore, Speculator" (⟨M°,5⟩). In Benjamin's analysis, the German baroque was an era that was indeed able to see death all around it: Christian eschatology was secularized into the passion of the world, a chain of historical disasters. Yet there remained a whisper of redemption within the melancholy gaze under which the world was revealed as a scattered path of emblems of death: although all secular hopes ended thus, the deepest contemplation of the world as infernally evil would for the baroque allegorist finally give way to reveal its opposite; the descent would end with the rise to redemption (1:406–9). As in Dante's rewriting of Vergil's Lethe, the about-face was possible only through the shift out of an aesthetic solution into a theological one.

This is the theory of allegory Benjamin brought to the *Passagen-Werk* as a theology of hell. It was, however, mediated through Marx, who, Benjamin found, provided the grounds for a materialistic interpretation of the baroque mode: "Baroque emblems can be understood as semi-manufactured products [*Halbfabrikate*], which, out of the stages of a process of production, became memorials of a process of destruction. . . . The death's-head of baroque allegory is a semi-manufactured product of the religio-historical process that Satan disrupts to the extent he is permitted" (J78,4). In a Marxian analysis, the baroque doctrine of *vanitas* is revealed as a protest against the corruption engendered by the rise of commodities. Brought to bear against the blossoming commodity culture of nineteenth-century Paris, such a theological reading proved a potent antidote to the secular illusions of technological utopia. If the baroque world had been threatened by the corruption of Satan, then Paris was shot through with it.

What existed for the baroque allegorist as a style—placing two fragments together, "this meaning to that picture"—had become the economic reality of this price to that commodity: "The fashion of meanings changes nearly as quickly as the price of commodities. In fact, price is the meaning of the commodity. . . . A hell rages in the souls of commodities, which are nevertheless apparently given peace by their price" (J80,2/J80a,1). In the baroque, corruption had meant valuing only worldly goods to the exclusion of the salvation of one's soul; now it meant perceiving worldly goods as that salvation in themselves. The key to the distinction lies in the final image: the meaning arbitrarily assigned to people or things by the allegorist always revealed the same thing—*vanitas*. The meaning or price of the commodity, whether person or thing, serves always to disguise the same thing: the hell (or death) it endows with the illusion of peace (or heaven-on-earth).

The allegorist, then, whose role it had been to descend into the corrup-

tion of the world in order to trick Satan out of his prize, now found
himself literally mortified—for alienation objectifies relations between
people as well as those with things—but looking better than ever—for
alienation gives commodities the illusion of an independent life.[14] Consequently, allegory could no longer exist as a style that contemplated its
object from a distance: "Baroque allegory views the corpse only from
without; Baudelaire represents [*vergegenwärtigt*] it from within" (J56,2).
The endless procession of corpses and mortified emblems of death became
an endless proliferation of always identical promises of novelty and progress. The critical element had been internalized and disguised: as an allegorist, Baudelaire continued to give it expression, but no longer as a death's-
head to contemplate; rather, he presented his lover as a death's-head, from
within, as it were. In his Paris, as in Marx's *Kapital*, we are in hell, and
thus, by extension, we are ourselves corpses, all the while believing ourselves in a heaven-on-earth.[15]

   Benjamin's nineteenth century is analogous to Dante's hell: every expression of the souls dwelling within it reveals the nature of their sin (in
Marxian terms, the fact of their reification), but only to the outside observer. The outside observer, however, is what was now lacking: Benjamin
suggests that allegory could flourish in the seventeenth century as a style
depicting the commodity because the commodity had not yet so deeply
ingrained itself within the society. Hence, the crux of the project was to
provide the structure of interpretation, the critical distance. Baudelaire
was to be the new Vergil, but it was only with difficulty that Benjamin
would be able to distinguish Baudelaire as Vergil from a possible choice
for a twentieth-century Dante, one who could descend and also return.
Baudelaire had pointed the way to the problem but had not himself been
willing or able to find the solution.

   The central question Benjamin sought to answer in the projected book
on the poet that grew out of the *Passagen-Werk* was how the antiquated
form of allegory could manifest itself uniquely in the nineteenth century
as the principal mode of the period's most important lyric work, *Les*

---

[14] The classic interpretation of Marx's theory of alienation is the chapter on reification in Georg Lukács, *Geschichte und Klassenbewußtsein*, 1923; trans. Rodney Livingstone, *History and Class Consciousness: Studies in Marxist Dialectics* (Cambridge,
Mass., 1985), 83–222, esp. 83–110. Benjamin began reading Lukács at Capri in the
summer of 1924, while drafting the *Trauerspiel* book, nearly a decade before he read
Marx proper.

[15] For Benjamin's reading of Marx on the nineteenth century as hell, see X7a, 3 and
GS 7:759.

Fleurs du mal (1:677).[16] His answer is that the allegorical way of seeing had become so deeply ingrained as reification that when Baudelaire wrote "tout pour moi devient allégorie," he was not establishing his peculiarity as a poet but, to the contrary, expressing the primary, albeit unconscious, mode of seeing of his time. In other words, like Dante's Vergil, for all his apparent difference from the other souls in hell, Baudelaire epitomized and shared in their plight.

As figured in Benjamin's notes, Baudelaire gives poetic and personal expression to the internalization of the baroque view of fallen nature as one of life in hell; in a convincing barrage of citation, Benjamin reconstructed the shift by tracing each image from the *Trauerspiel* book to its place in Baudelaire's writings. Laughter is the guiding motif, for, as Baudelaire claimed, citing Christ as his example, the wise and innocent do not laugh. Rather, it is the corrupt who do; hence, laughing children are corrupt, which is consistent with their closer proximity to nature, the source of corruption in Baudelaire's inverted scheme. Now, it is apparent that Baudelaire's conscious intent was to attack anything that society, and Christianity, held dear; it was Benjamin's insight to juxtapose the motifs of that attack with the earlier allegorical tradition while recasting both within a Marxian analysis of those motifs.[17]

Laughter remained in Baudelaire the mark of Satan. It was the aesthetic expression of the fallen nature of the baroque, internalized as if it were the earthly paradise, and it retained the ring of truth that reveals its allegorical heritage. "Laughter is smashed-up articulation" (J54,1), writes Benjamin, recalling the ruined fragments of baroque emblems. The metaphorical connection leads to his allegorical expression of the source of Baudelaire's "allegorische Anschauung" (allegorical intuition): the poet was led to allegory by the satanic laughter ringing in his ears (J53a,4). That is, he heard the internalized *promesse de bonheur* of capitalism for what it really was.

For Benjamin, Baudelaire's allegorical intuition would be manifested in the symptoms of satanic possession, the hell that raged in his soul. In the poem that seems to have set off the chain of analogies, Benjamin finds

---

[16] Cited from "Zentral Park" (*GS* 1:655–90), a collection of theoretical fragments from Benjamin's work on Baudelaire, most of which are found in some form or another in Konvolut J of the *Passagen-Werk*. Further citations are identified with the abbreviation *ZP*; trans. Lloyd Spencer, "Central Park," *NGC* 34 (Winter 1985): 32–58.

[17] See, for example, the first of a group of citations (N16,4–18,2) from Karl Korsch's work on Marx (read in manuscript [*GS* 5:1303]), in which Benjamin cites Korsch's discussion of Marx's concept of nature, which replaced nature as outside in relation to men (*ökonomische natura naturans*) with a nature defined as between men (*ökonomische natura naturata*)(N16, 4).

Baudelaire acting out the process of internalization of the technique of mortification whereby the baroque allegorists would produce their emblems. In "La Destruction," the poet describes how he swallows a demon who then throws before his eyes "des vêtements souillés, des blessures ouvertes / Et l'appareil sanglant de la Destruction" (soiled clothing, open wounds / and the bloody apparatus of Destruction).[18] The setting of allegory has moved, Benjamin writes, from the baroque court to the workshop of art.[19] He finds the products of the workshop in the subsequent poem of the collection, "Une Martyre," which presents the dismembered corpse of a woman lying in a bed, the severed head on the night table: "The allegorical intention has done its work on this martyr: she is smashed to bits" (J67a,7).

The *Trauerspiel* book had countered the prevailing critical evaluation of the German baroque by avoiding the question of aesthetic quality altogether in favor of a sociotheological analysis. Similarly, the presentation of Baudelaire here attacked the romantic myth of poetic creation: yes, Benjamin argues, creation in Baudelaire occurs in a private interior, and yes, composition is a true ordeal (here he cites the third preface to the *Fleurs du mal,* which finds the poet wondering out loud, Does one show the horrors of composition in public? [J56,4]). But, he continues, these two poems show us the "truth content" (*Wahrheitsgehalt*) behind the clichés: the workshop of art truly expresses the actions of the other workshops of the city; the subject is truly made object, literally mortified, smashed to bits (*zerstückelt*) by the apparatus of destruction, that is, by the allegorical intuition.

If the apparatus of destruction could be understood as the allegorical intuition, then Benjamin felt justified in understanding its workplace as the

---

[18] The phrase "l'appareil sanglant de la destruction" runs like a leitmotif through the two-hundred-page folder of notes on Baudelaire. It begins in J15a, 3, where Benjamin asks himself where the phrase occurs; recurs in 29,7, 56,4, and 65a,4; also in ZP 1:676; and peaks in the citation and close reading of the poem and its significance in the context of the *Fleurs du mal* (67a,7–68,2). Not coincidentally, it is in this part of the folder that Benjamin begins systematically to analyze baroque and Baudelairean allegory, rereading and citing the final chapters of his *Trauerspiel* book in this new context (cf. J53,5–57,3); see also the note to the Baudelaire book, "appareil sanglant de la destruction as aura of the allegory? and in the baroque?" (*GS* 7:757).

[19] Typically, this insight is given aphoristic form: " 'L'appareil sanglant de la Destruction' is the court of allegory" (J65a,4); and in *ZP:* " 'L'appareil sanglant de la Destruction'—these are the scattered household effects that lie at the feet of the whore in the innermost chamber of Baudelaire's poetry, and that have inherited the full powers of allegory" (1:676).

theater of capitalism. "Une Martyre" demonized the bourgeois interior; Baudelaire's project was to demonize all of Paris. It was a project with a long tradition: in the early Middle Ages, citizens of Paris, having paid the requisite sum of money and taken a vow of silence, would be led into the catacombs of their city and shown the Devil in all his infernal majesty (C2,1). The materialistic analysis updates Christian *allegoria in facto* by grounding the metaphors of descent in historical and sociological fact: the sum of money is translated as the system of capitalism, the vow of silence as the inhabitants' lack of knowledge of where they are, the catacombs as the arcades and narrow winding streets of central Paris before Haussmann.

Baudelaire's affinity to flaneurs and prostitutes was associated with the *Passagen-Werk* through the same process: these figures transformed the city into the sort of interior identified with the labyrinth. Just as the arcades, thresholds between private interior and public exterior, present the mythic site of the river Lethe in the dialogue between Fashion and Death, so does the demonized city have its Minotaur: "As is self-evident, an image of the Minotaur belongs in its center. It is not decisive that it bring death to the individual; rather, it is the image of the death-dealing forces that it embodies which is decisive. And this also is a novelty for the big-city dweller" (*ZP* 1:688).[20] Benjamin moves by analogy from Baudelaire's allegorical apparatus of destruction to the death-dealing force of the Minotaur at the heart of the capitalist city. With such images of mythic violence, he attempted to rework what he termed the purely destructive, regressive nature of Baudelaire's allegory into a disenchanting, progressive force against the society whence the violence was derived.

The endeavor is allusively figured in the image of the Minotaur, for it contains within it yet another journey of descent, with Theseus as a redemptive figure. Having essayed the labyrinth to kill the Minotaur, Theseus was able to retrace his steps with Ariadne's thread, saving the Minoans from the necessity of further tribute of human fodder for the Minotaur.[21] Benjamin allegorized the episode through the death-dealing force of

[20] For the flaneur and the labyrinth, see J61, 8: "The labyrinth is the true path for he who nevertheless will always arrive early enough at his goal. For the flaneur, this goal is the marketplace." For the prostitute, see J60, 5: "The whore is the costliest piece of plunder in the triumph of allegory—life which means death. This quality is the only one that cannot be bought off her, and for Baudelaire this is the only issue." Here, the connection is through the "death-dealing" force of the Minotaur itself.

[21] The Ariadne image was a familiar one for Benjamin: it structures the opening passages of the autobiographical memoir *Berliner Chronik* (Berlin chronicle), where Benjamin introduces as "Ariadnes" his first guides to the "labyrinth of the city": nurse-maids, Paris, and prostitutes (6:495, 469).

the Minotaur, analogous to the hell raging in the soul of the commodities, pacified by the continual human sacrifice that Marx would tell us is to be found in the unseen labor within the price. In its perfect mimesis of the Minotaur, Baudelaire's apparatus of destruction was intended to disenchant the illusion that masked its death-dealing force. Hence, Theseus suggests the redemptive corrective to follow Baudelaire's purely destructive allegorical intuition.[22]

Now, although the images bear witness to the desire Benjamin had to incorporate society's mythic power of destruction into his own work, he was careful to mediate that power. First, as we saw above, he derived the images historically from factors shown to be at work in the seventeenth century. Second, he gave them an explicitly Marxian, materialistic interpretation as the superstructural expression of economic reality. Baudelaire's rejection of the natural is both the logical extension of the seventeenth-century view of nature as a collection of emblems of death, and a genuine reaction to the fact that, in nineteenth-century capitalism, nature as such continued to exist only in the form of the phantasmagoria of commodities.

Benjamin found a parallel vision of a world turned infernal in Marx's image of the workplace as hell, which he cited, "The hidden sites of production, on the thresholds of which is to be read: 'No entry for unauthorized persons,' " commenting "cf. Dante's inscription on the gate of hell" (X7a,3). Benjamin proposes nature herself as a dialectical image: entry into capitalism is a rape of nature that not surprisingly mirrors the dialectical image of the prostitute. In its products, capitalism proposes as utopia the very material of nature it exploits in order to perpetuate itself. Benjamin did not fail to extend the interpretation back into superstructural production: if capitalism is really hell—in the negative terms of Marx's image—then the culture that understands its production in terms

---

[22] The same submerged dialectic of redemption appears if we follow the thread of Theseus further, for in addition to making the metaphorical descent of the labyrinth, he descended into the underworld itself, accompanied by Pirithous, to rescue Persephone after Hades had abducted her. (Theseus's descent is several times alluded to in *Aen.* 6, especially in Charon's fear that Aeneas is another Theseus.) The utopian element of the allegory of redemption is clearest here, for the rescue of Persephone was responsible in Greek myth for restoring the equilibrium of nature, which had gone awry from Demeter's mourning of her daughter. What better image to counter the reified and eternally repeated nature of capitalism than the myth of the origin of the natural passage of the seasons?

of the disinterested descent of contemplation actually participates, through this descent, in that same exploitation.[23]

Benjamin extended the argument elsewhere in his notes: not only the factories of capitalism but also metro stations, entrances to arcades—indeed, all doors and thresholds—suggest passages into the underworld, full of threat. At the same time, they continue to embody the desired threshold experience (*Schwellenerfahrung*). His pun on the anthropological *rite de passage* clarifies the point: the descent to hell has always mythologized male initiation; if that experience had come to mean solely Marx's image above, then it is not surprising that, as he says, his generation had become deficient in threshold experiences—after all, one cannot descend *from* hell. Nevertheless, Benjamin argued, the residue of such experiences inheres in the literal *rite de passage:* "Whoever enters an arcade covers the doorway in the opposite sense. (Or he betakes himself into the intrauterine world.)" (L5,1). The original sexual component of the descent as a rape of nature is exposed by the figure of the whore both as image of the exploitation of human nature and as mythic image of mother Nature.

Baudelaire's allegorical intuition was the crucial piece of the data of modernism, the vision of truth out of which Benjamin was to construct his *Inferno;* the difficulty remained in the return, the retooling (*Umfunktionierung*) of that negative truth into redemptive prophecy. Benjamin developed his understanding of Baudelaire as guide in the book planned as an essay-length "miniature" of the *Passagen-Werk* (5:1164) and begun in 1937. It was to have been in three parts and dialectical in structure: the first part would demystify the origins of Baudelaire's poetry and reveal its destructive nature through his concept of allegory, dealing with the reception of his poetry, his aestheticism, his role as melancholic, the image of the prostitute, and other themes derived from the twin sources of the *Trauerspiel* book (7:763–64) and the Paris of the poet's youth. The concept of allegory would return in the third part as a Marxian category for the production of dialectical images, pointing the way to revolution through a full-blown model of the *descensus ad inferos* able to reveal the

[23] Indeed, starting with the mythic violation of the mother (see Tom Phillips, trans. and illus. *Dante's "Inferno"* [New York, 1985], 284), the poetic descent to acquire knowledge has always been constructed through images of violence: Odysseus's pool of blood, the animals sacrificed by Aeneas to give luck to his descent, Dante's pre-descent prophecy of a *veltro* that will come to rip apart the she-wolf of avarice. Baudelaire expanded this motif into an art form. See, for example, the comparison of his lover to a rotting animal carcass in "Une charogne" ("A Piece of Carrion").

elusive means of return. Between question and answer, thesis and resolution, the second part of the book was to provide the mediating sociohistorical and philological data: the significance of Baudelaire was to emerge from the setting of Second Empire Paris.

This scheme grew out of the 1935 exposé of the *Passagen-Werk* written for the Institute for Social Research; indeed, the motto for the second part of the tripartite division of the section on Baudelaire reads, once again, "Facilis descensus Averno" (5:55). Benjamin's use of the topos of descent is evident both within the theoretical framework of the *Passagen-Werk* and in his techniques of research and composition. In other words, the sociohistorical research involved not only the Marxian descent into the facts of economics within the hell of capitalism but the theoretical descent from the contemplative gaze of the baroque allegorist of the proposed first part to Baudelaire's "empathy with commodities" (*Einfühlung in die Waren*).

The results of the emulation of Baudelaire's "empathy" are evident from Adorno's reaction to the 1935 exposé; for, not having had a good look at the project since Königstein, Adorno expected the immersion to result still in a baroque demystification and was unable to see any possibility of dialectical redemption out of such an apparently unguided descent. The motifs of chthonic Paris remained, but within the figure of Baudelaire; for Benjamin was already formulating hell not merely as the dialectical counterpart to heaven-on-earth but as the topos of descent, materialized into a dialectical image that would be able to encompass the regressive nature of the poet's relation to society (his coexistence with it in hell) as well as the progressive possibility of the redemption of prophecy still present even given the exposure of the form of the topos itself as exploitative.[24] Benjamin, in other words, wanted to avail himself of the rhetorical authority of the Augustinian and Dantean return while simultaneously grounding it materialistically: he wanted to use dialectics to resolve the inherent contradiction of the *descensus ad inferos*.

[24] Adorno still hoped to find chthonic Paris as the dialectical counterpart of the Michelet motto of chap. 2, "Chaque époque rêve la prochaine," and the corresponding Benjaminian concepts of dream image, dreaming collective, and utopia (see the Hornberg letter). The particulars of the debate are beyond the scope of this chapter. I merely note that Benjamin, apparently receptive to Adorno's criticism of the vagueness and danger of his terminology, substantially rewrote this passage in the 1939 exposé. My argument here is that the concept of hell was never limited to such a strategy of ideology critique, as is demonstrated by its appearance elsewhere in the 1935 exposé, in conjunction with, but not negation of, the corresponding concept of dialectical images, to the definition of which Adorno took equal exception.

It should not surprise us, then, that both Adorno's scathing reaction to the first finished portion—part 2—of the Baudelaire book and Benjamin's response were couched in infernal imagery. By way of dismissing Benjamin's claim for the book as a miniature model for the *Passagen-Werk*, Adorno reminded Benjamin of his statement at Königstein that each of the thoughts of the project had had to be wrenched from a realm in which madness reigned, and maintained that the unmediated presentation of facts in the Baudelaire chapter failed to do so (B 783, 580). Adorno's accusation that the essay had set itself up at "the crossroads of magic and positivism" (786, 582) implied, quite simply, that Benjamin had descended to hell and remained there.

The underground metaphorics are particularly strong in a "jest" in the same letter attributed by Adorno to his wife: "Gretel once joked that you inhabit the cavelike depths [*Höhlentiefe*] of your Arcades and that you shrink from finishing your study because you are afraid of having to leave what you have built [*den Bau verlassen zu müssen*]" (788, 583).[25] Benjamin apparently agreed with the substance of the criticism, responding that Adorno had indeed characterized the essay's methodology; he took issue only with Adorno's understanding of that methodology. The philosophical inquiry of the first part, Benjamin maintained, could be resolved only through the construction of monads out of the philological matter presented in the second. In other words, it was *only* at the crossroads of positivism and magic, only from the *Höhlentiefe*, that the phantasmagoria could be disenchanted into dialectical images.

It was not just the project that was concerned with hell; the metaphorics extended to the personal level as well. Hence, Adorno couched the critique as a Faustian accusation: "I took your idea of making the Baudelaire a model for the *Arcades* study extremely seriously, and I approached the Satanic scene [*Schauplatz*] much as Faust approached the phantasmagoria of the Brocken mountain when he thought that many a riddle would now be solved. May I be excused for having had to give myself Mephistopheles' reply that many a riddle poses itself anew?" (783, 579). To which Benjamin responded with his own allusion: "When you speak of a 'wide-eyed presentation of mere facts,' you characterize the genuine philological stance. This stance was necessary not only for the sake of results, but had to be embedded in the construction as such. . . . Philology is the examination of a text which proceeds by details and so magically fixates the reader

[25] There is likely here a veiled reference to Franz Kafka's story of obsessive rebuilding and securing of its burrow by an unidentified creature, "Der Bau" (1923–24, publ. 1931).

on it. What Faust took home in black and white is closely related to Grimm's devotion to small things. They share the magical element whose exorcism is reserved for philosophy, here for the final part" (793–94, 587–88). While Adorno identifies himself with Mephistopheles (lord but also permanent denizen of the underworld) and tackles the question of knowledge, Benjamin latches onto a detail and bends it for his own use, identifying himself with the one descending, returning, and finally saved. The allusion is to the student scene of the first part of the play, where the student responds to Mephisto's ironical instructions on study habits for the learning of metaphysics, "You don't have to tell me twice / I can tell how useful this will be; / For what you possess in black and white / you can carry home confidently."[26] Metaphysics grow out of methodology, and not vice versa. By changing the credit of the lines to Faust, pointedly retaining the character assigned him by Adorno, and selecting the very scene of the satanic pact for his counterallusion, Benjamin makes it clear that, if it is a role that suits him, it is nevertheless Adorno who wants to damn him for it.[27]

It was not at all that Adorno denied the identification of capitalism with hell or the critic's role as that of the demystifying allegorist; what he denied was the imagery of descent and the reemergence implied by it. They were arguing over two ways of representing hell. The methodology of part 2 was faulty to Adorno because of the outside viewpoint its representation required. Benjamin conceived of Baudelaire dialectically as a personification of Paris, a Vergil to lead him and his readers through hell and eventually to be subsumed and transcended by a prophetic and revolutionary return. Conversely, Adorno thought of Baudelaire as a historical object, the meaning of which was to disenchant the illusions of nineteenth-century capitalism through a purely immanent and negative ideology critique. His hell was material and not theological, philosophical and not allegorical, and consequently could not reconcile opposites. Dante, in contrast, *had* combined them; hence his importance to Benjamin as a model.

Benjamin's identification with the tradition of Dante is evident, as has been noted, in the choice of the topos of descent for a motto. He took pains, particularly in the spirited response to Adorno's scathing criticism

---

[26] Johann Wolfgang von Goethe, *Faust Part I,* trans. Peter Salm, 1962, rev. ed. (New York, 1985), 1964–67.

[27] It *is* that strong a letter, as is Adorno's. See, for example, the line excised in the *Briefe* and restored by Tiedemann in *GS* 1:1105, in which Benjamin uses a pseudonymous verse by Horkheimer on waiting for a letter to express the strong personal feelings brought on by the rejection of the manuscript.

of the Baudelaire draft, but also in earlier formulations of the book's structure, to outline the factual, historical nature of the second part within the context of the prophetic, if not redemptive, interpretation to be derived therefrom.[28] Even Benjamin had no illusions as to the poet's limitations as a guide, identifying Baudelaire's allegorical intuition as almost wholly destructive in form and distinguishing it from any hints he might give of the type of the twentieth-century allegorist (J57,3).[29]

Nevertheless, the history of the composition of the Baudelaire book documents Benjamin's apparently ever-greater withdrawal into the figure of the poet, a Dante turning back into Vergil. The shift is perhaps most evident in "Über einige Motive bei Baudelaire" (On Some Motifs in Baudelaire), the reorganization of the second part of the Baudelaire book ordered by Adorno and Horkheimer for the institute's house organ, *Zeitschrift für Sozialforschung,* and completed in August 1939. In it, Benjamin completely abandoned the methodology of the *Passagen-Werk* in favor of the direct application of contemporary theory and literature (Bergson, Proust, Freud) to the motifs of Baudelaire and the crowd.

Similarly, in the last surviving overall plan for the *Passagen-Werk* (1939), the motto "Facilis descensus Averno," as well as the motifs of chthonic Paris and the theory of dialectical images with the accompanying example of the prostitute, was gone, replaced by an interpretation of Baudelaire's poem "Les Sept vieillards" (The Seven Old Men). The 1939 exposé reevaluates the status of allegory by placing any residue of a theology of hell within a solely literary interpretation. Benjamin did not relinquish any of the earlier concepts; he merely grounded them within hell. So Baudelaire's nightmarish vision of a sequence of "infernal" (his adjective) and identical apparitions of a horrifying old man signifies the hellish nature of the phantasmagoria of novelty as the eternal return of the always-the-same.

---

[28] See the letter to Adorno of 12/9/38 (*GS* 1:1101–7; *B* 790–99, 585–92), and compare, for example, with the far more muted, concessive, and indirect (through Gretel) response of 8/16/35 to Adorno's equally strong criticism of the 1935 exposé (*B* 685–88, 506–8).

[29] Benjamin's choice of vocabulary in this 8/28/38 letter to the Adornos is noteworthy: "These two parts [1st and 3d] provide the armature: the first, Baudelaire's representation of allegory, the third its resolution in society." It will be noted that *Armatur* is the same word used by Benjamin to describe the appearance of the prostitute as dialectical image, corporified allegory (he will also discuss Baudelaire's decision to make allegory into "the armature of his poetry" in J53,2). The book would not only derive a theory of allegory out of the dialectical negation of Baudelaire; it would itself express that theory in its own dialectical movement.

This reading is mirrored in Benjamin's treatment of his most significant discovery of the late 1930s, Auguste Blanqui's theory of eternal return, in the forgotten book *L'Eternité par les astres* (Eternity through the stars, 1870). Benjamin wrote of it to Horkheimer, "If hell is a theological object, then this speculation can be called a theological one" (*B* 741). The "theology of hell" is Blanqui's new myth of an infinite number of lives based on the infinite number of stars. Benjamin found in Blanqui's "scientific" mythmaking an irony of which the career revolutionary, unlike Baudelaire, apparently remained unaware: the eternal repetition that appeared to him, writing in prison, as hellish, was a precise and profound demystification of the capitalist myth of progress.

Blanqui was more than a crackpot philosopher; he dramatically personified the fatal history of the failure of nineteenth-century revolution. That Blanqui, having participated in all three revolutions (1830, 1848, 1870) and imprisoned once again as an old man, was able to demythologize—without even being aware of having done so—the very system he had been attempting to overthrow for half a century, graphically demonstrated to Benjamin that an allegorical intuition in no way led to political action, or vice versa. The irony seems to have begun to carry over into the later conception of the project: once he had immanently grounded its concepts within the figures of Baudelaire and Blanqui, the category of hell appeared to have returned to the status of negation to which Adorno had so much desired to restrict it, and any hope of return seemed to be lost.

And yet Benjamin's only post-Baudelaire production, the theses "Über den Begriff der Geschichte" (1940), though written from the point of view of hell and resolutely pessimistic, in no way relegates theology to the nineteenth century, as might be expected from the analysis above. To the contrary, that Benjamin went to the effort of composing and assembling these texts at all at this point indicates a response to the situation just presented. The theses were, in fact, drafted from notes compiled in the *Konvolute*, particularly "N," throughout the gestation of the project and were intended by Benjamin as a methodological introduction to the Baudelaire book, if not to the project as a whole.[30] All evidence points to the

[30] Adorno maintains that they were part of the project as a whole ("Einleitung zu Benjamins *Schriften*," 1955, rpt. in *Über Walter Benjamin*, ed. Rolf Tiedemann [Frankfurt, 1990], 34–53; this citation, 45). Michel Espagne and Michael Werner, as part of their argument that the Baudelaire book was meant to replace the "abandoned" *Passagen-Werk*, cite two letters in which Benjamin refers to the theses as the "theoretical armature for the second essay on Baudelaire" ("Vom Passagen-Projekt zum 'Baudelaire': Neue Handschriften zum Spätwerk Walter Benjamins," *Deutsches Vierteljahrsschrift* 58:4 [1984]: 646–48; letters rpt. in *GS* 1:1130, 1135); that is, in order to

fact that Benjamin was not quite ready to relinquish the original premise of return behind the manifest descent of negation. Although not overtly utopian in the manner of the earliest notes to the project, the theses are nonetheless resolutely aimed at Benjamin's contemporaries in the 1930s, and aimed at redeeming Baudelaire's only positive legacy, the critique of progress.

There is not space here for a closer examination of the theses; I mention them at this point in order to assert the continued existence of a project beyond the Baudelaire book. For, as the miniature of the *Passagen-Werk,* it was to have had an exterior guide: Benjamin himself, for whom the project had been an autobiographical one all along. As representative of the generation born into the afterlife of Baudelaire's "modernity," he would descend into the past in order retrospectively to prophesy the future —his present, that is—and reconstruct that descent as an allegory of con-version for his contemporaries. By 1940, when Benjamin drafted the the-ses from earlier notes, the "prophecy" could no longer be anything but a last gasp before going under, but this does not change its basic form as an intervention in the present. Reclaiming the *figural* tradition of the *descen-sus ad inferos,* the theses telescoped the hell of the past into that of the present, thereby signaling that a solely negative, demystifying descent would never be sufficient in itself, for the critique of progress could only succeed if the past and the present could be brought together dialectically.

Through such a figural dialectic, Benjamin's project provides a model for reading a prophetic voice into a world of modernist allegory com-monly viewed as resolutely negative and language-bound. Not to prove that literature might be able actually to escape the bounds of language and directly address history, as was the avowed intent of many modernists, but to propose that a concern for the exterior world, an attempt to tran-scend its medium, forms an integral part of twentieth-century writing— something we have seen at work in both Céline and Woolf as well as in Weiss. The topos of manifest descent and implied return structures the modernist view of tradition: descent includes the recent past of the nine-teenth century in its figural data, and the mythopoetic past of the allegori-cal tradition in its representational structure of the autobiographical allegory of conversion. Return means a dialectical understanding of them as together they relate to and reread the present by rewriting the past. This

---

defend the second Baudelaire essay from Adorno's criticism of the first. For critical discussions of the status of the book and of Espagne and Werner's argument, see Michael W. Jennings, *Dialectical Images: Walter Benjamin's Theory of Literary Criti-cism* (Ithaca, 1987), 19–24, 215–19; and Buck-Morss 1989, 205–8.

concern may have a different significance than the medieval model, but it is only once that model has been wrested from a modernist medievalism that the present significance may be properly understood.

To evaluate the motifs of return within which the *Passagen-Werk* was to be framed, and their possibility and significance, with a view toward establishing a model for reading twentieth-century writing, we must now expand the scope of our study of Benjamin and examine his use of auto-biographical allegory in the more overtly topical material of the twenties and thirties: reviews, articles, and letters. For it is here that we find the polemical strategies through which he addressed his contemporaries and the ways in which these strategies are inextricably bound into the structure of the *Passagen-Werk* through the finally omitted, but still pronounced, words of the Sibyl, *Facilis descensus Averno*.

> The authentic image seems old, but authentic thought is new. It is of our time. This time seems paltry and taken for granted, but however it may seem, we must take it firmly by the horns if we are to be able to question the past. For it is the bull whose blood must fill the pit so that the spirits of the dead can appear at its edges. (*GS* 3:259)

> The problem of any truly current interpretation of Vergil—the possibility of humanism in our time. (321)

IT IS CLEAR from correspondence that for Benjamin the "representation of hell" entailed not just the thorough study of nineteenth-century Paris but the contemporary experience of the city as well. Such an experience, channeled through autobiographical themes but common to his generation, would itself prove to be the entry to the underworld, the gate to the past through which the present could be rewritten as a Marxian and materialistic one. Benjamin planned to represent hell through the autobiographical allegory of conversion he had constructed out of his public life from the days in the youth movement to his tenure as an influential journalist and critic in the late twenties. If Baudelaire was the guide who led Benjamin through his research, it was Benjamin himself who would recount his own return while guiding his contemporaries down into a past Paris through which he could represent and interpret the ciphers of the current crisis.[31]

---

[31] Nothing resembling a definitive biography of Benjamin has yet been written. Gershom Scholem's memoir *Walter Benjamin: Die Geschichte einer Freundschaft* (Frankfurt, 1975; trans. Harry Zohn, *Walter Benjamin: The Story of a Friendship* [New York, 1988]) remains essential; also useful are the shorter memoirs collected and

The conception of a representational framework for the data and images of the *Passagen-Werk* is strongest in 1940 (in the theses) and at the beginning stages of the project, for Benjamin was honing his polemical skills during the same years in the late twenties in which he was formulating the project. The connection is frequently expressed through a metaphorics of descent. Comparing the project to *Einbahnstraße (One-Way Street; 1926, publ. 1928; GS 4:83–148)*, an avant-garde collection of aphorisms, *Denkbilder*, dream protocols, and social criticism, he wrote, "In it, the profane motifs of *Einbahnstraße* will pass by in review hellishly intensified" (B 455, 322). The formulation of the project in terms of his earlier writings gives a key to the contemporary context in which Benjamin conceived what would often later come to appear as a solely historical project. In other letters of the twenties, Benjamin discussed the origin of *Einbahnstraße* in Paris, where he discovered its form (B 446, 315), and presented the *Passagen-Werk*, at this early juncture simply an article to be entitled "Pariser Passagen," as a further step in his argument *(Auseinandersetzung)* with the city (B 459, 325).

A focal point of the Parisian axis of *Einbahnstraße* and the *Passagen-Werk* was the French surrealists, about whom he wrote an article of both high praise and severe censure during 1928–29.[32] In the article, to which he referred in several letters as "a screen [*Paravent*] before the 'Pariser Passagen' " (B 491, 348; also 489, 347), Benjamin acknowledged the movement's innovation as one that could provide a "profane illumination" *(profane Erleuchtung)* through a dreamlike immersion in the stuff of everyday life, the kitsch and clichés of consumer society. The focus on the "profane" as a means of achieving insight into the problems of society furnished the structural principle of *Einbahnstraße* and inspired the early fragments of the *Passagen-Werk*.

---

translated in *On Walter Benjamin: Critical Essays and Recollections*, ed. Gary Smith (Cambridge, Mass., 1988). Critical biographies include Julian Roberts, *Walter Benjamin* (London, 1982); Richard Wolin, *Walter Benjamin: An Aesthetic of Redemption* (New York, 1982); Werner Fuld, *Walter Benjamin: Zwischen den Stühlen* (Frankfurt, 1981); Bernd Witte, *Walter Benjamin* (Reinbek bei Hamburg, 1985), trans. James Rolleston, *Walter Benjamin: An Intellectual Biography* (Detroit, 1991); Momme Brodersen, *Spinne im eigenen Netz: Walter Benjamin, Leben und Werk* (Buhl-Moos, 1990).

[32] "Der Surrealismus," first published in three installments in the *Literarische Welt* (1, 8, 15 Feb. 1929); rpt. in *GS* 3:295–310; in *Reflections*, trans. Edmund Jephcott (New York, 1986), 177–92 (hereafter cited by page number as *R*). On Benjamin and the surrealists, see Margaret Cohen, *Profane Illuminations: Walter Benjamin and the Paris of Surrealist Revolution* (Berkeley, 1993); and the essays by Jacques Leenhardt, Gianni Carchia, and Rita Bischof and Elisabeth Lenk in Wismann.

During the late twenties Benjamin suggested, "Once I have seized hold of it, then an old, in a manner of speaking rebellious, quasi-apocryphal province of my thought will be subjugated, colonized, controlled," just as the *Trauerspiel* book had closed the "canonical" cycle of *Germanistik* studies (B 470, 333). The "apocryphal" region not only covered "profane" subject matters of everyday life outside the province of academic studies but also signified Benjamin's recent discoveries of surrealism and Marxism, both of which, if already implicit in the *Trauerspiel* book, permeated *Einbahnstraße*. The *Passagen-Werk* was predicated on Benjamin's return to Paris as a genuine threshold experience (*Schwellenerfahrung*), a *rite de passage* into an alluring yet dangerous world that at this point in his mind held all the secrets of the coming revolution: this is the autobiographical allegory of conversion that frames the project's construction.

Traces of such an allegory are discernible in Benjamin's notes; they are particularly evident in the short piece "Passagen." This piece fairly explicitly demonstrates the intention (which would be far more hidden in the later notes) of allegorically returning to the present by descending from it into the past; it equally voices the roles—himself as guide and his generation as those descending—and introduces some of the key personifications. Benjamin begins the piece with an autobiographically voiced anecdote: his attendance of the opening of a new arcade in the Champs-Elysées, brightly lit and elegantly fitted, presenting the state of the form in the 1920s as totally affirmative and devoid of interest: "While here a new passageway was made ready for fashionable Paris, one of the oldest arcades in the city has disappeared: the Passage de l'Opéra, which has been swallowed up by the extension [*Durchbruch*] of the Boulevard Haussmann" (GS 5:1041). The dialectic of nineteenth-century Paris persists in the present: the always-the-same is being presented to the public as the latest rage, while the ruin of its original form (*Urbild*), now the expression of its truth content, is being irretrievably destroyed.

The allegory is fairly plain to see, for the Passage de l'Opéra, notes Benjamin elsewhere in an inspired pun, was the birthplace of surrealism ("Dada was Surrealism's father; an arcade was its mother" [C1,3; h°,1]). Louis Aragon's book, *Le Paysan de Paris* (1926; Paris peasant), a direct inspiration for the *Passagen-Werk*, was born out of the author's desire to preserve in literature the arcade that at that moment was being demolished.[33] The apparatus of its destruction, the Boulevard Haussmann, per-

---

[33] Aragon also stressed the necessity of preserving the arcade in writing, distinguished between its affirmative character in the nineteenth century and its radical surrealistic character in the present as ruin, and suggested the personification of the Boulevard Haussmann (*Le Paysan de Paris* [Paris, 1972], 19–22, 34–42).

sonifies the political destruction under Napoleon III of the possibility of revolution by means of driving wide boulevards through the narrow lanes and dark alleyways of old Paris. In the *Passagen-Werk,* Benjamin would comprehensively chronicle the ideological, political, and economic motives behind the Baron Haussmann's program of "strategic beautification." [34] The crux of the allegory is the figure of the moment of resistance that cannot be eradicated by the forces of capitalism. The Passage de l'Opéra lives on not as it was—the phantasmagoria repeated in its modern-day counterpart—but in the critical and utopian elements of its ruins, brought to light and preserved by Aragon. The autobiographical allegory suggests a frame for Benjamin's presentation of the data of the project in the form of dialectical images: the phantasmagorias of nineteenth-century Paris were to be demystified; at the same time, their dream elements were to be fragmented and recomposed into a critical vision of the present.

The *descensus ad inferos* always returns to the dead past, but at its heart lies the authority of a prophetic voice. [35] The danger inherent to such dream images was noted by Adorno in the Hornberg letter; as we have seen, it is already present in Homer and Vergil, and its paradoxes structure medieval descents and visions. Benjamin was intent on counteracting the mythification of prophecy; for him, the dream images of the nineteenth century were collective only in the sense of having been lived through by his generation—those who were children around 1900. Although the historical experience theoretically encompassed all social classes, Benjamin's allegory was aimed specifically at his own: the youth of the upper middle class, cut loose for the first time into the inferno of the real world by the First World War and the depression of the twenties. Hence the attraction of the surrealists: Benjamin was born in 1892, Breton in 1896, Aragon (in Paris) in 1897; the movement grew out of its members' Dada group, born in 1916 in response to the war. Hence the note made during

---

[34] By beginning with the new arcade and the extension of the boulevard, Benjamin conceded what in his day had come to be regarded as the aesthetic achievement of Haussmann. The cycle continues today, when both boulevards and arcades are integral parts of nostalgia for the "old Paris" being lost to the current capitalist nemesis of the international chain store and its garish neon.

[35] One aspect of the descent Benjamin made: in 1935 he wrote a letter to the director of the Bibliothèque Nationale requesting permission to descend into the library's *enfer* of forbidden books, emphasizing his scholarly research credentials (*GS* 5:1124–25). In a subsequent letter to a friend, he gloats over having successfully wangled the pass, apparently difficult to obtain (*B* 669, 493; *GS* 5:1126). It is, moreover, fitting that the *Passagen-Werk* itself owes its life to the fellow inhabitant of *l'enfer,* and another member of Benjamin's generation, Georges Bataille (b. 1897), who secreted the notes into some recess or other of the library for the duration of the war.

the composition of the 1935 exposé: "The experience of our generation: capitalism will not die of natural causes" (*GS* 5:1218). The generational experience was to ground historically the mythic tendencies of the prophetic voice.[36]

The descent into hell required only a Marxist; the return into prophecy called for an allegorist. Benjamin struggled to define the possibility of allegory in his time throughout work on the *Passagen-Werk;* what remained constant was the use of himself as an autobiographical vehicle for the experience of his generation. Interpretation of Benjamin's oeuvre, including the most theoretical pieces, risks compromising the foundation of the critical project when it ignores the presence of hidden autobiographical allegories. This was clear to Benjamin's first readers, especially Scholem and Adorno, who were attuned to the dialectic of autobiography and philology even in Benjamin's most theoretical writings.[37] Even during the

---

[36] Benjamin's critico-allegorical expression thus intersects with the sociology of knowledge of Karl Mannheim. See Mannheim's essay "The Problem of Generations," 1927; rpt. in *Essays on the Sociology of Knowledge,* ed. Paul Kecskemeti (New York, 1952), 276–322. Although there is common ground in their attribution of important ontological status to generational experience, there is little reference in Benjamin's work to Mannheim outside an early note of acquaintanceship and a dismissive remark in a 1937 letter to Horkheimer (*B* 727, 537). It is likely Benjamin shared the theoretical distaste of the Frankfurt School for Mannheim's grounding of intellectual history in underlying large structures. See John McCole, *Walter Benjamin and the Antinomies of Tradition* (Ithaca, 1993), 23–24; and Martin Jay, "The Frankfurt School's Critique of Karl Mannheim," in *Permanent Exiles: Essays on the Intellectual Migration from Germany to America* (New York, 1985), 62–78.

[37] Scholem's and Adorno's results differ greatly. A good place to begin examining the differences is generationally: Scholem (b. 1898), although somewhat younger than Benjamin, first met him in 1915, and their friendship deepened in the first years of the war and was irrevocably marked by it: "The observance of the second requirement [of friendship] was particularly easy for me: his utter aversion to discussing the political events of the day and occurrences of the war. . . . In those years, anyone who wished to have a closer association with Benjamin either had to share this attitude (as I did) or respect it. . . . We did discuss our basic attitude toward the war, but concrete events were never mentioned" (*Story of a Friendship,* 23). Both eventually received (questionable) medical dispensations from service—Benjamin's first letter following Scholem's exemption was the first to use his given name—and the friendship intensified when both lived in Bern in 1918–19. The equality of exchange continued to mark their relationship, notwithstanding various later differences. Adorno (b. 1903), in contrast, missed the war and came to know Benjamin as his first (and only) disciple. Roberts gives a refreshingly iconoclastic account of Adorno's early motions toward Benjamin (71–74), and the mentor/disciple relationship is clearly visible in the intellectually aggressive correspondence of the thirties, as well as in the later proprietary tone over the manuscripts. This should not in any way slight the magnitude of Adorno's *Auseinan-*

late twenties and until he was forced to flee Germany in 1933, the period when his career as a critic and journalist was at the height of its influence, Benjamin continued to address a small circle of friends, a larger circle of acquaintances, and at the most a particular social and intellectual class.[38]

The *Berliner Kindheit um 1900* (Berlin childhood around 1900), the revision of the earlier *Berliner Chronik* (Berlin Chronicle) into an autobiography of that class and that generation, expresses the historical and individual experience Benjamin took for granted in his readers.[39] Evidently, it was also received on these terms: as Erich Auerbach (born like Benjamin in Berlin in 1892) put it in a letter of 1935 from Florence on the way to a teaching position in Istanbul, "I greatly regret that we are not seeing your *Kindheitsbuch, which is also ours*, in its entirety."[40] This was the audience for whom the *Passagen-Werk* was conceived and to whose experience its images were coded. By reconstructing some sense of the experience in which Benjamin embedded his research during the *entre-deux-guerres*, we will be able to determine which elements of the project and its theories still qualify in turn to speak to our postwar present. To short-circuit the process, which had already led during Benjamin's lifetime to misunderstandings over the Baudelaire book and which continues to

---

dersetzung with the elder Benjamin's works, especially postmortem, but it goes a long way toward explaining the respective tones of the two critics, which in turn has had a lasting effect on their respective receptions of his writings.

[38] After fleeing to Paris in 1933, Benjamin continued (although with increasing difficulty) to attempt to reach this circle and class, publishing reviews under various pseudonyms for the next few years, as well as *Deutsche Menschen* (Switzerland, 1936; *GS* 4:149–233), an annotated collection of German letters from the eighteenth and nineteenth centuries. The title of this work was meant to allow it entry into the Third Reich, but its content was oppositional, an attempt, writes Adorno, "against the annihilation of the German spirit wholly degraded into ideology by the National Socialists. . . . It thought to uncover an underground [*unterirdische*] German tradition" ("Nachwort," in *Deutsche Menschen* [Frankfurt, 1962], rpt. in *Über Walter Benjamin*, 54–62; this quotation, 55).

[39] Benjamin worked on the *Berliner Kindheit* throughout his exile, completing the first revision in late 1933 and then returning to it as late as 1938, when he completed the last version, only recently uncovered in Paris (1st version, *GS* 4:235–304; latest version, *GS* 7:385–433).

[40] The two had met through their mutual friend Werner Kraft and had begun corresponding. Auerbach apparently read the twelve excerpts of the *Kindheitsbuch* published in the *Frankfurter Zeitung* of February and March 1935 (it is unclear whether Benjamin also sent him a copy of the manuscript). The letter continues with several comments on the *Passagen-Werk*, concluding, "This will be a document, if only there remain people who read documents" (Karl-Heinz Barck, "5 Briefe Erich Auerbachs an Walter Benjamin in Paris," *Zeitschrift für Germanistik* 9:6 [Dec. 1988]: 690; my emphasis).

haunt Benjamin studies, especially in the United States, means not to realize even what the goals of the project may have been.

It is not surprising that the fault line defining the polarities of Benjamin
criticism has been biographical. Already hinted at in Scholem's and
Adorno's portrayals, the image of Benjamin as a tragic, melancholic outsider defined the bitter polemics of the Benjamin revival in Germany in the
sixties, where he was either the last true German man of letters or a radical
Brechtian Marxist.[41] The English reception in the seventies, lacking such
an immediate political crisis, continued the same polemic within a more
purely academic context, as in the explicitly Marxist and Brechtian monographs by Eagleton and Roberts and translations of Benjamin's most ten-
dentiously Brechtian and Marxist writings in the film journal *Screen* and
in the *New Left Review*.[42] The American reception, without the political
charge of the German reception or the political intentions of the British
one, has been framed until recently by a simplified embrace of either
Adorno's or Scholem's version of the melancholic mystic.[43]

At the same time, the general romanticization of Benjamin on this
side of the Atlantic has led to the rejection of any biographical material
whatsoever. This is particularly evident in the influential appropriation of
Benjamin by the American deconstructionists. Focusing almost exclusively
on Benjamin's early work, especially the pre-Marxist parts of the *Trauerspiel* book and "Die Aufgabe des Übersetzers" (The Task of the Translator), and any later essay that can be read nostalgically ("Der Erzähler"
[The Storyteller], for example), these critics have not avoided biographical
romanticization but simply hypostasized it into a purportedly objective
and critical theory of language and allegory.[44] Despite the more even-

---

[41] Klaus Garber gives an excellent summary and bibliography of this and later stages
in Benjamin's reception, particularly in West Germany: "Etapes de la réception de
Benjamin," in Wismann, 917–84; for the sixties debate in West Germany, see 952–62.

[42] Terry Eagleton, *Walter Benjamin or Towards a New Criticism* (London, 1981);
translations: "A Short History of Photography," *Screen* 13:1 (1972); "A Radio Talk
on Brecht," *New Left Review* 123 (Sept.-Oct. 1980); "Goethe: The Reluctant Bourgeois," *New Left Review* 133 (May-June 1982).

[43] The following are exemplary: Susan Sontag's article "The Last Intellectual," *New
York Review of Books* 25:15 (12 Oct. 1978): 75–82; rpt. as intro. in *One-Way Street
and Other Writings*, by Walter Benjamin (London, 1979), and as the title essay in
Sontag, *Under the Sign of Saturn* (New York, 1980), 107–34; Steiner's introduction to
The Origin of German Tragic Drama (7–24); and Wolin's monograph.

[44] See, for example, Jacobs; Paul De Man, "Conclusions on Walter Benjamin's 'Task
of the Translator,'" *Yale French Studies* 69 (1985): 25–48; Miller; and Geoffrey
Hartman, *Criticism in the Wilderness: The Study of Literature Today* (New Haven,
1980), 63–85.

handed approaches seen in the special issues of *New German Critique*, in Jennings, and in Buck-Morss (1989), there remains an apparent reluctance to take Benjamin's work on its own terms by first accounting for the vexed role played by autobiography within it.[45]

For Benjamin, the present situation was neither absent from the study of the past nor in an unambivalent relationship with it. The idea of applying the theory of allegory in the *Trauerspiel* book to the present was a subtext of that work; it was a primary methodological assumption of the *Passagen-Werk* as well.[46] The autobiographical allegory functions on a dialectical model, structuring the movement of its reader between three determinant historical moments: Baudelaire, childhood around 1900, *entre-deux-guerres*. One theme in the *Passagen-Werk* explicitly manifests the generational tone of the dialectical chronology. Benjamin uses the key word *gauloiserie* to introduce Baudelaire's note on a "Wonderful conspiracy to be organized for exterminating the Jewish race," concluding that "Céline has continued this line. (Facetious murderer and robber!)" (J40,1).[47] If Benjamin's contemporaries, the surrealists, had led him to the nineteenth century, it was that epoch that would in return provide the substance of the critique of his contemporaries.

One line of descent from Baudelaire led to Céline (b. Paris, 1894); another became a critique of Ernst Jünger (b. 1895). Jünger emerges from a citation directly following the note above, of Baudelaire's criticism of the use of military metaphors: "The poets of combat. The literati of the avant-garde. This habit for military metaphors does not denote militant minds, but those made for discipline, that is to say, for conformity" (J40,2). This is the critical lexicon of Benjamin's review of Jünger's collection of paeans to the experience of the First World War, *Krieg und Krieger*

---

[45] For a bibliography of most full-length studies, and nearly all English-language essays up to 1988, see Smith 1988, 371–92.

[46] The clearest interior evidence of this intent in the *Trauerspiel* book is in the conclusion to the second part, "Trauerspiel und Tragödie," where Benjamin cites a description of the French writer Charles Péguy, who was killed in action in the First World War, as an example of the seventeenth-century type of the melancholic. The presence of such an intention, however, does not necessarily demonstrate Benjamin's resolve to apply baroque allegory *as such* to the avant-garde of the 1920s.

[47] The note reappears in the first Baudelaire essay as a description of the "culte de la blague" (cult of empty talk) and the mention of Céline's anti-Semitic pamphlet *Bagatelles pour un massacre (bagatelle* being a synonym for *blague*). In the letter to Horkheimer that also contains an important outline of the Baudelaire book (4 Apr. 1938; *B* 740–43, 558), Benjamin, criticizing Gide's dismissal of the pamphlet as banal, comments that it is precisely its banality that is dangerous.

(War and warriors), which responded to the perceived current decadence of Germany through the doctrine of *Totalmobilmachung:* the extension of wartime mobilization into every aspect of peacetime life.[48] A look at Benjamin's polemic against Jünger reveals the centrality of the war experience to his criticism, the use of generational metaphors to structure theoretical disputes, and consequently, the intimate relation of such polemics to the *Passagen-Werk.*

Within the context of a detailed critique of the premises of the book's arguments, Benjamin weaves a scathing polemic in response to what he considers "an unrestrained translation of the theses of l'art pour l'art into war itself" (*GS* 3:240; *TGF* 122), by means of a stylistic critique of Jünger's actions: "A falser tone could not be struck, nor clumsier words set to paper, nor more tactless words uttered." He quickly extends the criticism into a personal attack: "Only a suitor who embraces poorly is so loquacious. And indeed these authors embrace their thoughts poorly. They must repeatedly be brought back to them, and that is what we will do here" (3:241; 122). Now, related by analogy to Baudelaire's distinction between the use of military metaphors and the military mind, the amatory metaphor belongs to the Benjaminian constellation surrounding the comparison between sexuality and writing. The analogy extends from the early series of comparisons between books and whores in *Einbahnstraße*, "Nr. 13" (*GS* 4:109), to the Baudelairean thematic of writer as prostitute and prostitute as allegorical image in the *Passagen-Werk.*[49] As Benjamin applies it, the constellation is not resolutely negative but dialectical: he portrays the contributors as inadequate young lovers/writers while implicitly proposing himself as a superior one.

The same dialectical register is to be found in "Tankstelle" (Filling

---

[48] *Krieg und Krieger,* ed. Ernst Jünger (Berlin, 1930). Benjamin's review, "Theorien des deutschen Faschismus," first appeared in *Die Gesellschaft* 7:2 (1930): 32–41 (*GS* 3:238–50); trans. Jerolf Wikoff, "Theories of German Fascism," *NGC* 17 (Spring 1979): 120–28; cited hereafter as *TGF.* On Benjamin's critique in this review, see Ansgar Hillach, "The Aesthetics of Politics: Walter Benjamin's Theories of German Fascism," *NGC* 17 (Spring 1979): 99–119. On Jünger's role in the so-called Conservative Revolution in Germany between the wars, see Jeffrey Herf, *Reactionary Modernism: Technology, Culture, and Politics in Weimar and the Third Reich* (New York, 1984), esp. 18–48 and 70–108.

[49] It need hardly be noted that this is an old tradition. Procreative metaphors for writing go back to antiquity (see Curtius, 313–14). Benjamin attributes his particular modernist strain to Mallarmé (he cites the French poet's metaphor of the virgin page in *Einbahnstraße* to introduce a series of analogies between books and whores); the image of prostitution derives from Baudelaire or the surrealists.

Station), the first piece of *Einbahnstraße,* where, significantly, it is used to distinguish the two youthful types from an older generation of sterile impotence: "Under [present] circumstances true literary activity cannot aspire to take place within a literary framework—this is, rather, the habitual expression of its sterility [*Unfruchtbarkeit*]. Significant literary work can only come into being in a strict alternation between action and writing. . . . Opinions are to the vast apparatus of social existence what oil is to machines: one does not go up to a turbine and pour machine oil over it; one applies it to hidden spindles and joints that one has to know" (*GS* 4:85; *R* 61). The sterility of traditional literary activity is contrasted with the types of action of two avant-gardes: those, like Jünger's group above, who "stand before a turbine and pour machine oil over it," and those, like Benjamin, who know the correct nooks and crannies.[50]

Benjamin finishes off the stylistic critique of *Krieg und Krieger* with a Shakespearean flourish, uniting seduction, writing, and war:

We will however not tolerate anyone who speaks of war, yet knows nothing but war. Radical in our own way, we will ask: where do you come from? And what do you know of peace? . . . And, without waiting for you to answer: No! Not that you would then not be able to celebrate war, even more passionately than now; but to celebrate it *as* you do— of that you would not be capable. How would Fortinbras have testified for war? This can be deduced from Shakespeare's technique. Just as he reveals Romeo's love for Juliet in the fiery glow of its passion by presenting Romeo as in love from the outset, in love with Rosalinde, he would have had Fortinbras begin with a passionate eulogy of peace so enchanting and mellifluously sweet that, when at the end he raises his voice all the more passionately in favor of war, everyone would have wondered with a shudder: what are these powerful, nameless forces that compel this man, wholly filled with the bliss of peace, to commit himself body and soul to war?—But there is nothing of that here. (3:245–46; *TGF* 125–26)

Capping the amatory rhetoric with the counterexample of Romeo, Benjamin smoothly shifts for the conclusion back into the thematic register of war: the variety put forth by Jünger's writers will wreak the same ruin and destruction as did Hamlet, leaving Fortinbras, the Norwegian warrior-prince and the young Dane's contemporary, to pick up the pieces.

[50] Benjamin is appropriating a modernist topos. On the identification of women and technology within modernism, see Huyssen 1986, 65–81.

Certainly, there is a prophetic ring to the allegory, but it is equally concerned with the theoretical issues of the day: given that war (and for
Benjamin, this meant revolution) was necessary, how did one preach it to
the masses?

Hamlet is the quintessential melancholic qua allegorist in the *Trauerspiel* book, later updated for the nineteenth century as Baudelaire. Yet,
in the *Passagen-Werk*, Benjamin was careful to base his model of the
contemporary critic as historical materialist on a critique of this type (cf.
J57, 3; J66, 2): they may be suicidal Hamlets, but he will be Fortinbras,
who will reconstruct a new kingdom from the ruins of the old. Within
the generational similarity of the two ("Radical in our own way"), the
distinction between Hamlet's and Fortinbras's situations is simple but
precisely enunciated: Hamlet cleared away the debris of the past, revealing
his kingdom as corrupt, his parents as evil, while dooming himself in the
process. This role need not have been conscious—the baroque allegorists
did not know the meaning their mortificatory emblems would hold for the
twentieth century, nor was Baudelaire a revolutionary—but the madness
has nonetheless been cleared away (cf. N1, 4; G°, 3). In the same way, the
critique in "Theorien des deutschen Faschismus" uses the tragedy of those
writers to expose its roots in the previous generation (*l'art pour l'art*, to
give the example at hand); not, however, in order to return to that past
but to show its dangerous influence on the present and to clear the way to
the future.

Benjamin thus formulated polemics with his contemporaries as a dual
attack: against the dangerous alternatives they proposed and against the
outmoded status quo opposed by both. He used the same critical strategy
to distinguish himself rhetorically and theoretically from the mistakes of
those much closer to his own stance, especially the surrealists. We find the
following comment in a letter to Scholem on their relationship to the
Passagen-Werk: "In order to extricate the work from an overly ostenta-
tious proximity to the Surrealist movement, which is so understandable
and grounded as to prove fatal to me, I have had to extend it ever further
in my thoughts and make it so universal in its most particular and minutest
framework that it will enter into the *inheritance* of Surrealism, already in
a purely temporal sense, and, indeed with all the absolute power of a
philosophical Fortinbras" (*B* 483, 342; his emphasis). Unlike the ideo-
logues of *Krieg und Krieger,* ripe for polemic, for whom Benjamin merely
needed to formulate the proper framework, the surrealists had first to be
cast within that framework, disenchanted by the mortifying work of critique, so that Benjamin's work might enter into its inheritance. The twofold meaning of inheritance is instructive: technically, Fortinbras inherits

the kingdom directly from the dead king and queen, but only because of the actions and following the death of the legitimate heir, Hamlet.

The allegorical domain inherited by the surrealists (for it was they who had reclaimed it from oblivion) was the arcades; Benjamin could lay claim to them only by establishing his succession; to do so, he had first to establish his credentials as equal of the surrealists, then mortify their movement through critique, and carry on from there. The autobiographical framework of the *Passagen-Werk* is clearest in cases like that of the surrealists, for the description of strategy made to Scholem enacts the dual effect Benjamin intended the dialectical images to have on his readers—the manifest clearing away of illusion followed by the hidden synthesis into the present.

Their rediscovery of the arcades was the most apparent legacy of the surrealists' focus on the importance of the everyday and ephemeral as a means of understanding the world. Benjamin also learned from them the profane illumination to be achieved from viewing the world in an altered state of consciousness, of which the phylogenetic model was the dream state. In the surrealism essay, he criticized them for continuing to cling to "a number of pernicious romantic prejudices" in their aesthetic of "the artist *én état de surprise*" (*GS* 2:307; *R* 189), which he characterized in notes at the same time as "mythologizing" (H°, 17; also N1, 9). At the same time, Benjamin argued that such new forms of perception met the needs created in a collective body now being reorganized through technology and thus could eventually lead to revolution (cf. 2:310; 192).

One manifestation of Benjamin's shift in emphasis brought about by universalizing the particular is the concept of the dreaming collective. Benjamin regarded Jung's mythicization of the collective as analogous to the surrealists' mythicization of dreams.[51] His goal, in contrast, was a demythicized awakening, and he literalized this metaphor for the collective as the revolutionary awakening from the sleep of capitalism. The surrealism essay concludes with the image of a man's face turned into that of an alarm clock "that rings sixty seconds long every minute," the transcendence of reality "as put forth by the Communist Manifesto" (2:310; 192). If the dream could be extended to the collective, then so could the guidelines for its interpretation, as Benjamin set out to do in the *Passagen-Werk*.

At the same time, as the chronological scheme cited at the start of the chapter confirms, Benjamin chose nineteenth-century Paris because his dreams were rooted in its ruins: "Awakening as a gradual process, which

---

[51] Buck-Morss discusses this facet of Benjamin's thought in depth in 1989, 253–86.

asserts itself in the life of the individual as in that of a generation. Sleep as its primary stage. A generation's experience of youth [*Jugenderfahrung*] has much in common with the experience of dreams [*Traumerfahrung*]" (F°, 7). The generational specificity of this experience gave it objective validity for him and his contemporaries: "The fact that we were children in this time belongs for me with its objective picture" (M°, 16; also K1a, 2). Benjamin found evidence of such a fact in Kafka's repeated literary glimpses of the family interior: "And this experience is an inalienable quality of his, and only his—and thus our—generation, because only for it does the terrifying furniture of the beginnings of high Capitalism fill up the scenes of its brightest childhood experiences" (K°, 27).

Given the fact that certain members of his generation had already begun producing images of its awakening, Benjamin's project was twofold. First, the potential of such images (of surrealism and Jünger, for instance) required evaluation and, generally, mortification.[52] Benjamin noted, for example, that "in the writings of the Surrealists and in the new book by Heidegger [*Sein und Zeit*], one and the same crisis manifests itself in both possibilities of resolving it" (S1, 6).[53] Then, along with, or rather in the rubble left by such a critique, the rest of the generation would be awakened through dialectical images composed out of the dream material and memory traces left behind by the wake-up call.

Benjamin was in no doubt as to the nature of the alarm. In a note to the *Passagen-Werk*, he presented its general form in the abstractly autobiographical language of the *Berliner Kindheit*: "When we must rise early for a day of traveling, it can happen that, disinclined to wrest ourselves from sleep, we dream that we are getting up and getting dressed. The bourgeoisie dreamed such a dream in *Jugendstil*, fifteen years before history resoundingly awakened it" (S4a,1). In the passage of fifteen years from Benjamin's childhood to his youth can also be found the passage from *Jugendstil* to *Jugendbewegung* (youth movement), which was to practice the reintegration of all spheres of life analogous to *Jugendstil*'s reintroduction of technology into art.[54] Benjamin was a prominent mem-

---

[52] For an extended effort to use Benjamin instead as the medium for a stylistic rapprochement of the surrealists and Jünger, see Karl-Heinz Bohrer, *Die Ästhetik des Schreckens* (Munich, 1978).

[53] Born in 1889, Heidegger was Benjamin's senior by a mere three years.

[54] Benjamin makes the connection in the same folder, suggesting *Jugendbewegung* as the working out of *Jugendstil*: "Perhaps one ought to try, pursuing Jugend*stil* until its consequences in the Jugend*bewegung*, to take this observation up to the threshold [*Schwelle*] of the war" (S5, 3; his emphasis).

ber of a particularly radical and pacifist branch of the youth movement during the prewar years, and he experienced a profound shock when his mentor, Gustav Wyneken, endorsed the war.[55] It is no accident, then, that Benjamin reacted so violently to Jünger's book of responses to the *Kriegserlebnis*, the war experience: this was the battle for their generation. If that was their defining moment, their rite of passage (as the sexual metaphor makes abundantly clear), then nothing could be more dangerous than a false image of it.

Benjamin had begun constructing his own image of the *Kriegserlebnis* by 1917. In an early essay on *The Idiot*, he concluded with the rather strong misreading of "Dostoevsky's great complaint: the collapse of the youth movement" (*GS* 2:240). Benjamin sent the essay to his new friend Scholem, who perceived that the figure hidden behind Benjamin's reading of Prince Myshkin was the poet Fritz Heinle, another member of the youth movement and Benjamin's closest friend at the time, who had committed suicide with his lover Erika Seligson following the declaration of war.[56] Benjamin, evidently elated by his new friend's perceptiveness, immediately answered Scholem that the misreading indeed signaled the existence of a hidden autobiographical allegory and that Scholem had correctly deciphered its generational-historical meaning (Scholem 1981, 49).

Benjamin had established Heinle's suicide as the crux of a generational allegory of the foundering of the youth movement. Over the years, the *figura* gradually accrued each additional meaning in Benjamin's understanding of the generational experience and the role of the *Kriegserlebnis* within it. He continued to ground strong readings in submerged autobiographical allegories from Charles Péguy as image of the modern melancholic to the breakup of his marriage in the epochal essay on Goethe's *Wahlverwandtschaften* (*Elective Affinities*); in conjunction with his discovery of both Marxism and surrealism in the 1920s, he also buried such allegories in the structural foundations of *Einbahnstraße*.[57] The third piece of that work takes up Heinle's suicide again, but with

[55] See his "leavetaking" letter to Wyneken, 3 Mar. 1915 (*B* 120–22, 75–76).
[56] For a well-researched account of Heinle's life, if a somewhat superficial analysis of its meaning for Benjamin, see Erdmut Wizisla, " 'Fritz Heinle war Dichter': Walter Benjamin und sein Jugendfreund," in *"Was nie geschrieben wurde, lesen": Frankfurter Benjamin-Vorträge*, ed. Lorenz Jäger and Thomas Regehly (Bielefeld, 1992), 115–31. See also the following special issues: *aut aut*, n.s., 189–190 (1982), and *Akzente* 31 (Munich, 1984).
[57] Benjamin saw Péguy as perhaps the closest to himself of any modern writer (*B* 217, 147). For the subtext of the essay "Goethes *Wahlverwandtschaften*," see Scholem 1981, 93–94, 102, 111; see also Witte, 44.

added symbolic weight. Written in three parts, each composed as a dream, it is entitled as a whole with an address, "Nr. 113," and given an epigraph: "The hours that hold the figure and the form / Have run their course within the house of dreams" (4:86; R 62).⁵⁸ The address and the metaphor of the house of dreams give the same architectural metaphor for the layers of a dream that Benjamin would use in the *Passagen-Werk;* it extends here to the titles of the three parts: "Cellar" [*Souterrain*], "Vestibule," and "Dining Room."⁵⁹

We begin underground, with the dream of a reconciliation with the here-unnamed Heinle, introduced by a general statement on the assault by enemy bombs on the house of life and depicting the dream as a tempestuous renewal of friendship and brotherhood dreamed on a night of despair. It concludes with the shock of recognition: "But when I awoke it became clear to me that what despair had brought to light like a detonation was this person's corpse, which had been walled up there and meant: whoever one day lives here should in no way resemble him/it [*ihm*]" (GS 4:86; R 63). By the late twenties, Benjamin had firmly wedded the new philosophical concept of the shock of awakening to the figure of Heinle.

Solely in terms of language, however, the dream is little different from a 1925 dream allegory of the war experience by Jünger; what may seem clichéd about the latter also brings out a peculiarity of Benjamin's style that is not often enough noticed: his images are constructed primarily out of cliché, or "dream kitsch," as he called it in the context of the surrealists (GS 2:620–22). The stylistic use of cliché figures in Benjamin's generational allegory just as the experience of childhood does: both are part of the shared past. A comparison with Jünger's use of the same material reveals several interesting points: first, that the *Kriegserlebnis,* both in its clichés and in its trauma, indeed provided something like a shared generational experience; second, that on a formal level, the literary experimentation of the left-wing Benjamin is fairly indistinguishable from that of the right-wing Jünger; third, and consequently, that any means of differentiation will have to take into account not just formal qualities but also biographical and historical ones.

Here is Jünger's piece, from *Das abenteuerliche Herz* (1929; The adventurous heart), a collection of dream protocols, aphorisms, and critical reflections very similar in form to *Einbahnstraße:*

⁵⁸ Werner Kraft, a friend of Benjamin's from 1915 onward, suggests that the verses are either Benjamin's or Heinle's ("Über einen verschollenen Dichter," *Neue Rundschau* 78 [1967]: 615–16, quoted in GS 4:915).
⁵⁹ See folders K ("Dream City and Dream House, Dreams of the Future, Anthropolog⟨ical⟩ Nihilism, Jung") and L ("Dream House, Museum, Fountain Hall").

One evening, in bed, the rain pouring down, the person of a close acquaintance who had died the previous year came to mind. I saw him in various situations—small, distinguishing features [*bezeichnende Eigen-arten*] emerged as the memory came to life; for a moment, he appeared alive and about to come within reach, until clearheaded composure suddenly called to mind the facts of his death. This sudden collision of the living with the dead somehow deeply moved and shook my inner balance, and it was in fact the need for complete clarification that wrenched my thoughts out into the dark rain-besmirched corner of some churchyard, and sent them to penetrate the loose earth and search into the coffin: "While I am lying here in warmth, you are lying there at the same time—strange, that I have not yet thought about you for the whole year." . . . Whenever I read in the newspaper about a judicial/forensic [*gerichtlich*] disinterment, I, a completely grown [*erwachsener*] man, am overcome with astonishment—that we are actually striking corpses this way.[60]

The pieces share the manifest meaning of awakening to the memory of the death of a friend; both bodies are buried underground; the generational memory invoked is identical. Stylistically, Jünger's generational allegory is fairly sophisticated. It is structured around three central wordplays, *Eigenarten, gerichtlich,* and *erwach(s)ener* (grown/awake), which provide the key to its interpretation.[61] If the ideological difference between the two writers is already apparent from the double meaning of *Eigenarten*, it is not as easy as might be expected to establish those differences within the use of language. Such an effort consequently becomes even more impera-tive: for once the romanticized image of Benjamin the outsider has been dispelled, his relationship to his own time must be differently defined.

This definition is the role of the autobiographical allegory whose traces we find more or less hidden throughout Benjamin's writings; we need only reconstruct it according to his directions. First of all, Benjamin's piece evokes the *Kriegserlebnis* as the latent content ("Souterrain") of our inter-pretation; it is mediated through the dream symbolism of the house at "Nr. 113." Whereas Jünger's dream operates as a straightforward allegory of the need to work through the loss of the war embodied in the soldier, Benjamin's is framed within a further register of cliché: the dream symbol-ism of the house setting. This structure of the kitsch of the interiors of his

---

[60] Ernst Jünger, *Das abenteuerliche Herz* (Berlin, 1929), 92; rpt. in vol. 9 of *Sämtliche Werke*, 18 vols. (Stuttgart, 1978-).

[61] *Eigenarten*, which under National Socialism referred to racial characteristics, pro-vides a generational allegory of Jünger's own: beneath the image of his fellow soldier's distinguishing features lies the figure of his solidarity.

childhood mediates the impact of the war, in which, after all, Benjamin, unlike Jünger, did not fight.[62]

The strong rhetoric of Benjamin's piece is manifestly in service not of the *Kriegserlebnis* but of the more generic symbolism of the basement as the unconscious, the return of a lost friend and the longed-for reconciliation thereof as a working-through of the shock of death. Employed skillfully, as they are here, these clichés still strike a chord, just as do those of the *Berliner Kindheit*. But Benjamin's images are not merely a question of language; we have already identified the unnamed friend as Heinle and thus the interment as a mediated version of Jünger's immediate *Kriegserlebnis* above: the encounter with a casualty of war. Whereas Jünger's piece

---

[62] One could certainly ask to what extent their experiences remain comparable. Benjamin's position, evident in the constant presence of his privileged childhood, is that the experience, grounded in the shock of the war, remains the same even if certain objective situations vary. Certainly, his critique of *Krieg und Krieger* stemmed from his hostility to its authors having fought willingly in the war. For him, there had been only two morally pure alternatives: to be exempted (able to depend on monetary support from his parents, Benjamin faked illness and spent the war in Switzerland) or to kill oneself (the choice Heinle made; it is unlikely he could have afforded to take Benjamin's option). Conversely, the very similarity of the two pieces is evidence that Benjamin was on the right track, and, of course, Jünger's generally aristocratic bearing (most noticeable in his valorization of the attitude of detachment, or *désinvolture*) would set him closer to Benjamin's class (with the important exception of the latter's Jewish background), again accounting for the extra hostility. If so, one would have to determine exactly to what extent Benjamin and those like him were subject to the psychological effects of the *Kriegserlebnis* analyzed by Klaus Theweleit as having helped pave the way toward National Socialism and which Benjamin had already seen at work in Jünger's volume (*Männer-Phantasien*, 2 vols. [Reibek bei Hamburg, 1980]; trans. Stephen Conway, *Male Fantasies*, 2 vols. [Minneapolis, 1987, 1989]). Those elements of Benjamin's writing and thought that are closest to Jünger—his embrace of technology, his fascination with destruction and apocalypse, and even their clichéd appeals to the brotherhood of their generation—all fall within this complex. To be sure, Benjamin conceived his efforts, and thus are they being read here, as different responses to that shared experience and shared psychological trauma. Yet as much care must be taken in discovering the similarities as the differences, for only once the former have been defused can the latter be freed for use. I am aware of one overtly psychoanalytic interpretation of Benjamin, by Beth Sharon Ash, "Walter Benjamin: Ethnic Fears, Oedipal Anxieties, Political Consequences," *NGC* 48 (Fall 1989): 2–42. Ash regards Benjamin's destructive side from the point of view of a collective response to anti-Semitism, drawing sweepingly negative conclusions as to the benefits of reading his works. While Benjamin's Jewishness certainly needs to be accounted for, his particular fascination with technology and images of masculine destruction calls for further critical analysis as well.

descends from and returns again to "clearheaded composure," however, Benjamin's "Nr. 113" begins underground as the necessary prelude to climbing upstairs; in the allegory of conversion the subject is awake and clearheaded only at the end of the journey.

Upstairs, the "Vestibule" and "Dining Room" are inhabited by another venerable symbol—the figure of Goethe—and their narratives take the form of childhood fantasies. The first, in Goethe's house, ends with the narrator's discovery of his name entered in the visitor's book, "with big unruly children's writing" (*GS* 4:87; *R* 63). The second takes place in a study unknown to him yet known to be that of Goethe, who presents the narrator a gift, seats him at a table set for the narrator's relatives and even his ancestors, and, finally, moves him to tears by his weakness (*GS* 4:87; *R* 63). The manifest symbolic content of Goethe's figure puts "Souterrain" in a new light, as an allegory of the process, the art, and the profession of writing in the house of tradition (or fame): Heinle's figure unites *Kriegserlebnis* with the practice of literature.

In this allegory, the main floor of the house is the realm of Goethe, the clichéd yet enduring symbol of German letters, in all their propriety, success, conservatism, and maturity, and in all the ambivalence they generate in a youthful modernist writer. Unlike the opening nightmare, these two dreams, as befits their setting above-ground, are fairly straightforward wish fulfillments. Remaining within the dream symbolism, we have the following interpretation: the manifest part of the dream structure of the house, the furnished rooms in which one lives and plies one's craft, is the visible process of creation, clear, simple, and neither profound nor terribly striking—although elegantly formulated, as one would expect from someone in Goethe's tradition. The force, emotion, and shock come up from the unconscious through the dream part of the house, the material buried by the author in his cellar which will come to light at the proper moment in the text, illuminating its meaning. Thus, at best, does Benjamin's text read without the individual or generational allegory: a well-wrought, perhaps profound, yet wholly classical product.

To be sure, we may at this point remember the particular interpretation given by Benjamin to the interior in the note above on Kafka: "Because only for it does the terrifying furniture of the beginnings of high Capitalism fill up the scenes of its brightest childhood experiences" (K°, 27). This is the house into which Benjamin manifestly moves and in which he was already inscribed as a child. Here, then, is the surface material, the clichés of his as well as of Jünger's youth, but not the shock. Heinle, the figure of that shock, was not just a friend and member of the youth movement; Scholem reports that Benjamin considered him "the purest lyric poet of

his generation" (1981, 17). So "Nr. 113" identifies the essentially dual
nature of Heinle as a cipher: he embodies the fate of the youth movement
(victims of the war) but equally, and inseparably, the difficulty of writing
about it, for lyric was killed along with youth.

Kriegserlebnis, the problem of expressing it, and the shared language of
one's parents' furniture: this is the constellation out of which the images
of the *Passagen-Werk* are derived. Heinle's meaning as the common
thread of Benjamin's autobiographical allegory became further constel-
lated when Benjamin made his first explicit attempt to recall it in the
Berliner Chronik in 1932. He begins with Ernst Joel, a link between the
past and the present, a former opponent from youth movement days encountered again in the late twenties and now supervising his experiments
with hashish:

> So his image appears to me at this stage only as an answer to the
> question whether forty is not too young an age at which to evoke the
> most important memories of one's life. For this image is already now
> that of a dead man, and who knows how he might have been able to
> help me cross this threshold [*den Übergang über diese Schwelle erleicht-
> ern*], with memories of even the most external and superficial things?
> ... It was in Heidelberg, during what was undoubtedly self-forgetful
> work, that I tried to summon up, in a meditation on the nature of the
> lyric, the figure of my friend Fritz Heinle, around whom all the happen-
> ings in the Meeting House [*im Heim*] arrange themselves and with
> whom they vanish. Fritz Heinle was a poet, and the only one of them all
> whom I met not "in real life" [*"im Leben"*] but in his work. He died at
> nineteen, and could be known in no other way. (*GS* 6:477; *R* 17).[63]

If the dream pieces of *Einbahnstraße* are allegories of the process of awakening—the descent to the underworld—then the later description of
Heinle in the *Berliner Chronik* is Benjamin's attempt to describe the process of remembrance that will make sense of the shock of that dream—
the return to the open air of history.

Benjamin's obsession with Heinle represents both a personal coming-
to-terms with the tragedy of his youth and a historical connection with
the experience of his generation in the tragedy of the war; it is an attempt
to find a means of representing it as well as a common ground from which

---

[63] The "Meeting House" (*das Heim*) was the site of youth movement meetings and
power struggles as well as of Heinle and Seligson's suicide. The suicide note read, "You
will find us lying in the meeting house [*im Heim*]" (6:478).

to receive the attempts of others. Each shift in Benjamin's life situation or critical stance is reflected by a shift in his expression of Heinle's legacy. This legacy is most concretely manifest in the unrealized attempts Benjamin made to publish what he believed to be the sole surviving manuscript of Heinle's poems. Heinle's death, Scholem writes, moved the poet into "the realm of the sacrosanct" (1981, 17). Benjamin did not mean it lightly, then, when, writing from Paris, he told Scholem that the only inconsolable loss from the books and papers left behind in Berlin (and much else, including manuscripts of Benjamin, was also lost) was that of Heinle's notebooks.[64] The progression is as accurate as it is elegantly figured. If the man had fallen victim to the First World War, it suited the allegory that his memory should fall victim to the Nazis, lending the individual force to the famous words of the sixth thesis on the concept of history, "Only that historian will have the gift of fanning the spark of hope in the past who is firmly convinced that *even* the dead will not be safe from the enemy if he wins" (*GS* 1:695; *I* 255; his emphasis).

If Heinle's figure describes the arc of Benjamin's attitude toward his work and his generation, then we find its peak, the moment at which Benjamin succeeded in digging up the memory, woven into the moment at which he discovered the arcades. In the surrealism essay, Benjamin cites Breton's description of a bar that he is "inconsolable . . . no longer to be able to have known": " 'It's quite dark, with arbors like impenetrable tunnels—a drawing room on the bottom of a lake'—there is something that brings back to my memory that most uncomprehended room in the old Princess Café. It was the back room on the second floor, with couples in the blue light. We called it the 'anatomy school' ['*die Anatomie*']; it was the last locale for love" (*GS* 2:301; *R* 183). If Breton's prose is already a figure for the Paris of the *Passagen-Werk* and Baudelaire ("The Paris of

---

[64] He would return to this theme. In a letter of 1 Nov. 1938, he wrote to Gretel Adorno that the notebooks of both Heinles (he had befriended Fritz Heinle's brother Wolf, also a poet, who died in the thirties, penniless, in spite of Benjamin's epistolary and other efforts to raise money for him), his "irreplaceable archive of the history of the youth movement, and ultimately also my youthful works [*Jugendarbeiten*] . . . have been destroyed" (*B* 780–82; 578–79). The thought process whereby Benjamin connected and hierarchized these topics is clear. We can also mention the will written by Benjamin when contemplating suicide on Ibiza in 1932 (around his fortieth birthday), which survives in the Potsdam archive and which Scholem reproduced in part in his memoir of Benjamin: "My entire estate contains in addition to my own writings primarily the work of the brothers Fritz and Wolf Heinle. . . . These comprise not only the Heinles' manuscripts but also my edited handwritten copies of their works" (quoted in 1981, 175–76).

his poems is a submerged city, more submarine than subterranean" [*GS* 5:55; *R* 157]), the "we" of the conjured memory is Heinle and the link is his poetry: until recently, one of the only known lines of his oeuvre was a verse out of "Princess Café" cited in the *Berliner Chronik,* "Türen führen Kühle über durch Gesang" (Doors draw coolness over through the song [*GS* 6:483; *R* 24]). The threshold image of the door that perhaps (along with the mnemonic quality of the sounds) caused the verse to stick in Benjamin's mind conjures up the same alien environment of the "anatomy school."

Once the threshold was passed, there was a new setting in the café and a new meaning for Heinle, now in memory: "Later, when this epoch was long since closed, I sat long evenings there, close to a jazz band, discreetly consulting sheets and slips of paper, writing my *Origin of German Trauer-spiel.* When one day a new 'renovation' set in, turning the Prince Café into Café Stenwyk, I gave up. Today it has sunk into the level of a beerhouse" (*GS* 6:484; *R* 24). Beginning with the construction of the Prince(ss) Café as a Berlin arcade where the countersurrealism of Benjamin and Heinle was born, it is not difficult to read in these last lines an autobiographical allegory for the respective trajectories of Benjamin's generation as a whole and his own class of Jewish intellectuals, as traced through the receding presence of Heinle and as reflected in the frame of the *Passagen-Werk:* from the shared experience of childhood and the adolescent "anatomy room," tragically cut short by the shock of the war; to the solitary jazz cellar and the attempt at academic respectability; to the Stenwyk of the former and the alienation of the latter; and, finally, to the beerhouse on the one hand and exile in Paris on the other, Heinle's memory annihilated as completely as the decor of the café. Heinle's death marks the end of the first period; his lyrics memorialize it. His memory as a dream cipher of death punctuates the *Trauerspiel* book and *Einbahnstraße* and suggests the *rite de passage* of the *Passagen-Werk.* The loss of his manuscripts parallels Benjamin's recovery of him on paper in the *Berliner Chronik:* by 1933 the alarm had sounded for Benjamin, and Heinle was the emblem of what had been lost and what must now be remembered, the aegis under which the images of the arcades were conceived.

Autobiographical memories as such play little part in the notes to the *Passagen-Werk;* two have received excellent readings.[65] A third recounts a dream that establishes another link between Heinle and the *Passagen-Werk,* again through the door:

[65] See the "Bullrich-Salz" episode (G1a,4) in Buck-Morss 1989, 462n (which is cited as the only childhood memory in the notes); and Jennings's analysis (119–20) of the "Place du Maroc" anecdote (P1a,2).

From dreams, we are all acquainted with doors that, out of fear, won't close [*den Schrecken nichtschließender Türen*]. To be precise: these are doors that appear to be shut without being so. I learned about this phenomenon in an intensified manner in a dream where a ghost appeared to me and a friend in the window of the ground floor of a house we had to sweep. And as we went further along, it accompanied us from the inside of all the houses. It went through every wall and always remained even with us. I saw this, although I was blind. The conduct that we make through arcades is also at bottom this sort of ghostly path [*Gespensterweg*], along which doors give way and walls soften. (L2,7)

Especially noteworthy is the expansion of the situation of "Nr. 113" into an explicit threshold between individual and collective (the ghost goes from house to house), and Benjamin's conclusion, in which the arcade is defined as the site of our ability to act as the ghost; that is, particularly in the rare autobiographical setting, to give the shock of the wake-up call ourselves, as Benjamin intends here.[66]

This is consistent with the movement from the personal *Berliner Chronik* to the generational *Berliner Kindheit;* it was only in the 1930s that Benjamin fully developed what he learned through them into a materialistic theory of awakening. Although he had muted much of the collective dream imagery, he would still write to Adorno in 1940, "Why should I hide from you that I found the root of my 'theory of experience' in a childhood memory" (*B* 848, 629). Heinle as emblem provided the bridge between the childhood around 1900 and the present of the thirties, albeit only by personifying the rift between them.

Heinle's many manifestations in Benjamin's published and unpublished writings describe an autobiographical allegory of the process that the *Passagen-Werk* was to enact collectively, through the mechanism of the dialectical image. If Heinle had begun as the cipher for the collapse of the youth movement, that collapse eventually revealed itself to Benjamin to be a *figura* of the shock that befell his generation; it was the final moment of the childhood begun around 1900. If Heinle's figure was later buried, that was only emblematic of the shock itself: nascent in the twenties, only to burst forth in the upheavals of the early thirties. So did it resurface in dreams in the late twenties, and Benjamin did not fully recover its meaning (at least on paper) until the early thirties—moments before, in other words, it was too late to act and it would be gone for good. Heinle's only remains are in the traces of Benjamin's writings; it is no accident that the

---

[66] The piece is dated by the editor as pre-1935, so we can assume it was composed after "Nr. 113" and either before or contemporaneous with the childhood memoirs.

final episode is analogous to the one Benjamin constructed around Aragon and Haussmann in the first short draft of the *Passagen-Werk,* "Pariser Passagen": even if the man and his works were destroyed, their allegorical significance could still be preserved in the dialectical images of the *Passagen-Werk* which, if too late to get to utopia, could at least restore to memory the alarm for it.

The medieval model of the topos of *descensus ad inferos* as the site for the creation of the autobiographical voice demonstrates several things: the necessarily rhetorical nature of the assumption of prophetic authority; the subtle modulations by which an individualized voice may be created through citation, allusion, and translation; the ability to move back and forth between history and myth, fact and fiction, macrocosm and microcosm. Benjamin theorized the model as we have seen it at work in twentieth-century literature; as with its medieval predecessors, the theory is simultaneously representational, a second descent. The inability to return in modernism was no longer predicated on the prohibition of *allegoria in facto* for writers of pagan fictions; from Baudelaire onward, individual creative authority was perhaps the only given that did remain.

The problem became, rather, on what authority to base the move to transcendence, how to translate the individual allegory of conversion into a collective one. The medieval move was resolutely to shift out of a temporal scheme into God's eternal present; the modern planted itself just as resolutely within history. We have seen the autobiographical voice weaving itself through novels, essays, pamphlets, diaries, and letters—sometimes wholly personal, sometimes wholly generational in form. The moments when we find the topos of *descensus ad inferos* invoked are moments of tension between the two: the places where Céline establishes his authority as eyewitness of history; where Woolf founds a new tradition of writing; where Benjamin shows us that the descent to Paris is simultaneously the awakening to the reality of 1940, the remembrance of the past simultaneously the realization that the memory could disappear irrevocably at any moment.

Marx perhaps best explained the power of the image of the underworld to an inhabitant of modern Western society: if we are already in hell, then it is in this world as well that we must seek the way back out. Hence, every descent in modern literature has at least an inkling of return, every timeless myth a counterimage of the history behind it. Many, as Benjamin suggested, need only be disenchanted, the ideology behind the myth revealed. As exemplary figures, Céline and Woolf show whither into history the autobiographical allegory leads once deciphered, the directions that conscious manipulation of the topos might take. Given a firmer grasp of the mechanisms of the modernist descent, it becomes possible to begin to separate the images of our criticism from it. We saw in Weiss's rereading of Dante the effects of the descent into modernism from the standpoint of the present; by way of conclusion, I next raise the possibility of a criticism of both medieval and modern literature that would move beyond the persistently modern paradigms seen at work in the previous chapters.

6

The Descent into History, or Beyond a Modernism of Reading: Heaney and Walcott

Larkin's shade surprised me. He quoted Dante:

"Daylight was going and the umber air
Soothing every creature on the earth,
Freeing them from their labours everywhere.

I alone was girding myself to face
The ordeal of my journey and my duty
And not a thing had changed, as rush-hour buses

Bore the drained and laden through the city.
I might have been a wise king setting out
Under the Christmas lights—except that

It felt more like the forewarned journey back
Into the heartland of the ordinary.
Still my old self. Ready to knock one back.

A nine-to-five man who had seen poetry."
      —Seamus Heaney, "The Journey Back"

Hell was built on those hills. In that country of coal
without fire, that inferno the same colour
as their skins and shadows, every labouring soul

climbed with her hundredweight basket, every load for
one copper penny, balanced erect on their necks
that were tight as the liner's hawsers from the weight. . . .

Kneel to your load, then balance your staggering feet
and walk up that coal ladder as they do in time,
one bare foot after the next in ancestral rhyme.
      —Derek Walcott, *Omeros*

PRESENT-DAY CRITICISM continues to labor under myths of modernism that postwar writers such as Weiss, Heaney, and Walcott have already put behind them. If we approach the modernist allegory of conversion obliquely, it becomes possible to discern what those myths continue to consist of and why they might persist. Such an approach involves examining some of the modernists who fit less easily into the standard critical poles of high modernism versus the historical avant-garde. Herein lies an explanation for the absence of the obvious modernist *descensi ad inferos* of Joyce, Rilke, Mann, Proust, Broch, or Kafka from this book. In different ways, Benjamin, Woolf, and Céline lay claim to being transcendent writers while simultaneously revealing the contradiction of such a claim. Their use of the *descensus ad inferos* emphasizes the cultural and historical role of transcendence within modernity; consequently, they suggest ways of discovering similar traces within the polarized reception of the more canonical writers.

At the same time, we have been able to discover these tensions at work in Céline's postwar trilogy, Woolf's *A Room of One's Own* and *Orlando*, and Benjamin's *Passagen-Werk* because we have not been satisfied with reading their versions of descent through the lens of a modernist vision of Dante. Instead of accepting the "theologized" Dante inherited from romanticism, it has been possible to place him within the contradictions of a medieval tradition on the one hand and a postwar rereading of the *Commedia* on the other. To be sure, it is through Dante that the model of the allegory of conversion influenced modernists, but it is precisely the representation of past models that is most subject to rewriting. Dante provides not simply a "theology of style," an ontology of writing as creation, but a highly contradictory compression of the old antinomies of pagan/Christian, poetry/truth, myth/history, microcosm/macrocosm into a form in which they remained legible to modernity.

Benjamin can play a similar role for a contemporary reading of modernism, finding in Baudelaire the inversion of Dante in industrial capitalism, and in Paris a new site for the underworld. The nineteenth-century obsession with the underground in all its variations became synthesized with the Dantean hell of literary tradition into a model of descent both autobiographical (for a generation born in that century's last decade) and mythic. The First World War crystallized this model around a historical catastrophe. We began with the example of Céline (of the same generation as Benjamin and Woolf but outliving them by two decades) to see how the Second World War performed a similar function: the trenches were displaced by Germany and its death camps as the hell to be reckoned with, the source of horror and of knowledge, the source of damnation and of

prophetic authority. The ideological thrust of the descent to the underworld could not be more strikingly demonstrated for a postwar audience.

A child of the *entre-deux-guerres,* Weiss suggested that modernism no
longer constitutes our present and thus can be contextualized as our past
in order to provide a new model of descent for the postwar writer, starting
with a new contextualization of Dante. Weiss thus focused on the possibility of analyzing high modernism and the historical avant-garde as artistic
counterparts to the war. That is to say, he set his sights on 1945 as a
manifestation of hell within history, the culmination of a thirty-year inferno, while matching that image with the mythic update of Dante as high
modernist. The literary tradition, the genealogy to be reckoned with in the
descent for poetic authority, would now run up to and through Joyce,
Kafka, and the other writers explored by Coppi, Heilmann, and the narrator on their way to the *Commedia.* Our Dante and our Middle Ages,
Weiss told us, are a modernist creation.

The degree to which this is true and the degree to which the myths of
modernism continue to inform not contemporary literature but contemporary criticism is demonstrated, among other places, in Beryl Schlossman's
recent book, *The Orient of Style: Modernist Allegories of Conversion.*
Schlossman invokes Dante to support her theory of a modernist "theology
of style": "What I am calling the 'allegory of conversion' in these readings
is the representation of an investment in style" (4). This is the modernist
Dante, a Dante after Céline's heart: allegory is conflated with artistic
creation, the prophetic vision with the act of writing, and language with
style. Instead of the mediation between myth and history suggested by
her definition, Schlossman's allegory of conversion simply accepts Dante's
claim to be God at face value and then uses it to ground similar claims by
Baudelaire, Flaubert, and Proust. Art is made the object rather than the
vehicle of worship, and the artist becomes the originator rather than the
vehicle of truth. Criticism of modernism—and consequently renderings of
a history still seen as culminating in modernism—continue uncritically to
force a choice exclusively between two stances: either the artist is simply
a tool of history (superstructure as direct reflection of base) or she or he is
absolute master of it (art with the power to change life directly).

Like Dante's *Commedia,* I would argue, high modernism is potentially
far more dialectical than such antinomies allow and did in fact allegorize
the means by which it created its illusion of transcendence while still
availing itself of the mythic force of that illusion. Thus, we are beginning
to be able again to notice (as Christine de Pizan, for example, was able to
do some five hundred years ago) that if Dante turned himself into God, he
also wrote an allegory about how he did it. To be able to see this in Dante

means that we are beginning to be able to distance ourselves from a quintessentially modernist reading of Dante as the poet of transcendence. Consequently, we should maintain a similar distance from a modernist conflation of vision with writing, of life with representation that depends on the acceptance of a continuous, homogeneous account of literary history as the ever-greater autonomization of art (or, conversely, of the simple identity of art with ideology and of ideology with politics).

A differently inflected reading of Dante and medieval allegory results in a reading of modernism no longer determined by such a teleology. This will not occur, however, as long as modern literary history is dominated by a view of Dante's *Commedia* as a *summa* of the Middle Ages that transcends its limitations as it transcends the bounds of art, or as long as a composite image of the high modernists comes to seem to the postwar writer and the postwar critic as a pinnacle, the *non plus ultra* of autonomous art. What appears in one reading as the solely derivative approach of a Christine de Pizan to the *descensus ad inferos* can be seen from another angle to generate meaning out of Dante as the model of what cannot be duplicated.[1] Christine incorporated this insight within the dynamics of an autobiographical allegory. In a rather stunning creative achievement, she grafted the topos of modesty to those of descent, sailing, and city-founding, creating an extended metaphorical framework that allowed her to conjure up a female *translatio studii,* an entire tradition, where it had scarcely previously existed.

The formal structure of Weiss's use of Dante is similar to Christine's (as it is to Woolf's in the reading given in Chapter 4): both are creating a tradition ex nihilo. Weiss's Dante is no longer Christine's, however; if Christine showed what could be done with the allegorical structures built up and out from Vergil through Augustine to Dante, Weiss excavated modernism, recasting it as a tradition far different from what it had been reified into. Dante as guide through the *entre-deux-guerres* becomes the new nadir of the descent to the underworld, the point toward which history converges and whence it struggles to return. Weiss's reading signals a crucial insight: namely, that modernist art from Baudelaire to Benjamin, from Flaubert to Woolf, has passed away as absolutely as the century of history encompassed by it. This means two things. First, any experience

---

[1] The alternative is equally predicated on placing Dante in the past. Boccaccio and Petrarch, for example, take on Dante as predecessor, slaying the father by denying the *Commedia.* The *Decameron* concerns itself solely with the "judgment of man"; Petrarch refuses to acknowledge that he had even read Dante. Cf. Menocal, 135–53, 178–203.

of this art and its context is of necessity wholly mediated through memory, through representation, and thus wholly within the purview of literary creation. Second, and consequently, any study, depiction, or recreation of it equally involves, consciously or not, the subsequent attempt to translate it into the present.

Modernism, in other words, is no more a viable model for conceptualizing the present than is Dante's theology or his political theory. Indeed, one of the reasons to read modern literature based on a medieval model is to suggest that, as a part of the same past, it bears more in common with the Middle Ages than with our own time. I am being polemical, to be sure, but the results, I think, demonstrate the validity of the point. With the conflict between pagan and Christian as with the expressionism debate—as the reconstruction of it by Weiss discussed in Chapter 3 shows—the question is no longer who was right but how the terms of the discussion translate into those of the present. Thus Christine troped the conflict between *allegoria in verbis* and *in facto* as an issue of gender. She retained the shell of an established, but past, discourse, complete with selected metaphorics and ready-made *auctoritas,* and animated it to allegorize her concerns. Transformation without explicit but with allegorical alteration: this is the strategy of Christine, of Woolf, of Rauschenberg, and of Weiss. The authority residing in the formal and affective quality is retained but translated into new meanings.

The vehicle whereby the illusion of authenticity is created while being called into question is the autobiographical voice. It is the self-conscious signal of the process enacted to some extent by any writing dealing with the past: retelling history recreates it as something other than it was. To what degree are Christine's genealogy of women's history, Woolf's tradition of Judith Shakespeare, and Weiss's chronicle of the resistance less true than those of Matheolus, Prof. Von X, or postwar Germany? One answer is to ask the converse: to what degree have ancient Rome, the *dolce stil novo,* and Céline's style been determined by their recreation through the autobiographical voices of Vergil, Dante, and Destouches? Benjamin famously tells us that "there is no document of civilization that is not at the same time a document of barbarism" (*GS* 1:696; *I* 256); especially in the current critical climate, we must remind ourselves that the converse is equally true. To conceive of the autobiographical voice as a guide for negotiating the past and the problems inherent in returning to it is to remain constantly alert to the inevitable process whereby history is written as myth and myth transformed into history.

I do not mean by this simply to reinvoke the postmodernism debates of the eighties. As Buck-Morss suggests, the chronological polarity between "formalist 'modernism' " and "historically eclectic 'postmodernism' " is in fact the hypostasization of two partially true political positions within capitalism: "If modernism expresses utopian longing by anticipating the reconciliation of social function and aesthetic form, postmodernism acknowledges their nonidentity and keeps fantasy alive" (1989, 359). We can identify these two poles with the two attitudes taken toward the return in the *descensus ad inferos:* transcendent or self-limiting. But it is more important to realize that the descent highlights not one or the other of these positions but their interdependence, the tension between them. The antinomies, in other words, are not simply going to go away. The price of authority will always be deviation from the truth; life will never dissolve into art, and art will never dissolve into life. Moreover, the relationship between the two is always changing and always changeable.

What Weiss and, as we see below, Heaney and Walcott signal is that modernism, as part of our past, as mythology, has become eminently changeable. We need both to be aware of this and to take advantage of it. For them, the passing of modernism has meant not a swing into the opposite position of postmodernism but the necessity of recasting past myths into forms amenable to the end of this century. Criticism must cease to use art to attempt to change the present or to live in the past, and begin to search it for versions of the past of which we are not yet aware, and for versions of it whose mythic features we should be more suspicious of.

The phenomenon described by Buck-Morss remains fully at work not so much in the production of art but in its consumption by a criticism still trapped within bygone myths. This is particularly evident in the persistence of the notion that we remain able to recreate the totality of any modernist writer in an unmediated embrace. The veritable cults that have grown up in recent decades around Céline, Woolf, and Benjamin (to cite only those modernist writers treated in this book) are the most apparent symptom of the myth of the accessibility of the modern. Scholem, Brecht, and Adorno may have fought over Benjamin—that was their present history that they were attempting to affect directly—but if we continue merely to empathize with his melancholy or to subscribe to his translation of messianism into criticism, we are falling for a myth that will change nothing in the world, while also missing the opportunity to rewrite Benjamin's history using his insights as the basis for something that might at least improve our understanding of it. One of the salutary features of Weiss's final novel is its central insight that modernism failed absolutely in what it set out to do, and so our role is not to identify with it but to perform a postmortem in order to rescue an account that might serve us better than the modernists were served by theirs.

In the chapter on Céline, to give one example, I began by showing
how the mythification of the postwar style unavoidably involves tacit
acceptance of the premises and existence of the pamphlets; that they are
drawn, so to speak, from the same well. This is not, then, immediately to
recommend jettisoning an oeuvre that can still be claimed as one of the
most influential and brilliant of the century. Rather, it is to focus attention
on the hard decisions necessitated by reading Céline, on the fact that
ethical decisions inhere within the reading process; that, in the case of
Augustine or of Weiss, literature reinvents history each time it is read, or,
even more so, each time it is taught or written about. Few probably still
wholeheartedly believe in the primary modernist myth that art has the
power immediately to affect its present surroundings. Nevertheless, what
the wholesale embrace or discarding of this particular myth continues to
obscure is a different hypothesis: that art has the power to change not the
present but the past. Once we follow the lead of the so-called postmodern
artists and set down modernism as part of that past, we may indeed deny
ourselves a mythified present with which to identify, but we gain in return
an abundance of new ways of recreating its history and an extended perspective on our present context.

By way of conclusion, I want briefly to place two further examples of
recent literary descents—those of Seamus Heaney and Derek Walcott—
alongside that of Peter Weiss and the other postwar readings examined
here in order to sketch some of the new perspectives and new views of
history that suggest themselves when return from the nadir of modernism
is predicated on casting modernism as past and gone.

THE PUBLISHED *Auseinandersetzung* of Heaney with Dante dates back
to 1979, when he included a translation of the Ugolino episode (*Inf.* 32–
33) in *Field Work*. It intensified in the long eponymous central poem of
Station Island (1985), in which Heaney staged what he has called "a
sequence of dream encounters" with dead friends and dead predecessors
such as Joyce on the island known as St. Patrick's Purgatory. His most
recent collection, *Seeing Things* (1991), is particularly interesting in this
regard. It begins with "The Golden Bough," Heaney's translation of Aeneid 6.98–148, and concludes with "The Crossing," his translation of
Inferno 3.82–129. The collection unfolds, in other words, in the space
between the plucking of the golden bough—the evocation and authorization of descent—and the descent itself—the crossing of the Styx on
Charon's bark by virtue of that authorization. In between lies the single
shift that creates the poetry it frames: during the passage from the first
episode to the last, Heaney crosses from one poet to the next, from Vergil's
evocation to Dante's rewriting of the subsequent descent.

The present-day context of this space is defined in the opening poem of the collection proper, "The Journey Back," which begins, "Larkin's shade surprised me. He quoted Dante."[2] Heaney's down-to-earth and sardonic predecessor then cites the scene that falls between golden bough and Charon, the poignant opening of *Inferno* 2. His "translation" of Larkin is precisely analogous to Dante's of Vergil: creating within the shell, beneath the mask of the authoritative version. "The Journey Back" does not erase the palimpsest of translation but reveals it by extending it, bringing it up-to-date for a contemporary poet. Larkin quotes Dante's words, but in Heaney's translation. Larkin then continues with his "own" words; after all, the only words admitted as Heaney's are the debut: "Larkin's shade surprised me. He quoted Dante." Why the elaborate gesture of *auctoritas*? Heaney has Larkin give him the prophetic nod; the layers of self-consciousness peel back from the allegory of conversion ("I might have been a wise king setting out / Under the Christmas lights") to reveal ascent into the everyday: "except that / It felt more like the forewarned journey back into the heartland of the ordinary."

This is the difficult return forewarned by the Sibyl in the opening translation; it brings, however, not the birth of a messiah or the coming of the Roman empire but the attempt to recover reality through the concrete description of "A nine-to-five man who had seen poetry." Heaney's poetry is celebrated for its focus on simple, rural, Irish details; nevertheless, we should not be carried away: the "poetry" Heaney has Larkin say he has seen is not, within the context of the poem, the outside world but his own translation of the *Inferno*. The poetry that summons up the forewarned journey back is the result of a minute attention to a palimpsest of words: Heaney's translation of Larkin's translation of Dante's translation of Vergil.

This is neither a Bloomian recession of oedipal aggression nor postmodern intertextuality; rather, it is the careful uncovering of the incessant recreation of history that occurs in words just as it does in things. Heaney discovers poem after poem in the space of a field, a bog; he always also finds it in words (*"Claritas.* The dry-eyed Latin word / Is perfect for the carved stone of the water" ["Seeing Things"]); and he finds it—from Vergil to Larkin—within four hundred verses of *Aeneid* 6. The space for descent has been enormously compressed within the moment of waiting at the shore to cross, but the resultant concentration opens up each moment into a historicity stretching over and recreating two thousand years of history.

Translation enacts the piling of meaning within each thing seen, re-

[2] Seamus Heaney, *Seeing Things* (New York, 1991).

trieved and recreated not by unfolding the narrative but by digging out the layers of meaning inhering in the words themselves. For an Irish poet working in English, such a project has always an oblique angle to it, just as Joyce remade the language as Dublin's history in his writings: as his shade "tells" Heaney in a form of terza rima in *Station Island,* " 'Who cares,' / he jeered, 'anymore? The English language / belongs to us.' " [3] For the Santa Lucian poet Derek Walcott, the angle is even more steeply oblique between the language and the history he will recreate within it, but the maneuver functions just as much as an excavation: the call to represent the poetry of the island arises from the history unearthed out of the image of the descent to the underworld.

Walcott concludes the first book of *Omeros* with an extended adaptation of Aeneas's meeting with Anchises as an imagined reunion of the autobiographically voiced narrator with his long-dead father, illegitimate son of a Warwickshire colonist. From "the Bard's county," in other words, as the narrator's father tells us: the topos of descent continues to serve its function as the allegorical framework for negotiating the Western literary tradition. Walcott weaves the long tradition of the topos into his poem, from the Homeric *nekuia* contained within the title, through the Vergilian meeting of father and son, to the Dantean reminiscence of the three-verse stanzas. In case we thought these stanzas were mere coincidence, we need only turn to the moment when the narrator and his father descend to the wharf to view the women loading coal onto the cargo ships, where we find Walcott subtly shifting into terza rima. First, as they catch sight of the ships and the father remembers the same image from his childhood ("Hell was built on those hills"), Walcott interlocks the tercets with alternating rhymes. Next, in the final section of the chapter and of book 1 (13.3), as the father transforms the infernal image of exploitation into a poetic mission for his son, the alternating rhymes blossom for a few crucial pages into full-fledged terza rima. There is one break in this scheme: "Kneel to your load, then balance to your staggering feet / and walk up that coal ladder as they do in time, / one bare foot after the next in ancestral rhyme." With the break of the rhyming couplet, Walcott signals his divergence from the European model: "only by its stages / like those groaning women will you achieve that height / whose wooden planks in couplets lift your pages / higher than those hills of infernal anthracite." [4]

Walcott does not pastiche Dante and Vergil any more than his poem's title conceit pastiches Homer and Joyce; rather, the couplet that interrupts

[3] Seamus Heaney, *Station Island* (New York, 1985), 93.
[4] Derek Walcott, *Omeros* (New York, 1990), 75.

the Dantean rhyme recreates the image of the *descensus ad inferos*. The dual past of Walcott's British and West Indian heritage is dually expressed within the image of descent. The truth with which he returns is simultaneously the poetic authority of Vergil, Dante, and the Bard, and the colonial oppression of his island. Walcott introduces the image of the native history he needs to remember within the imagery of the underground—not only in the figurative language of the "infernal anthracite" but in the fact of the mines lurking behind it. In so doing, he renders the truth that history and myth, the past that records oppression and the past that offers the means of representing that oppression, are inextricably linked. Moreover, he renders it through purely formal, linguistic means: the shared metaphorics of the underground powerfully realize the shared genealogy of barbarism and art.

By interweaving the two strands of his poem, the substance to be represented and the means of representing it, Walcott does not change the present. He neither ends the continuing economic exploitation of Santa Lucia nor makes himself complicit with it by using the means of the exploiter to render it. Rather, he uses the metaphorical analogy between two histories to allegorize (that is, to bring into the open) the historical affiliation. He develops his poetic heritage through the *translatio studii* from his English grandfather through his father to himself as child and as mature poet (and consequently from Homer through Vergil through Dante through Joyce to Walcott). That history of culture is simultaneously a continuity of barbarism:

> . . . Look, they climb, and no one knows them;
> they take their copper pittances, and your duty
>
> from the time you watched them from your grandmother's house
> as a child wounded by their power and beauty
> is the chance you now have, to give those feet a voice.
>
> (75–76)

He will neither change that barbarism nor abet it, but in a brilliant recasting of descent and return, he gives it a voice.

His structure comes out of the European *translatio studii;* for his substance, Walcott memorializes the unknown oppression, hell cast in the terms of his country's history. He uses the Western myth to unearth the history, and the Western history to recast that history into a mythic past to be remembered by his contemporaries. Book 2 of *Omeros* recounts this colonial history, the source of the underground metaphorics of Santa

Lucia, through the colonial crossing aboard *The Marlborough* of Major Plunkett's ancestor and namesake. The poem continues in book 3 with the intertwined history of the island's other inhabitants: at sea in his fishing boat, Achilles is led from the ghost of his father's face by a sea swift back to the Africa from which Afolabe was taken as a slave. The narrator's descent of book 1 frames and contextualizes the descent of his characters as aspects of his own genealogy split off into the historical pasts of the island.

As in the case of Heaney, my discussion can only touch the surface of these contemporary translations of the descent, but I want to stress two points. First, in a way similar to what we saw Christine and Woolf doing, the topos functions as a personification of a constellation of questions about the version of Western literary tradition accepted at the time. In other words, it provides the means to concretize the vast power, authority, and scope of that tradition within a representable metaphorical structure. This leads to the second point: with contemporary writers, the personification has again been updated, to include the modernist form of the tradition, and, further, it is more and more clearly bracketed as simultaneously excluding, exploiting, and rendering comprehensible a rapidly unfolding panorama of non-Western culture. The descent to the underworld, then, reveals both the genealogy within Western tradition and its infernal effect on non-Western history. The return, consequently, is both a newly recast Western tradition and the authority to be independent from it. It epitomizes the totalizing Western cultural structures in the modernist obsession with transcendence, revealing and recasting both forms as mythic renderings of history in need of reevaluation.

Contemporary literature, if not perhaps reaching the peaks as which we continue to regard modernism, seems to have come to terms with the fact that such peaks exist only so long as modernism remains fixed in the present and hence unchangeable. Such an assumption, in contrast, is precisely what contemporary criticism seems for the most part to have remained trapped within. Consequently, it oscillates between one pole wherein everything is an allegory of life (politics), and the other pole wherein everything everywhere can mean anything else (complete autonomy): art as identity or art as nonidentity; or, more to the point, criticism as identity or criticism as nonidentity. During the course of this book I have suggested one way in which art serves as a vehicle of mediation between these antinomies. The phenomenon I have called the autobiographical voice and the mechanism I have identified as the *descensus ad inferos* are simply the devices whereby readings that dissolve these antinomies can be brought to light and readings that negotiate them can be recognized as such. It is not so much a new reading of modernism that is at the heart of this project but an end to a modernism of reading. What I propose, finally, is a nonmodernist reading of the Middle Ages, a nonmodernist reading of postmodernism, and, perhaps most important, a nonmodernist reading of modernism itself.

Bibliography

Adorno, Theodor W. *Über Walter Benjamin.* Ed. Rolf Tiedemann. Frankfurt: Suhrkamp Verlag, 1990.
——. *Versuch über Wagner.* 1952. Frankfurt: Suhrkamp Verlag, 1974.
——. *In Search of Wagner.* Trans. Rodney Livingstone. London: NLB, 1981.
Alter, Robert. *The Art of Biblical Narrative.* New York: Basic Books, 1981.
Anderson, William. *Dante the Maker.* London: Hutchinson, 1980.
Apollonio, Mario. "Il canto XIV dell'*Inferno.*" In *Lectura Dantis Scaligera* 1. Florence: Le Monnier, 1967–68. 451–78.
Aragon, Louis. *Le Paysan de Paris.* 1926. Paris: Gallimard, 1972.
Ash, Beth Sharon. "Walter Benjamin: Ethnic Fears, Oedipal Anxieties, Political Consequences." *NGC* 48 (Fall 1989): 2–42.
Auerbach, Erich. *Dante, Poet of the Secular World.* Ed. Theodore Silverstein. Trans. Ralph Manheim. 1961. Chicago: University of Chicago Press, 1988. Originally published as *Dante als Dichter der irdischen Welt.* Berlin: De Gruyter, 1929.
——. "Figura." *Neue Dantestudien* (Istanbul, 1944): 72–90. Rpt. in *Scenes from the Drama of European Literature.* Trans. Ralph Manheim. New York: Meridian, 1959. 11–76.
——. *Mimesis: The Representation of Reality in Western Literature.* Trans. Willard R. Trask. 1953. Princeton: Princeton University Press, 1968. Originally published as *Mimesis.* Bern: Franke, 1946.
Augustine, Saint (Aurelius Augustinus). *Opera.* CCSL. Turnhout: Brepols, 1954–.
——. *The City of God.* Trans. Henry Bettenson. New York: Pelican, 1972.
——. *Confessions.* Trans. William Watts. 1631. 2 vols. Loeb Classical Library. Cambridge: Harvard University Press, 1977.
——. *Confessions.* Trans. R. S. Pine-Coffin. New York: Penguin, 1961.
——. *On Christian Doctrine.* Trans. D. W. Robertson Jr. Library of Liberal Arts. Indianapolis: Bobbs-Merrill, 1958.
Ausführliches Lexikon der Griechischen und Römischen Mythologie. Ed. W. H. Roscher. 6 vols. Leipzig: Teubner, 1890–97.
Bakhtin, Mikhail. *Rabelais and His World.* 1965. Trans. Helene Iswolsky. Bloomington: Indiana University Press, 1984.
Baldanza, Frank. "Orlando and the Sackvilles." *PMLA* 70 (1955): 274–79.

Barbi, Michele. *Problemi di critica dantesca. Prima serie 1893–1918.* Florence: Sansoni, 1934.

Barck, Karl-Heinz. "5 Briefe Erich Auerbachs an Walter Benjamin in Paris." *Zeitschrift für Germanistik* 9:6 (Dec. 1988): 688–94.

Barolini, Teodolinda. *Dante's Poets: Textuality and Truth in the "Comedy."* Princeton: Princeton University Press, 1984.

——. *The Undivine Comedy: Detheologizing Dante.* Princeton: Princeton University Press, 1992.

Bassi, Domenìco. "Sant' Agostino et Virgilio." *Annale dell'Istruzione Media* 6 (1930): 420–31.

Baudelaire, Charles. *Oeuvres.* Ed. Y.-G. Le Dantec. 2 vols. 1931–32. Paris: Gallimard, 1954.

Beer, Jeanette M. A. "Stylistic Conventions in *Le Livre de la mutacion de Fortune.*" In Richards, 124–36.

Bell, Quentin. *Virginia Woolf: A Biography.* 2 vols. New York: HBJ, 1972.

Benjamin, Walter. *Briefe.* Ed. Theodor W. Adorno and Gerschom Scholem. 1966. Frankfurt: Suhrkamp Verlag, 1978.

——. *Correspondence.* Trans. Manfred R. Jackson and Evelyn M. Jackson. Chicago: University of Chicago Press, 1994.

——. *Gesammelte Schriften.* Ed. Rolf Tiedemann and Hermann Schweppenhäuser. 7 vols. 1974–89. Frankfurt: Suhrkamp Verlag, 1991.

——. "Central Park." Trans. Lloyd Spencer. *NGC* 34 (Winter 1985): 32–58.

——. *Illuminations.* Ed. Hannah Arendt. Trans. Harry Zohn. New York: Schocken, 1969.

——. *One-Way Street and Other Writings.* Trans. Edmund Jephcott and Kingsley Shorter. London: NLB, 1979.

——. *The Origin of German Tragic Drama.* Trans. John Osborne. 1977. London: NLB, 1985.

——. *Reflections.* Ed. Peter Demetz. Trans. Edmund Jephcott. 1978. New York: Schocken, 1986.

——. "Theories of German Fascism." Trans. Jerolf Wikoff. *NGC* 17 (Spring 1979): 120–28.

Bennett, Arnold. *Arnold Bennett: The "Evening Standard" Years: "Books and Persons," 1926–1931.* Ed. Andrew Mylett. Hamden, Conn.: Archon, 1974.

——. *The Author's Craft and Other Critical Writings by Arnold Bennett.* Ed. Samuel Hynes. Lincoln: University of Nebraska Press, 1968.

——. *Our Women: Chapters in the Sex Discord.* London, 1920.

Bérard, Victor. *Les Navigations d'Ulisse.* 4 vols. Paris: Librairie Armand Colin, 1929.

Bernard Silvestris. *Commentum quod dicitur Bernardi Silvestris super sex libros "Eneidos" Virgilii.* Ed. Julian W. Jones and Elizabeth Frances Jones. Lincoln: University of Nebraska Press, 1977.

——. *Commentum super sex libros "Eneidos" Virgilii.* Ed. Wilhelm Riedel. Greifswald, 1924.

——. *The Commentary on the First Six Books of the "Aeneid" by Bernardus*

Silvestris. Trans. Earl G. Schreiber and Thomas E. Maresca. Lincoln: University of Nebraska Press, 1979.

——. *The Commentary on Martianus Capella's "De Nuptiis Philologiae et Mercurii" Attributed to Bernardus Silvestris*. Ed. Haijo Jan Westra. Studies and Texts, 80. Toronto: Pontifical Institute of Medieval Studies, 1986.

——. *Cosmographia*. Ed. Peter Dronke. Leiden: Brill, 1978.

——. *Cosmographia*. Trans. Winthrop Wetherbee. New York: Columbia University Press, 1973.

Bernfeld, Susan Cassirer. "Freud and Archaeology." *American Imago* 8 (1951): 107–28.

Bishop, E. L. "The Shaping of Jacob's Room: Woolf's Manuscript Revisions." *Twentieth Century Literature* 32:1 (Spring 1986): 115–35.

Blanchard, Joël. "Christine de Pizan: Les raisons de l'histoire." *Le Moyen Age* 92 (1986): 417–36.

——. "Compilation and Legitimation in the Fifteenth Century: *Le Livre de la Cité des Dames.*" Trans. Earl Jeffrey Richards. In Richards, 228–49. Originally published as "Compilation et légitimation au XVe siècle." *Poétique* 19 (1988): 139–57.

Bloomfield, Morton, ed. *Allegory, Myth, and Symbol*. Harvard English Studies, 9. Cambridge: Harvard University Press, 1981.

Boccaccio, Giovanni. *Tutte le opere di Giovanni Boccaccio*. Ed. Vittore Branca. 12 vols. Verona: Mondadori, 1967.

——. *Concerning Famous Women*. Trans. Guido Guarino. New Brunswick: Rutgers University Press, 1963.

Bodkin, Maud. *Archetypal Patterns in Poetry*. London: Oxford University Press, 1963.

Bohrer, Karl-Heinz. *Die Ästhetik des Schreckens*. Munich: Carl Hanser, 1978.

Borges, Jorge Luis. *El jardín de senderos que bifurcan*. 1941. In *Ficciones*. Buenos Aires: Emecé, 1956.

——. *Textos cautivos*. Barcelona: Tusquets, 1986.

——. *Borges: A Reader*. Ed. Emir Rodriguez Monegal and Alistair Reid. New York: Dutton, 1981.

Bosco, Umberto. "Il canto XIV dell'*Inferno.*" In *Nuove Lettere* 2. Florence, 1968. 47–74.

Brabant, Margaret, ed. *Politics, Gender, and Genre: The Political Thought of Christine de Pizan*. Boulder, Colo.: Westview Press, 1992.

Brabant, Margaret, and Michael Brint. "Identity and Difference in Christine de Pizan's *Cité des Dames.*" In Brabant, 207–22.

Brodersen, Momme. *Spinne im eigenen Netz: Walter Benjamin, Leben und Werk*. Buhl-Moos: Elster Verlag, 1990.

Brooks, Robert A. "*Discolor Aura*: Reflections on the Golden Bough." *American Journal of Philology* 54 (1953): 260–80.

Brown, Peter. *Augustine of Hippo*. Berkeley: University of California Press, 1967.

Brownlee, Kevin. "Discourses of the Self: Christine de Pizan and the *Rose.*" *Romanic Review* 79:1 (Jan. 1988): 199–221.

——. "Literary Genealogy and the Problem of the Father: Christine de Pizan and Dante." Robert Branner Forum for Medieval Art. Columbia University. 27 Oct. 1991.

Brunel, Pierre. *L'Evocation des morts et la descente aux enfers.* Paris: SEDES, 1974.

Buck-Morss, Susan. *The Dialectics of Seeing: Walter Benjamin and the "Arcades Project."* Cambridge: MIT Press, 1989.

——. *The Origins of Negative Dialectics: Theodor W. Adorno, Walter Benjamin, and the Frankfurt Institute.* New York: Free Press, 1977.

Buffière, Félix. *Les Mythes d'Homère et la pensée grecque.* 1956. 2d ed. Paris: "Les Belles Lettres," 1973.

Burmeister, Hans-Peter. *Kunst als Protest und Widerstand: Untersuchungen zum Kunstbegriff bei Peter Weiss und Alexander Kluge.* EH, 1st ser., 824. Frankfurt: Peter Lang, 1985.

Burrow, J. A. *The Ages of Man: A Study in Medieval Writing and Thought.* Oxford: Oxford University Press, 1986.

Cantor, Norman. *Inventing the Middle Ages: The Lives, Works, and Ideas of the Great Medievalists of the Twentieth Century.* New York: William Morrow, 1991.

Céline, Louis-Ferdinand. *Bagatelles pour un massacre.* Paris: Denoël, 1937.

——. *Ballets sans musique, sans personne, sans rien.* Paris: Gallimard, 1959.

——. *Les Beaux draps.* Paris: Nouvelles Éditions Françaises, 1941.

——. *Céline et l'actualité, 1933–1961: Cahiers Céline 7.* Ed. Jean-Pierre Dauphin and Pascal Fouché. Paris: Gallimard, 1986.

——. *D'un château l'autre.* 1957. In *Romans II.* Ed. Henri Godard. Paris: Gallimard, 1974.

——. *Castle to Castle.* Trans. Ralph Manheim. New York: Dell, 1968.

——. *L'Ecole des cadavres.* Paris: Denoël, 1938.

——. *Entretiens avec le professeur Y.* 1955. In *Romans IV.* Ed. Henri Godard. Paris: Gallimard, 1993.

——. *Conversations with Professor Y.* Trans. Stanford Luce. Hanover, N.H.: University Press of New England for Brandeis University Press, 1986.

——. *Féerie pour une autre fois.* 1952. In *Romans IV.*

——. *Féerie pour une autre fois II: Normance.* In *Romans IV.*

——. *Guignol's band I.* 1944. In *Romans III.* Ed. Henri Godard. Paris: Gallimard, 1988.

——. *Guignol's Band.* Trans. Bernard Frechtman and Jack T. Nile. 1954. New York: New Directions, 1969.

——. *Guignol's Band II.* 1964. In *Romans III.*

——. *Mea culpa.* 1936. In *Oeuvres de L.-F. Céline,* vol. 3. Paris: Balland, 1967. 337–47.

——. *Mort à crédit.* 1936. In *Romans I.* Ed. Henri Godard. Paris: Gallimard, 1981.

——. *Death on the Installment Plan.* Trans. Ralph Manheim. New York: New Directions, 1966.

———. "Morceaux choisis: *Bagatelles pour un massacre* (Le livre de la semaine)." *Je Suis Partout* (4 March 1938), 8.

———. *Nord.* 1960. In *Romans II.*

———. *Rigodon.* 1969. In *Romans II.*

———. *La vie et l'oeuvre de Philippe-Ignace Semmelweis.* 1924. In *Semmelweis et autres écrits médicaux: Cahiers Céline.* Ed. J.-P. Dauphin and H. Godard. Paris: Gallimard, 1977.

———. *Voyage au bout de la nuit.* 1932. In *Romans I.*

———. *Journey to the End of the Night.* Trans. Ralph Manheim. New York: New Directions, 1983.

Chenu, M. D. "Involucrum: Le mythe selon les théologiens médiévaux." *AHDLMA* 22 (1956): 75–79.

Christine de Pizan. *L'Avision-Christine.* Ed. Mary Louise Towner. Washington, D.C.: The Catholic University of America, 1932.

———. *Le Débat sur le "Roman de la Rose."* Ed. Eric Hicks. Paris: Champion, 1977.

———. "L'Epistre Othea." In "Classical Mythology in the Works of Christine de Pisan, with an edition of 'L'Epistre d'Othea' from the manuscript Harley 4431." Halina Didycky Loukopoulos. Ph.D. diss., Wayne State U, 1977. 152–289.

———. "The *Livre de la Cité des Dames* of Christine de Pizan: A Critical Edition." Ed. Maureen Curnow. Ph.D. diss., Vanderbilt University, 1975.

———. *The Book of the City of Ladies.* Trans. and ed. Earl Jeffrey Richards. New York: Persea, 1982.

———. *Le Livre de la Mutacion de Fortune.* Ed. Suzanne Solente. 4 vols. Société des Anciens Textes Français. Paris: Picard, 1959–66.

———. "*Le Livre des Trois Vertus* of Christine de Pisan." Ed. Lore Loftfield De-bower. Ph.D. diss., University of Massachusetts, 1979.

———. *The Treasure of the City of Ladies or The Book of the Three Virtues.* Trans. Sarah Lawson. Harmondsworth: Penguin, 1985.

———. *Le Livre du Chemin de long estude.* Ed. Robert Püschel. Berlin, 1881.

———. *Oeuvres poétiques de Christine de Pisan.* Ed. Maurice Roy. 3 vols. Paris, 1886–96.

Clark, Raymond J. *Catabasis: Vergil and the Wisdom Tradition.* Amsterdam: B. R. Grüner, 1979.

Clausen, Wendell. "An Interpretation of the *Aeneid*." *Harvard Studies in Classical Philology* 68 (1964): 139–48.

Coffin, H. C. "The Influence of Vergil on St. Jerome and on St. Augustine." *Classical World* 17 (1923): 70–75.

Cohen, Margaret. *Profane Illuminations: Walter Benjamin and the Paris of Surrealist Revolution.* Berkeley: University of California Press, 1993.

Cohen, Robert. *Bio-Bibliographisches Handbuch zu Peter Weiss' "Ästhetik des Widerstands."* Hamburg: Argument Verlag, 1989.

———. *Versuch über Weiss' "Ästhetik des Widerstands."* New York University Ottendorfer Ser., n.s. 33. Bern: Peter Lang, 1989.

Coleridge, Samuel Taylor. *The Collected Works.* Kathleen Coburn, gen. ed. 16 vols. Princeton: Princeton University Press, 1987.

Compagnon, Antoine. *La seconde main ou le travail de la citation.* Paris: Seuil, 1979.

Comparetti, Domenico. *Vergil in the Middle Ages.* Trans. E. F. M. Beinecke. 2d ed. 1903. Rpt. Hamden, Conn.: Archon, 1966. Originally published as *Virgilio nel medio evo.* 2d rev. ed. Florence: B. Seeber, 1896.

Couliano, I. P. *Out of This World: Otherworldly Journeys from "Gilgamesh" to Albert Einstein.* Boston: Shambhala, 1991.

Courcelle, Pierre. *"Les Confessions de Saint Augustin" dans la tradition littéraire: antécédents et posterité.* Paris: Etudes Augustiniennes, 1963.

———. *Lecteurs païens et lecteurs chrétiens de "l'Énéide."* 2 vols. Mémoires de l'Académie des Inscriptions et Belles-Lettres, n.s. 4. Paris: Institut de France, 1984.

———. *Late Latin Writers and Their Greek Sources.* Trans. Harry E. Wedeck. Cambridge: Harvard University Press, 1969. Originally published as *Les lettres grecques en Occident de Macrobe à Cassiodore.* Rev. ed. Paris: Editions de Boccard, 1948.

Croce, Benedetto. *The Poetry of Dante.* Trans. Douglas Ainslie. 1922. Rpt. Mamaroneck, N.Y.: Paul P. Appel, 1971. Originally published as *La Poesia di Dante.* 2d rev. ed. Bari: Laterza, 1921.

Curtius, Ernst Robert. *European Literature in the Latin Middle Ages.* Trans. Willard R. Trask. Bollingen Ser., 36. 1953. Princeton: Princeton University Press, 1973. Originally published as *Europäische Literatur und lateinisches Mittelalter.* Bern: Francke, 1948.

Damrosch, David. *The Narrative Covenant: Transformations of Genre in the Growth of Biblical Literature.* 1987. Ithaca: Cornell University Press, 1991.

Dante Alighieri. *La Commedia secondo l'antica vulgata.* Ed. Giorgio Petrocchi. 4 vols. Società Dantesca Italiana. Mondadori: Edizione Nazionale, 1966–68.

———. *La Divina Commedia.* Ed. Charles Grandgent. 1933. Rev. ed. Charles S. Singleton. Cambridge: Harvard University Press, 1972.

———. *The Divine Comedy.* Trans. and comm. Charles S. Singleton. 6 vols. 1977. Princeton: Princeton University Press, 1980–82.

———. *Convivio.* Ed. Cesare Vasoli. In *Opere minori.* Vol. 1, pt. 2. Vol. 5 of *La letteratura italiana: Storia e testi.* Milan: Ricciardi, 1979.

———. *Dante's "Convivio."* Trans. W. W. Jackson. Oxford: Clarendon, 1909.

———. *Epistole.* Ed. Arsenio Frugoni and Giorgio Brugnoli. In *Opere minori.* Vol. 2.

———. *Monarchia.* Ed. Bruno Nardi. In *Opere minori.* Vol. 2.

———. *Vita nuova.* Ed. Domenico De Robertis. In *opere minori.* Vol. 1, pt. 1.

———. *Dante's "Vita Nuova."* Trans. Mark Musa. Bloomington: Indiana University Press, 1973.

Daugherty, Beth Rigel. "The Whole Contention between Mr. Bennett and Mrs. Woolf, Revisited." In Ginsberg and Gottlieb, 269–94.

Dauphin, Jean-Pierre. *Louis-Ferdinand Céline: Essai de bibliographie des études en langue française consacrées à Louis-Ferdinand Céline, I: 1914–1944.* Paris: Minard, 1977.

Dauphin, Jean-Pierre, and Pascal Fouché. *Bibliographie des écrits de Louis-Ferdinand Céline.* Paris: Bibliothèque de Littérature Française Contemporaine de l'Université de Paris VII, 1985.

Delany, Sheila. "History, Politics, and Christine Studies: A Polemical Reply." In Brabant, 193–206.

——. "Mothers to Think Back Through: Who Are They? The Ambiguous Example of Christine de Pizan." In *Medieval Texts and Contemporary Readers,* ed. Laurie A. Finke and Martin B. Shichtman. Ithaca: Cornell University Press, 1987. 177–97.

——. *Writing Woman: Women Writers and Women in Literature Medieval to Modern.* New York: Schocken, 1983.

De Man, Paul. *Blindness and Insight.* 2d rev. ed. Minneapolis: University of Minnesota Press, 1983.

——. "Conclusions on Walter Benjamin's 'Task of the Translator.'" *Yale French Studies* 69 (1985): 25–48.

Derval, André, ed. *70 Critiques de "Voyage au bout de la nuit," 1932–35.* Paris: IMEC, 1993.

Dieterich, Albrecht. *Nekyia: Beiträge zur Erklärung der neuentdeckten Petrusapokalypse.* 1893. 2d ed. Annot. R. Wünsch. Leipzig: Teubner, 1913.

Dronke, Peter. "Bernardo Silvestre." In *Enciclopedia Virgiliana.* 5 vols. Rome: Istituto della Enciclopedia Italiana, 1984.

——. *Fabula: Explorations into the Uses of Myth in Medieval Platonism.* Mittellateinische Studien und Texte, 9. Leiden: Brill, 1974.

Eagleton, Terry. *Walter Benjamin or Towards a New Criticism.* London: NLB, 1981.

Eliot, T. S. *Selected Essays.* New York: Harcourt, Brace, 1950.

——. "A Talk on Dante." 1950. Rpt. in *Dante in America: The First Two Centuries,* ed. A. Bartlett Giamatti. Binghamton, N.Y.: Medieval and Renaissance Texts, 1983. 219–27.

Enciclopedia Dantesca. 6 vols. Rome: Istituto dell'Enciclopedia Italiana, 1970–78.

Erbse, Hartmut. *Beiträge zum Verständnis der "Odyssee."* Berlin: De Gruyter, 1972.

Espagne, Michel, and Michael Werner. "Vom Passagen-Projekt zum 'Baudelaire': Neue Handschriften zum Spätwerk Walter Benjamins." *Deutsches Vierteljahrsschrift* 58:4 (1984): 593–657.

Farinelli, Arturo. *Dante e la Francia dall'età media al secolo di Voltaire.* 2 vols. Milan: Hoepli, 1908.

Fenster, Thelma. "Did Christine Have a Sense of Humor? The Evidence of the *Epistre au Dieu d'Amours.*" In Richards, 23–36.

Ferrante, Joan M. *The Political Vision of the "Divine Comedy."* Princeton: Princeton University Press, 1984.

Fichter, Andrew. *Poets Historical: Dynastic Epic in the Renaissance.* New Haven: Yale University Press, 1982.

Fletcher, Angus. *Allegory: The Theory of a Symbolic Mode.* Ithaca: Cornell University Press, 1964.

Forster, E. M. "Virginia Woolf." In *Two Cheers for Democracy.* New York: Harcourt, Brace & World, 1942. 242–58. Rpt. in Sprague, 14–25.

Fox, Alice. "Literary Allusion as Feminist Criticism in *A Room of One's Own.*" *Philological Quarterly* 63:2 (Spring 1984): 145–61.

Freccero, John. *Dante: The Poetics of Conversion.* Ed. Rachel Jacoff. Cambridge: Harvard University Press, 1986.

Freeman, Michelle. "Problems in Romance Composition: Ovid, Chrétien de Troyes, and the *Romance of the Rose.*" *Romance Philology* 30 (1976–77): 158–68.

Freud, Sigmund. *The Complete Letters of Sigmund Freud to Wilhelm Fliess, 1877–1904.* Ed. and trans. Jeffrey Moussaieff Masson. Cambridge: Harvard University Press, 1985.

———. *The Standard Edition of the Complete Psychological Works of Sigmund Freud.* Ed. and trans. James Strachey with Anna Freud. 24 vols. London: Hogarth Press, 1953–74.

Fuld, Werner. *Walter Benjamin: Zwischen den Stühlen.* 1979. Rev. ed. Frankfurt: Fischer, 1981.

Fulgentius, Fabius Planciades. *Opera.* Ed. Rudolf Helm. Leipzig: Teubner, 1898.

———. *The Exposition of the Content of Vergil According to Moral Philosophy.* In *Medieval Literary Criticism,* ed. and trans. O. B. Hardison, Jr. New York: Ungar, 1974. 69–80.

———. *Fulgentius the Mythographer.* Trans. Leslie G. Whitbread. Columbus: Ohio State University Press, 1971.

Garber, Klaus. "Etapes de la réception de Benjamin." In Wismann, 917–84.

Gardiner, Eileen, ed. *Visions of Heaven and Hell before Dante.* New York: Italica Press, 1989.

Geist, Johann Friedrich. *Arcades: The History of a Building Type.* Based on a trans. by Jane O. Newman and John H. Smith. Cambridge: MIT Press, 1983. Originally published as *Passagen—Ein Bautyp des 19. Jahrhunderts.* Munich: Prestel-Verlag, 1979.

Gerlach, Ingeborg. *Die Ferne Utopie: Studien zu Peter Weiss' "Ästhetik des Widerstands."* Aachen: Karin Fischer Verlag, 1991.

Gibault, François. *Céline 1: 1894–1932: Le Temps des espérances.* Paris: Mercure de France, 1977.

———. *Céline 2: 1932–1944: Délires et persécutions.* Paris: Mercure de France, 1985.

———. *Céline 3: 1944–1961: Cavalier de l'Apocalypse.* Paris: Mercure de France, 1985.

Gilbert, Sandra M., and Susan Gubar. *The Madwoman in the Attic: The Woman Writer and the Nineteenth-Century Literary Imagination.* New Haven: Yale University Press, 1979.

———. *No Man's Land: The Place of the Woman Writer in the Twentieth Century.* Vol. 1, *The War of the Words.* New Haven: Yale University Press, 1988.

Ginsberg, Elaine, and Laura Moss Gottlieb, eds. *Virginia Woolf: Centennial Essays.* Troy, N.Y.: Whitston, 1983.

Godard, Henri. *Poétique de Céline.* Paris: Gallimard, 1985.

Goethe, Johann Wolfgang von. *Werke.* Ed. Erich Trunz. 14 vols. Hamburg ed. 11th rev. ed. 1949–67. Munich: Beck Verlag, 1978.

Götze, Karl-Heinz, and Klaus Scherpe, eds. *"Die Ästhetik des Widerstands" lesen.* Argument Sonderband, 75. Berlin: Argument Verlag, 1981.

Hagendahl, Harald. *Augustine and the Latin Classics.* 2 vols. Studia Graeca et Latina Gothoburgensia 20. New York: Humanities Press, 1967.

Haiduk, Manfred. *Der Dramatiker Peter Weiss.* Berlin: Henschelverlag, 1977.

Hartman, Geoffrey. *Criticism in the Wilderness: The Study of Literature Today.* New Haven: Yale University Press, 1980.

Haug, Walter, ed. *Formen und Funktionen der Allegorie.* Stuttgart: Metzler Verlag, 1979.

Hauvette, Henri. *Etudes sur la "Divine Comédie."* Paris: Champion, 1922.

Heaney, Seamus. *Field Work.* New York: FSG, 1979.

——. *Seeing Things.* New York: FSG, 1991.

——. *Station Island.* New York: FSG, 1985.

Herf, Jeffrey. *Reactionary Modernism: Technology, Culture, and Politics in Weimar and the Third Reich.* New York: Columbia University Press, 1984.

Herman, William. "Virginia Woolf and the Classics." In Ginsberg and Gottlieb, 257–68.

Heubeck, Alfred, and Arie Hoekstra. *A Commentary on Homer's "Odyssey."* Vol. 2, *Books IX-XVI.* Oxford: Clarendon, 1989.

Hewitt, Nicholas. *The Golden Age of Louis-Ferdinand Céline.* Leamington Spa, UK: Oswald Wolff Books, 1987.

Hillach, Ansgar. "The Aesthetics of Politics: Walter Benjamin's Theories of German Fascism." *NGC* 17 (Spring 1979): 99–119.

Himmelfarb, Martha. *Tours of Hell: An Apocalyptic Form in Jewish and Christian Literature.* Philadelphia: University of Pennsylvania Press, 1983.

Hindman, Sandra. *Christine de Pizan's "Epïstre Othéa": Painting and Politics at the Court of Charles VI.* Toronto: Pontifical Institute of Medieval Studies, 1985.

Hoffmann, Charles G. "Fact and Fantasy in *Orlando:* Virginia Woolf's Manuscript Revisions." *Texas Studies in Language and Literature* 10:3 (Fall 1968): 433–44.

Hollander, Robert. *Allegory in Dante's "Commedia."* Princeton: Princeton University Press, 1969.

——. *Studies in Dante.* Ravenna: Longo, 1980.

Homer. *The Odyssey.* Trans. A. T. Murray. 2 vols. 1919. Loeb Classical Library. Cambridge: Harvard University Press, 1976.

——. *The Odyssey.* Trans. Richard Lattimore. New York: Harper, 1965, 1967.

Horkheimer, Max, and Theodor W. Adorno. *Dialektik der Aufklärung: Philosophische Fragmente.* 1944. Frankfurt: Fischer, 1969.

——. *Dialectic of Enlightenment.* Trans. John Cumming. New York: Continuum, 1972.

Huot, Sylvia. "Seduction and Sublimation: Christine de Pizan, Jean de Meun, and Dante." *Romance Notes* 25 (1985): 361–73.

Huyssen, Andreas. *After the Great Divide: Modernism, Mass Culture, Postmodernism.* Bloomington: Indiana University Press, 1986.

———. "After the Wall: The Failure of German Intellectuals." *NGC* 52 (Winter 1991): 109–43.

———. "Paris/Childhood: The Fragmented Body in Rilke's *Notebooks of Malte Laurids Brigge.*" In *Modernity and the Text,* ed. Andreas Huyssen and David Bathrick. New York: Columbia University Press, 1989. 113–41.

Hynes, Samuel. "The Whole Contention between Mr. Bennett and Mrs. Woolf." *Novel* (Fall 1967): 34–44.

Jacobs, Carol. "Walter Benjamin's Image of Proust." *MLN* 86:6 (1971): 910–32. Rpt. in *The Dissimulating Harmony: The Image of Interpretation in Nietzsche, Rilke, Artaud, and Benjamin.* Baltimore: Johns Hopkins University Press, 1978. 87–110.

Jacoff, Rachel, and Jeffrey T. Schnapp, eds. *The Poetry of Allusion: Virgil and Ovid in Dante's "Commedia."* Stanford: Stanford University Press, 1991.

Jauss, Hans Robert. *Alterität und Modernität der mittelalterlichen Literatur.* Munich: Wilhelm Fink, 1977.

———. "The Literary Process of Modernism from Rousseau to Adorno." 1983. Trans. Lisa C. Roetzel. *Cultural Critique* 11 (Winter 1988–89): 23–61.

———. *Studien zum Epochenwandel der ästhetischen Moderne.* Frankfurt: Suhrkamp Verlag, 1989.

Jay, Martin. *Permanent Exiles: Essays on the Intellectual Migration from Germany to America.* New York: Columbia University Press, 1985.

Jeanroy, Alfred. "Boccace et Christine de Pisan, le *De Claris Mulieribus,* principale source du *Livre de la Cité des Dames.*" *Romania* 48 (1922): 92–105.

Jeauneau, Edouard. "L'Usage de la notion d'*integumentum* à travers les gloses de Guillaume de Conches." *AHDLMA* 24 (1957): 35–100.

Jennings, Michael W. *Dialectical Images: Walter Benjamin's Theory of Literary Criticism.* Ithaca: Cornell University Press, 1987.

Johnson, W. R. *Darkness Visible: A Study of Vergil's "Aeneid."* Berkeley: University of California Press, 1976.

Jones, J. W. "The So-Called Silvestris Commentary on the *Aeneid* and Two Other Interpretations." *Speculum* 64:4 (1989): 835–48.

Joyce, James. *Ulysses.* 1922. New York: Random House 1961.

Jünger, Ernst. *Sämtliche Werke.* 18 vols. Stuttgart: Klett-Cotta, 1978-.

Kantorowicz, Ernst. *The King's Two Bodies: A Study in Medieval Political Theology.* Princeton: Princeton University Press, 1957.

Kaplan, Alice Yeager. *Reproductions of Banality: Fascism, Literature, and French Intellectual Life.* Minneapolis: University of Minnesota Press, 1986.

Kenney, Edwin J., Jr. "The Moment, 1910: Virginia Woolf, Arnold Bennett, and Turn of the Century Consciousness." *Colby Library Quarterly* 13 (1977): 42–66.

Kirk, Geoffrey Stephen. *The Songs of Homer.* Cambridge: Cambridge University Press, 1962.

Kluge, Alexander, and Oskar Negt. *Geschichte und Eigensinn.* Frankfurt: Zweitausendeins, 1981.

Knopp, Sharon E. " 'If I Saw You Would You Kiss Me?' Sapphism and the Subversiveness of Virginia Woolf's *Orlando.*" *PMLA* 103:1 (Jan. 1988): 24–34.

Knowles, Sebastian D. G. *A Purgatorial Flame: Seven British Writers in the Second World War.* Philadelphia: University of Pennsylvania Press, 1990.

Krance, Charles. "Louis-Ferdinand Céline." In *The Twentieth Century, Part I.* Vol. 6 of *A Critical Bibliography of French Literature,* ed. D. Alden and R. A. Brooks. Syracuse, N.Y.: Syracuse University Press, 1980. 743–65.

Krause, Rolf. *Faschismus als Theorie und Erfahrung: "Die Ermittlung" und ihr Autor Peter Weiss.* EH, 1st ser., 541. Frankfurt: Peter Lang, 1982.

Kreutz, Irving. "Mr. Bennett and Mrs. Woolf." *Modern Fiction Studies* 8 (Summer 1962): 103–15.

Kristeva, Julia. *Powers of Horror: An Essay on Abjection.* Trans. Leon S. Roudiez. New York: Columbia University Press, 1982. Originally published as *Pouvoirs de l'horreur: Essai sur l'abjection.* Paris: Seuil, 1980.

Kroll, Josef. *Beiträge zum Descensus ad Inferos.* Königsberg, 1922.

———. *Gott und Hölle: Der Mythos vom Descensuskampfe.* Studien der Bibliothek Warburg, 32. Leipzig: Teubner, 1932.

Kuspit, Donald. "A Mighty Metaphor: The Analogy of Archaeology and Psychoanalysis." In *Sigmund Freud and Art: His Personal Collection of Antiquities,* ed. Lynn Gamwell and Richard Wells. New York: Abrams, 1989. 133–51.

Landau, Marcus. *Hölle und Fegfeuer in Volksglaube, Dichtung und Kirchenlehre.* Heidelberg: Winter Verlag, 1909.

Le Goff, Jacques. *The Birth of Purgatory.* Trans. Arthur Goldhammer. Chicago: University of Chicago Press, 1984. Originally published as *La Naissance du purgatoire.* Paris: Gallimard, 1981.

Lesser, Wendy. *The Life below Ground: A Study of the Subterranean in Literature and History.* Boston: Faber & Faber, 1987.

Lewis, C. S. *The Allegory of Love: A Study in Medieval Tradition.* 1936. New York: Oxford University Press, 1963.

Lewis, Thomas S. W. "Combining 'The Advantages of Fact and Fiction': Virginia Woolf's Biographies of Vita Sackville-West, Flush, and Roger Fry." In Ginsberg and Gottlieb, 257–68.

Lewis, Wyndham. *Blasting and Bombardiering: An Autobiography (1914–1926).* 1937. 2d rev. ed. 1967. London: Calder, 1982

———. *Men without Art.* 1934. Ed. Seamus Cooney. Santa Rosa, Ca.: Black Sparrow Press, 1987.

Lindner, Burkhardt. "Ich Konjunktiv Futur I oder die Wiederkehr des Exils." In Götze and Scherpe, 85–94.

———. "Between Pergamon and Plötzensee: Another Way of Depicting the Course of Events: An Interview with Peter Weiss." Trans. Christian Rogowski. *NGC* 30 (Fall 1983): 107–26. Originally published as "Peter Weiss im Gespräch mit Burkhardt Lindner: Zwischen Pergamon und Plötzensee oder Die andere Darstellung der Verläufe." In Götze and Scherpe. 150–73.

——. "Hallucinatory Realism: Peter Weiss' *Aesthetics of Resistance, Notebooks,* and the Death Zones of Art." Trans. Luke Springman and Amy Kepple. *NGC* 30 (Fall 1983): 127–56. Originally published as "Halluzinatorischer Realismus: *Die Ästhetik des Widerstands,* die *Notizbücher* und die Todeszonen der Kunst." In Stephan, 164–204.

Lipking, Joanna. "The Manx Cat Again." *Virginia Woolf Miscellany* 23 (Fall 1984): 2–3.

Little, Judy. "*Jacob's Room* as Comedy: Virginia Woolf's Parodic *Bildungsroman.*" In *New Feminist Essays on Virginia Woolf,* ed. Jane Marcus. Lincoln: University of Nebraska Press, 1981. 105–24.

Livingstone, Rodney, ed. and trans. *Aesthetics and Politics.* London: NLB, 1977.

de Lubac, Henri. *Exégèse médiévale.* 4 vols. Paris: Editions Montaigne, 1959–64.

Lucan (Marcus Annaeus Lucanus). *Lucan.* Trans. J. D. Duff. Loeb Classical Library. Cambridge: Harvard University Press, 1928.

Luce, Stanford, and William Buckley. *A Half-Century of Céline: An Annotated Bibliography, 1932–1982.* New York: Garland, 1983.

Lucian. *Selected Satires of Lucian.* Ed. and trans. Lionel Casson. 1962. New York: Norton, 1968.

Lukács, Georg. *History and Class Consciousness: Studies in Marxist Dialectics.* Trans. Rodney Livingstone. Cambridge: MIT Press, 1985. Originally published as *Geschichte und Klassenbewußtsein.* 1923. In *Frühschriften II,* vol. 2 of *Werke.* 15 vols. Neuwied: Luchterhand Verlag, 1968.

MacDonald, Ronald. *The Burial-Places of Memory: Epic Underworlds in Vergil, Dante, and Milton.* Amherst: University of Massachusetts Press, 1987.

Macrobius, Ambrosius Aurelius Theodosius. *Opera.* Ed. James Willis. 2 vols. Leipzig: Teubner, 1963.

——. *The Commentary on Scipio's Dream.* Trans. W. H. Stahl. New York: Columbia University Press, 1952.

——. *Les Saturnales.* Ed. and trans. Henri Bornecque. 2 vols. Paris: Garnier Frères, 1937.

——. *The Saturnalia.* Trans. P. V. Davies. New York: Columbia University Press, 1969.

Majumdar, Robin, and Allen McLaurin, eds. *Virginia Woolf: The Critical Heritage.* London: Routledge & Kegan Paul, 1975.

Mannheim, Karl. *Essays on the Sociology of Knowledge.* Ed. Paul Kecskemeti. New York: Oxford University Press, 1952.

Marcus, Jane. " 'The Niece of a Nun': Virginia Woolf, Caroline Stephen, and the Cloistered Imagination." In Marcus, 7–36.

——. *Virginia Woolf and the Languages of Patriarchy.* Bloomington: Indiana University Press, 1987.

——, ed. *Virginia Woolf: A Feminist Slant.* Lincoln: University of Nebraska Press, 1983.

Marrou, Henri-Irène. *Saint Augustin et la fin de la culture antique.* 4th ed. Paris: Editions de Boccard, 1958.

Martianus Capella. *De Nuptiis Philologiae et Mercurii*. Ed. A. Dick and J. Préaux. Stuttgart: Teubner, 1978.

——. *The Marriage of Philology and Mercury*. Trans. W. H. Stahl and R. Johnson. Vol. 2 of *Martianus Capella and the Seven Liberal Arts*. New York: Columbia University Press, 1977.

Marx, Karl. *Werke*. 41 vols. Berlin: Dietz Verlag, 1956–74.

——. *Capital*. Vol. 1. 1867. Trans. Ben Fowkes. New York: Penguin, 1990.

——. *Grundrisse: Introduction to the Critique of Political Economy*. Trans. Martin Nicolaus. New York: Random House, 1973.

——. *Surveys from Exile*. Ed. David Fernbach. New York: Vintage, 1974.

Mazzotta, Giuseppe. *Dante, Poet of the Desert: History and Allegory in the "Divine Comedy."* Princeton: Princeton University Press, 1979.

McCarthy, Patrick. *Céline*. New York: Penguin, 1975.

McCole, John. *Walter Benjamin and the Antinomies of Tradition*. Ithaca: Cornell University Press, 1993.

McLeod, Glenda. "Poetics and Antimisogynist Polemics in Christine de Pizan's *Le Livre de la Cité des Dames*." In Richards, 37–47.

Menocal, María Rosa. *Writing in Dante's Cult of Truth: From Borges to Boccaccio*. Durham: Duke University Press, 1991.

Merkelbach, Reinhold. *Untersuchungen zur "Odyssee."* Vol. 2. Zetemata 2. Munich: Beck, 1969.

Meuli, Karl. *Gesammelte Schriften*. Vol. 2. Basel: Schwabe, 1975.

Miller, J. Hillis. "The Two Allegories." In Bloomfield, 355–70.

Miller, Jacqueline T. *Poetic License: Authority and Authorship in Medieval and Renaissance Contexts*. New York: Oxford, 1986.

Minnis, A. J. *Medieval Theory of Authorship*. 2d ed. Philadelphia: University of Pennsylvania Press, 1988.

Missac, Pierre. *Walter Benjamin's Passages*. Trans. Shierry Weber Nicholsen. Cambridge: MIT Press, 1995. Originally published as *Passage de Walter Benjamin*. Paris: Seuil, 1987.

Morgan, Alison. *Dante and the Medieval Other World*. Cambridge: Cambridge University Press, 1990.

Muray, Philippe. *Céline*. Paris: Seuil, 1981.

Murrin, Michael. *The Allegorical Epic*. Chicago: University of Chicago Press, 1980.

——. *The Veil of Allegory*. Chicago: University of Chicago Press, 1969.

Nagy, Gregory. *The Best of the Achaeans*. Baltimore: Johns Hopkins University Press, 1979.

Nilsson, M. P. *Geschichte der griechischen Religion*. Vol. 3, pt. 1. Munich: Beck 1967.

Nugent, S. Georgia. *Allegory and Poetics: The Structure and Imagery of Prudentius' "Psychomachia."* Studien zur klassischen Philologie, 14. Frankfurt: Peter Lang, 1985.

Oesterle, Kurt. "Dante und das Mega-Ich: Literarische Formen politischer und ästhetischer Subjektivität bei Peter Weiss." In *Widerstand der Ästhetik? Im*

Anschluß an Peter Weiss, ed. Martin Lüdke and Delf Schmidt. *Literaturmagazin* 27. Reinbek bei Hamburg: Rowohlt, 1991. 45–72.

O'Meara, John. "Augustine the Artist and the *Aeneid*." In *Mélanges Offerts à Mademoiselle Christine Mohrmann.* Utrecht: Spectrum, 1963. 252–61.

Ostrovsky, Erika. "Louis-Ferdinand Céline: Creator and Destroyer of Myths." In *Critical Essays on Louis-Ferdinand Céline,* ed. W. K. Buckley. Boston: G. K. Hall, 1989. 92–100.

Owen, Craig. "The Allegorical Impulse: Toward a Theory of Post-Modernism." *October* 12 (Spring 1980): 67–86, and 13 (Summer 1980): 59–80. Rpt. in *Art after Modernism,* ed. Brian Wallis. New York: Godine, 1984. 203–35.

Pagliaro, Antonino. *Ulisse: Ricerche semantiche sulla "Divina Commedia."* 2 vols. Messina-Florence: G. D'Anna, 1967.

Paratore, Ettore. "Il canto XIV dell'*Inferno*." In *Lectura Dantis romana.* Turin: Società editrice internazionale, 1959.

Parry, Adam. "The Two Voices of Vergil's *Aeneid*." *Arion* 2:4 (Winter 1963): 66–80.

Paulys Realencyclopädie der classischen Altertumswissenschaft. Ed. Georg Wissowa, Wilhelm Kroll, and Kurt Witte. Stuttgart: Metzler, 1893-.

Pépin, Jean. *Dante et la tradition de l'allégorie.* Conférence Albert-Le-Grand, 1969. Montreal: Institut d'Etudes Médiévales, 1970.

———. *Mythe et allégorie: Les origines grecques et les contestations judéo-chrétiennes.* 2d rev. ed. Paris: Etudes Augustiniennes, 1976.

Philippy, Patricia A. "Establishing Authority: Boccaccio's *De Claris Mulieribus* and Christine de Pizan's *Livre de la Cité des Dames*." *Romanic Review* 77:3 (1986): 167–94.

Phillips, Tom, trans. and illus. *Dante's "Inferno."* New York: Thames & Hudson, 1985.

Pike, David L. "*Facilis descensus Averno*: Allegory and the Autobiographical Voice, Medieval and Modern." Ph.D. diss., Columbia University, 1993.

Prudentius (Aurelius Prudentius Clemens). *Prudentius.* Trans. H. J. Thomson. 2 vols. Loeb Classical Library. Cambridge: Harvard University Press, 1969.

Quilligan, Maureen. *The Allegory of Female Authority: Christine de Pizan's "Cité des Dames."* Ithaca: Cornell University Press, 1991.

———. *The Language of Allegory: Defining the Genre.* 1979. Ithaca: Cornell University Press, 1992.

Rauschenberg, Robert. *Thirty-Four Drawings for Dante's "Inferno."* 1959–64.

———. *Werke, 1950–1980.* Exhibition Catalog. Staatliche Kunsthalle Berlin, 1980.

Reinhardt, Karl. *Von Werken und Formen: Vorträge und Aufsätze.* Godesberg: H. Kupper, 1948.

Reno, Christine. "The Preface to the *Avision-Christine* in ex-Phillips 128." In Richards, 207–27.

———. "Virginity as an Ideal in Christine de Pizan's *Cité des Dames*." In *Ideals for Women in the Works of Christine de Pizan,* ed. Diane Bornstein. Detroit: Michigan Consortium for Medieval and Early Modern Studies, 1981. 69–90.

Richards, Earl Jeffrey. "Christinè de Pizan and Dante: A Reexamination." *Archiv für das Studium der neueren Sprachen und Literaturen* 137 (1985): 100–11.

———. *Dante and the "Roman de la Rose": An Investigation into the Vernacular Narrative Context of the "Commedia."* Beihefte zur Zeitschrift für romanische Philologie, 184. Tübingen: Niemayer, 1981.

———. "French Cultural Nationalism and Christian Universalism in the Works of Christine de Pizan." In Brabant, 75–94.

———. "Sexual Metamorphosis, Gender Differences, and the Republic of Letters: Or, Androgyny as a Feminist Plea for Universalism in Christine de Pizan and Virginia Woolf." *Romance Languages Annual* 2 (1990): 146–52.

———, ed. *Reinterpreting Christine de Pizan.* Athens: University of Georgia Press, 1992.

Roberts, Julian. *Walter Benjamin.* London: Macmillan, 1982.

Said, Edward W. *The World, the Text, and the Critic.* Cambridge: Harvard University Press, 1983.

Salloch, Erika. *Peter Weiss' "Die Ermittlung": Zur Struktur des Dokumentartheaters.* Frankfurt: Athenäum Verlag, 1972.

———. "The *Divina Commedia* as Model and Anti-Model for *The Investigation* by Peter Weiss." *Modern Drama* 14 (1971): 1–12. Translation of chapter 3 of *Peter Weiss' "Die Ermittlung."*

Sarolli, G. R. *Prolegomena alla "Divina Commedia."* Florence: Olschki, 1971.

Schaefer, Josephine O'Brien. *The Three-fold Nature of Reality in the Novels of Virginia Woolf.* Studies in English Literature 7. The Hague: Mouton & Co., 1965.

Scherpe, Klaus R. "*Die 'Ästhetik des Widerstands'* als *Divina Commedia:* Peter Weiss' künstlerische Vergegenständlichung der Geschichte." In Wolff, 88–99.

———. "Reading the *Aesthetics of Resistance:* Ten Working Theses." *NGC* 30 (Fall 1983): 97–105.

Schibanoff, Susan. "Taking the Gold Out of Egypt: The Art of Reading as a Woman." In *Gender and Reading: Essays on Readers, Texts, and Contexts,* ed. Elizabeth A. Flynn and Patrocino P. Schweikart. Baltimore: Johns Hopkins University Press, 1986. 83–106.

Schlack, Beverly Ann. *Continuing Presences: Virginia Woolf's Use of Literary Allusion.* University Park: Pennsylvania State University Press, 1979.

———. "Fathers in General: The Patriarchy in Virginia Woolf's Fiction." In Marcus, 52–77.

Schlossman, Beryl. *The Orient of Style: Modernist Allegories of Conversion.* Durham: Duke University Press, 1991.

Scholem, Gerschom. *Walter Benjamin: The Story of a Friendship.* Trans. Harry Zohn. 1981. New York: Schocken, 1988. Originally published as *Walter Benjamin: Die Geschichte einer Freundschaft.* Frankfurt: Suhrkamp Verlag, 1975.

Schwartz, Beth C. "Thinking Back through Our Mothers: Virginia Woolf Reads Shakespeare." *ELH* 58:3 (Fall 1991): 721–46.

Sieburth, Richard. "Benjamin the Scrivener." In Smith 1989, 13–37.

Silverstein, Theodore. Review of *Commentum quod dicitur Bernardi Silvestris super sex libros "Eneidos" Virgilii,* ed. Jones and Jones. *Speculum* 54:1 (1979): 154–57.

———. ed. *Visio Sancti Pauli*. Studies and Documents, 4. London: Christophers, 1935.

Singleton, Charles S. *Dante's "Commedia": Elements of Structure*. 1954. Baltimore: Johns Hopkins University Press, 1977.

———. *Journey to Beatrice*. 1958. Baltimore: Johns Hopkins University Press, 1977.

Smalley, Beryl. *The Study of the Bible in the Middle Ages*. 2d ed. Oxford: Oxford University Press, 1952.

Smith, Gary, ed. *Benjamin: Philosophy, Aesthetics, History*. Chicago: University of Chicago Press, 1989.

———, ed. *On Walter Benjamin: Critical Essays and Reflections*. Cambridge: MIT Press, 1988.

Smith, Pauline. *The Beadle*. London: Jonathan Cape, 1926.

Söllner, Alfons. *Peter Weiss und die Deutschen*. Opladen: Westdeutschen Verlag, 1988.

Sontag, Susan. "The Last Intellectual." *New York Review of Books* 25:15 (12 Oct. 1978): 75–82. Rpt. as title essay in *Under the Sign of Saturn*, by Sontag. New York: FSG, 1980. 107–34.

Spence, Sarah. *Rhetorics of Reason and Desire: Vergil, Augustine, and the Troubadours*. Ithaca: Cornell University Press, 1988.

Sprague, Claire, ed. *Virginia Woolf: A Collection of Critical Essays*. Englewood Cliffs, N.J.: Prentice-Hall, 1971.

Statius, Publius Papinius. *Statius*. 2 vols. Trans. J. S. Mozley. Loeb Classical Library. 1928. Cambridge: Harvard University Press, 1982.

Stecopoulos, Eleni, with Karl D. Uitti. "Christine de Pizan's *Livre de la Cité des Dames:* The Reconstruction of Myth." In Richards 48–62.

Steiner, George. "Cry Havoc." *New Yorker* (1971). Rpt. in *Extraterritorial: Papers on Literature and the Language Revolution*. New York: Atheneum, 1976. 35–46.

———. Introduction to *The Origin of German Tragic Drama*, by Walter Benjamin. London: NLB, 1985. 7–24.

Steiner, Gerd. "Die Unterweltsbeschwörung des *Odyssee* im Lichte hethitischer Texte." *Ugarit-Forschungen* 3 (1971): 265–83.

Stephan, Alexander. " 'Ein großer Entwurf gegen den Zeitgeist': Zur Aufnahme von Peter Weiss' *Ästhetik des Widerstands*." In Stephan 346–66.

———, ed. *Die Ästhetik des Widerstands*. Suhrkamp Taschenbuch Materialien. Frankfurt: Suhrkamp Verlag, 1983.

Stock, Brian. *Myth and Science in the Twelfth Century: A Study of Bernard Silvester*. Princeton: Princeton University Press, 1972.

Strabo. *The Geography of Strabo*. Trans. H. L. Jones. 8 vols. Loeb Classical Library. Cambridge: Harvard University Press, 1969.

Strubel, Armand. "Allégorie *in verbis* et *in facto*." *Poétique* 23 (1975): 342–57.

Theweleit, Klaus. *Male Fantasies*. Trans. Stephen Conway with Erica Carter and Chris Turner. 2 vols. Minneapolis: University of Minnesota Press, 1987, 1989. Originally published as *Männer-Phantasien*. 2 vols. Reibek bei Hamburg: Rowohlt, 1980.

Thornton, Agathe. *People and Themes in Homer's "Odyssey."* London: Methuen, 1970.

Tomkins, Calvin. *Off the Wall: Robert Rauschenberg and the Art World of His Time.* New York: Doubleday, 1980.

Van Dyke, Carolynn. *The Fiction of Truth: Structures of Meaning in Narrative and Dramatic Allegory.* Ithaca: Cornell University Press, 1985.

Varese, Claudio. "Canto XIV." In *Letture dantesche: "Inferno,"* ed. Giovanni Getto. Florence: Sansoni, 1955. 251–66.

Vegio, Maffeo. *Maphaeus Vegius and His Thirteenth Book of the "Aeneid": A Chapter on Vergil in the Renaissance.* Ed. Anna Cox Brinton. Stanford: CA: Stanford University Press, 1930.

Vergil (Publius Vergilius Maro). *The Aeneid.* Trans. Robert Fitzgerald. 1983. New York: Vintage, 1990.

——. *Aeneid VI.* Ed. and trans. Eduard Norden. Leipzig, 1903.

——. *Virgil.* Trans. H. Rushton Fairclough. Rev. ed. 2 vols. Loeb Classical Library. Cambridge: Harvard University Press, 1978.

Vitoux, Frédéric. *Céline: A Biography.* Trans. Jesse Browner. New York: Paragon House, 1992. Originally published as *Vie de Céline.* Paris: Grasset, 1988.

Vogt, Jochen. *Peter Weiss.* Rowohlt Monographien. Reinbek bei Hamburg: Rowohlt, 1987.

Vormweg, Heinrich. *Peter Weiss.* Ed. *Text und Kritik.* Munich: Beck, 1981.

Walcott, Derek. *Omeros.* New York: FSG, 1990.

Walters, Lori. "Fathers and Daughters: Christine de Pizan as Reader of the Male Tradition of *Clergie* in the *Dit de la Rose.*" In Richards, 63–76.

——. "The Woman Writer and Literary History: Christine de Pizan's Redefinition of the Poetic *Translatio* in the *Epistre au Dieu d'Amours.*" *French Literature Series* 16 (1989): 1–16.

Weiss, Peter. *Abschied von den Eltern.* Frankfurt: Suhrkamp Verlag, 1961.

——. *Die Ästhetik des Widerstands.* 3 vols. 1975, 1978, 1981. Frankfurt: Suhrkamp Verlag, 1988.

——. *Fluchtpunkt.* Frankfurt: Suhrkamp Verlag, 1962.

——. *Exile.* Trans. E. B. Garside, Alastair Hamilton, and Christopher Levenson. New York: Delacorte, 1968. Originally published as *Abschied von den Eltern* and *Fluchtpunkt.*

——. *Der Maler Peter Weiss: Bilder, Zeichnungen, Collagen, Filme.* Exhibition Catalog, Bochum Museum. Berlin: Frölich & Kaufmann, [1980].

——. *Notizbücher, 1960–1971.* 2 vols. Frankfurt: Suhrkamp Verlag, 1982.

——. *Notizbücher, 1971–1980.* 2 vols. Frankfurt: Suhrkamp Verlag, 1981.

——. *Peter Weiss im Gespräch.* Ed. Rainer Gerlach and Matthias Richter. Frankfurt: Suhrkamp Verlag, 1986.

——. *Rapporte.* Frankfurt: Suhrkamp Verlag, 1968.

——. *Rapporte 2.* Frankfurt: Suhrkamp Verlag, 1971.

——. *Stücke I.* Frankfurt: Suhrkamp Verlag, 1976.

——. *The Investigation.* Trans. Jon Swan and Ulu Grosbard. New York: Atheneum, 1966.

Wetherbee, Winthrop. *Platonism and Poetry in the Twelfth Century: The Literary Influence of the School of Chartres*. Princeton: Princeton University Press, 1972.

Whitman, Jon. *Allegory: Dynamics of an Ancient and Medieval Mode*. Cambridge: Cambridge University Press, 1988.

Willard, Charity Cannon. *Christine de Pizan: Her Life and Works*. New York: Persea, 1984.

Williams, Raymond. *The Politics of Modernism: Against the New Conformists*. Ed. Tony Pinkney. London: NLB, 1989.

Williams, Rosalind. *Notes on the Underground: An Essay on Technology, Society, and the Imagination*. Cambridge: MIT Press, 1990.

Wismann, Heinz, ed. *Walter Benjamin et Paris: Colloque international, 27–29 juin 1983*. Paris: Cerf, 1986.

Witte, Bernd. *Walter Benjamin: An Intellectual Biography*. Trans. James Rolleston. Detroit: Wayne State University Press, 1991. Originally published as *Walter Benjamin*. Rowohlt Monographien. Reinbek bei Hamburg: Rowohlt, 1985.

Wizisla, Erdmut. " 'Fritz Heinle war Dichter': Walter Benjamin und sein Jugendfreund." In *"Was nie geschrieben wurde, lesen": Frankfurter Benjamin-Vorträge*, ed. Lorenz Jäger and Thomas Regehly. Bielefeld: Aisthesis Verlag, 1992. 115–131.

Wohlfarth, Irving, ed. "Second Special Issue on Walter Benjamin." *NGC* 39 (Fall 1986).

Wolf, F. A. *Prolegomena to Homer*. 1795. Trans. and ed. Anthony Grafton, Glenn W. Most, and James E. G. Zetzel. Princeton: Princeton University Press, 1985.

Wolff, Rudolf. *Peter Weiss: Wirk und Wirkung*. Sammlung Profile 27. Bonn: Bouvier, 1987.

Wolin, Richard. *Walter Benjamin: An Aesthetic of Redemption*. New York: Columbia University Press, 1982.

Woolf, Virginia. *Between the Acts*. 1941. New York: HBJ, 1969.

——. *Books and Portraits*. Ed. Mary Lyon. New York: HBJ, 1977.

——. *The Common Reader: First Series*. 1925. Ed. Andrew McNeillie. Annot. ed. New York: HBJ, 1984.

——. *The Diary of Virginia Woolf*. Ed. Anne Olivier Bell, with Andrew McNeillie. 5 vols. New York: HBJ, 1977–84.

——. *The Essays of Virginia Woolf*. Ed. Andrew McNeillie. 6 vols. New York: HBJ, 1987-.

——. *Jacob's Room*. 1922. New York: HBJ, 1978.

——. *The Letters of Virginia Woolf*. Ed. Nigel Nicolson and Joanne Trautmann. 6 vols. New York: HBJ, 1975–80.

——. *Mrs. Dalloway*. 1925. New York: HBJ, 1953.

——. *Night and Day*. 1919. New York: HBJ, 1948.

——. *Orlando: A Biography*. 1928. Ed. Brenda Lyons; notes, Sandra Gilbert. Harmondsworth: Penguin, 1993.

——. *A Room of One's Own*. 1929. New York: HBJ, n.d.

———. *To the Lighthouse.* 1927. New York: HBJ, 1955.
———. *The Voyage Out.* 1920. New York: HBJ, 1948.
———. *The Waves.* 1931. New York: HBJ, 1978.
———. *The Years.* 1937. New York: Harcourt, Brace, and World, 1965.
Zaleski, Carol. *Otherworld Journeys: Accounts of Near-Death Experience in Medieval and Modern Times.* New York: Oxford University Press, 1987.
Ziolkowski, Theodore. *Virgil and the Moderns.* Princeton: Princeton University Press, 1993.

Index